Corpus Analysis in Different Genres

This collection sheds light on the ways in which corpus linguistics and the use of learner corpora might be applied to the study of academic discourse, revealing linguistic and rhetorical patterns and insights into variation across a range of disciplinary genres. Organized into three sections, the book highlights key tools and methodologies in corpus analysis to study such features as discourse markers, lexical bundles, linguistic complexity, lexico-grammatical conventions, and modality in studies of academic discourse, both in a second language and in English for specific purposes. The volume features examples from disciplinary genres not often covered in the existing literature, including MA theses, academic book reviews, and online student forums. Taken together with the study of learner corpora, the book demonstrates the impact of corpus linguistic tools in better understanding linguistic patterns of specific languages and language use and in turn, their role in helping to identify the needs of language learners. The book will be of interest to students and scholars in corpus linguistics, applied linguistics, and English for Specific Purposes.

María Luisa Carrió-Pastor is a professor of English language at the Department of Applied Linguistics at the Universitat Politècnica de València, Spain.

Routledge Studies in Applied Linguistics

Cantonese as a Second Language
Issues, Experiences and Suggestions for Teaching and Learning
Edited by John Wakefield

The Social Lives of Study Abroad
Understanding Second Language Learners' Experiences through Social Network Analysis and Conversation Analysis
Atsushi Hasegawa

Defining and Assessing Lexical Proficiency
Agnieszka Leńko-Szymańska

Global Perspectives on Project-based Language Learning, Teaching, and Assessment
Key Approaches, Technology Tools, and Frameworks
Edited by Gulbahar H. Beckett and Tammy Slater

Referring in a Second Language
Studies on Reference to Person in a Multilingual World
Edited by Jonothan Ryan and Peter Crosthwaite

Aspects of Language Development in an Intensive English Program
Alan Juffs

First Language Influences on Multilingual Lexicons
Edited by Paul Booth and Jon Clenton

Corpus Analysis in Different Genres
Academic Discourse and Learner Corpora
Edited by María Luisa Carrió-Pastor

For more information about this series, please visit: https://www.routledge.com/Routledge-Studies-in-Applied-Linguistics/book-series/RSAL

Corpus Analysis in Different Genres

Academic Discourse and Learner Corpora

Edited by
María Luisa Carrió-Pastor

Routledge
Taylor & Francis Group
NEW YORK AND LONDON

First published 2020
by Routledge
605 Third Avenue, New York, NY 10017

and by Routledge
2 Park Square, Milton Park, Abingdon, Oxon, OX14 4RN

First issued in paperback 2022

Routledge is an imprint of the Taylor & Francis Group, an informa business

Publisher's Note
The publisher has gone to great lengths to ensure the quality of this reprint but points out that some imperfections in the original copies may be apparent.

Library of Congress Cataloging-in-Publication Data
A catalog record for this title has been requested

ISBN: 978-0-367-41716-1 (hbk)
ISBN: 978-0-367-49993-8 (pbk)
ISBN: 978-0-367-81590-5 (ebk)

DOI: 10.4324/9780367815905

Typeset in Sabon
by codeMantra

Contents

Contributors

Francisco Alonso-Almeida
Universidad de Las Palmas de Gran Canaria

Francisco J. Álvarez-Gil
Universidad de Las Palmas de Gran Canaria

Ana Bocanegra-Valle
Universidad de Cádiz

María Luisa Carrió-Pastor
Universitat Politècnica de València

Jesús Fernández-Domínguez
Universidad de Granada

Miguel Fuster-Márquez
Universitat de València

Davide Simone Giannoni
Universidad de Bérgamo

Isabel Herrando-Rodrigo
Universidad de Zaragoza

Sanja Vakanjac Ivezić
University of Osijek

Alisa Kriukova
Saint Petersburg State University

Barbara Kružić
University of Osijek

Eva M. Mestre-Mestre
Universitat Politècnica de València

Anna Montesinos-López
Universitat Politècnica de València

Francisco Núñez-Román
Universidad de Sevilla

Javier Pérez-Guerra
Universidad de Vigo

Elena Quintana-Toledo
Universidad de Las Palmas de Gran Canaria

Francesca Romero-Forteza
Universitat Politècnica de València

Margarita Esther Sánchez Cuervo
Universidad de Las Palmas de Gran Canaria

David Sánchez-Jiménez
CUNY New York City College of Technology

Hanna Skorczynska
Universitat Politècnica de València

Višnja Pavičić Takač
University of Osijek

Chiara Tasso
Universidad Católica de Valencia San Vicente Mártir

Milagros Torrado-Cespón
Universidad Internacional de La Rioja

Introduction

María Luisa Carrió-Pastor

The analysis of different genres provides a wider perspective of language patterns. This is the reason why corpus analysis is frequently used as a method to provide evidence on the study of language patterns. Observation and the identification of similar ways of constructing the different structures of language are the basic aspects that linguists use to establish the rules that govern language. Linguists use a corpus-driven methodology to provide evidence about the observed occurrences; thus, the results show that scientific and objective data is provided to withdraw the conclusions or findings, convincing readers that conclusions are the fruit of an objective analysis. This book focuses on the use of corpus analysis to study different genres, paying special attention to academic discourse and learner corpora to thoroughly show the way the reader of this book can put into practice research using corpus methodology.

In this volume, corpora are used to identify the rhetoric and linguistic patterns used in academic English for specific purposes, to show analysis on discourse markers used in English as a second language, and to recognise linguistic patterns in second language acquisition through the use of learner corpora. This edited book contains two sections: the first one is devoted to the analysis of academic discourse of different genres and the second focuses on the analysis of learner corpora compiled from academic settings.

In the section devoted to the study of academic discourse, readers will discover diverse perspectives of the contributing authors such as the use of a corpus of academic book reviews, the analysis of lexical bundles and modal verbs, the study of phraseological units, etc. In the section focused on learner corpora, readers will discern extensive discussions of issues, including language proficiency, teaching lexical bundles, anxiety, emotions, etc.

The main themes are the use of corpus methodology in the analysis of discourse markers, English for specific purposes, and the use of learner corpora to improve language acquisition. The main objectives are, on the one hand, to help researchers and scholars understanding the different language patterns among different genres, providing the latest advances in the study of corpus analysis, and, on the other, to show language teachers expert analysis based on the study of learner corpora that could help them to develop specific activities for their teaching.

This book will appeal to researchers and teachers of language who will find this work thought-provoking, instructive, and informative. It makes a valuable contribution to the field of corpus linguistics, focusing on the use of this methodology to study the patterns and implications of specific genres and on its use to identify the needs of language learners. It offers detailed case studies as well as theoretical aspects related to the use of corpus linguistics applied to the study of academic language and learner corpora. The authors of the different chapters are experienced practitioners and eminent scholars that explore the way corpus linguistics is applied to provide objective evidence of language patterns. The chapters of the book trace topics such as lexical studies, qualitative analysis data software, modal verbs, linguistic complexity, lexicogrammatical and generic conventions, identification of emotion, anxiety in learner corpora, etc. In sum, this collection of essays invites readers to consider critical questions such as the use of corpus analysis to improve language learning and to identify language patterns.

As stated before, the book comprises two sections: one entitled "Corpus studies on academic discourse" and the second one "Studies on learner corpora". The first section includes eight chapters that study different genres in academic language. The first chapter, authored by María Luisa Carrió-Pastor, is entitled "Variation in the use of self-mentions in different specific fields of knowledge in academic English". The author focuses on the comparison of discourse markers, specifically self-mentions, to carry out a corpus analysis of research papers. She explains that the internal structure of a genre within a particular academic context in English may constrain the forms of the linguistic resources and the functional values they assume in discourse. Metadiscourse analysis studies academic communication, and so several researchers such as Mauranen (1993), Hyland and Tse (2004), Dahl (2004), Hyland (2005), and Ädel (2006) have indicated the different characteristics of language in specific settings. The hypothesis of this chapter is that researchers do not always use English language in the same way as the choice of rhetorical devices varies depending on the specific field of knowledge. Also, the choice of metadiscourse devices changes within the same genre, in this case, academic papers. The objectives of this chapter are to identify if writers show an authorial persona, establish their credentials, or present themselves as a group of researchers and to identify variation in the use of English self-mentions in the three different disciplines. Fifty scientific papers from the specific fields of knowledge of engineering, medicine, and linguistics were compiled and analysed. The three corpora were used to study variation in the use of self-mentions in the specific fields; the occurrences were extracted from the corpora and compared. Results were analysed and evidenced by the initial hypothesis that variation exists in the use of self-mentions in the genre of scientific papers, and this may be the result of conceptual and organisational differences among disciplines.

The second chapter, entitled "The expression of gratitude in the prefaces of academic books in linguistics", whose author is Francisco Alonso-Almeida, focuses on the analysis of academic books, specifically the expression of gratitude in academic books in linguistics. The corpus is composed of prefaces found in books published from the year 2000 to 2019 in the field of linguistics. The author questions the purpose of the preface, if this is the indication of both the purpose and the scope of the book. The author believes that the communicative goal of the preface genre is academic and promotional, and although the corpus of this genre may not be lengthy in the number of tokens, it exhibits extraordinary evidence as to the language of appraisal and affect, and thus, thanking expressions. In this chapter, the way writers express their gratitude for any help or support obtained from third parties in their prefaces is explored. Thus, the form of thanking expressions and their functions in the corpus compiled are described and evidence is provided about their variation.

Chapter 3 focuses on another genre, book reviews. It is entitled "Criticism in Russian academic book reviews of the soviet and post-soviet periods", and it is authored by Alisa Kriukova, who investigates how criticism is expressed in this genre in the 1980s and the 2010s in the most reputable Russian linguistic journal, *Issues in Linguistics* (*Voprosy Jazykoznanija*). To make the data comparable, additional criteria were introduced; that is, only the reviews on monographs in which both the author and the reviewer are from the same academic community, that is Soviet or Russia, were selected. In this chapter, critical attitude is defined in terms of 'critical acts', that is, instances of criticism targeted at different aspects of the book under review. The author tagged the negative critical acts and calculated the proportion of criticism in the whole text, the targets of critical acts, and the instances of hedging and intensification for every book review. Finally, the critical acts were classified and the soviet and modern periods were compared. The results indicated that instances of both criticism and its intensification were more frequent in the 2010s reviews, while the reviews of the 1980s are generally less critical, which means a tendency to a more critical attitude towards a book under review. In this chapter, it was observed that the use of personal attribution, praise-criticism pairs, and hedges has changed in the two periods compared, but means of intensification of criticism did not suffer significant changes.

In Chapter 4, whose authors are Elena Quintana-Toledo and Margarita Esther Sánchez Cuervo and is entitled "Modal verb categories in medical abstracts", the genre analysed is abstracts in academic papers. The authors are conscious that modality has been widely investigated, but they focus on recent approaches to modality that show modals may also convey attitudinal qualifications regarding the speaker's position towards his/her text, that is, stancetaking. Thus, modal auxiliaries come to fulfil a wide range of textual, rhetorical, and interactional functions in a text, so modality may be broadly understood as the domain of attitudinal qualifications and the speaker's evaluation of what is being said. In this chapter, the authors study the most frequent modal verb types in medical abstracts. As modals may be used with a variety of functions determined by contextual factors, their goal is to unveil how they are deployed in the corpus compiled and to describe the type of modal meanings exhibited. Furthermore, they provide insight into the communicative functions of modals in this genre and specific field of knowledge. As the genre chosen for this study is the abstract section of the chapter, the authors identified a massive use of dynamic and epistemic modals that showed dynamic possibility and epistemic possibility and probability. It was noticed in the examples from the corpus that this combination allows authors to present their ideas and external facts without really imposing their views.

Chapter 5, entitled "A disciplinary analysis of fairly in late modern English scientific writing" and authored by Francisco J. Álvarez-Gil, analyses the academic texts of the Corpus of History English Texts and the Corpus of English Texts on Astronomy, two sub-corpora within the Coruña Corpus of English Scientific Writing (1700–1900). The author focused on the study of the uses and functions of the adverb *fairly* to see whether it shows epistemic or evidential nuisances in scientific discourse and whether the variable of discipline might have some effect on the category of this adverb in these historical texts. His intention is to explore how this adverb contributes to the elaboration of meaning of whatever nature and thus, a corpus-based quantitative and qualitative analysis was performed to offer a categorisation of this adverb in these sub-corpora, and to show whether there are disciplinary differences in the use and functions of this adverb in this period of the English language. He also analysed the syntactic context of this adverb, since it has some important effects on its pragmatic functions. This chapter adopts a diachronic perspective within the arena of historical pragmatics. Its conclusions indicate that 'fairly' presents different meanings and functions in the two corpora analysed; for example, it was used both to mitigate and to strengthen propositional content.

In Chapter 6, "An analysis of lexical bundles in academic journal descriptions", Davide Simone Giannoni studies the genre of academic journals. This author considers that the way academic journals portray their mission and values is a source of interesting insights. This author uses a corpus drawn from leading international journals in the same discipline and investigates multi-word sequences as an indicator of generic and disciplinary proclivities. The analysis focused on three- to four-word sequences, classified by function and divided into referential, discourse organising, and stance bundles. Referential bundles were the most frequently used in the corpus analysed. The author points out that variation across disciplines was found to be limited and this fact suggested a degree of formulaic standardisation in the language of academic editors and most of the bundles were associated with self-evaluative meanings.

In Chapter 7, "Collaborating with disciplinary experts in corpus compilation processes", Isabel Herrando-Rodrigo explains how to compile corpora in the medicine. She emphasises the importance of using authentic corpora and explaining how to compile these corpora in an accurate way. She points out that scholars and professionals are nowadays encouraged to disseminate new knowledge and findings among different audiences and through different channels mainly hosted on the internet. The study of how to recode discourse practices is important to show scholars how to process texts. This chapter may help medical doctors to cast light onto how knowledge transferred, being embedded on the internet, is being nowadays shaped. Thus, this contribution raises awareness about why linguists should turn to authentic texts and professionals' expertise describing a process of corpora gathering based on an ethnographic approach. The process suggested by the author is to go from context to text and back to context, framing more consistent linguistic analyses.

The following chapter, the last of this section, number 8, "Researching academic genres, language and discourse with computer-assisted qualitative data analysis software", whose author is Ana Bocanegra-Valle, emphasises the capabilities of computer-assisted qualitative data analysis software and investigates the advantages of using two particular packages, ATLAS.ti and NVivo for the analysis of qualitative data. This chapter explores and discusses scholarly articles in the field of English for specific and academic purposes that were published in renowned journals and employed these two software packages. The analysis of these studies contributes to mapping the main features of computer-assisted qualitative research in the field and reveals that the research of the language, discourse, and genres that occur in academic settings can be efficiently supported and successfully enhanced by current software.

In the second section, "Studies on learner corpora", ten chapters are included that focus on the use of corpora in different genres to help teachers and learners to improve the acquisition of a foreign language. The first chapter of this section, Chapter 9, is entitled: "A corpus-driven exploration of discourse markers in L2 academic texts" and authored by Višnja Pavičić Takač, Barbara Kružić, and Sanja Vakanjac Ivezić. It focuses on the analysis of texts written by learners of English and German and studies text coherence and the way this can be influenced by a number of factors, including the use of discourse markers. The authors state that L2 users tend to overuse, misuse, or misplace discourse markers.

This erroneous use is attributed to their insufficient knowledge of stylistic constraints on the choice of connectors, especially in formal styles, and to their lack of awareness of what constitutes a coherent text in the target language. They are conscious that these assumptions have not been fully confirmed mainly because of few studies that included a small number of languages. Thus, this study aims at exploring the use of discourse markers in academic argumentative essays written by non-native users of two foreign languages, English and German, who share their mother tongue. The issues addressed are two-fold and include the similarities and differences in discourse markers use between English and German L2 texts, and the extent to which an erroneous use of discourse markers causes coherence disruption. It is used as a corpus tool to analyse L2 academic texts; thus, this contributed to a better understanding of how coherence is established, reduced the subjectivity of qualitative approaches to text coherence analyses, and allowed for cross-linguistic comparisons of patterns of rhetorical organisation. The results are acquisitional, focusing on the fact that non-native language users encounter a number of problems when using discourse markers to establish text coherence. Also, methodological problems are studied; specifically, how to correct errors should be treated prior to corpus analyses and whether corpus analyses may point to coherence breaks.

Chapter 10, authored by Francisco Núñez-Román and entitled "Personal metadiscourse markers in a corpus of final degree dissertations in education sciences", analyses final degree dissertations and offers the initial results of a research focused in the use of personal metadiscoursive markers in a corpus of Final Degree Dissertation in Education Sciences. To that end, a corpus of 130 FDD on Primary Education Degree belonging to 16 Spanish universities, named TFE-Prim, has been built. TFE-Prim is divided into three sub-corpora according to the typology of FDD: didactics proposals, researches, and review of literature. After establishing a list of metadiscursive elements from the taxonomies proposed by Salas Valdebenito (2015), Ädel (2006), and Hyland (2005), a quantitative and qualitative analysis has been carried out in order to answer two questions: Are the use of PMM determined by the typology of FDD? and which are the main discursive functions of PMM in an FDD? The findings show, first, that PMM are more frequent in FDD concerning research, and second, that there is a preference for some discursive functions focused in organising the text at the expense of discursive functions focused in reflecting about the topic or engaging the reader. An implication of this is the necessity of developing the author's awareness in assuming their voice inside a specific discursive community.

In Chapter 11, "Interactional metadiscourse features in the written production made by Spanish EFL learners", written by Chiara Tasso, essays written by Spanish learners of English were compiled and studied.

This chapter presents a study of interactional metadiscourse features in the written production in English made by Spanish learners with a C1 level of language proficiency, taking into account the levels of the Common European Framework of Reference for Languages. The motivation behind this work was the verification of the lack of research which analyses how Spanish learners of English use interactional features in written texts. Thus, this chapter aims to examine the use and distributions of metadiscourse interactional features in the learner corpora compiled. In order to meet this objective, a corpus of essays was manually compiled. The methodology followed to respond to the general objective was a combination of quantitative and qualitative analyses of the corpus. Results allowed us to identify the interactional metadiscourse features that EFL Spanish learners master at C1, as well as their specific needs.

In Chapter 12, "Intercultural rhetoric in the written academic discourse: the rhetorical function of citation in English and Spanish by college students and expert writers", whose author is David Sánchez-Jiménez, the practice of citation in an academic setting in two cultural communities, the American and the Spanish, is explained. The main objective of this research is to determine what the rhetorical functions of citations in the master's thesis of American and Spanish students written in their native language are, as well as in scientific articles of American and Spanish professional writers in Applied Linguistics. The author used a computational text analysis of the rhetorical functions of citations arranged in a typological classification. The results obtained from this research indicate that the different cultural conventions in the compositions highlight differences not only in the texts written in English with respect to the Spanish group, but likewise show rhetorical characteristics identifiable to professional academic discourse and to postgraduate students.

In Chapter 13, "Measuring linguistic complexity and proficiency in learner and native academic English", Javier Pérez-Guerra investigates linguistic complexity in learner academic language. The notion of complexity is approached by considering a number of lexical, structural, and syntactic features as generated by computational tools. The hypotheses are that learner academic language deviates from native language as regards linguistic complexity, and proficient learner language involves a greater degree of complexity. The data on second language academic language are retrieved from the Written Corpus of Learner English, which includes academic writings by Spanish university students from the A2 to the C2 level of the Common European Framework of Reference for Languages. The mother tongue data comprise A-level essays extracted from the Louvain Corpus of Native English Essays. The software used are Coh-Metrix and the L2 Syntactic Complexity Analyzer. Principal Component Analysis and an ordered logistic regression analysis are used to determine the most significant groupings of features (or variables) in the dataset.

In Chapter 14, "A new linguistic corpus in Catalan and the teaching of languages for specific purposes at university", Anna Montesinos-López and Francesca Romero-Forteza present a pioneer research project in the teaching of specialised languages in Catalan, within the framework of higher education. By establishing a corpus produced by students of specialised subjects in Catalan, the linguistic shortcomings and behaviours shown by the students of said subjects can be inferred. The programme of educational action for the corresponding subjects is then based on the collected corpus, in order to address the needs of Catalan language students in the technical/scientific domain.

Chapter 15, "Overused bundles in the written academic English of Spanish EFL students", authored by Miguel Fuster-Márquez and Jesús Fernández-Domínguez, identifies and classifies overused bundles in the written academic tasks of Spanish university students of English Studies and Translation at the University of Valencia. This is done by means of a frequency-driven corpus methodology. For that purpose, CASTLE, a corpus of about half a million words, has been analysed and compared with the findings in two native corpora. One of them, ACUV, is a corpus with over one million words containing research articles written by expert native writers; the other is a selection of BAWE, containing over one million words of novice writing whose first language is English. The distributional data of the spoken conversational component of the BNC, accessed through the BNCWeb, has also been used in this analysis. Their findings show that a sizeable number of four-word bundles represent extreme cases of overuse, i.e. fairly unconventional sequences which are absent from the native corpora we have compared them with. Among other features, most of these bundles are personalised stance discourse sequences where writer visibility plays an important role.

Chapter 16, "Verbs of vision in academic discourse: variations in the use of their non-literal senses in L1 expert, L1 non-expert and L2 non-expert writing", is authored by Hanna Skorczynska. She focuses on the variations of the non-literal senses of three verbs of vision: 'regard', 'see', and 'view' in three corpora: English L1 expert writing, English L1 non-expert writing, and English L2 non-expert writing. The non-literal senses of the verbs express major mental activities involved in scientific enquiry and perform important discourse functions in academic texts. Previous studies pointed to areas of difficulty for English L2 non-expert writers with regard to the use of lexical verbs. Taking into account that the usage of literally and non-literally used words differs in terms of their frequencies and lexico-grammatical patterns, this research provides a close scrutiny of the frequency of the non-literal 'regard', 'see', and 'view', as well as the data on the variations of three non-literal senses of 'see' together with the syntactic structures used in three corpora. The findings not only point to cases of overuse and underuse of forms and structures in L2 non-expert writing, but also unveil a complex picture of variations that deserve to be further studied.

Chapter 17, "Showing emotion in academic discourse. A pragmatic analysis", by Eva M. Mestre-Mestre, focuses on the analysis of master's thesis. She indicates that academic discourse is starting to display some changes in issues such as the way authors show themselves and establish rapport with their audiences. These changes need to be acknowledged and learned by non-native English speakers who wish to be competent and proficient in this field. This also affects teachers, who need to include them in their instructions. It appears that pragmatic competence is one of the most difficult to acquire, albeit by proficient L2 students, and thus these changes increase the greater degree of difficulty for non-native English speakers who choose to write their research in English. The study analyses the expression of emotions found in texts written in English by native and non-native English speakers. In particular, a corpus of Masters Theses is analysed. Findings show that strategies used in the L1 and the L2 are dissimilar, thus implying a need for further analysis and pedagogical implications.

Finally, this section and the whole book close with Chapter 18, "Proofreading, the net and foreign language anxiety in the use of apology formulae in an online forum. A learner corpus study", written by Milagros Torrado-Cespón. This author points out that the use of internet as a medium of instruction has changed the way students write. This chapter analyses the productions of university students in online forums which are part of their final mark and where they use English as a vehicular language. In this case, they seem to forget proofreading before sending their posts and the solution is writing another post apologising for their mistakes. The lack of proofreading, the influence of social networks, typing, and foreign language anxiety are the basis to understand students' performances in this type of tasks. As a result, it is important to advise students to revise their online productions to maintain a certain standard in written language.

All these chapters focus on the study of different genres, specifically, in the way authors organise discourse and the use of corpus analysis in language teaching. The reader of this volume can observe how language patterns change depending on the genre studied and the way corpora are used to provide objective results. The core message of this manuscript is that the diversity of genres studied here shows different ways of communication, providing clear signals that this research provided insights that would not have been possible had this book not been researched, written, and this argument developed.

References

Ädel, A. (2006). *Metadiscourse in L1 and L2 English*. Amsterdam/Philadelphia: John Benjamins.

Dahl, T. (2004). Textual metadiscourse in research articles: a marker of national culture or of academic discipline? *Journal of Pragmatics* 36, 1807–1825.

Hyland, K. (2005). *Metadiscourse: Exploring Interaction in Writing*. London: Continuum.

Hyland, K. and Tse, P. (2004). Metadiscourse in academic writing: a reappraisal. *Applied Linguistics* 25/2, 156–177.

Mauranen, A. (1993). *Cultural Differences in Academic Rhetoric: A Textlinguistic Study*. Frankfurt: Peter Lang.

Salas Valdebenito, M. (2015). Una propuesta de taxonomía de marcadores metadiscursivos para el discurso académico-científico escrito en español. *Revista Signos* 48/87, 95–120.

Section 1

Corpus Studies on Academic Discourse

1 Variation in the Use of Self-Mentions in Different Specific Fields of Knowledge in Academic English

María Luisa Carrió-Pastor

1 Introduction

In this chapter, several aspects are taken into account. This study analyses the way in which writers show an authorial persona, establish their credentials, or present themselves as a group of researchers. It is a corpus-driven analysis and so the challenges involved in the identification, tagging, and comparison of rhetoric strategies used in academic English are also considered.

The theoretical background of this study is functional, following the main aspects described by Halliday and Matthiessen (2014). From this starting point, I focus on the analysis of the rhetorical strategies used in academic language with the aim of identifying patterns that pinpoint differences in different specific fields of knowledge. For this study, I selected the specific fields of knowledge of engineering, also known as belonging to hard sciences, linguistics, which can be included in the field of soft sciences, and finally medicine, a research area that combines characteristics from both hard and soft sciences. The taxonomy used to identify discourse markers is based on previous studies on metadiscourse by Thompson (2001) and Hyland (2005b), who identified two categories and ten sub-categories that determined the way writers present their findings to readers. Metadiscourse has been analysed by many researchers such as Mauranen (1993), Hyland and Tse (2004), Dahl (2004), Hyland (2005b, 2015, 2017), Ädel (2006), Vande Kopple (2012) and Carrió-Pastor (2016). Most of the research conducted to date has focused on identifying characteristics of metadiscourse in academic English. The different discourse markers are identified and discussed to establish the different patterns of academic English and the way writers should use language to convince readers about their findings. In this chapter, academic discourse is studied to identify the way writers refer to themselves taking into account different fields of knowledge, not different languages. Few studies have focused on this aspect, so I consider this gap should be filled in order to identify whether the writers show their authorial persona.

This study is part of a broader project which aims to identify and analyse metadiscursive strategies in English and Spanish, funded by the Spanish Ministerio de Economía y Competitividad (reference FFI2016-77941-P). The project aims to analyse metadiscourse strategies used in English and Spanish in academic language in several disciplines, to detect variation in the use of Spanish and English in linguistics, medicine, and engineering, and to identify whether papers written in English and Spanish use metadiscourse devices in an appropriate way.

Thus, the main objective of this chapter is to show that researchers do not present themselves and promote their own research in the same way, as self-representation in writing varies depending on the particular field of knowledge. The specific objectives are, first, to detect the frequencies of first person singular and first person plural self-mentions in academic research papers; second, to identify whether writers show an authorial persona, establish their credentials, and portray themselves as individuals or as a group of researchers; and finally, through the functional classification of self-mentions, to study whether the representation of identity changes within the same genre of academic English in the specific knowledge areas of engineering, medicine, and linguistics.

2 Metadiscourse: Self-Mentions

Pragmatics is a field of research that emphasises the importance of the addressee in the act of communication. In this sense, apart from being proficient in the syntactic and lexical aspects of a language, speakers should also be aware of pragmatic features such as irony, mitigation, humour, boosting, engagement, etc. Sometimes, it can be observed that communication is not successful due to the imposition of certain rules of a given culture on another one or to not being aware of the cultural implications of a language and to the difficulties in intracultural communication when a speaker is monolingual and does not understand the interlocutor's pragmatic intentions. In this sense, I believe that communicative competence should include pragmalinguistic competence, that is, being able to use a proper form to communicate, and sociopragmatic competence, that is, to choose the right meaning to avoid intercultural errors.

Focusing on academic writing, it is well known that the use of devices within a particular context in English may restrain the meaning and functional values of some words in specialised discourse, but sometimes variation occurs, as has been stated in several studies (Carrió-Pastor and Muñiz 2013, 2015a, 2015b, Carrió-Pastor 2014, 2016). Specifically, the prominence of metadiscourse in academic communication has been emphasised by several researchers such as Crismore (1989), Vande Kopple (1985, 2002), Crismore, Markkanen, and Steffensen (1993),

Mauranen (1993), Hyland and Tse (2004), Dahl (2004), Hyland (2005b, 2015, 2017), Ädel (2006), and Gillaerts and de Velde (2010).

Citing Hyland (2015: 1):

> Metadiscourse is the interpersonal resources used to organize a discourse or the writer's stance toward either its content or the reader. [...] while some researchers restrict this to features that help organize the text as text, others take a wider view and see it as the ways speakers and writers project themselves into their discourse to signal their understanding of their material and their audience.

In this sense, the latter position of metadiscourse helps us to carry out a cross-cultural exploration of interpersonality and to explore not only the text but also the way in which writers influence their readers and the way we convince others about our findings in academic research discourse. In this position, we follow the studies of Crismore (1989), Vande Kopple (1985, 2002), Hyland and Tse (2004), Hyland (2005b), and Kawase (2015).

One aspect that has also been considered important by most of the researchers that focus on metadiscourse is the different categorisation or the taxonomies that are related to metadiscourse. Studies by Hyland and Tse (2004), Hyland (1998, 2005b), Mur Dueñas (2011), Hu and Cao (2011), and Kawase (2015) propose the identification of the different metadiscourse devices and their classification into categories and sub-categories taking into account their functional nature. These authors divide metadiscourse devices into two main categories:

a Interactive devices, which aim to organise the information depending on the needs and expectations of the listener.

b Interactional devices, which intend to stimulate interaction between the speaker and the listener.

In this chapter, I focus on interactional devices to study how writers manage to describe their self-representation to readers in academic papers. The category of interactional devices is divided into five subcategories (Mur Dueñas 2011: 3070):

- Hedges: features which limit the writer's full commitment to what is stated in a proposition and which may be the result of certain pragmatic conventions in academic writing.
- Boosters: features which highlight the writers' certainty and conviction about a proposition and which may be the result of certain pragmatic conventions in academic writing.
- Attitude markers: items which show the writer's affective evaluation of given parameters or entities.

- Engagement markers: elements through which scholars bring the readers into the text, involving them in the negotiation of academic knowledge. These include personal pronouns, question forms, directives and asides.
- Self-mentions: explicit signals of the authorial persona of the scholar(s). They feature self-references and self-citations.

In particular, my interest in this chapter lies in the last sub-category, self-mentions, which have mainly been analysed to identify specific characteristics in specific genres in English (Hyland 2001, 2002, 2003, 2005a, 2011, Beke 2005, Harwood 2005, Salas Valdebenito 2015, Albalat-Mascarell and Carrió-Pastor 2019, Peng 2019, Qin and Uccelli 2019) or to compare different patterns of the use of self-mentions in different languages (Vassileva 2000, Flottum, Dahl and Kinn 2006, Mur Dueñas 2007, 2011, Carciu 2009, Molino 2010, Chávez Muñoz 2013).

The sub-category of self-mentions includes any kind of reference to the author or authors of a research paper. These metadiscourse markers "[...] manifest an authorial voice through which they [scholars] can portray themselves as expert, reliable members of a given disciplinary community" (Mur Dueñas 2007: 144). Self-mentions are essential in academic discourse because they indicate the degree of the speaker's presence in a given discourse, measured by the incidence of first person singular and plural pronouns and their corresponding adjectives. They include personal references such as *I*, *me*, *my*, *myself*, *exclusive we/our*, *our*, *ourselves*, *us*, and self-citations.

Self-mentions can be seen as part of the persuasive strategies used by researchers to convince others about the importance of their findings, allowing writers to emphasise and seek agreement for their contributions. Thus, it can be seen as a rhetorical strategy that should be mastered by researchers as it connects with the "desire to present oneself as an informed and reliable colleague, strongly identifying oneself with a particular view to gain credit for one's individual perspective or research decisions" (Hyland 2005a: 106).

Self-mentions are considered critical features of persuasion in academic writing, being associated with the construction of a credible *ethos* that is used to convince readers of the validity of the research being reported in a research paper. Specifically, the use of the first person pronoun in singular form has been the focus of many studies. As an example, Tang and John (1999) take into account the seminal work of Ivanic (1998: 307) to distinguish different uses of the first person pronoun in academic writing:

> [t]here is a continuum from not using 'I' at all, through using 'I' with verbs associated with the process of structuring the writing, to using 'I' in association with the research process, and finally to using 'I' with verbs associated with cognitive acts.

The reflexive form of this pronoun has also drawn attention, as Starfield and Ravelli's study (2006: 231) shows. For them, the reflexive *I* allows authors to "create a powerful textual self" that manages to convey authority "through its explicit attention to autobiography" and its presentation of the author as a "subject within the research process". Tang and John (1999) illustrate the different uses of the first person pronoun in academic writing in the taxonomy shown in Figure 1.1, from the least to the most authoritative authorial presence.

The different roles and identities of the taxonomy identified by Tang and John (1999) are defined in the following way:

a The representative: "a generic first-person pronoun, usually realised as the plural 'we' or 'us', that writers use as a proxy for a larger group of people" (Tang and John 1999: 27).
b The guide through the essay: "the person who shows the reader through the essay (...), locates the reader and the writer together in the time and place of the essay, draws the reader's attention to points which are plainly visible or obvious within the essay" (Tang and John 1999: 27).
c The architect: "foregrounds the person who writes, organizes, structures, and outlines the material in the essay" (Tang and John 1999: 28).
d The recounter of the research process: "describes or recounts the various steps of the research process" (Tang and John 1999: 28).
e The opinion-holder: "the person who shares an opinion, view or attitude (for example, by expressing agreement, disagreement or interest) with regard to known information or established facts" (Tang and John 1999: 28).
f The originator: "It involves the writer's conception of the ideas or knowledge claims which are advanced in the essay" [...] "it calls for the writer to present or signal these as *new* in the essay" (Tang and John 1999: 29).

No 'I'	'I' as representa-tive	'I' as guide	'I' as architect	'I' as recounter of research process	'I' as opinion-holder	'I' as originator

Least powerful authorial presence → *Most powerful authorial presence*

Figure 1.1 Tang and John's (1999: 29) taxonomy of the first person singular.

Later, Sheldon (2009: 261) indicates that the use of the first person singular is crucial, "revealing the researcher's critical reflections on the intellectual value of the research".

She went further by identifying two subtypes of reflexive *I* in Spanish and English: the narrative self, comprising anecdotal accounts that connect the researcher with the study, and the explicatory self, stressing the engagement of the individual with the research.

However, Kawase (2015: 122) focuses on the use of *we/our* and also indicates, in the analysis of introductions, that self-mentions are used "to describe insufficient aspects of previous knowledge" and to present themselves as the researchers who could not obtain the desired results in previous studies.

Focusing on the use of self-mentions in specific settings, Harwood (2005: 1213) identifies the self-promotional use of the pronouns *I* and *we* in four specific areas of knowledge in academic English. He pays attention to self-citation, as

> reference to one's previous work is a powerful weapon in the quest for disciplinary ratification and credibility, showing that the researcher is in the vanguard of research and is working on issues which are preoccupying the discipline at the time of writing.

Additionally, it can be observed in this study that self-references are used to self-promote research, to alert readers about the research done by the authors, to create a research space, to highlight innovation, to show how previous difficulties have been overcome, to repeat claims and results, and to show that the work of the authors deserves to be taken seriously. Furthermore, Mur Dueñas (2007) focuses on the specific use of the personal pronoun *we* in business management research papers and identifies eight rhetorical functions: (a) explaining a procedure, (b) making a claim or statement, elaborating an argument, (c) stating a hypothesis, an expectation, or a wish, (d) stating a goal or purpose, (e) showing results or findings, (f) assessing the limitations of their research, (g) assessing the strengths of their research, and (h) outlining the steps followed in the research article.

This analysis takes into account the taxonomy of Tang and John (1999) to show how writers foreground their knowledge claims and represent themselves to readers in three specific fields of knowledge, that is, engineering, medicine, and linguistics. I have adapted their proposal to the identification of the self-mentions *I*, *me*, *my*, exclusive *we*, *our*, and *us*. A corpus-driven, quantitative analysis has been carried out based on the findings extracted with a semi-automatic tagging tool and a qualitative analysis was applied to the rhetorical functions found. The procedure followed is described in the sections below.

3 Corpus

The corpus for this study comprises 150 research papers from the fields of engineering, medicine, and linguistics (50 from each of them). Only research papers based on applied linguistics were included in the corpus to ensure comparability. The papers were taken from journals included in Journal Citation Reports (JCR), in the indexes of 2016 and 2017.

The papers were written mainly by native English speakers. This was guaranteed by the names and affiliation of the authors and in the cases of multiple-authorship, at least 60% of the authors should be native speakers of English. Although this aspect is quite difficult to verify, these were the only available criteria and it should be added that the published papers meet native-speakers' standards as they were reviewed by the editors and revised by the authors prior to their publication, and this may guarantee the representativeness of the language used by the authors in the three specific settings.

Table 1.1 shows the data of the corpus compiled:

Table 1.1 Data of the corpus compiled

Overall	*Engineering*	*Medicine*	*Linguistics*	*Total*
Tokens	265,901	197,834	244,746	1,635,951
Running words	3,654,489	3,378,225	3,894,061	10,926,775

Although the number of research journals compiled was the same for each discipline, the tokens in each paper were different, the papers related to medicine being shorter than the ones related to engineering and linguistics. In order to prepare the research papers for analysis with a semi-automatic tool, the articles in pdf format were converted into txt format. In this process, the tables, figures, images, references, formulae, etc., were eliminated from the corpus.

4 Method

The three corpora compiled were used to study the variation in the use of self-mentions and the specific characteristics of research papers specialised in linguistics, medicine, and engineering. Once compiled, the three corpora were uploaded in the tagging tool METOOL. This tool was designed by Constantin Orasan, a member of the Research Institute for Information and Language Processing of the University of Wolverhampton. The tool identifies metadiscourse devices, which are tagged by the members of the research project funded by the Spanish government with reference FFI2016-77941-P. The tool is mainly used for the identification and tagging of rhetorical devices in academic discourse, although it has also been used to identify metadiscourse devices in other genres. In this chapter, the self-mention devices used in the three corpora were identified and tagged, taking into account the use of self-mentions in the context. The devices found in the corpus from the sub-category of self-mentions were: *I*, *me*, *my*, exclusive *we*, *our*, and *us*. The devices *myself* and *ourselves* were not found in the corpora analysed and I decided not to include self-citations in order to focus on the pronouns that indicate self-mention. Also, the mentions to the authors of the paper such as 'this paper' and 'this author' were not identified as my interest lies in the different use of first person singular versus first person plural in research papers and, thus, in the differences that we can identify in specific fields of knowledge. The occurrences were then extracted from the three corpora and contrasted to show a synchronic variation in academic discourse using the tagging tool METOOL. Figure 1.2 shows the way metadiscourse devices are detected and tagged.

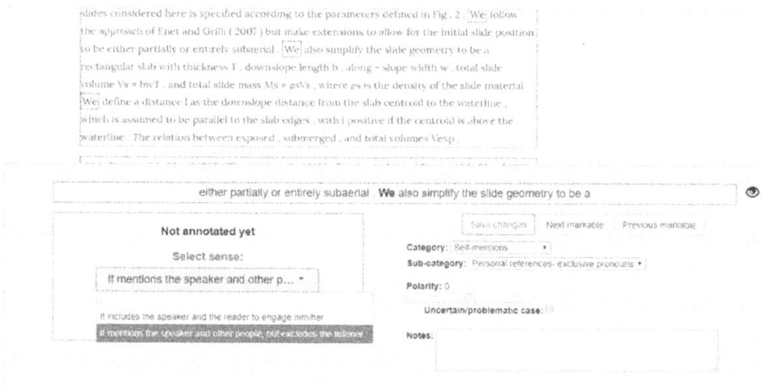

Figure 1.2 Annotation of self-mentions in the engineering corpus.

The tool automatically identifies the self-mentions in the texts, which are highlighted in yellow. Then, the tagger selects one meaning from the display (see the bottom of the figure), followed by a category, a sub-category, and finally saves the changes. If the metadiscourse marker is a problematic case, the tagger can tick the box and there is also the possibility of identifying the polarity of a discourse marker. Additionally, there is a box in which the tagger can comment on the incidences. After this tagging process, the researcher can then analyse the results of the tagged corpora. The number of occurrences can be seen by selecting the different sub-categories or one particular self-mention device can also be selected.

In Figure 1.3, the occurrences identified in the field of linguistics are shown in their context. The researcher can check the sense selected, the category, and whether the annotator inserted any notes. The full text in which the self-mentions were found can also be accessed through the function 'go to annotation'.

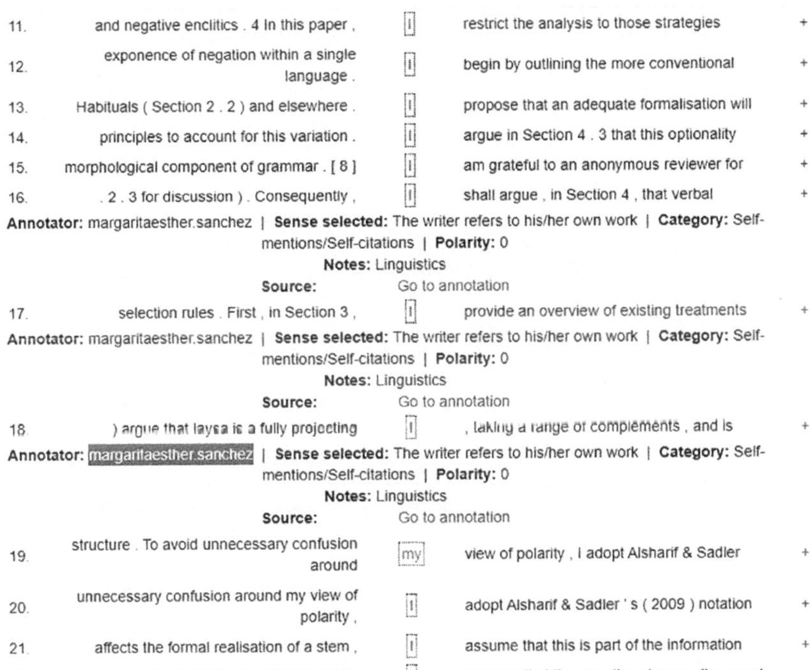

11.	and negative enclitics . 4 In this paper ,	I	restrict the analysis to those strategies	+
12.	exponence of negation within a single language .	I	begin by outlining the more conventional	+
13.	Habituals (Section 2 . 2) and elsewhere .	I	propose that an adequate formalisation will	+
14.	principles to account for this variation .	I	argue in Section 4 . 3 that this optionality	+
15.	morphological component of grammar . [8]	I	am grateful to an anonymous reviewer for	+
16.	. 2 . 3 for discussion) . Consequently ,	I	shall argue , in Section 4 , that verbal	+

Annotator: margaritaesther.sanchez | **Sense selected:** The writer refers to his/her own work | **Category:** Self-mentions/Self-citations | **Polarity:** 0
Notes: Linguistics
Source: Go to annotation

17.	selection rules . First , in Section 3 ,	I	provide an overview of existing treatments	+

Annotator: margaritaesther.sanchez | **Sense selected:** The writer refers to his/her own work | **Category:** Self-mentions/Self-citations | **Polarity:** 0
Notes: Linguistics
Source: Go to annotation

18.	) argue that laysa is a fully projecting	I	, taking a range of complements , and is	+

Annotator: margaritaesther.sanchez | **Sense selected:** The writer refers to his/her own work | **Category:** Self-mentions/Self-citations | **Polarity:** 0
Notes: Linguistics
Source: Go to annotation

19.	structure . To avoid unnecessary confusion around	my	view of polarity , I adopt Alsharif & Sadler	+
20.	unnecessary confusion around my view of polarity ,	I	adopt Alsharif & Sadler ' s (2009) notation	+
21.	affects the formal realisation of a stem ,	I	assume that this is part of the information	+

Figure 1.3 Occurrences of self-mention I in linguistics.

In this way, the annotators can be sure they have spotted the correct use of metadiscourse devices, as they can check the meaning of the annotated marker twice. This tool was designed taking into account that corpus tagging is not an easy process and nowadays linguistic elements are identified, but it is difficult to disambiguate their meaning. This is a thorough process that requires precision in the identification of markers and sometimes, depending on the ambiguity of the marker, training is necessary. Annotation currently includes structure tagging, grammar tagging, lexical tagging, etc., but the main concern of natural language processing is to identify the correct meaning of a word in a given context, to disambiguate the meaning of some words, to automate the process, and to obtain higher reliability in tagging.

Additionally, the functional meaning of self-mentions was checked in the corpora and the different rhetorical functions were identified and examples were discussed. The proposal of Tang and John (1999) was initially used for the analysis, adapting it to the findings of this study. These authors proposed this taxonomy for the classification of pronominal discourse functions, but here I adapt the taxonomy to the rhetorical functions of the self-mentions found in the corpora, i.e. *I*, *me*, *my*, exclusive *we*, *our*, and *us*.

Once the total occurrences of self-mentions in the three corpora had been obtained, the results were divided into the different functions of self-mentions identified in the analysis. The occurrences were then normalised to 10,000 words, as the numbers of tokens of the three corpora were different. After normalising the results, the data were compared and examples of the most frequent or singular occurrences were discussed in the results section. Finally, conclusions were drawn.

5 Results

This section is divided into two subsections: one that includes the frequency of use of first person self-references and another that explains the functional analysis of first person self-references. As indicated earlier, the taxonomy used to classify the functions of self-mentions is the one proposed by Tang and John (1999).

5.1 Frequency of Use of First Person Self-References

Table 1.2 shows the total number of self-mentions found in the three corpora of the three specific fields of knowledge. The total numbers of sentences and tokens have also been added to compare the way authors organise academic discourse in engineering, medicine, and linguistics.

Table 1.2 Results of the corpora analysed

	Occurrences Engineering	*Occurrences Medicine*	*Occurrences Linguistics*	*Total occurrences*
Self-mentions	684	970	2,212	3,866
Number of sentences	18,546	15,546	16,813	50,905
Number of tokens	265,901	197,834	244,746	1,635,951

It can be observed that the numbers of tokens and sentences in the three corpora are different, with a higher number in the engineering corpus, followed by the linguistics and medicine corpora. The total number of self-mentions (*I*, *me*, *my*, exclusive *we*, *our*, and *us*) found in the three corpora was 3,866. It should be noticed that in the linguistics corpus, we found more occurrences than in medicine and engineering. When analysing the corpora, it was observed that most linguistics papers were single-authored, whereas all the medicine and engineering papers were mainly multi-authored. This can be seen when the occurrences of self-mentions were classified in the different markers: *I*, *my*, *me*, exclusive *we*, *our*, and *us*. Table 1.3 indicates that there are differences among the three corpora. Some of them, such as the use of the first person singular, are quite frequent in linguistics, but they are seldom used in medicine and never used in engineering.

Table 1.3 Occurrences and normalised frequencies of first person self-mentions

Field of knowledge	*Occurrences I (normalised 10,000)*	*Occ. my (norm. 10,000)*	*Occ. me (norm. 10,000)*	*Occ. exclusive we (norm. 10,000)*	*Occ. our (norm. 10,000)*	*Occ. us (norm. 10,000)*	*Total occurrences (normalised 10,000)*
Engineering	0 (0.00)	0 (0.00)	0 (0.00)	505 (18.99)	150 (1.88)	26 (0.97)	681 (25.61)
Medicine	3 (0.15)	4 (0.20)	10 (0.50)	599 (30.27)	318 (16.07)	36 (1.81)	970 (49.03)
Linguistics	149 (6.08)	175 (7.15)	77 (3.14)	982 (40.12)	606 (24.76)	223 (9.11)	2,212 (90.37)
Total	152 (0.92)	179 (1.09)	87 (0.53)	2,086 (12.75)	1,074 (6.56)	285 (1.74)	3,863 (23.61)

The most frequent self-mention used in the three corpora is the subject pronoun exclusive *we*. This fact indicates that most papers are multi-authored or that authors use *we* as an academic way of referring to a single author, and is a way of being politer and of hiding the writer's face to avoid criticism from others. Hyland (2001) and Mur Dueñas (2007) also mention the cases of *we* used in single-authored academic papers, indicating that the purpose of the authors is to emphasise their role as authors.

Sometimes, this self-mention may be considered a form of the *royal we*, and used to include other people that have not contributed to the paper but are working with the author on this theory. The use of *we* instead of *us* indicates that the author is not claiming authority, he/she is avoiding possible criticism with the use of *royal we*. The use of the authorial *we* is very common in academia for single-authored papers as a way to avoid showing vanity and to be humble. That is also the reason for the use of the passive voice in many academic papers instead of the first person pronoun. The results extracted from the analysis indicate that this is not the case in linguistics, due to the high number of single-authored papers and I also believe that the knowledge of the mechanisms of language makes linguists more conscious of the importance of using first person singular pronouns when they are the only author of an analysis. Additionally, given the nature of the linguistics experiments, there are more experiments carried out by one author than by several authors.

Thus, the exclusive pronoun *we* is the most frequent in the three corpora and, consequently, the possessive pronoun *our* and the object pronoun *us* are also frequently used. In contrast, the subject pronoun *I* is used in linguistics more frequently than in medicine (it was only found in one single-authored paper) or engineering. Consequently, the possessive pronoun *my* and the object pronoun *me* were used mainly in the field of knowledge of linguistics.

If we observe the total frequencies of self-mentions found in the three corpora, it can be observed that linguists used more self-mentions to refer to their findings (90.37), procedural choices, or views, with the aim of creating their identity and projecting a positive and reliable self to the reader. Medical doctors also used (49.03) self-mentions quite frequently to self-promote in academic writing, but most occurrences, as in engineering, were found in the use of the first person plural pronoun and possessive adjective. In the case of medicine and engineering, the papers in which the authors used fewer self-mentions, the way to describe the experiments, the method, the results, or the objectives was basically by using the passive voice.

5.2 Functional Analysis of First Person Self-References

The functions of the self-mentions (based on the taxonomy of Tang and John 1999) identified in the study are described in this section with examples to discuss the specific rhetorical purposes for which authors make their persona explicit. Only examples of the first person plural are going to be discussed, given that none or very few occurrences were found in the fields of knowledge of engineering and medicine.

Here, the first category identified by Tang and John (1999), "The representative", was not found. Authors use this function to speak in general, to explain that this is a general fact and, consequently, it reduces the speaker to a non-entity, and this is the less powerful role. In the three corpora analysed, no occurrences were found with this role, as in the specific domains of engineering, medicine, and linguistics, writers show a more powerful role, as they describe their own research and need to position themselves as authors, making their authorial presence explicit. Authors represent themselves, they do not wish to represent others or describe their research in general, and they put forth a stance that performs a visible role in their specific field of knowledge.

5.2.1 The Guide

This function, which entails guiding the reader through the research paper, is the most frequent in the three corpora analysed. Below, it can be seen in Examples 1–3 from the corpora that in the three specific fields of knowledge, writers use *we* to draw readers' attention to some aspects that make them follow the argumentative discourse of the writers. This function is useful to connect ideas and explain the logical procedure followed in the research described. The authors of academic papers explain the different steps of the research (see Example 1), describe the method used (Example 2), or comment on the results of the analysis (Example 3).

Example 1- "*We* now consider several scenarios with different levels of knowledge about the type of the next task, the lower and upper..." [Eng. 19]
Example 2- "*We* used descriptive statistics to describe the baseline and post-UV light installation keyboard cultures." [Med. 02]
Example 3- "In (14a) *we* compare the number of students Amy knows with the number Dan knows." [Ling. 02]

Tang and John (1999: 28) explain that "since the reader as guide is always implicitly or explicitly accompanied by the reader, this particular usage of the first person pronoun is usually realized in the plural, inclusive form of we or us". I consider that the self-mention *we* in the corpus analysed in this study is used as exclusive, not inclusive as mentioned by these authors. Inclusive *we* includes the reader in the communication process and so it may be considered to have the function of an engagement marker. It is not a self-mention, which is considered exclusive and refers to the writers, not to the readers. The authors describe the study and guide the readers, but they refer to all the participants in the study, and they do not include the readers in Examples 1–3. Thus, I use this category of self-mentions but consider that it refers to all the authors of the academic paper.

Moreover, it was observed that the subject pronoun *we* was mainly used as the guide, while the object pronoun *us* was sometimes used with the role mentioned by Tang and John (1999). This function, which was expressed with *let* + *us*, was detected in the corpora of engineering and linguistics, not in the medicine corpus. Example 4 shows this role in engineering:

Example 4- "Let *us* consider the event that the system functions for the next task it has to perform, denoted by S. Let". [Eng. 14]

In this example, it seems that the writer includes the reader in the narration of the paper, as the form let + pronoun is used to express a suggestion that includes you and the other people. Nevertheless, I think that writers try to transmit a dynamic or more informal way or they even use *let* as an imperative, as in the example found in linguistics, shown in Example 5:

Example 5- "Let *us* check that all (poet) does satisfy the accusative extension condition" [Ling. 14]

In the research papers analysed, the third function described by Tang and John (1999: 28), i.e. the architect, who "foregrounds the person who writes, organizes, structures, and outlines the material in the essay", was quite similar to the role of guide in the corpora analysed. Thus, the decision was made to merge the categories of the guide and the architect in the former, as in the corpora analysed, it was almost impossible to differentiate these two functions.

5.2.2 *The Recounter of the Research Process*

In the three corpora, the function of recounter was found in all the texts analysed.

The writers explain, mostly in the methodology section, the way material was collected, the process used in the method, etc. Examples 6–8 illustrate the way writers explain the process of the research and their role as the recounters of the research process.

Example 6- "*We* propose observational techniques to assess increases in risk levels and decide when it is necessary to update the risk management approach or deploy emergency measures" [Eng. 09]
Example 7- "*We* used descriptive statistics to describe the baseline and post-UV light installation keyboard cultures". "We interviewed participants from 2 units" [Med. 02]
Example 8- "*We* generated displays like those in Figure 3... For *our* target items, the player either made all 12 baskets...". [Ling. 07]

The writers describe the research steps and the process they used to get their results and to provide an answer to the objectives of the experiment.

5.2.3 *The Opinion Holder*

Academic language entails having an opinion and convincing others about this way of understanding a particular aspect of science. Thus, in the three corpora analysed, we found self-mentions with the function of opinion holder. Most of the authors use this function to explain the novelty of their experiments and their agreement or disagreement with previous studies. This category was found in the introduction, results, and conclusions sections of the research papers. Examples 9–11 show some of the opinion holder roles found in the three corpora:

Example 9- "We therefore believe using the Jabiru data is the best option available" [Eng. 08]
Example 10- "*We* know of only a single paper to date that has directly compared QoL after maxillectomy between obturators and flaps". [Med. 24]
Example 11- "In addition, *we* present evidence that these correlations can be improved if the set of refinements is lexically constrained, in keeping with broadly neo-Gricean views". [Ling. 03]

This function was performed in our corpora by the subject pronoun *we* or, in the linguistics papers, also by the first person singular pronoun *I*, as in Example 12:

Example 12- "In addition to the standard types e for individuals and t for truth values, *I* assume types p and v for space-points and real numbers, respectively". "*I* argue that loci should not be analyzed as..." [Ling. 12]

Linguists use the first person singular pronoun to explain their opinion and to compare this opinion with those of other researchers. This is one of the most important roles of academic writers: to fix a position and to use an experiment that justifies that they are right about their beliefs.

5.2.4 The Originator

This is the most powerful role that a writer can have in an academic paper. The authors explain that they create the experiment and that they show the results of their hypothesis and objectives. In this sense, writers show that they advance in science with their experiments and they are considered part of academia and they originate knowledge that is shared with other colleagues and society. Example 13 shows the way an author in the field of linguistics vindicates his/her ideas and the way he/she contributes to understanding language:

Example 13- "For this reason, *I* call the indexical field proposed in Figures 5 and 6 a "non exhaustive indexical field," as it includes many of the social qualities associated with intervocalic [z] without claiming to include all its possible social meanings. Niceness, confidence, and localness, on the one hand, and education and class, on the other, were combined in *my* statistical analysis due to correlations in listener evaluations." [Ling 17]

Examples 14 and 15 also show examples of authors playing the role of originator:

Example 14- "*We* propose an observational technique to assess...". "Furthermore, we also found in that study..." [Eng. 15]
Example 15- "*We* found substantial variation in mortality...". "Here we demonstrate that transplantation of...". [Med. 34]

Authors choose this role as the originator mainly in the results and conclusion sections of the research papers. Writers refer to research processes and outcomes in order to highlight their findings and indicate the way the objectives are answered in the research paper. Carciu (2009) explains that in the corpus she analysed, "the combination of 'we' and 'our' in Discussion sections seems to suggest reasons of pragmatic politeness". In our three corpora, this function of politeness was not identified. Authors use *we*, *us*, and *our* in the discussion sections to show that they are the originators of the findings they describe in the academic paper. Their interest lies in highlighting their role as academics and knowledge searchers.

6 Conclusions

The main objective of this chapter was to use quantitative and qualitative analyses to demonstrate that researchers do not present themselves and refer to their own research in the same way in different specific settings. In fact, it was shown that self-representation in academic writing varies in frequencies and in the roles that authors transmit to readers. The powerful authorial presence of academic writers was studied in order to identify patterns and to observe whether the functions identified by Tang and John (1999) and also used by other researchers in their studies (Carciu 2009, Chávez Muñoz 2013) could be spotted in three domains: engineering, medicine, and linguistics.

In this analysis, the use of first person singular and first person plural self-mentions in academic research papers was discussed and it was discovered that first person singular pronouns were only used in linguistics. This is due to the fact that there were a higher number of single-authored research papers in linguistics, while in engineering and medicine all the papers were multi-authored. But it should be noted that even when papers on linguistics were single-authored, the writers sometimes used the first person plural pronoun as a self-mention. This may be due to the use of the plural form to hide their face using the *royal we* as an impersonal form.

In the results section, it was seen that writers show an authorial persona and establish their credentials in all three fields of knowledge. In linguistics, they portray themselves as individuals and use first person singular pronouns to describe their research. In medicine and engineering, as papers are multi-authored, they use self-mentions that reflect them as a group of researchers, but the function identified by Tang and John (1999), in which inclusive *we* was considered part of the functional classification of self-mentions, was not included in the analysis as I believe it belongs to the category of engagement markers and it has another function in text. In this study, I only took into account the references to the author, not to the reader, although some examples have been discussed.

Finally, it was seen that the representation of identity did not change within the same genre of academic English in the specific areas of knowledge of engineering, medicine, and linguistics, that is, in hard and soft sciences, as the functions identified and adapted from the taxonomy of Tang and John (1999) were used in the three corpora. Only four roles, i.e. guide, opinion holder, recounter, and originator, were identified in the corpora analysed. The functions of architect and representative were not found or the occurrences were similar and very difficult to distinguish. It was clear from the analysis that academic writers from the specific fields of engineering, medicine, and linguistics wish to mention that they are the authors of their work and that they prefer to adopt a more powerful authorial presence in their research. When comparing the results of this chapter with previous research mentioned in the theoretical background, it can be observed that authors are more aware that they work hard to write and communicate their research and thus they prefer to highlight this fact, using self-mentions in all the sections of the research paper.

In future research, I think that it could be interesting to compare these results with the use of impersonal forms in academic papers and also to study self-citations in order to have a full picture of the way writers construct their authorial persona.

References

Ädel, A. (2006). *Metadiscourse in L1 and L2 English.* Amsterdam/ Philadelphia: John Benjamins.

Albalat-Mascarell, A. and Carrió-Pastor, M. L. (2019). Self-representation in political campaign talk: A functional metadiscourse approach to self-mentions in televised presidential debates. *Journal of Pragmatics* 147, 86–99.

Beke, R. (2005). El metadiscurso interpersonal en artículos de investigación. *Revista Signos* 38, 7–18.

Carciu, O. M. (2009). An intercultural study of first-person plural references in biomedical writing. *Ibérica* 18, 71–92.

Carrió-Pastor, M. L. (2014). Cross-cultural variation in the use of modal verbs in academic English. *Sky, Journal of Linguistics* 27, 153–166.

Carrió-Pastor, M. L. (2016). A contrastive study of interactive metadiscourse in academic papers written in English and in Spanish. In F. Alonso Almeida, L. Cruz García and V. González Ruiz (Eds.), *Corpus-based studies on language varieties*, pp. 89–114. Bern: Peter Lang.

Carrió-Pastor, M. L. and Muñiz Calderón, R. (2013). Variation of English business e-mails in Asian countries. *Ibérica* 26, 55–76.

Carrió-Pastor, M. L. and Muñiz Calderón, R. (2015a). A contrastive analysis of metadiscourse features in business e-mails written by non-native speakers of English. *Procedia. Social and Behavioral Sciences* 173, 214–221.

Carrió-Pastor, M. and Muñiz Calderón, R. (2015b). Identification and causes of lexical variation in Chinese Business English. *English Today*, 31, 10–15.

Chávez Muñoz, M. (2013). The "I" in interaction: Authorial presence in academic writing. *Revista de Lingüística y Lenguas Aplicadas* 8, 49–58.

Crismore, A. (1989). *Talking with readers: Metadiscourse as rhetorical act.* New York: Peter Lang.

Crismore, A., Markkanen, R., and Steffensen, M. S. (1993). Metadiscourse in persuasive writing: A Study of Texts Written by American and Finnish University Students. *Written Communication* 10/1, 39–71.

Dahl, T. (2004). Textual metadiscourse in research articles: A marker of national culture or of academic discipline? *Journal of Pragmatics* 36, 1807–1825.

Flottum, K., Dahl, T. and Kinn, T. (2006). *Academic voices. Across languages and disciplines.* Amsterdam: John Benjamins.

Gillaerts, P. and Van de Velde, F. (2010). Interactional metadiscourse in research article abstracts. *Journal of English for Academic Purposes* 9, 128–139.

Halliday, M. A. K. and Matthiessen, Ch. (2014). *Halliday's introduction to functional grammar.* London: Routledge.

Harwood, N. (2005). Nowhere has anyone attempted... In this article I aim to do just that. A corpus-based study of self-promotional I and we in academic writing across four disciplines. *Journal of Pragmatics* 37, 1207–1231.

Hu, G. and Cao, F. (2011). Hedging and boosting in abstracts of applied linguistics articles: A comparative study of English and Chinese medium journals. *Journal of Pragmatics* 43, 2795–2809.

Hyland, K. (1998). Persuasion and context: The pragmatics of academic metadiscourse. *Journal of Pragmatics* 30, 437–455.

Hyland, K. (2001). Humble servants of the discipline? Self-mention in research articles. *English for Specific Purposes* 20, 207–226.

Hyland, K. (2002). Authority and invisibility: Authorial identity in academic writing. *Journal of Pragmatics* 34, 1091–1112.

Hyland, K. (2003). Self-citation and self-reference: Credibility and promotion in academic publication. *Journal of the American Society for Information Science and Technology* 54(3), 251–259.

Hyland, K. (2005a). A convincing argument: Corpus analysis and academic persuasion. In U. Connor and T. A. Upton (Eds.), *Discourse in the professions: Perspectives from corpus linguistics*, pp. 87–112. Amsterdam: John Benjamins.

Hyland, K. (2005b). *Metadiscourse: Exploring interaction in writing.* London: Continuum.

Hyland, K. (2011). Projecting an academic identity in some reflective genres. *Ibérica* 21, 9–30.
Hyland, K. (2015). Metadiscourse. In Karen Tracy, Cornelie Ilie and Todd Sandel (Eds.), *The international encyclopedia of language and social interaction*, pp. 1–11. New York: John Wiley and Sons.
Hyland, K. (2017). Metadiscourse: What is it and where is it going? *Journal of Pragmatics* 113, 16–29.
Hyland, K. and Tse, P. (2004). Metadiscourse in academic writing: A reappraisal. *Applied Linguistics* 25/2, 156–177.
Ivanic, R. (1998). *Writing and identity. The discoursal construction of identity in academic writing.* Amsterdam: John Benjamins.
Kawase, T. (2015). Metadiscourse in the introductions of PhD theses and research articles. *Journal of English for Academic Purposes* 20, 114–124.
Mauranen, A. (1993). *Cultural differences in academic rhetoric: A textlinguistic study.* Frankfurt: Peter Lang.
Molino, A. (2010). Personal and impersonal authorial references: A contrastive study of English and Italian Linguistics research articles. *Journal of English for Academic Purposes* 9, 86–101.
Mur Dueñas, P. (2007). 'I/we focus on…': A cross-cultural analysis of self-mentions in business management research articles. *Journal of English for Academic Purposes* 6, 143–162.
Mur Dueñas, P. (2011). An intercultural analysis of metadiscourse features in research articles written in English and in Spanish. *Journal of Pragmatics* 43, 3068–3079.
Peng, J.-E. (2019). Authorial voice constructed in citation in literature reviews of doctoral theses: Variation across training contexts. *English for Academic Purposes* 37, 11–21.
Qin, W. and Uccelli, P. (2019). Metadiscourse: Variation across communicative contexts. *Journal of Pragmatics* 139, 22–39.
Salas Valdebenito, M. (2015). Una propuesta de taxonomía de marcadores metadiscursivos para el discurso académico-científico escrito en español. *Revista Signos* 48, 95–120.
Sheldon, E. (2009). From one I to another: Discursive construction of self-representation in English and Castilian Spanish research articles. *English for Specific Purposes* 28/4, 251–265.
Starfield, S. and Ravelli, L. J. (2006). "The writing of this thesis was a process that I could not explore with the positivistic detachment of the classical sociologist": Self and structure in New Humanities research theses. *Journal of English for Academic Purposes* 5/3, 222–243.
Tang, R. and John, S. (1999). The 'I' in identity: Exploring writer identity in student academic writing through first person pronoun. *English for Specific Purposes* 18, 23–39.
Thompson, G. (2001). Interaction in academic writing: Learning to argue with the reader. *Applied Linguistics* 22, 58–78.
Vande Kopple, W. (1985). Some exploratory discourse on metadiscourse. *College Composition and Communication,* 36, 82–93.
Vande Kopple, W. (2002). Metadiscourse, discourse and issues in composition and rhetoric. In E. Barton and G. Stygall (Eds.), *Discourse studies in composition*, pp. 91–113. Cresskill, NJ: Hampton Press.

Vande Kopple, W. (2012). The importance of studying metadiscourse. *Applied Research in Linguistics* 1/2, 37–44.

Vassileva, I. (2000). *Who is the author? A contrastive analysis of authorial presence in English, German, French and Bulgarian academic discourse.* Sankt Augustin, Germany: Asgard Verlag.

2 The Expression of Gratitude in the Prefaces of Academic Books in Linguistics

Francisco Alonso-Almeida

1 Introduction

The present chapter discusses a fundamental aspect of academic writing, i.e. the expression of thanking, even if its presence in research documents does not represent, strictly speaking, a contribution to scientific development. Expressing gratitude in academic discourse seems to maintain and enhance social ties with other scholars and institutions in a call for acceptance in the academia. There is an important gap in the study of thanking in scholarly research, as put forward in Leithart (2014: 2):

> Gratitude is *de rigueur* for academics themselves: No academic book is complete without acknowledgements that fairly drip with gratitude (not, of course, to say flattery or obsequiousness). But the academics who express gratitude do not seem much interested in analysing it.

In research books, an ideal place to show gratitude is the prefatory material, as Bhatia has identified that one well-defined function of prefaces is to serve "academic as well as promotional purposes" (1997: 183). For this study, I have compiled texts from books in the field of linguistics, which were published in the chronological period 2000–2019, as I shall explain below.

Gratitude and the act of thanking are certainly known ideas in society, and everybody has an intuition about what this is. The way in which gratitude is articulated by a speaker and received by a hearer remains, therefore, personal. There exists, however, certain routinisation of thanking expressions, e.g. *thanks!* and *thank you!*, and this is evidence of the importance society gives to the acknowledgement of benefits. Originality is also possible. Much of this originality comes from variation in the way in which common stock phrases for communicating thanks are combined in order to adjust a particular expression to the communicative situation and needs. I shall comment on routinised expressions and variation in the corpus compiled, and the pragmatics of using these thanking expressions.

Understanding the concept of gratitude requires a multidisciplinary approach, as this notion is not exclusively linguistic, even if language might help to share and spread the emotion. Feeling grateful for something is fundamental in establishing and keeping social bonds, as everybody enjoys appreciation of their generous involvement and support in accomplishing something for another person. The idea of thanks is central to religion, as put forward in Leithart (2014: 14 ff), and the way in which gratitude is perceived is somehow different for reasons of misuse. In this context, subjugation may arise from the corrosive religious idea that sharing is virtuous and deserves no acknowledgement, as God is the ultimate benefactor. The reverse is also damaging, and gratitude for the benefits received may represent a tight bond that might be enslaving if wrong use of donating a favour is adopted by benefactors. As seen, contradicting positions may lead to turn gratitude into a bad sentiment. This has an obvious echo in all spheres of social life, and academic research is one of them. Scholars use thanking expressions for a variety of reasons, other than merely true appreciation, and the connection of gratitude with politeness and facework seems to be essential in their own notion of the term.

The concept of gratitude will be discussed in Section 2, along with some other related terms, including politeness. Section 3 presents a description of the corpus used for extracting examples of thanking expressions in prefaces. A definition of the genre is also in order in this section. The analysis of the texts and a discussion of the results are given afterwards. Finally, the conclusion section is offered.

2 Gratitude and Related Notions. What Gratitude Is and the Forms It Takes

Expressing one's gratitude towards a particular aspect of life or of human behaviour is certainly within those positive emotions a human being can experience (Watkins, 2014: 2). Showing one's gratitude towards some kind of help or support of any kind seems to be in order in scientific writing, but those feelings of appreciation are apparently not so common in life, as one may initially think. That is noted in Fagley (2018: 1), who states that gratitude is a continuum in which some people feel appreciation for some kind of benefits received at one end, while others do not feel positive in this respect at the other end. Regardless of this binary sense, gratitude can be understood, as described below:

> Gratitude is an emotion, the core of which is pleasant feelings about the benefit received. At the cornerstone of gratitude is the notion of *undeserved merit*. The grateful person recognizes that he or she did nothing to deserve the gift or benefit; it was freely bestowed... The benefit, gift, or personal gain might be material or nonmaterial

> (e.g., emotional or spiritual). Gratitude is other-directed—its objects include persons, as well as nonhuman intentional agents (God, animals, the cosmos; Solomon, 1977). It is important that gratitude has a positive valence: It feels good
>
> (Emmons & Mccullough, 2004: 5)

A related concept, as already suggested earlier, is *appreciation*. This has been reported as "a disposition that plays an important role in psychological well-being and the building and maintenance of social bonds" (Adler & Fagley, 2005: 80). In the case of academic writing, this support of the social side represents much of the work done by linguists (Kampf & Danziger, 2019: 13), and they, therefore, dedicate part of their texts to express polite behaviour in the elaboration and presentation of meaning. This might have a twofold function. One could be to attenuate the extent of their claims, and the other is to indeed indicate solidarity by acknowledging some kind of help or support. The opposite can have negative effects, as pointed out in Cui (2012: 753), as the lack of appreciation may result in the damage of group ties among the members of a particular academic community. In this context, the expression of thanks and its relationship with politeness stands clear (cf. Díaz Pérez, 2005). Golato (2005: 116) raises this point, and sees some connection between compliments and thanking, as the former represents "an expression of gratitude". Indeed, she contends that compliments are "used for affiliatory or face-maintaining moves" (2005: 116). It remains to be explained the exact nature of the relationship between politeness and thanking, and whether the effects of showing gratitude and appreciation are assessed differently according to the recipients' own evaluation of the thanking formula. This is touched upon in Section 2.1.

Acknowledgements are related to the expression of thanking, and they constitute an essential aspect of scholarly writing to the extent that they often have their own separate sections in academic books and theses, as pointed out in Hyland (2004: 305). Acknowledgements are defined as "formulations that take on an intermediate position between the internal contents of the ethnography and the people and relationships outside it" (Ben-Ari, 1987: 65). Another strategy to show recognition and appreciation is *mentions*. This is included in Hyland (2004: 314 ff) and represents a rhetorical device that has to do with name-dropping of individuals involved to any extent in the research carried out. In Hyland's analysis of dissertation's acknowledgements, the function of mentions is apparently twofold: (a) to gain the acceptance of the thesis, and (b) to "contribute to gaining the writer credit and ease the examination process for the student" (2004: 316).

The expressions of thanking described in this section are all quite common in the scientific literature as strategies which clearly seem to have a focus on an ethical side of research. With these, the author seeks to accredit some kind of support in the development of their research. There also seems to be another less ethical motivation, albeit reasonable in the academia environment, and that is to gain credibility through collegiality. The fact that the names of a number of people whose scholarly contribution is relevant for the scientific community appear *passim* in academic texts may trigger some benefits for the authors. The connection of this function with politeness stands opposite to the authors' true reaction for the help granted, and so this may be rather seen as an act of impoliteness (see Locher & Bousfield, 2008).

2.1 *The Relationship between Politeness and the Expression of Thanking*

Politeness and impoliteness are well-known concepts in the arena of applied linguistics, as the way in which information is presented has a clear impact on its reception. Leech (2014: 3) defines politeness, as follows:

> Politeness, in this broad sense, is a form of communicative behavior found very generally in human languages and among human cultures; indeed, it has been claimed as a universal phenomenon of human society. What it means to be polite (...) is to speak or behave in such a way as to (appear to) give benefit or value not to yourself but to the other person(s).

Regardless of the universal nature of politeness, which is not within the scope of this chapter, this definition of politeness emphasises the social side of this phenomenon. Politeness strategies enable communication in different spheres of life, including those in which positions are not always a matter of reconciliation. In the scientific domain, politeness seems mandatory, as scholars are very often engaged in vigorous debates, which require some degree of respectful behaviour in order (a) to be able to present new information in a modest way without imposing a particular view, and (b) to be able to show disagreement following the same manners. This is linked to the notion of 'face', developed in Brown and Levinson (1987: 2), which barely corresponds to the personal and public images individuals want for themselves or for others. In this context, three strategic alternatives are in order: positive politeness, i.e. "the expression of solidarity", negative politeness, i.e. "the expression of restraint", and off-record politeness, i.e. "the avoidance of unequivocal impositions" (Brown & Levinson, 1987: 2).

The relation between the expression of thanking and facework raises some issues. Watts (2003: 66), following Leech's work (2014 [1983]) on politeness, states that showing one's gratitude seeks to "maximise praise of *other*", and that obviously means strong support of the other's esteem. If second thoughts are considered, the act of thanking could be regarded as impolite, and that could be the case of insincere gratitude. There are cases in which the beneficiary declares a debt of gratitude which is not real in order to gain some benefits in return. One clear example is the use of mentions by means of which the writer gets the profits of dropping a big name, i.e. an important linguist or critic, even if this person has not contributed in any way to the development of the book. This may, of course, threaten the positive-face want of the mock benefactor. Mentions may also serve as a means to boasting of their own academic background so as to suggest the supposed quality of the book, edited or written.

Acknowledging the help of a benefactor also appears to threaten the integrity of the writer's face, as he/she declares a debt of any kind to the benefactor. According to Brown and Levinson (1987: 67), this declaration of humbleness by the writer attempts against the writer's own face. The opposite also holds, and the benefactor may think that the help or support given does not deserve so much praise, as pointed out in Brown and Levinson (1987: 67): "acceptance of H's thanks or H's apology (S may feel constrained to minimize H's debt or transgression, as in 'It was noting, don't mention it'.)". In my corpus, this aspect is difficult to prove because it lacks the promptness and interaction of the conversation, as we shall see. The formulas deployed are, however, similar, especially those corresponding to what Watts (2003: 169) labels as highly conventionalised utterances, e.g. *thank you*.

2.2 The Form and Function of Thanking Formulae

There are various ways in which someone may express their gratitude, as pointed out in Jautz (2013) and Ohashi (2013), among others. Following Aijmer (1996), Jautz (2013: 11) mentions two types of thanking strategies: one according to a continuum of explicitness, e.g. *thanks*, and the other according to a continuum of emotionality, e.g. *I must thank you*. The act of thanking was described by Searle (1969) in the following terms: "When I thank someone, I imply that the thing I am thanking him for has benefited me (or was at least intended to benefit me)" (Searle, 1969: 65). In the same line, Searle (1969: 65) states that "To thank, welcome or congratulate counts as an expression of gratitude ^ pleasure (at H's arrival), or pleasure (at H's good fortune)", and a thanking speech act, therefore, involves specific rules in order to fulfil its function, as shown in Table 2.1:

The prototypical thanking formulae present the performative *thank*, either alone or in combination with intensifiers, e.g. *thanks a lot*, as said in Holmes (1984) and Aijmer (1996: 46). In addition, other more elaborate formulas are used to convey the writers' appreciation, namely *to be grateful, to be indebted, to express my gratitude*, to mention a few. In general, in this study, I have followed a function-to-form approach in

Table 2.1 Searle's types of rules for 'thank (for)'

Propositional content	*Past act A done by H*
Preparatory	*A* benefits *S* and *S* believes *A* benefits *S*
Sincerity	*S* feels grateful or appreciative for *A*
Essential	Counts as an expression of gratitude or appreciation

the sense that routinised thanking expressions are identified along with other less common expressions of gratitude.

Thanking formulae fulfil other functions than expressing gratitude in order to meet certain interactional demands. Defying the Searlean rules for the expression of gratitude given in Table 2.1, thanking for a future action can also be possible to indicate different interactional needs. Jautz (2013: 12) lists some functions of thanking routines: (a) to show acceptance and refusal of an offer, e.g. *I'm sorry, but I can't, thanks!*, (b) to show courtesy, e.g. *Thanks for calling*, (c) to show irony, see Jacobsson (2002: 64), e.g. *Nice of you, thank you!*, and (d) to indicate discourse organisation, e.g. as a closing formula in dialogues.

Thanking routines and other routines have certain contextual features, and these are grouped in frames, according to Aijmer (1996: 27), which she defines, as follows:

> The frame should be regarded as a hypothesis about speakers' stereotypic knowledge of a situation and how this knowledge is organized in the long-term memory... People have frames for 'rooms' or 'houses', as well as for linguistic facts like noun phrases, and there are probably also frames for thanking, apologizing, etc.

She argues that the frames used to express gratitude "represent the language users' knowledge of the social rules of thanking" (Aijmer, 1996: 75). The definition of the frame for thanking she has outlined presents some situational parameters concerning the setting, the participants, and the types of thanking. The use of intensifiers, for example, in routinised thanking expressions is seen as variation from the standard situation, as also pointed out in Aijmer (1996: 76–77). Following Holmes (1984: 185 ff), Aijmer (1996) argues that the presence of intensifiers in thanking strategies indicates variables pertaining to social hierarchy, as also noted in Lytvyn (2002: 116): "Thus the social relation of the participants and the inherent properties of the object of gratitude work together to determine the degree of gratefulness that should be expressed in a given situation". Thus, pragmatically, the expressions of thanking are elaborated differently depending on the variables involved in the act of thanking so as to adjust the thanking expression to the communicative situation.

3 Corpus and Method

The data taken as evidence for my analysis is taken from prefaces given in books in the domain of linguistics published between 2000 and 2019 in leading academic publishers. Prefaces have been defined as one well-established genre found earlier in (edited) books and monographs as a way of introduction. Azar (2012: 150) states that the "[m]aterial normally included in a preface section consists of reasons for undertaking the book, methodology, acknowledgements, and sometimes permissions granted for the use of previously published material". Bhatia (1997: 164) describes the function of prefaces, as "To outline the general purpose and scope of the book, often indicating steps leading to the preparation of the book. (Communicative purpose (s) – academic as well as promotional)".

This information represents, as Bhatia (1997: 189) claims, the two major rhetorical moves which constitute the genre. Asghar et al. (2015: 60) are more descriptive and mention up to fourteen moves in prefaces. Azar (2012: 153) identifies only four rhetorical moves in his corpus of prefaces in academic textbooks in the domain of linguistics. These are: *M1: Establishing the needs of the readership, M2: Establishing orientations, M3: Introducing chapters and scope, and M4: Acknowledgements.* These are different from the six moves described in Mohsenzadeh (2013: 320) in his study of English prefaces in literature books: *1-General statement/description, 2-The significance, 3-The purpose, 4-Type of reader, 5-Information about the chapters or other volumes,* and *6-More explanation.* As seen, there seems to be a lack of a unified idea as to the number of rhetorical moves a preface is made up of. Be it as it may, what stands clear from these structure representations is the fact that all these scholars have detected both the persuasive and the acknowledging functions of prefaces.

In my analysis, I have not attempted an identification of the moves to provide my own selection of rhetorical moves, as I was only concerned with the expression of thanking, often included in the move number 4 in Azar's description.

All the texts in my corpus are written in English by native and non-native speakers. I believe that these texts have been edited to display good use of the language by native speakers in those cases of non-native authorship. I should say here that identification of origin based only in the authors' surnames is rarely safe, because, beneath a Spanish surname, one may find a London-born speaker. The reverse also happens, and someone with a British surname may have been living for years abroad and his/her English is L2 acquired during schooldays.

The number of prefaces compiled amounts to 72 of varying length, with a total of 199,215 words. For the analysis of the texts, I have used the *CasualConc* suite for retrieving cases of thanking expressions in order to draw quantitative data and to excerpt examples of these expressions for analysis and illustration. A first step was required in order to identify thanking expressions, other than *thank*-routines and *grateful*-routines, to tag each of them for later computation. The analysis of results provides information concerning the form of these expressions. More careful examination was essential in order to determine their functions and pragmatic significance.

4 Thanking Expressions in Prefaces in Linguistics Books

In this section, I include the results drawn from the analysis of the corpus. Information concerns the forms, the functions, and the pragmatics of thanking expressions. I will consider each one, in turn.

4.1 The Form of Thanking Formulae

The analysis of the corpus of prefaces returns 141 cases of thanking expressions and reveals the degree of variation as to the formal characteristics of these expressions. For the sake of clarity, I have grouped all instances according to its more salient features, and the results are displayed in Figure 2.1:

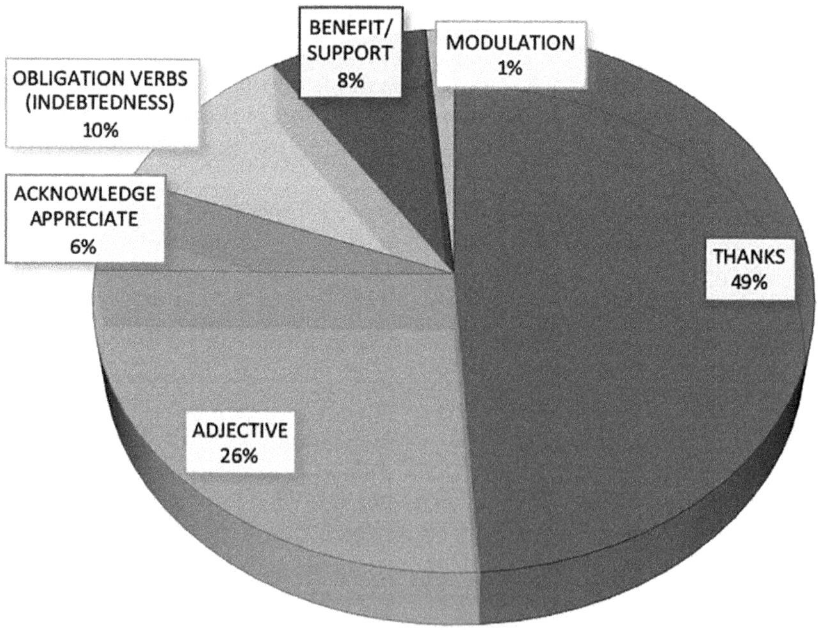

Figure 2.1 Groupings of thanking expressions by a salient formal feature.

As shown in this figure, the most common thanking strategies in the compilation of prefaces are those containing the word *thank*, either as a verb or as a noun, with 49% of the instances. The structure with embedded *would like to* appears to be the most frequent in the text, with almost 30 out of the 69 expressions of gratitude. Other common strategies from a formal perspective are the use of *thanks* preceded by an intensifier and followed by an NP. The use of intensifiers is common in these devices, as I shall explain in due course. The following list gives other frequent templates of thanking expressions by order of number of occurrences (brackets mean optionality; slanting bar means one or the other):

1 THANKS + VP + NP: In addition, my thanks go to various colleagues who have helped me with their expertise in areas which interface with Irish English (acknowledgements are given at the appropriate points in the book) (Hickey, 2007).
2 THANK YOU + (TO NP) / (INTENSIFIER): Thank you so much (Meierkord, 2012).
3 (INTENSIFIER) THANKS + TO BE + DUE TO + NP: Also, again thanks are due to the R Development Core Team and many contributors to bugfixes and packages for R and, also again, to R. Harald Baayen for exposing me to R the first time (Gries, 2013).
4 I/WE + THANK + (NP) + (FOR + V-ING) / (NP): The editors... particularly thank Dr Shihoko Yamamoto for producing the bibliography of Professor Akimoto's works (Kytö et al., 2010).

Structures containing an adjective to indicate gratitude are also very frequent (26%) in the corpus. Even if there is much variation in the form of expressions with adjectives, the following template is by far the commonest one:

5 I/WE + TO BE + (INTENSIFIER) + ADJECTIVE + (TO + NP) + (THAT-CLAUSE) + (FOR NP): I am very grateful to Roger Lass for his careful and critical reading of several versions of this book. His comments caused me to consider more deeply the implications of my research (Romaine, 2009).

The next group in frequency (10%) represents those containing verbs entailing some kind of internal obligation or necessity, as seen in the following templates:

6 I/WE + WISH/WANT TO + VERB OR EXPRESSION OF GRATITUDE + (INTENSIFIER) (NP) + (PP): We wish to thank the anonymous reviewers of the volume for insightful suggestions and constructive criticism, and John Benjamins Publishing Co.

for including the volume in Pragmatics & Beyond New Series (Taavitsainen et al., 2000).

7 WE + OWE + INTENSIFIER + (DEBT OF) GRATITUDE: We owe a special debt of gratitude to Brigitta Flick and to Elena Rhind, for helping us organise the Workshop in a most efficient manner (Aikhenvald & Dixon, 2014).

8 I/WE + TO BE INDEBTED + TO NP + FOR + V-ING: We are also indebted to the English Departments at the Universities of Helsinki and Stockholm for their support (Taavitsainen et al., 2000).

Another group of thanking expressions corresponds to the *support* (noun) and *profit* (verb) series, and it represents 8% of the cases in the corpus of prefaces. Some templates here are these:

9 I + PROFIT + FROM + NP + WITH + (NPs): I have particularly profited from my discussions with Elizabeth Traugott about socio-historical linguistics (Romaine, 2009).

10 SUPPORT + VP: Brigitta Flick's support and editorial assistance was, as always, invaluable (Aikhenvald & Dixon, 2014).

The fifth group refers to sequences containing the verbs *acknowledge*, *appreciate*, and *deserve*. This group corresponds to a total of 6% of the cases, and some examples of templates in this set are the following:

11 WE + (INTENSIFIER) + ACKNOWLEDGE + NP: We gratefully acknowledge [THANK] financial assistance from the Faculty of Arts and Social Sciences and from the Cairns Institute at James Cook University (Aikhenvald & Dixon, 2014).

12 I + INTENSIFIER + APPRECIATE + NP: I really appreciate [THANK] his encouragement and many useful references that he directed me to (Sztencel, 2018).

13 NP + DESERVE + (INTENSIFIER) + GRATITUDE/MENTION: Raj Mesthrie, his wife, and daughter deserve a special mention (Meierkord, 2012).

The least frequent group (1%) represents those which present modulation of the propositional content, as exemplified in this template:

14 PP + NP + MODAL + V: Without your support, I could never have completed this project (Collins, 2009).

In terms of explicitness and emotionality, there seems to be no difference between these two ways of conveying gratitude, as shown in Figure 2.2, and both types appear in equal ratios.

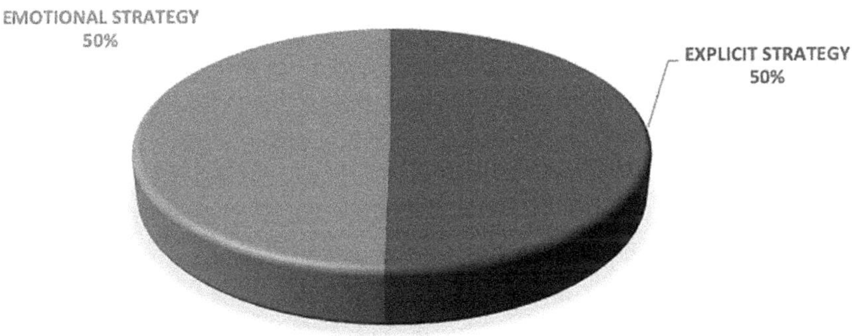

Figure 2.2 Explicit thanking expressions and emotionality thanking expressions.

Examples of explicit strategies in the corpus include a direct address to the benefactor, as shown in the following examples:

15 Thanks, Jane (Dixon, 2005).
16 Thank you, Christof, Simon, and David for bearing with me during the process of writing this volume (Meierkord, 2012).

Explicit thanking expressions in the corpus may also carry specific intensifiers, as in these instances:

17 *Many* thanks also to the anonymous reviewers commissioned by Cambridge University Press (Meierkord, 2012).
18 A *very* special word of thanks to Jan Blommaert, Jonathan Culpeper, Marina Dossena, and Ingrid Tieken-Boon van Ostade (Pahta et al., 2010).
19 A *very* big thank you goes to Amanda Parsonage, for her assistance and cheerful support during the preparation of the final manuscript (Aikhenvald & Dixon, 2014).

Emotional thanking strategies show more variation and creativity than explicit strategies. This includes references to specific actions and references to degrees of moral responsibility in acknowledging some benefits, including meeting certain conditions at the moment of writing, as seen in the following examples:

20 I am particularly conscious of debts to the work and/or comments of Jack Aitken, Michael Benskin, Juliette Blevins, Derek Britton… (Smith, 2007).

21 And last but not least, I want to say how lucky I have always been with the sound and commonsense advice of Kuif's agency (Forceville & Urios-Aparisi, 2009).

22 I have particularly profited from my discussions with Elizabeth Traugott about socio-historical linguistics (Romaine, 2009).

23 To him I am also indebted for providing me with a very supportive environment at Erfurt University (Meierkord, 2012).

4.2 The Functions and the Pragmatics of Thanking Formulae

Figure 2.3 includes the various functions thanking formulae fulfil in the corpus of prefaces. It is not surprising that receiving feedback during the process of writing or editing seems to be the most wanted and appreciated help (29%). The following most frequent thanking devices are those for showing appreciation to colleagues with 16% and those for showing gratitude for facilitating work. Other common functions are showing gratitude for editorial support and showing personal appreciation occurring in 12% and 11% of the cases, respectively. The other remaining 16% of thanking expressions are distributed in the following way: (a) acknowledging financial support, (b) showing gratitude for contributing in an edited monograph, (c) showing appreciation for active help in revising the manuscript, (d) acknowledging institutional support, and (e) showing gratitude to linguists for earlier literature. I comment and show examples excerpted from our corpus in the following sections.

As pointed out earlier, many are the functions of thanking expressions in the corpus, if the general pragmatic idea is that of conveying politeness. The reasons for this might be diverse, as each occasion may seek to meet a particular interest ranging from pure and sincere gratitude to a more convenient and academic gratitude significance. It is important to note here that I have not detected any thanking expressions used to indicate a joking or ironic attitude (cf. Jautz, 2013: 138 ff). I would like to point out at this stage that thanking expressions, regardless of their form, seem to have different uses in our corpus of prefaces with respect to other genres, especially in the oral medium. Lytvyn (2002: 118), for instance, has identified a segmentation function of thanking expressions. In this context, she claims that "thank you" in British English is used as "a punctuation mark of interaction" (2002: 118). This use, for instance, has not been recorded in our corpus. In general, the thanking expressions identified are used to show appreciation for material benefits and for immaterial benefits, as I shall explain in due course. This terminology echoes Coulmas' dimensions (1981: 74) concerning the expression of gratitude, but my target is, however, very different and my view concerning the motivations of thanking is deliberately less comprehensive in this chapter. The grouping of thanking expressions according to the nature of the benefit received into (a) thanking material

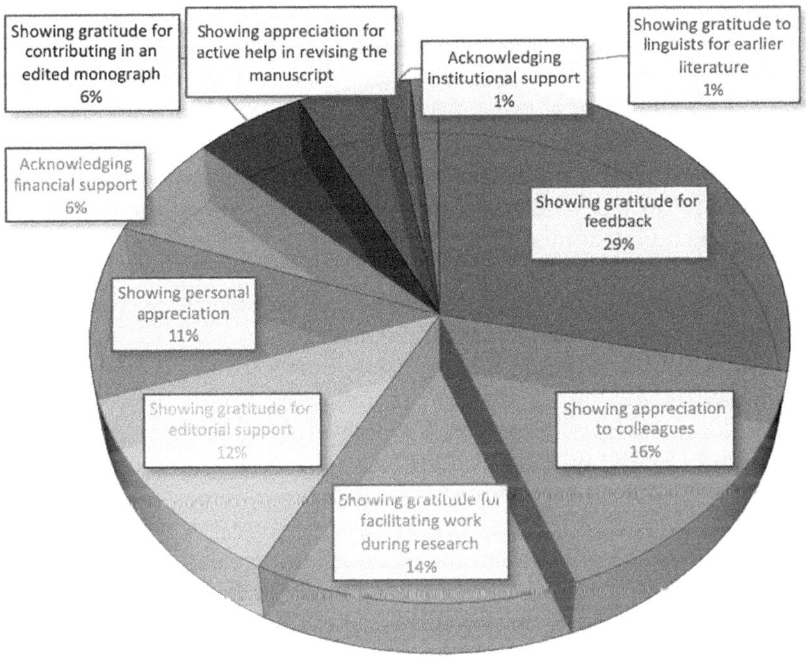

Figure 2.3 The functions of thanking expressions in prefaces.

benefits and (b) immaterial benefits seems to work well for the data excerpted from the corpus of prefaces.

4.2.1 Thanking Material Benefits

An important part of writing or editing an academic book relies on the support and the work of others, and thanking all the help received from people and institutions is a primary aim of the prefaces compiled, and this is in agreement with Bhatia's (1997) academic and promotional functions of the genre, as pointed out in Section 3. The authorial interest of acknowledging material benefits is evinced by the occurrence of thanking expressions with this function, which in our corpus amounts to 68% of the cases. These include the devices whose aim is the following: (a) receiving feedback during the process of writing or editing, (b) showing gratitude for facilitating work, (c) acknowledging financial support, (d) showing gratitude for contributing in an edited monograph, (e) showing appreciation for active help in revising the manuscript, (f) acknowledging institutional support, and (g) showing gratitude to linguists for earlier literature.

4.2.1.1 SHOWING GRATITUDE FOR FEEDBACK

Feedback is an integral part of the publication process. Whether this is received through discussions with colleagues and friends prior to submission, or through the editor's report based on the referees' opinions after submission, this is frequently seen as beneficial for the final draft. This appreciation is shown in different ways, and there is no one single case in our corpus that may lead us to think that expressions of gratitude for feedback are not sincere. In the following instances, the authors use different formulas to meet this function:

24 We are grateful for the participant feedback we received at various conferences (Nevalainen et al., 2018).
25 The work has benefited from discussions with many linguists over the years, including Rodney Huddleston, Pieter Seuren, Robert Eagleson, Edgar Schneider, Geoffrey Leech, Stig Johansson, and Michael Halliday (Collins, 2009).

While Nevalainen et al. in (24) opt for the prototypical *to be grateful for* leaving the identity of the benefactors unrevealed, Collins in (25) also shows his appreciation for the benefits of feedback, but the identity of benefactors has been disclosed this time. Obviously, the implications for the reader are different in terms of authority, and therefore, on social distance. Granting that both cases fulfil their gratitude function, the example in Nevalainen et al. seems to be less involved in seeking colleagues' solidarity, while Collins' example finds solidarity through the mention of certain important names, surely on the basis of Collins' own honesty for the help specified and his true admiration to the celebrated scholars he mentions. In this context, the hierarchical position with respect to his readers might be assumed to be higher than in Nevalainen et al.'s instance, even if none of these authors intended to evince a hierarchical position.

4.2.1.2 SHOWING GRATITUDE FOR FACILITATING WORK

Authors also tend to show their gratitude for the help they have received during the preparation of the book. Cases of this are given below:

26 Grateful acknowledgement is made to the following sources for permission to reprint material in this book (Ruiz de Zarobe & Jiménez Catalán, 2009).
27 We are grateful to the Wellcome Library and to Catherine Draycott, for giving us permission to publish pictures from the Wellcome collections, and to Julianne Simmons, for suggesting the interesting range of pictures to us, many of which have not been used as book illustrations before (Taavitsainen & Pahta, 2011).

28 I am grateful to Sidney Greenbaum for allowing me, once again, to work in the offices of the Survey (Palmer, 1990).

In all these cases, authors are thankful for some specific material they have been able to have access during research, e.g. reprinted material in (26), permission to publish pictures in (27), and for being able to work in the offices of the Survey in (28). The forms of these thanking formulae are not distinct from those described earlier for feedback. In all these three instances, the adjective *grateful* appears either in attributive or predicative position and so the authors explicitly make manifest their appreciation. The examples in (27) and (28) also provide more details concerning the benefits obtained and the benefactors. From a pragmatic perspective, the authors seek to express pure politeness and keep social ties safe this way. In the specific case of (27), the thanking device also serves the purpose of clearing any responsibility for the selection of images to Julianne Simmons, thus preserving her public image from future scholarly interpretations concerning the images included in the book.

The majority of the examples identified as belonging to this category contain names of people, many of which are reputed linguists, who have directly helped authors in any way, other than feedback, e.g. invitation to an institution, for the preparation of a bibliographic list, for acceptance as a member of a scholarly network, for providing data for analysis, etc. It seems logical, then, that these people should be openly mentioned, and association with degrees of social proximity between the authors and their audience cannot, therefore, be categorically established.

4.2.1.3 ACKNOWLEDGING FINANCIAL SUPPORT

These formulae are used to show the authors' appreciation for grants or other means of financial support received. The majority of the forms with this function contain the words *grateful(ly)*, *acknowledge*, and *thank*, as in (29)–(31), even if variation has also been registered, as in (32) and (33):

29 We gratefully acknowledge financial assistance from the Faculty of Arts and Social Sciences and from the Cairns Institute at James Cook University (Aikhenvald & Dixon, 2014).

30 We would also like to thank the Department of English at the University of Helsinki for financial aid in editing the book (Taavitsainen & Pahta, 2011).

31 We are grateful to NorFA for providing funds which allowed us to organise the Symposium, and to the Swedish Council (Taavitsainen et al., 2000).

32 Other sources of funding have also in part supported our work, including project funding provided by the Academy of Finland and the Universities of Helsinki and Jyväskylä (Nevalainen et al., 2018).

33 This project would not have been possible without the Academy of Finland and University of Helsinki funding for the Research Unit for the Study of Variation, Contacts and Change in English (Nevalainen et al., 2018).

Pure gratitude is extremely unclear, as statement of financial endowment is mandatory, and this is normally explicitly stated in the grant submission forms. In other words, saying thanks is an obligation regardless the amount of money received may cover the full expenses of research or only the partial costs. Actually, some principal researchers of funded projects elaborate the exact thanking formula that they distribute later to the project members for addition in their publications. At a more pragmatic level, mentioning financial support may be related to prestige. Funded research seems to be associated with established standards of quality, as research material following from grants can be evaluated by committees of experts, and this is seen as a guarantee of excellence.

4.2.1.4 SHOWING GRATITUDE FOR CONTRIBUTING IN AN EDITED MONOGRAPH

The expressions in this category usually include *we (would like to) thank…, we are grateful…, my/our thanks + verb*, as in (33) and (35). The only cases with *owe* and *are due* to underline some kind of moral obligation are given in (36) and (37), respectively:

34 My thanks go the contributors of this volume for their help and co-operation, to Danielle Hickey for her careful copy-editing and layouting work (Jucker, 2009).

35 We thank all of the authors included here, for taking part in the Workshop, for getting their chapters on time (Aikhenvald & Dixon, 2014).

36 But, of course, we owe our greatest gratitude to the contributors of this volume for their effort, understanding, and punctuality during the editing process as well as their good humour in which they responded to our questions (Palander-Collin et al., 2017).

37 Our thanks are due first and foremost to all the authors, the quick and the dead, whose work is collected here (Aarts et al., 2004).

The formulation of gratitude using an explicit thanking strategy, as in (35), or an emotional thanking strategy, as in (36), tends to unambiguously indicate an earnest feeling to the contributors. The monograph would not be obviously the same without their participation. In addition, beyond intended acts of politeness and linguistic courtesy, these expressions encompass some evaluative language items which may seek to emphasise their authenticity: *greatest gratitude, their effort, (their) understanding, first and foremost,* among others. The indication of moral duty in (36) and (37) is also a proof of authorial commitment towards these acts of thanking, namely *we owe our gratitude* and *our thanks are due to*, respectively.

4.2.1.5 SHOWING APPRECIATION FOR ACTIVE HELP IN REVISING THE MANUSCRIPT

Forms used to indicate this function can be given using the performative verb *thank*, as in (38), or as a noun, as in (39) or it can be indirectly expressed, as in (40):

38 I would also like to thank Bob Le Page, who very kindly read a first draft of the book; I have incorporated some of his suggestions and comments in this revised version (Romaine, 2009).

39 She read it and offered comments that I appreciated. Thanks, Jane (Dixon, 2005).

40 The editing process benefited highly from the very careful work of Zahra Amirsad, Bridget Fonkeu, Verena Minow, Heiko Schittek, Jude Ssempuuma, Barbara Stauch, and Eva Zumhasch (Meierkord, 2012).

The function "showing appreciation for active help in revising the manuscript" is very much related to the function "showing gratitude for feedback", although the type of activity both acknowledged represents different collaborative levels. Revising manuscripts is a very time-consuming task. From a pragmatic standpoint, the type of relationship one may see between the authors and the benefactors is closer than in those cases in which feedback for improving some elaboration of an idea is given.

4.2.1.6 ACKNOWLEDGING INSTITUTIONAL SUPPORT

All the forms related to this type of thanking expressions contain *thank* (verb) or *to be grateful*. The function represented here alike the "acknowledgement of financial support" function represents some kind of moral obligation for the benefits received, albeit indirectly, from some institutional action. That is the case of (41):

41 I'd also like to thank the University of Cambridge for giving me a sabbatical leave in 2005–2006, which made it possible for me to finish the book (Roberts, 2007).

4.2.1.7 SHOWING GRATITUDE TO LINGUISTS FOR EARLIER LITERATURE

Examples of the "showing gratitude to linguists for earlier literature" function are the following:

42 So a note of thanks as well to Michael Halliday, for his close attention to interpersonal meaning in language and for his design of the roomy theory that inspired this research (Martin & White, 2005).
43 We are, of course, greatly indebted to these colleagues, and to all the functional linguists and educational linguists of the so-called Sydney School who gave value to our work (Martin & White, 2005).

This function is certainly challenging to evaluate in pragmatic terms. The appreciation of others' work is certainly welcome and shows signs of scholarly courtesy and modesty the very least. In fact, this function places the benefactors in a higher position in the academic rank by crediting their work and professional careers. Example (42) shows a direct reference to the legendary linguist Prof. Michael Halliday. This mention may have meant, in principle, additional benefits for the volume, but still, this thankful expression seems rather to contextualise the volume, while it also argues for a sincere expression of appreciation for Halliday's scholarly legacy. The example in (43) from the same source feels more conversational due to the presence of the sequence "of course", and the authors do not address someone in particular, but a group of people working in a same area of linguistics. This positions the authors as members of this group of linguists.

It is interesting, though, that this thanking expression contains the verbal form *are indebted*, which, as Watkins et al. (2006: 218 ff) explain, refers to a more unpleasant state than gratitude, being this a very positive feeling. Indebtedness means that the beneficiary must repay for the benefits at any time. They argue, however, that indebtedness, or even the notion of obligation in the act of thanking, and gratitude are used as synonyms by scholars in the social sciences (2006: 218). This seems to be the case in the samples excerpted from our corpus, but my interpretation leans towards a positive side of the terms, as no sense of compensation for the benefits declared has been detected. The use of *owe* in (36) and *are due* in (37) represents the same case of indebtedness. However, thanking formulae with embedded deontic expressions (*would like to, thanks are due to, want to,* etc.) obviously serve to air that some help or support has been received. The truth is that this type of expressions and the other thanking expressions in the same fashion also serve to discharge and relieve the beneficiary of the burden of feeling constant gratitude. There is, therefore, no further commitment to compensate for the help or the support. The transaction, if one can call this social and linguistic event this way, ends up without any expectation of any further exchange from any of the parties. In linguistics, synonymy is seen as an acceptable stylistic choice, even if a more convenient interpretation of a term like *indebted* in a thanking expression must rest at the expenses of additional cognitive efforts.

4.2.2 *Thanking Immaterial Benefits*

Thanking immaterial benefits represent 32% of the functions of the thanking expressions in the corpus, and these correspond to the functions: showing appreciation to colleagues, showing gratitude for editorial support, and showing personal appreciation. It is not hard to see that these formulae want to maintain social bonds with institutions and colleagues on one side, and with families and close friends on the other. The benefits thanked represent aspects leading to solidarity and personal appreciation, and they seek to trigger a different emotional reaction by appealing to the "human" side of the writers or the editors of the monograph. Not in vain, aspects of the daily routines are given within the formulation of thanking formulae: *Last but not least I wish to thank my family for surrendering the dining room table to my piles of books, papers and data* (Collins, 2009).

4.2.2.1 SHOWING APPRECIATION TO COLLEAGUES

The forms representing this function are many and cover almost the majority of templates designed in Section 4.1. Examples are the following:

44 Finally, our home teams deserve a special word of thanks for their support and understanding (Taavitsainen et al., 2011).
45 Thanks also to our SFL colleagues around the world who have engaged so helpfully with our ideas at meetings (Martin & White, 2005).
46 I would like to thank my colleagues (Forceville & Urios-Aparisi, 2009).

This function does not really indicate gratitude towards any precise activity or towards identifiable individuals. The authors, as can be seen in all the examples given earlier, say thanks for such general aspects as *their support and understanding* and *engaged so helpfully with our ideas at meetings* in (44) and (45), respectively. In the case of (46), the reason for being grateful is not given at all. In general, these expressions seem to emerge as an expected routine in the preface genre in order to show some kind of concern for the others, and not necessarily as factual and global expressions of thankfulness. An obvious gain, however, is that social distance is reduced, as the use of the forms *our* and *my* in *our home teams*, in *our SFL colleagues*, and in *my colleagues* visually place the authors as members of the groups mentioned.

4.2.2.2 SHOWING GRATITUDE FOR EDITORIAL SUPPORT

The function "showing gratitude for editorial support" specifies appreciation for the editorial commissioned editors' moral support, patient, encouragement, enthusiasm, etc., as in the following examples:

47 I am also very grateful to Helen Barton of Cambridge University Press, for her tolerance and understanding in putting up with a dilatory and distracted author, to Rosina Di Marzo, to Jill Lake for her skilful and tactful copy-editing, and to Philip Riley for his meticulous proofreading (Smith, 2009).
48 I wish to thank Christian Mair from the editorial committee for this Rodopi series for his welcome encouragement (Collins, 2009).
49 We would like to thank our editor, Lesley Riddle, who patiently waited for the completion of this book (Kress, 2001).

At the core of these acknowledgements is the desire to give prominence to the editorial house for the publication of their monographs through some gratitude shown to their commissioned editors. Pragmatically, saying thanks in this context appears to be a duty, although not a moral duty, strictly speaking. There could be cases where showing gratitude for this editorial support comes from a true desire for specific benefits, as in (49).

4.2.2.3 SHOWING PERSONAL APPRECIATION

Showing personal appreciation is expected to be the most authentic thanking expressions of all, at least from an emotional perspective. The truth is that showing gratitude to family, friends, and close colleagues is anything but required from this group of people. The kind of help obtained embodies support at a psychological level through generous family and friends care. This stands evident in the following instances from the corpus:

50 Most of all, however, it is my family without whose loving support I couldn't have written this book. Thank you, Christof, Simon, and David for bearing with me during the process of writing this volume, for tolerating many physical and mental absences, and for reminding me of the many other joys of life (Meierkord, 2012).
51 Lastly, I would like to express my immense gratitude to my family for their constant love and support, and their confidence in me (Murray, 2017).
52 My family has been involved in this book in many ways, and I would like to thank them for their loving support throughout the study and the writing phases (Norris, 2011).

53 Completing this project would have also been impossible without the unwavering support of my husband Piotr as well as friends and colleagues Indu, Kate, Rachel, and Chris. Thank you (Sztencel, 2018).

Feelings are key concepts in these thanking expressions, and especially the feeling of love. In general, the authors show themselves more vulnerable and less composed. The obvious consequence of this function is the reduction of social distance and therefore bonds tighten. The idea behind this function is not to show appreciation to the people mentioned but to show appreciation for having them, hence the vulnerability referred to previously, as put forward in Fagley and Adler (2012: 181–182):

> Relishing time with co-workers, friends or family and additionally, expressing appreciation to them, gets at the heart of interpersonal appreciation. It is not being grateful *to* them for what they have done for one, or for anything specific that they have given one. It is being grateful *for* them. It is appreciating their presence in one's life, feeling lucky to have them. When people appreciate one another and recognize what they have in each other, they strengthen social bonds and enhance their effectiveness in the many endeavors they pursue.

5 Conclusion

This chapter has addressed the expression of gratitude in a corpus of prefaces excerpted from linguistics books. Results have shown that there are certain routinised thanking expressions along with creative thanking expressions. These forms may or may not carry intensifiers to enhance the perspective. The functions of these expressions of gratitude are varied, but they generally seek to show appreciation to people (colleagues, friends, family, and other linguists) for help and support of any type, and to institutions for (financial) support. Thanking formulae is very convenient to indicate politeness, and these, therefore, are used to avoid potential face risks by acknowledging the benefits to benefactors. In this sense, these expressions represent symptoms of academic modesty and, to some extent, of academic honesty.

In terms of truth, it is certainly difficult to determine the genuineness of these expressions, but I have found no strong linguistic evidence allowing me to suspect against the authenticity of the feelings exhibited in these thanking speech acts. Some thanking expressions, e.g. acknowledging financial support, may, however, represent an institutionalised action rather than a voluntary action. One important conclusion concerning the use of gratitude expressions is their potential to reflect the beneficiary's position within the scholarly traditions and groups. In this line, I have also shown that using these expressions is useful to specify social distance. Similarly, the information contained in thanking speech acts allows readers to infer meanings other than gratitude, e.g. humbleness, collegiality, credibility, and prestige, among others.

References

Aarts, B., Denison, D., Keizer, E. & Popova, G. (2004). *Fuzzy Grammar.* Oxford: Oxford University Press.

Adler, M. G., & Fagley, N. S. (2005). Appreciation: Individual Differences in Finding Value and Meaning as a Unique Predictor of Subjective Well-Being. *Journal of Personality*, *73*(1), 79–114. doi:10.1111/j.1467-6494.2004.00305.x.

Aijmer, K. (1996). *Conversational Routines in English. Convention and Creativity.* doi:10.4324/9781315845128.

Aikhenvald, Alexandra Y. & Dixon, R. M. W. (2014). *The Grammar of Knowledge. A Cross-Linguistic Typology.* Oxford: Oxford University Press.

Asghar, S., Asghar, Z., & Mahmood, M. (2015). A Genre Analysis of Preface Sections of Textbook. *Journal of Education and Practice*, *6*(7), 58–63.

Azar, A. S. (2012). *The Self-Promotion of Academic Textbooks in the Preface Section: A Genre Analysis*, *34*(2), 147–165.

Ben-Ari, E. (1987). On Acknowledgements in Ethnographies. *Journal of Anthropological Research*, *43*(1), 63–84. doi:10.1086/jar.43.1.3630467.

Bhatia, V. K. (1997). Genre-Mixing in Academic Introductions. *English for Specific Purposes*, *16*(3), 181–195. doi:10.1016/S0889-4906(96)00039-7.

Brown, P., & Levinson, S. (1987). Politeness: Some Universals in Language Usage. In *Cambridge University Press.* doi:10.2307/3587263.

Collins, P. (2009). *Modals and Quasi-Modals in English.* Amsterdam, New York: Rodopi.

Coulmas, F. (1981). Poison to your soul: thanks and apologies contrastively viewed. In Coulmas, F. (Ed.). *Conversational Routine: Explorations in Standardized Communication Situations and Prepatterned Speech* (pp. 69–91). The Netherlands: Mouton Publishers.

Cui, X. (2012). A Cross-linguistic Study on Expressions of Gratitude by Native and Non-native English Speakers. *Journal of Language Teaching and Research*, *3*(4), 753–760. doi:10.4304/jltr.3.4.753-760.

Díaz Pérez, F. (2005). The Speech Act of Thanking in English: Differences between Native and Non-native Speakers' Behaviour. *ES: Revista de Filología Inglesa*, *25*, 91–102.

Dixon, R. M. W. (2005). *A Semantic Approach to English Grammar.* Second edition. Oxford: Oxford University Press.

Emmons, R. A., & Mccullough, M. E. (2004). *The Psychology of Gratitude* (R. A. Emmons & M. E. Mccullough, eds.). Oxford: Oxford University Press.

Fagley, N. S. (2018). Appreciation (Including Gratitude) and Affective Well-Being: Appreciation Predicts Positive and Negative Affect Above the Big Five Personality Factors and Demographics. *SAGE Open*, *8*(4). doi:10.1177/2158244018818621.

Fagley, N. S., & Adler, M. G. (2012). Appreciation: A Spiritual Path to Finding Value and Meaning in the Workplace. *Journal of Management, Spirituality & Religion*, *9*(2), 167–187. doi:10.1080/14766086.2012.688621.

Forceville, C. J., & Urios-Aparisi, E. (2009). *Multimodal Metaphor.* Berlin, New York: Walter de Gruyter.

Golato, A. (2005). *Compliments and Compliment Responses. Grammatical Structure and Sequential Organization*. Amsterdam, New York: John Benjamins Publishing Company.

Gries, S. (2013). *Statistics for Linguistics with R. A Practical Introduction*. Berlin, Boston: Walter de Gruyter.

Hickey, R. (2007). *Irish English. History and Present-Day Forms*. Cambridge: Cambridge University Press.

Holmes, J. (1984). Modifying Illocutionary Force. *Journal of Pragmatics*, *8*(3), 345–365. doi:10.1016/0378-2166(84)90028-6.

Hyland, K. (2004). Graduates' Gratitude: The Generic Structure of Dissertation Acknowledgements. *English for Specific Purposes*, *23*(3), 303–324. doi:10.1016/S0889-4906(03)00051-6.

Jacobsson, M. (2002). Thank You and Thanks in Early Modern English. *ICAME Journal*, *26*, 63–80.

Jautz, S. (2013). *Thanking Formulae in English*. doi:10.1075/pbns.230.

Jucker, A. H. (2009). *Early Modern English News Discourse*. Amsterdam, New York: John Benjamins.

Kampf, Z., & Danziger, R. (2019). "You Dribble Faster Than Messi and Jump Higher Than Jordan": The Art of Complimenting and Praising in Political Discourse. *Journal of Politeness Research*, *15*(1), 1–24. doi:10.1515/pr-2016-0044.

Kress, G. (2001). *Multimodal Teaching and Learning: The Rhetorics of the Science Classroom*. London, New York: Continuum.

Kytö, M., Scahill, J., & Tanabe, H. (2010). *Language Change and Variation from Old English to Late Modern English. A Festschrift for Minoji Akimoto*. Bern, Berlin: Peter Lang.

Leech, G. (2014). The Pragmatics of Politeness. In *The Pragmatics of Politeness*. doi:10.1093/acprof:oso/9780195341386.001.0001.

Leithart, P. J. (2014). *Gratitude. An Intellectual History*. Waco, TX: Baylor University Press.

Locher, M. A., & Bousfield, D. (2008). Introduction: Impoliteness and Power in Language. In D. Bousfield & M. A. Locher (Eds.), *Impoliteness in Language: Studies on its Interplay with Power in Theory and Practice* (pp. 1–13). doi:10.1515/9783110208344.0.1.

Lytvyn, O. (2002). Semantics and Pragmatics of Thanks and Apologies in English Discourse. *Management and Sustainable Development*, *17*(2), 115–120.

Martin, J. R. and White, P. R. R. (2005). *The Language of Evaluation. Appraisal in English*. New York: Palgrave Macmillan.

Meierkord, C. (2012). *Interactions across Englishes. Linguistic Choices in Local and International Contact Situations*. Cambridge: Cambridge University Press.

Mohsenzadeh, H. (2013). Rhetorical Move Structure of Literature Book Prefaces in English and Persian. *Mediterranean Journal of Social Sciences*, *4*(4), 317–324. doi:10.5901/mjss.2013.v4n4p317.

Murray, S. E. (2017). *The Semantics of Evidentials*. Oxford: Oxford University Press.

Nevalainen, T., Palander-Collin, M., & Säil, T. (2018). *Patterns of Change in 18th-century English. A Sociolinguistic Approach* (T. Nevalainen, M. Palander-Collin, & T. Säily, eds.). Amsterdam, Philadelphia: John Benjamins Publishing Company.

Norris, S. (2011). *Identity in (Inter)action. Introducing Multimodal (Inter)action Analysis*. Göttingen: De Gruyter.

Ohashi, J. (2013). Thanking and Politeness in Japanese. In *Thanking and Politeness in Japanese*. doi:10.1057/9781137009876.

Pahta, P., Nevala, M., Nurmi, A., & Palander-Collins, M. (2010). *Social Roles and Language Practices in Late Modern English*. Amsterdam, Philadelphia: John Benjamins.

Palmer, F. (1990). *Mood and the English Modals*. New York, London: Routledge.

Palander-Collin, M., Ratia, M., & Taavitsainen, I. (2017). *Diachronic Developments in English News Discourse*. Amsterdam, Philadelphia: John Benjamins.

Roberts, I. (2007). *Diachronic Syntax*. Oxford: Oxford University Press.

Romaine, S. (2009). *Socio-Historical Linguistics Its Status and Methodology*. (Drist edition 1982). Cambridge: Cambridge University Press.

Ruiz de Zarobe, Y., & Jiménez Catalán, R. M. (2009). *Content and Language Integrated Learning Evidence from Research in Europe*. Bristol, Buffalo, Toronto: Multilingual Matters.

Searle, J. R. (1969). *Speech Acts: An Essay in the Philosophy of Language*. Cambridge: Cambridge University Press.

Smith, J. J. (2007). *Sound Change and the History of English*. Oxford: Oxford University Press.

Smith, J. J. (2009). *Old English. A Linguistic Introduction*. Cambridge: Cambridge University Press.

Sztencel, Magdalena. (2018). *Semantics, Pragmatics and Meaning Revisited. The Case of Conditionals*. Cham: Springer.

Taavitsainen, I., Melchers, G., & Pahta, P. (2000). *Writing in Nonstandard English*. Amsterdam, Philadelphia: John Benjamins.

Taavitsainen, I., & Pahta, P. (2011). *Medical Writing in Early Modern English*. Cambridge: Cambridge University Press.

Watkins, P. C. (2014). *Gratitude and the Good Life*. Dordrecht: Springer Netherlands.

Watkins, P. C., Scheer, J., Ovnicek, M., & Kolts, R. (2006). The Debt of Gratitude: Dissociating Gratitude and Indebtedness. *Cognition and Emotion*, *20*(2), 217–241. doi:10.1080/02699930500172291.

Watts, R. J. (2003). *Politeness*. Cambridge: Cambridge University Press.

3 Criticism in Russian Academic Book Reviews of the Soviet and Post-Soviet Periods

Alisa Kriukova

1 Introduction

During the past thirty years, Russia has witnessed considerable socio-historical changes which have influenced, among other spheres, the tradition of Russian academic community. This tradition and its evolution are embodied in the texts created by members of the academic community: in particular, in academic reviews, which are not only one of the academic genres but also one of the most important forms of contemporary academic expertise and a part of academic communication (Stepanov, 2016: 82–92).

Interest to the analysis of academic book reviews is a relatively new phenomenon: it first appeared within the framework of the research direction "English for academic purposes", which developed actively in the 1980s and 1990s of the twentieth century. During decades of its evolution, this field has expanded a lot and naturally has got outside the boundaries of just one language. Reviews of papers on this subject can be read, for example, in Martín-Martín & Burgess, 2004: 171–175 or in Stepanov, 2016.

Analysis of book reviews traditionally includes description of their compositional and semantic features and/or comparison of book reviews differing from each other in some aspect. As a whole, papers dedicated to the analysis of reviews can be classified into several groups. The division is made according to the main point of the author's attention throughout the study, and some papers can be attributed to more than one group as they look closely into several problems at a time. Particularly, the main lines of research in the analysis of academic book reviews include studies of evaluation in texts of countries with a different cultural (and scientific) tradition (for example, in Moreno & Suarez, 2008; Itakura & Tsui, 2011), sometimes in reviews written by male vs. female authors (Römer, 2005), as well as diachronic studies. This chapter belongs to this last mentioned type, investigating an expression of evaluation in two time periods and elaborating analysis of the changes taking place.

In general, papers on the discussed topic focus on changes occurring in the tradition of academic writing during a period of time (Salager-Meyer & Defives, 1998) or, in particular, of criticism and its targets in reviews of different time periods (Salager-Meyer et al., 2003; 2007). In the latter paper (Salager-Meyer et al., 2007), the authors investigate evolution of the expression of criticism. The study is based on a corpus of 100 French reviews on medical papers: half published between 1890 and 1900, and half between 1990 and 2000 (Salager-Meyer et al., 2007: 1761). According to their results, critical book reviews are more frequent in the first period than in the second, although this difference is not statistically significant. Moreover, "unhedged CRs [instances of criticism] are significantly more frequent" over the first period (16% of the total number of CRs recorded during that time) than they are over the second period (2.3% of the total number of CRs recorded during that time, $p = .0034$) (Ibid.: 1765). However, both in the whole corpus and in each of the periods, indirect critical acts outnumber direct ones.

The former of the two mentioned papers (Salager-Meyer et al., 2003) investigates both diachronic and inter-cultural aspects of the study of reviews. The results show that although French and Spanish researchers are generally more critical and tend to express criticism more directly than their English counterparts, the reviews written in recent years reflect an evolution of the expression of negative evaluation. Thus, in Spanish and French reviews, the number of instances of "direct" criticism was decreasing over a few years preceding the study (Salager-Meyer et al., 2003).

As we can see, there are both synchronic and diachronic differences in the ways of expressing criticism. Synchronic are usually culturally conditioned, while diachronic are a consequence of evolution of the genre and its conventions over time.

The aim of the present study, in turn, is to look into the expression of criticism in two different contexts: the USSR in the 1980s and contemporary Russia, as these contexts reflect not only a change over time that occurred within the same culture, but significant social and even cultural changes witnessed by the academic community over the past 30–40 years as a result of a shift in the historical context. In order to carry out such research, first I needed to analyse the features that characterise the expression of negative evaluation in the reviews of the two periods, and then to determine in what aspects these texts differ from each other and whether the differences can be accounted for by historical and social changes.

2 Data

In the study, I focus on two time periods: the decade of the 1980s and the latest decade, starting from 2010. The choice of these two periods roots primarily from the assumption that extensive changes in the socio-historical context have influenced the ways in which negative evaluation is expressed. The 1980s indicate the ending of the previous historical era of the country's development (the last full decade of the USSR), the era that was characterised by a stable, long-established scientific tradition reflecting the state of the academic community. As concerns the texts of the second period under review (2010s), they reflect the contemporary tradition of the Russian academic community.

The study is based on the reviews of the 1980s and the 2010s published in the journal "*Issues in Linguistics*", which is one of the most reputable Russian linguistic periodicals. The total amount of thirty reviews in Russian was analysed: fifteen from each period. Importantly, to achieve maximum possible homogeneity of the data and to make it comparable, additional selection criteria were introduced within the already stated timeframes. First, only reviews on monographs were chosen (in contrast to, for example, dictionaries and manuals). Second, collected volumes were excluded from the study: the entire text of a book should be written as a whole by one or several authors. The reason for this limitation is that collective works tend to be more heterogeneous than single- or multi-authored, and in such editions, criticism is usually directed at parts written by different authors individually rather than to the book as a whole, as a solid work. For instance, a reviewer might evaluate some chapters of the book highly while criticising others, written by other authors. As a result, the final review might lack uniformity and resemble several small independent reviews. Hence, reviews on collective monographs were withdrawn from the study.

The third requirement was for both the reviewer and the author of the monograph to belong to the same academic community (Soviet or Russian). The reason is that if the book under review does not match this criterion, it leads to some (probably inevitable) changes in the conceptual side of the review: criticism is less likely to be directed at some aspects of the book at which it would be, in other circumstances. For example, a person reviewing a book written not in his/her native language might fail to notice some stylistic defects of the narration. This could be a factor affecting the results and distorting them; thus, to escape this, limitations in the selection of reviews were introduced.

3 Theoretical Concepts

3.1 Criticism and Critical Acts

The study of criticism constitutes a part of a broader field of analysing evaluation in general or, within my object of study, a bit more specific sub-field of evaluation in academic discourse (see, for example, Hood, 2010). In this chapter, I limit myself to a most specific part of it – that is, criticism in academic reviews, and do not touch upon broader topics. For more detailed information on academic evaluation, see Hyland & Diani, 2009 and chapters in Tognini-Bonelli & Camiciotti, 2005.

In the present section, some notions used in the following parts of the research are clarified. Thus, in papers on the analysis of academic reviews, criticism is usually defined as negative evaluation targeted at some aspect of the work under review (for example, in Itakura & Tsui, 2011 and Salager-Meyer et al., 2007). By a critical act, one instance of criticism is understood.

Moreover, in the abovementioned research (Salager-Meyer et al., 2007), the authors distinguish three types of criticism according to its targets: conceptual, textual, and contextual. Conceptual criticism, as the authors write, is directed towards the very content of the book under review (e.g. omission or repetition of ideas, superficial comments, etc.); textual criticism is voiced at formal aspects of the book, such as stylistic issues, book layout, visual presentation, etc. And by contextual criticism, the authors mean evaluation targeted neither at the content nor at the design of the book, but rather at some external phenomena (e.g. historical, social, or political environment) (Salager-Meyer et al., 2007: 1763). This distinction will be needed for the further course of our study.

3.2 Mitigation of Criticism

Mitigation is a very common move spread across almost all genres of discourse: it is as universal as the politeness theory suggested by Brown and Levinson (Brown & Levinson, 1987), within which the need for mitigation can be accounted for. This need arises when one participant of a communicative situation feels that his/her message might bear a face-threatening effect for another participant if delivered directly. In this case, mitigation can be used to make the "dangerous" part less pronounced. While specific manifestations of politeness depend on conventions of a particular community, it is generally used as strategic conflict avoidance and social indexing (Kasper, 1990).

Mitigation is employed a lot, especially when a certain amount of criticism needs to be delivered. Thus, it is employed by teachers giving feedback to students (Hyland & Hyland, 2001), editors formulating suggestions to writers (Mackiewicz & Riley, 2003), and, among other situations, by reviewers critically evaluating some piece of academic writing. Critical evaluation in such cases might appear in either overt or mitigated form, depending on the intention of the reviewer. Overt criticism is found in those instances when negative evaluation is expressed without the use of any resources to soften it, and in this case the critical act is regarded as direct in contrast to an indirect, or mitigated. The term *mitigation devices*, therefore, is used to denote linguistic means by which the reviewer softens negative evaluation and minimises the face-threatening effect it might have.

For example, in (1), taken from one of the studied reviews, the following cases of softening can be pointed out: lexical mitigation ("*somewhat questionable*"), the use of the subjunctive mood in the expression of criticism, and the decrease in the categoricalness of the judgement (the use of *perhaps* instead of, for example, obviously).

1 *Neskol'ko somnitel'no razgranichenie absolyutivnyh (korova bodaetsya) i refleksivno-posessivnyh vzaimnyh konstrukcij (Avtor dolzhen publikovat'sya).* [...] *Vozmozhno, bolee nadezhnym byl by drugoj kriterij: tol'ko absolyutivnye, no ne refleksivno-posessivnye konstrukcii nedopustimy v sovershennom vide.*

The distinction between absolute («Корова бодается», 'a cow horns') and reflexive-possessive reciprocal constructions («Автор должен публиковаться», 'an author should be published') is somewhat questionable. [...] Perhaps a different criterion would be more reliable: only absolute, but not reflexive-possessive constructions are impossible in the perfective aspect.

Martín-Martín in his dissertation looks closely into mitigation in English and Spanish academic writing and distinguishes several strategies that are implemented with the help of various linguistic devices (Martín-Martín, 2004: 112–117):

- Indetermination strategy, when a shade of uncertainty, vagueness, and lesser clarity is attributed to the judgement. This strategy includes epistemic modality, as well as approximators of quantity, frequency, degree, and time.
- Strategy of camouflage hedging – with the means of metalinguistic operators, i.e. parenthetical words and expressions that indicate the position from which the author evaluates the truth of the statement ("*it is obvious that*", "*strictly speaking*", "*to some extent*", "*in fact*", etc.).
- Subjectivisation strategy that includes the use of the first-person pronouns along with the verbs of cognition or performative verbs, which indicates that the evaluation is a personal opinion of the author, and shows respect for an alternative point of view. Besides, a part of this strategy are adjectival and adverbial expressions that emphasise quality, such as "*extremely interesting*", "*particularly important*", "*promising results*", etc., which are used to convince the reader that the expressed claim is true and/or important.
- Depersonalisation strategy consists in authors minimising their presence in texts by using impersonal, agentless, and passive constructions to spare themselves the responsibility for the truthfulness of propositions.

Different kinds of mitigation strategies are discussed also in Caffi, 1999. For research dedicated to mitigation in Russian, see, for example,

Namsaraev (1997), where the author investigates correlation between hedging and linguistic spheres such as modality, metadiscourse, and the pragmatics of politeness, and classifies main functions and strategies of hedging.

4 Methodology

Drawing upon the theoretical background, the method of the study can be summarised as follows:

> Once the data had been collected, manual analysis was made. First, quantitative characteristics were recorded: I calculated the number of critical acts encountered in the reviews and the correlation between a critical part of a review and the rest of the text. Besides, instances of direct vs. indirect criticism were singled out and their proportion counted. After that, the qualitative part of the analysis was carried out. Specifically, targets of criticism were identified for every critical act, the tactics used by the reviewers to mitigate or intensify expression of critical attitude were determined, as well as linguistic means correlating with these tactics–e.g. lexical/ grammatical/ syntactical markers. Finally, the Soviet and the modern periods were compared on the basis of the research made.

To provide a more detailed account of how all the steps of the research were performed, some comments need to be made. Thus, during the recording of instances of negative evaluation in each of the chosen reviews, additional considerations were regarded. Particularly, critical acts were included into the study on the condition that the target of criticism is the book under review itself: its content or design. In other words, only conceptual and textual criticism was taken into account, while the third type (contextual, following the division made in Salager-Meyer et al., 2007) was not, which means that instances of criticism whose target is outside of the book under review were not recorded as critical acts. This decision is based on the criterion of compulsoriness. In line with the conventions of the genre, the reviewer has to pay attention to nearly all the drawbacks of the book under review, including its content and formal aspects. Therefore, expressing evaluation of these aspects is expected from any reviewer, while, however, paying attention to some external phenomena that can theoretically provoke criticism is not required from the reviewer and depends solely on his/her personal decision. For this reason, such instances were excluded from the present study.

Thus, examples similar to (2) were not analysed in the course of the research, as the target of the critical comment here lies outside the book under review. On the contrary, examples similar to (3) meet the stated requirement and, consequently, were recorded as critical acts.

2 *[...] teoreticheskij uroven' rossijskoj frazeologii – za ochen' nebol'shimi isklyucheniyami – ostaetsya otnositel'no nevysokim.*
[...] theoretical level of Russian phraseology – with very few exceptions – remains relatively low.

3 *Avtory, vklyuchiv ehtu glavu v knigu, ne opredelilis' v polnoj mere s teoreticheskim statusom vvodimogo formalizma.*
The authors, in spite of including this chapter in the book, haven't decided upon the theoretical status of the formalism they are introducing.

Likewise, every instance of criticism directed at one particular aspect of the book was registered as one critical act (even if it contained several examples from the book), and criticism directed at various aspects was recorded as several independent critical acts, even within a single sentence. Example (4) can illustrate this rule: in this sentence, three critical acts were recorded, by the number of different targets of criticism found there.

4 *Mozhno obratit' vnimanie i na bolee chastnye nedochety ehtogo solidnogo issledovaniya: problematichnost' predlagaemyh kriteriev polnoty osvoeniya literaturnoj leksiki v govore (str. 131); [...] traktovku sochetanij s «dat'» 8 (str. 195–196); protivorechiya tematicheskoj klassifikacii leksiki.*
Less significant shortcomings of this important research could also be indicated: the problematic nature of the proposed criteria for completeness of mastering literary vocabulary in a dialect (p. 131); [...] the interpretation of combinations with «дать» [dat', 'give'] *(p. 195–196); the contradiction of the thematic classification of vocabulary.*

Thus, the main criterion on which the decision whether to register a particular expression as a separate critical act or not depended was for the potential instance of criticism to convey completed idea, which correlates with the possibility to be taken out of context preserving its meaning, as in (4).

After all critical acts and their targets had been recorded, the next objective was to figure out how negative evaluation can be expressed, and particularly how it is strengthened and softened. In every critical act, the means of intensification and mitigation of criticism were identified. However, these means are not always employed: for example, in (5), the reviewer does not use neither mitigating nor strengthening tactics:

5 *Est' v knige i netochnosti, i opechatki (ukr. принцыпы vm. принципи — str. 30; мезанизм vm. механизм — str. 133; E. Едличка vm. A. Едличка — str. 73; cheshsk. Brezi jalovice vm. brezi jalovice — str. 292 i dr.)*

> *There are some inaccuracies as well as misprints in the book (Ukranian принцuпы instead of принцuпu — p. 30; мезанизм instead of механизм — p. 133; Е. Едличка instead of А. Едличка— p. 73; Czech Brezi jalovice instead of brezi jalovice — p. 292 etc.)*

It should be noted, besides, that there is no direct correlation between the number of critical acts and instances of intensification and mitigation of criticism. First, because a critical act can be expressed without employing these tactics, as in the example provided earlier. Second, within one critical act, both mitigation and intensification of evaluation can occur. Moreover, in some cases, mitigation is expressed outside of a particular critical act, ahead of it or later on, sometimes referring to more than one critical act.

All in all, a few consecutive steps were performed in order to obtain a clearer understanding of the features characterising each period. The results of the analysis are presented in the following section together with the comparison of the two periods.

5 Results

5.1 Amount of Criticism

After recording critical acts, calculations were made of the percentage of criticism in each review by the number of characters (see Table 3.1). It was found that in the modern reviews, criticism is usually more extended: the median value of the percentage of criticism for the period of the 2010s is 20% compared to 13.25% for the reviews of the 1980s. The quantity of critical acts is also greater in the modern reviews: there proved to be 152 critical acts in the reviews of the 2010s and 113 critical acts in the reviews of the 1980s.

The difference in the length of the reviews is explicit too: the average figures are 14,780 symbols for the 1980s. vs. 20,900 symbols for the 2010s. The median value for the 1980s amounts to 14,540 symbols, while for the 2010s, it is 18,132 symbols. This means we can argue that modern reviews tend to be longer and contain more criticism than Soviet reviews.

Table 3.1 Quantitative results: amount and length

	1980s	*2010s*
Percentage of criticism, median value	13,25%	20%
Critical acts	113	152
Length of reviews, median value	14,540 symbols	18,132 symbols

5.2 Targets of Criticism

The next step was to classify the targets of negative evaluation in order to identify which aspects of the work are criticised. It was discovered that most of the criticism is aimed at the content of the work, and only 10% of all critical acts are targeted at its formal aspects, such as mistypes, stylistic errors, inconsistency of references to literature, lack of tables, lack of subject index, etc. There is no difference between the two periods in this aspect.

Within the class of conceptual criticism, several subclasses have been distinguished. These include methodology (17%, see ex. (6)), results (15%, see ex. (7)), individual drawbacks – when the reviewer disagrees, for example, with one particular comment/interpretation (23%, see ex. (8)), coverage of the material (18%, see ex. (9)), narrative logic (14%, see ex. (10)), and "other" – instances that could not be included in other subclasses (13%).

6 *Predlozhennaya zhe avtorom procedura otdeleniya prilagatel'nyh ot sushchestvitel'nyh putem substantivacii sobstvenno prilagatel'nyh (v otlichie ot tak nazyvaemyh sklonyaemyh prilagatel'nyh) pri pomoshchi otnositel'no-ukazatel'nogo mestoimeniya (sr. prilag. tang «uzkij»— sushch. ye tang, bukv, «kotoryj uzkij», str. 15) kazhetsya izlishnej i iskusstvennoj v rabote istoricheskogo plana.*

A procedure proposed by the author – the procedure of separating adjectives from nouns by substantivizing proper adjectives (in contrast to so-called declining adjectives) with the help of a relative-demonstrative pronoun (compare adj. tang 'narrow'— n. ye tang, literally "which is narrow", p. 15) seems superfluous and artificial in a historical work.

7 [...] *Samo nalichie sovremennyh suffiksov prilagatel'nyh protivorechit kategoricheskomu vyvodu avtora, chto v kurdskom yazyke «utracheny dazhe te nemnogochislennye formal'nye kriterii vydeleniya prilagatel'nyh v otdel'nuyu chast' rechi, kotorye sushchestvovali v drevneiranskom».*

[...] *The very presence of modern suffixes of adjectives contradicts the categorical conclusion of the author that in the Kurdish language "even those few formal criteria for separating adjectives into an independent part of speech that existed in ancient Iranian are no longer applicable".*

8 *Ne sovsem udachnym predstavlyaetsya i sam termin «partikuly». Prinimaya ego, my slovno otrezaem sebya ot nerusskoyazychnoj lingvistiki, poskol'ku perevod dannogo termina na drugie yazyki krajne zatrudnitelen.*

The term «нартикулы» itself does not seem quite apt. By accepting it we seem to separate ourselves from non-Russian linguistics as translating this term to other languages is extremely difficult.

9 *K sozhaleniyu, vsego lish' odin abzac posvyashchen sootnosheniyu intonacii i klassov slov.*

Unfortunately, only one paragraph is dedicated to the relation of intonation and word classes.

10 *V dannom sluchae, ob"yasnenie nedifferencirovannosti imen v sovremennom kurdskom yazyke edinstvom drevneiranskih tipov skloneniya sushchestvitel'nyh i prilagatel'nyh predstavlyaetsya neskol'ko rasplyvchatym, nedogovorennym, mysl' ostaetsya nerazvitoj, kak by oborvannoj.*

In this case, the explanation of the non-differentiation of nouns in the modern Kurdish language by the unity of declination types of nouns and adjectives in the Ancient Iranian seems somewhat vague, unclear, the thought is not developed, as though cut short.

According to the calculated percentages, individual drawbacks constitute the most frequent target of criticism in the analysed texts. The possible explanation is that disagreement between the reviewer and the author is more likely to arise in particular observations than in global ideas – at least because a book usually has a very limited number of the latter compared to the former. Besides, even if the reviewer highly evaluates the book under review in general, and neither methodology nor results attract criticism, there most likely will be an example with the interpretation of which the reviewer can disagree, as it is practically impossible for the author and the reviewer to share 100%-similar opinions and intuitions. There is another fact in our findings that proves this suggestion: in the analysed data, there were several reviews with overall small amount of criticism where the only few critical acts were targeted at what was later in the course of the study defined as "individual drawbacks".

Summarising the findings concerning the aspects of the book at which reviewers aim critical comments, it can be underlined that in the studied corpus, conceptual criticism was nine times as frequent as textual criticism. Importantly, negative evaluation targeted at the content of the book can be classified into several groups, which are individual drawbacks, coverage of the material, methodology, results, and narrative logic, listed from the most frequent to the least.

5.3 Intensification of Negative Evaluation

It might be of interest to look closer at the picture created by quantitative and qualitative assessments of negative evaluation: from the number of

Table 3.2 Quantitative results: intensification of criticism

	1980s	*2010s*
Quantity of critical acts	25	65
Quantity of instances	28	93

critical acts in which criticism is intensified (see Table 3.2) or softened to the ways and tactics that help reviewers express negative evaluation. According to the findings, intensification of criticism is found in 25 (out of 113) critical acts in the 1980s and in 65 (out of 152) critical acts in the 2010s. A total of 28 instances were recorded in the reviews of the 1980s, and 93 instances in the reviews of the 2010s. The values of both parameters indicate a drastic change to a more relentless expression of negative evaluation.

In the majority of cases, intensification is expressed lexically: *serious doubts*, *especially undesirable*, etc. However, in both periods, some unexpected examples were discovered, when intensification of criticism is achieved with the help of tropes, such as comparison ("*like a phantom*", ex. 11), metaphor ("*scattered in the reviewed edition with a bountiful hand*", ex. 12), and irony (ex. 13), as well as a quotation from literature (ex. 14).

11 *V izlozhenii prisutstvuyut otdel'nye neyasnosti v tom, chto kasaetsya dialektnogo chleneniya v dannom areale. Ya imeyu v vidu dakskij* [...] *yazyk, kotoryj, kak nekij fantom, to poyavlyaetsya v knige, to ischezaet.*

There are certain ambiguities concerning the dialectal division in the area present in the narration. I mean Dacian language [...], *which, like a phantom, appears in the book from time to time and then disappears.*

12 *Razberem nemnogie iz primerov, predstavlyayushchih soboj sblizheniya po sozvuchiyu, razbrosannye v recenziruemom izdanii shchedroj rukoj.*

Let us look attentively at just a few of the examples which really are just comparisons based on consonance, scattered in the reviewed edition with a bountiful hand.

13 *Inogda sushchestvennaya mysl' vyskazyvaetsya v slishkom kategorichnoj forme. Naprimer, «protivopostavlenie fatiki i informatiki priznaetsya chrezvychajno sushchestvennym prakticheski vsemi yazykovedami mira» (s. 209). Mozhet byt', otricayut ehto protivopostavlenie i nemnogie, no ogromnoe chislo lingvistov prosto ne dumayut o nem, zanimayas' inymi problemami.*

Sometimes an important thought is expressed in a too categorical form. For example, "the opposition of fatics and information science is recognised as extremely significant by almost all linguists of the world" (p. 209). Perhaps, this opposition is disclaimed by very few linguists, but a huge number of them just do not think about it, occupying themselves with different problems.

14 *Ehto nevol'no zastavlyaet vspomnit' rekomendaciyu Sergeya Dovlatova: «Ne pishi ty ehpohami i kataklizmami! Ne pishi ty strastyami i lokomotivami! A pishi ty... bukvami – A, B, V...»*

This involuntarily makes us recall Sergei Dovlatov's recommendation: "Do not write epochs and cataclysms! Do not write passions and locomotives! And do write... letters - A, B, C..."

The tactics for expression critical attitude mentioned earlier stand out against the general stylistics of the academic discourse. Such unconventional means of intensifying negative evaluation offer a promising field for further research.

5.4 Mitigation of Negative Evaluation

As to the mitigation of criticism, it occurs in 70 critical acts in the total of 109 instances in the 1980s, and in 89 acts in 155 instances in the 2010s (see Table 3.3).

In spite of the fact that the difference between the periods in this aspect is not as radical as it is with the intensification of criticism, there are still more instances of mitigation of criticism than of its intensification. Consequently, the means of conveying mitigation are also more diverse. In Table 3.4, five most frequent mitigation strategies for both periods are represented. Examples illustrating them are provided below.

The mitigation devices mentioned in the table require an explicit comment. Hedging is the use of specific lexical items (like "*somewhat*", "*a bit*", "*quite*", and others) to lessen the face-threatening effect of a critical comment. Personal attribution (such as "*to my mind*", "*perhaps*", etc.) mitigates criticism by indicating subjectivity of the judgement, specifying that it represents the reviewer's personal opinion, not an objective quality of the book. Praise-criticism pair is a combination of negative and positive evaluations in order to mitigate criticism. Either the positive is put in the forefront, the reviewer

Table 3.3 Quantitative results: mitigation of criticism

	1980s	*2010s*
Quantity of critical acts	70	89
Quantity of instances	109	155

Table 3.4 Frequent mitigation devices

1980s	*2010s*
1 Personal attribution, see (15)	1 Personal attribution, see (15)
2 Hedging, see (15)	2 Hedging, see (15)
3 Praise-criticism pairs, see (16)	3 Praise-criticism pairs, see (16)
4 Remark in the form of advice to the author, see (17)	4 Critical act put in a footnote / in brackets, see (18)
5 Insignificance of the defect, see (19)	5 Justifiability of the defect, see (20)

emphasises some of the merits of the book under review, and then mentions the drawbacks, or vice versa, so that a critical act is followed by praise.

Example (15) illustrates such mitigation devices as personal attribution ("*in my opinion*") and hedges ("*not quite correct*"); example (16) shows a praise-criticism pair. In (17), criticism is expressed as an advice to the author with the use of the subjunctive mood. Negative evaluation in example (18) is mitigated as it is enclosed in parentheses, which has an effect of lesser importance, while in (19), the insignificance of the previously mentioned shortcomings is pointed out, and in (20) there is a justification of the appearance of a defect.

15 *Vprochem, na nash vzglyad, ne sovsem verno prichislyat' k takim obrazovaniya tipa «byt' bolee royalistom» – oni otmecheny i v arhaichnyh upotrebleniyah i blizki k konstrukciyam tipa on «bolee akter, chem pisatel'», gde bolee vystupaet v znachenii 'v bol'shej stepeni'.*

However, in my opinion, it is not quite correct to categorise in that way formations like «быть более роялистом» ('to be more of a royalist'): they have been recorded in archaic uses and are close to constructions like «он более актер, чем писатель» ('he is more of an actor than of a writer'), where "more" means 'in a greater degree'.

16 *Pri tom, chto knigu otlichaet yarkaya individual'nost', i bolee togo – izyashchestvo oformleniya (vplot' do oglavleniya i numeracii stranic), izlozhenie, k sozhaleniyu, soprovozhdaetsya nebrezhnostyami, kotorye neredko zatrudnyayut vospriyatie teksta.*

Although the book is characterised by originality and, moreover, an elegant design (up to the table of contents and page numbering), the narration is, unfortunately, accompanied by negligence that often causes difficulties in the perception of text.

17 *Sledovalo by takzhe avtoru recenziruemoj raboty soslat'sya na te razdely kollektivnogo truda «Opyt istoriko-tipologicheskogo*

issledovaniya iranskih yazykov» (I—II, M., 1975), v kotoryh rassmatrivayutsya grammaticheskie kategorii kurdskogo yazyka.

The author should have also referred to those sections of the collective work "Historico-Typological Study of the Iranian Languages" (I-II, M., 1975) where grammatical categories of the Kurdish language are addressed.

18 *Ishcha naibolee tochnye slova i stremyas' k mezhdunarodnomu standartu v oboznachenii tekh ili inyh stilistiko-poehticheskih i lingvisticheski yavlenij, X. R. Kurbatov neredko daet v skobkah ih ehkvivalenty, vnosit utochneniya v tradicionnoe terminoupotreblenie (zdes' otmetim, chto v takoj nasyshchennoj terminami knige byl by ves'ma umesten predmetnyj ukazatel').*

Seeking the most accurate words and aiming at the international standard in denomination of stylistic-poetic and linguistic phenomena, Kh. R. Kurbatov often gives their equivalents in parentheses, adding clarifications to the traditional terminology (here it should be pointed out that in such book filled with terminology, a subject index would be very appropriate).

19 *Vse podobnye sluchai, esli ih kolichestvo ne prevoskhodit nekotorogo poroga, vryad li mogut rassmatrivat'sya kak pretenzii.*

All such cases, if their number does not exceed a certain limit, can hardly be considered problems.

20 *Poskol'ku my i sejchas ploho umeem otlichat' yazyk ot dialekta, estestvenno sdelat' skidku na nekotoruyu opravdannost' takogo nerazlicheniya dlya drevnego perioda i dlya reliktovogo yazyka.*

Since we still do not entirely know how to distinguish a language from a dialect, it is natural to take into account that such non-distinction for the ancient period and for the relict language can be justified.

As seen in Table 3.4, three most frequent devices are typical for both periods. The differences between the 1980s and the 2010s start revealing from the fourth and the fifth positions that demonstrate mitigation devices that are frequent for one of the periods and rare or even not observed in the other: remark in the form of advice to the author, critical act put in a footnote / in brackets, insignificance of the defect, and its justifiability. Among those that have not been included in the table, such mitigation devices as, for instance, expressing criticism in the form of a rhetorical question or attributing problematic issues to the objectives of future studies can be mentioned. However, they are a lot less frequent in both periods than the seven discussed earlier.

If we return to example (5), repeated here as (21), now we have justification to classify the instances of mitigation found there into the mentioned categories. "*Somewhat questionable*" will then be assigned to the hedges and "*perhaps*" will be included into the "personal attribution" group. The subjunctive mood could theoretically be referred to the group "remark in the form of advice to the author". However, there is a subtle difference between this example and example (17): although they both suggest a possible way to improve something in the reviewed books, only in the latter is the author openly addressed – as a consequence, the former example is less direct, so I tend to assign these two cases into different groups of mitigation devices.

21 *Neskol'ko somnitel'no razgranichenie absolyutivnyh (korova bodaetsya) i refleksivno-posessivnyh vzaimnyh konstrukcij (Avtor dolzhen publikovat'sya).* [...] *Vozmozhno, bolee nadezhnym byl by drugoj kriterij: tol'ko absolyutivnye, no ne refleksivno-posessivnye konstrukcii nedopustimy v sovershennom vide.*

The distinction between absolute («Корова бодается», 'a cow horns') and reflexive-possessive reciprocal constructions («Автор должен публиковаться», 'an author should be published') is somewhat questionable. [...] *Perhaps a different criterion would be more reliable: only absolute, but not reflexive-possessive constructions are impossible in the perfective aspect.*

The provided figures show that in consistency with other parameters, there are more instances of mitigation in the reviews of the 2010s. Besides, if compared with the intensification of criticism, mitigation is a more typical move for reviewers, and there are various linguistic means that help them soften negative evaluation: from lexical to clausal and even graphic markers.

6 Conclusions

According to the collected data, there are a greater number of critical acts in the modern material. At the same time, reviews of the 2010s tend to be longer in general, which makes the quantity of critical acts not a representative number. However, the figures showing the median value of the percentage of criticism allow us to make a more relevant observation: statistically, larger parts of modern reviews contain critical comments, meaning there is more criticism in them compared to the reviews of the 1980s, even considering the difference in their length.

Speaking of targets of criticism, most of the cases found in the corpus are attributed to the conceptual criticism, with only a few directed at formal aspects of the book under review. The considerable number of critical acts targeted at the content of the books reviewed gives an opportunity to make a further distinction within the class of conceptual criticism: all such instances are categorised into several subclasses – individual drawbacks, coverage of the material, methodology, results, and narrative logic.

Interestingly, sometimes reviewers choose unconventional ways to convey negative attitude: metaphors, vivid comparisons, irony, or quotations from fiction. This serves as an illustration of creative use of language that can be encountered even within such seemingly rigid genre of academic writing as reviews.

A tendency to a more critical attitude towards the work under review discussed earlier is supported by another figure as well: instances of intensification of criticism are also more frequent in the modern reviews (three times more frequent than several decades ago). Thus, in terms of both the amount of criticism and the tactics of its expression, modern reviews tend to be more critical and more abrupt. In spite of that, from a general perspective, in both periods, most critical acts are expressed indirectly, i.e. with the use of mitigating strategies, as politeness is one of the conventions of the genre of academic reviews.

As for a more detailed analysis of mitigation devices, a few "core" means that are most (and equally) frequent in both periods can be identified, which are personal attribution, hedging, and praise-criticism pairs. These are well-established strategies in the tradition of academic discourse in Russia, while the rest are more typical for one or another of the periods and demonstrate alternating trends in mitigating criticism.

The results appear quite noteworthy and deserve consideration, especially the observations about the increased amount and relative directness of criticism in modern reviews, since this picture is evidently not universal. In contrast to what has been found in Russian material, in other diachronic studies, a decrease in the amount of criticism and an augmentation in its indirectness is observed in more modern reviews (see, for example, Salager-Meyer et al., 2003; 2007). Perhaps, this specific feature in the evolution of criticism expression in Russia can be explained by the fact that in the 1980s within the USSR, there were not as many linguistic schools as in the Western academic community and the Soviet academic sphere was not particularly open to other traditions. However, it has changed and has become more welcoming to Western ideas, and besides in modern times, there are many coexisting schools and trends. This fact results in reviewers being more critical to their colleagues now than they used to be, because in the current situation, they are more likely to hold to different points of view on linguistic issues. Another reason that can possibly account for the differences observed is the greater openness and transparency of the Russian academic community nowadays in general, which leads to a freer expression of criticism. However, both assumptions need a further, more consistent verification on the material of Russian academic reviews.

References

Brown, P., & Levinson, S. C. (1987). *Politeness: Some Universals in Language Usage*. Cambridge: Cambridge University Press.

Caffi, C. (1999). On mitigation. *Journal of Pragmatics*, 31/7, 881–909.

Hood, S. (2010). *Appraising Research: Evaluation in Academic Writing*. London: Springer.

Hyland, F., & Hyland, K. (2001). Sugaring the pill: Praise and criticism in written feedback. *Journal of Second Language Writing*, 10/3, 185–212.

Hyland, K., & Diani, G. (2009). Introduction: Academic evaluation and review genres. In *Academic Evaluation*. London: Palgrave Macmillan, 1–14.

Itakura, H., & Tsui, A. B. M. (2011). Evaluation in academic discourse: Managing criticism in Japanese and English book reviews. *Journal of Pragmatics*, 43/5, 1366–1379.

Kasper, G. (1990). Linguistic politeness: Current research issues. *Journal of Pragmatics*. 14/2, 193–218.

Mackiewicz, J., & Riley, K. (2003). The technical editor as diplomat: Linguistic strategies for balancing clarity and politeness. *Technical Communication*. 50/1, 83–94.

Martín-Martín, P. (2004). *A genre-analytic study of English and Spanish research article abstracts in the experimental social sciences*. Universidad de La Laguna, PhD Thesis.

Martín-Martín, P., & Burgess, S. (2004). The rhetorical management of academic criticism in research article abstracts. *An Interdisciplinary Journal of the Study of Discourse*. 24/2, 171–196.

Moreno, A. I., & Suárez, L. (2008). A study of critical attitude across English and Spanish academic book reviews. *Journal of English for Academic Purposes*. 7/1, 15–26.

Namsaraev, V. (1997). Hedging in Russian academic writing in sociological texts, in Markkanen, R. & Schröder, H. (eds.). *Hedging and Discourse. Approaches to the Analysis of a Pragmatic Phenomenon in Academic Text*. Berlin: Walter de Gruyter, 64–81.

Römer, U. (2005). 'This seems somewhat counterintuitive, though…': Negative Evaluation in Linguistic Book Reviews by Male and Female Authors, in Tognini Bonelli, E. & Del Lungo Camiciotti, G. (eds.). *Strategies in Academic Discourse*. Amsterdam: John Benjamins, 97–115.

Salager-Meyer, F., & Defives, G. (1998). From the gentleman's courtesy to the scientist's caution: A diachronic study of hedges in academic writing (1810–1995), in Fortanet, I., Posteguillo, S., Palmer, J. C. & Coll, J. F. (eds.). *Genre Studies in English for Academic Purposes*. Castelló de la Plana: Publicaciones de la Universitat Jaume I, 133–172.

Salager-Meyer, F., Alcaraz Ariza, M. A., & Zambrano, N. (2003). The scimitar, the dagger and the glove: Intercultural differences in the rhetoric of criticism in Spanish, French and English medical discourse (1930–1995). *English for Specific Purposes*. 22/3, 223–247.

Salager-Meyer, F., Alcaraz Ariza, M. A., Pabón Berbesí, M. (2007). Collegiality, critique and the construction of scientific argumentation in medical book reviews: A diachronic approach. *Journal of Pragmatics*. 39/10, 1758–1774.

Stepanov, B. (2016). Crisis of the genre: Book reviews in studies of scholary communication. *Laboratorium*. 8/1, 82–106.

Tognini-Bonelli, E., & Camiciotti, G. D. L. (Eds.). (2005). *Strategies in Academic Discourse* (Vol. 19). Amsterdam: John Benjamins Publishing.

4 Modal Verb Categories in Medical Abstracts[1]

Elena Quintana-Toledo and Margarita Esther Sánchez Cuervo

1 Introduction

The enormous growth not only of the scientific community worldwide but also of their production, i.e. published research papers above all in electronic format, seems to make both natural and practical that nowadays scientists read "abstracts as short, concise, complete and accurate sources of information" (Salager-Meyer, Alcaraz-Ariza and Lewin 2014: 221). This holds particularly true in the field of medicine where practitioners are supposed to have a quick access to huge amounts of information in order to keep up-to-date with the latest advances. In this sense, Hyland (2004: 63) highlights the role of the abstract as a crucial step for the reader as it may or may not encourage him/her to continue reading the whole paper. Abstract writing, then, is a significant stage in letting others know about the originality of your research and your competence within your discipline, both of which would contribute to building up your credibility in the scientific community. As such, abstracts stand as an interesting genre for analysing what modal verbs reveal about their authors.

This chapter seeks to explore the attitudinal qualifications conveyed by the use of modal verbs in a corpus of medical abstracts. In so doing, we try to characterise this textual genre within this specific discipline in terms of the most frequently used modal verbs and their meanings in relation to authorial stancetaking. Even though definitions of stancetaking generally differ in their scope giving rise to both broad and narrow notions of the term, it is also true that they all tend to focus on language by highlighting the functions and the contexts in which stance items occur. Hyland (2005: 176), for example, defines stance "as an attitudinal dimension and includes features which refer to the ways writers present themselves and present their judgements, opinions, and commitments. It is the way that writers intrude to stamp their personal authority onto their arguments and step back and disguise their involvement". In this sense, modal verbs obviously play a role in conveying the speaker's or writer's evaluation of the propositional content. Such an evaluation "may relate to certainty, obligation or desirability or any of a number of other sets of values" (Thompson and Hunston 2000: 5). The relationship between stance and/or evaluation and modality is so tight that Thompson and Hunston (2000: 5) take modality to be a subcategory of evaluation.

We use corpus linguistics methodology to analyse our body of data and to excerpt material to exemplify modal senses. As it is the abstract section of the paper, we predict a massive use of dynamic and epistemic modals to show (i) dynamic possibility, whose function is to show potentiality, and (ii) epistemic possibility/probability. This combination allows authors to present their ideas and external facts without really imposing their views. The paper is structured as follows. The next section describes the corpus of study paying special attention to the abstract genre in medical science journals. Section 3 describes the theoretical framework for our analysis of modal verb categories. Section 4 presents our findings and the analysis together with the pragmatic interpretation. Finally, the conclusions drawn from the study are indicated.

2 Corpus Description

The corpus contains 48 abstracts belonging to medical research papers. They are part of a larger corpus which is currently being compiled and annotated by researchers working on the project "Identification and Analysis of Metadiscourse Strategies in Spanish and English" (IAMET) at the Universidad Politécnica de Valencia. This larger corpus contains complete research papers in English and Spanish in engineering, linguistics, and medicine. They have been randomly selected from several databases of scientific journals and the compilers have ensured that they were all written by native speakers of the two languages. Journals included are *Cancer Epidemiology*, *Cardiovascular Radiation Medicine*, *Clinical Pediatric Emergency Medicine*, *JMIR Public Health and Surveillance*, and *Journal of Psychiatric Research*, among others. The abstracts were processed so as to be analysed with *AntConc* by Anthony Lawrence. However, manual analysis was in order too so as to disambiguate certain modal meanings.

The abstract is a relatively new genre within health sciences professional literature. According to the Ad Hoc Working Group for Critical Appraisal of the Medical Literature (1987: 600), it was not until the sixties that abstracts started to be usually found in medical journals and periodicals. Bhatia (1993: 78) defines the abstract as "a description or factual summary of the much longer report, and is meant to give the reader an exact and concise knowledge of the full article". Salager-Meyer (1990: 367) has referred to the function of the abstracts as "chrystalisation"; Swales (1990: 179) as "distillation"; and

Kaplan et al. (1994: 405) as simply a "summary" of an associated text. Berkenkotter and Huckin (1995: 34) point out that scientific abstracts have several functions: they facilitate information access, encapsulate the most important material of the article, and frame the reading of the whole article.

Once abstracts were considered as integral parts of the research articles, they started to be placed at the beginning of the paper and started to have a more or less defined structural organisation. Samraj (2005: 145) observes that the micro-structure of the abstracts depends on the macro-structure of the research article they precede. The traditional four-move structure, namely (i) purpose, (ii) methods, (iii) results, and (iv) conclusions (Bhatia 1993; Brenton 1996), has generally been accepted. Hyland (2005: 67) posits that this schema "offers a fairly robust, if rather general, classification for cross-disciplinary comparison if we admit a certain flexibility". In the field of medicine specifically, abstracts have evolved in such a way that many journals currently advise their prospective authors to use structured abstracts, where certain sections have to be contained in them. In the case of the abstracts analysed for the purposes of the present paper, some of them show the structured format where the headings are typographically indicated: Background, Methods, Results, and Conclusions.

3 Modality and Stancetaking

In their work *The Language of Evaluation. Appraisal in English*, Martin and White (2005: 33–35) relate stance with the interpersonal in language and the subjective presence of speakers or writers towards both the material that they present and the people to whom they address said material. They speak about appraisal, involvement, and negotiation as the three major discourse semantic resources which interpret interpersonal meaning. In particular, appraisal is thoroughly examined in Martin and White's book and includes three interacting domains: attitude, engagement, and graduation:

1 Attitude has to do with our feelings, emotional reactions, and judgements of behaviour and evaluation of things.
2 Engagement is concerned with sourcing attitudes and the variety of voices which exist in discourse.
3 Graduation is interested in grading phenomena which allow the amplification and diminishing of categories.

In a similar vein, Englebretson (2007: 1) considers stance as the study of language according to the functions for which it is used and bearing in mind the contexts in which language takes place. The author

(Englebretson 2007: 15–19) explains that the theory about stance has been largely associated with the terms of subjectivity, evaluation, and interaction. For example, he quotes Lyons (1994: 13) when saying that locutionary subjectivity is the "expression of himself or herself in the act of utterance", or "self-expression in the use of language". As to evaluation, Thompson and Hunston (2000: 5) define it as "the expression of the speaker or writer's attitude or stance towards, viewpoint on, or feelings about the entities or propositions that he or she is talking about. That attitude may relate to certainty or obligation or desirability or any of a number of other sets of values". Likewise, Biber et al.'s (1999: 966) definition of stance connects the notions of subjectivity and evaluation in that it includes "personal feeling, attitudes, value judgments, or assessments". With respect to interaction, Englebretson (2007) and White (2003) emphasise its relation to the intersubjectivity of language.

Among the various markers of stance that can be found in lexis and grammar, adverbials have provided a good source (Biber and Finegan 1988, 1989; Conrad and Biber 2000; Downing 2002), and the grammar of modals, which is our concern in this paper, has also been extensively researched by several authors (cf. Lyons 1977; Coates 1983; Palmer 1990; Thompson and Hunston, 2000). Martin and White (2005: 104–110) include the study of modals and evidentials within the engagement system, which contains dialogically expansive formulations by which speakers or writers establish that their position entails one of several other positions and, as a result, other possibilities are available.

In general, modality has been broadly defined as any speaker's modification of a state of affairs which includes the dimensions of tense and aspect (Perkins 1983: 6; Palmer 1986: 9). Nuyts (2006: 1) narrows this definition and refers to modality as a semantic subfield within the wider domain of TAM (tense-aspect-modality) categories. Modality is also regarded as a grammatical domain which expresses diverse attitudinal qualifications like evidential, epistemic, or deontic (Cornillie and Pietrandrea 2012: 2109). Other approaches have considered modality bearing in mind the following distinctions:

1 It can be defined as the category that expresses the speaker's attitude towards the propositional content of his/her utterance.
2 It is the category which qualifies the factuality of an utterance.
3 It has to do with the opposition between possibility and necessity.
4 It indicates the speaker's subjectivity.

Cornillie and Pietrandrea (2012: 2111) agree that modal auxiliaries are polyfunctional in that modal verbs like *can*, *may*, and *must* combine dynamic, deontic, and epistemic (evidential) readings which differ depending on the context of use. This polyfunctionality is due to the complex communicative strategies that occur between speaker and hearer and their co-participants. Nuyts (2006: 3–6) speaks about three basic dimensions of modality which correspond to three of the readings posed earlier:

1 Dynamic modality is characterised as an attribution of a capacity to the subject-participant of the clause or as a property of the first argument of the predicate, or of the controlling participant in the state of affairs which is usually the agent. Apart from ability, this category comprises the meaning of a need or necessity for the first-argument participant.
2 Deontic modality has been traditionally associated with permission and obligation. It also indicates the degree of "moral desirability of the state of affairs" expressed in the utterance that is typical of the speaker but that can also account for others' assessments.
3 Epistemic modality has to do with the degree of probability of the state of affairs. It refers to the speaker's estimation of the likelihood that the state of affairs that he/she states in the clause applies in the world. This type of modality is contained into a scale which goes from certainty through probability and neutral possibility that indicates that the state of affairs is real.

Nuyts (2006: 8–11) acknowledges categories on the margins of modality where he includes evidentiality, which he defines as an indication of the nature of the sources of information of the speaker. The author mentions several categories of the source of this information, such as:

- The one perceived through the speaker's organs which is often called experiential.
- The one indirectly deduced through directly perceived information (inferential) or coming from other general background knowledge (reasoned).
- The one received from other hearsay or reportative categories.

This author adds that the relation between evidentiality and epistemic modality is often problematic because there is a logical connection between the fact that epistemic judgements are based on evidence, and evidentials refer to types of said epistemic judgements. As a result, evidential categories often denote some degree of probability of the state of affairs. Other scholars such as de Haan (1999) consider that evidentiality and epistemic modality are separate categories in that the former affirms the evidence and the latter specifies an evaluation of the evidence. For Cornillie (2009: 46–47), "evidentiality refers to the reasoning processes that lead to a proposition and epistemic modality evaluates the likelihood that this proposition is true". Despite the reasons which exist to differentiate both categories, this author (Cornillie 2009: 59) explains that epistemic evaluation is not always connected with a specific mode of knowing. Although the recognition of the status of the evidence may differ, it does not necessarily imply an epistemic evaluation of likelihood. Similarly, for Alonso Almeida (2015: 392–393), there are occasions on which both evidential and epistemic interpretations of the same expression are possible. In this line, he explains that the evidential reading of modal verbs which may derive from a contextual use does not necessary involve epistemic judgement. This author explains that evidentiality reflects the source of information, whereas subsequent meanings such as commitment and reliability become second place effects which are prompted by the communicative situation which surrounds the hearer. As a result, evidential strategies are interpreted in the context where they occur, and further semantic and pragmatic values such as the epistemic one may be added.

4 Analysis of the Modal Categories

The analysis of the modal categories is presented following a descending order from the most numerous occurrences to the least numerous into *may*, *can*, *could*, *should*, *will*, *might*, *would*, and *must*. Each example is examined in relation to the specific section of the abstract wherein it is inserted and the explanations are accordingly related. Figure 4.1 shows the distribution of the deontic, dynamic, and epistemic senses of modal verbs in our corpus. Just as we expected, epistemic and dynamic interpretations prevail expressing possibility and potentiality, respectively. While epistemic modals allow writers to present knowledge cautiously and so anticipate possible objections to their research, dynamic modals emphasise the potentiality of the research to be applicable somewhere else or the capability of certain circumstances to obtain.

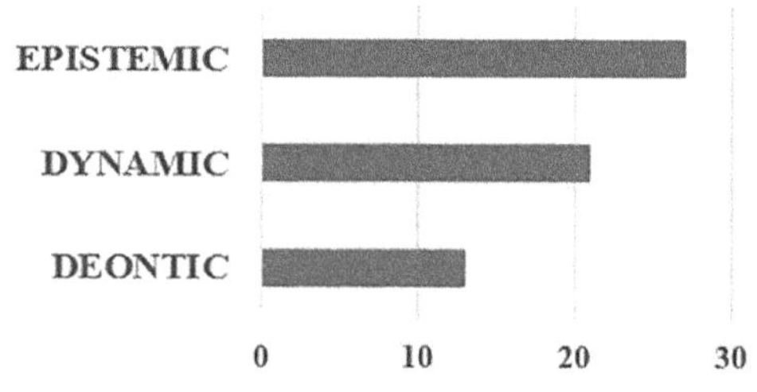

Figure 4.1 Distribution of modal senses in corpus.

4.1 May

May is by far the most frequent modal in the abstracts analysed. The types of meanings exhibited are epistemic and dynamic, being the epistemic ones the most frequent of the two with 15 occurrences. The remaining 3 instances of *may* have been labelled as dynamic.

> (1) Previous studies have reported an association between depression and psychotic experiences, but little is known about what drives this co-occurrence. This study tests the hypothesis that exposure to trauma and bullying ***may*** strengthen the relation between depression and psychotic experiences. [EPI]
>
> (2) The association between depression and psychotic experiences was significantly stronger among respondents who were victims of both bullying and sexual violence compared to those who experienced either exposure alone, or who were not exposed to either form of victimization. These findings suggest that cumulative exposure to trauma and victimization ***may*** contribute to the co-occurrence of depression and psychotic experiences. [EPI]
>
> (3) State-of-the-art metabolomic technologies give us the ability to measure thousands of metabolites in biological fluids or biopsies, providing us with a metabolic fingerprint of individual patients. These metabolic profiles ***may*** serve as diagnostic and/or prognostic tools that have the potential to significantly alter the management of CVD. [DYN]

May has been prototypically considered to be a hedge (Hyland 1998: 116). According to Collins (2007: 478), epistemic *may* tends to be used subjectively in the sense that it indicates the attitude of the speaker towards the information presented in terms of a lack of knowledge about its truth, rendering the utterance as an expression of a possibility. In addition, *may* can also have a dynamic interpretation derived from a potentiality for action depending on external circumstances (Facchinetti 2003: 303). In general, the dynamic possibility interpretations of *may* tend to be minor if compared with those of *can*, both of which bear a strong resemblance, as shown in Coates (1983), Biber et al. (1999), and Collins (2009), among others. Our results also show this tendency.

The epistemic value of *may* in examples (1) and (2) has to do with the authorial lack of commitment to the truth value of the proposition. In (1), *may* is used in the background/introduction/purpose section of the abstract where the authors point to the aim of the article. They do so by formulating the assumption taken as the starting point for the research, and that is the impact of bullying and trauma on a subject's suffering from both depression and psychosis. As such, the hypothesis is a tentative possibility yet to be tested. In (2), the modal verb is used in the results section. The findings are presented with less than certainty, not only because of the occurrence of the modal verb but also because of the epistemic lexical verb *suggest*. According to Hyland (1998: 120), *suggest* is an epistemic judgement verb which "reflect[s] appraisals by the speaker of the factive status of events". In our example, *suggest* indicates that the results are presented as a conjecture. Both in (1) and (2), authors prefer to present the information with caution avoiding imposing their claims not even when they are reporting their findings.

The dynamic sense of *may* in (3) is derived from the potential of the metabolic profiles mentioned to be used as diagnostic and prognostic tools in the management of cardiovascular diseases. Having this dynamic interpretation associated, the sentence can be paraphrased by "it is possible for" with no significant difference in meaning as noted by Collins (2009: 94). Huddleston (1971: 298) observes that the dynamic possibility sense in which *may* is used in examples like (3) does not have to do with authorial uncertainty, but rather with the fact that the situation described sometimes applies. This is called "qualified generalization", which is defined as a generalisation which "is said to apply to at least some members of the relevant population, but that it is not guaranteed to hold for all members".

4.2 *Can*

Can appears 11 times. Six occurrences of this category are used in the introductory section of the abstract, which contains the purpose of the study and shows the background from which the researchers stand their position. Two modal forms are presented in the methods section and 3 in the final part which renders the conclusions of the investigation.

> (4) Perturbations in cardiac energy metabolism are major contributors to a number of cardiovascular pathologies. In addition, comorbidities associated with cardiovascular disease (CVD) ***can*** alter systemic and myocardial metabolism, often contributing to the worsening of cardiac function and health outcomes. [DYN]
>
> (5) Translation of this research to the clinic via genetic system ***can*** precisely group affected patients according to molecular etiology, and identify individuals without evidence of disease who are at high risk for developing cardiomyopathy. [DYN]
>
> (6) More patients are required before we ***can*** conclude that the potential survival benefit of such measures may outweigh any adverse effects. [DYN]

This modal verb is usually examined within the domain of dynamic modality (Palmer 1991: 7–10) which is related to the expression of volition and ability. Perkins (1982: 252) defines this modality as "the disposition of certain empirical circumstances with regard to the occurrence of the same event". It also deals with the subject's physical or mental powers and with situations which are conditioned by circumstances external to the subject (Facchinetti 2003: 304). For Carrió-Pastor (2012: 122–123), the idea of potentiality which is part of dynamic modals is very useful in scientific writing in order to "describe the functions and uses of gadgets and substances that are able to, and has the potential of being actualised".

In example (4), belonging to the opening part, the author points out the disposition of "comorbidities associated with cardiovascular disease" to alter "systemic and myocardial metabolism". The tendency of this health problem to "often" contribute to the worsening of the patients' condition is used in a dynamic sense to indicate factuality rather than the assessment of the likelihood of the proposition to be true (Alonso Almeida 2015: 396). Likewise, the author advances previous knowledge upon the subject in order to inform the audience at this point of his/her study. Alongside the dynamic meaning, an evidential interpretation is also possible. *Can* shows an inferential deductive reasoning supported by the idea in the previous utterance. The additive expression "in addition" reinforces this inferential process.

In (5), the excerpt can be part either of the introduction or the methods section, in which case the authors describe the likely step that occurs from the research to the clinic through the genetic system which "can precisely group" patients prone to developing cardiomyopathy. The inclusion of the adverb "precisely" reinforces the notion that patients will be indeed safely diagnosed.

The idea of potentiality is also evident in (6) which is found, on this occasion, in the conclusion section of the abstract. Here, the author reveals the necessity to have "more patients" so as to be sure that "the potential benefits" of the measures that he/she is going to show in the article "may outweigh any adverse effects". In this sense, the appreciation of the factuality of the state of affairs needs further empirical evidence. However, contrary to the previous examples, the author's stance in the conclusion appears to be more tentative and subject to further research.

4.3 Could

This modal can be first referred to as both the past form and the backshifted counterpart of *can* (Collins 2009: 106–108). For Collins (2009: 116), the dynamic meaning of *could* entails a pragmatic extension of its hypothetical use, and the utterance wherein it is inserted is used to transmit a speech act that is different from a plain assertion as it occurs with the two examples described below. Gresset (2003:88) claims that this modal can be used to refer to a hypothesis which is made because the utterer has reasons for doing it. When this is the case, the epistemic value that is attached to *could* corresponds to the basic root meaning of *can*. Similarly, this hypothetical meaning of *could* is related to a counterfactual result by means of which something that did not happen could have happened.

This modal auxiliary occurs 10 times. Five instances are present in the introductory section of the abstract, only one in the method part and 4 occurrences in the conclusion. As it happens in the extracts with *can*, the examples with *could* represent a dynamic meaning which provides an appreciation of the factuality of the state of affairs based on previous research of the subject. In the examples, the speech acts can be analysed as wishes on the utterers' part rather than strict statements. For example, in (7), the meaning of *could* in the concluding lines of the abstract is mainly dynamic since the author(s) have presented their experience "of launching the adult clinic" and they have proved that it is an effective way in which "cross-covering doctors could refer patients" for a review. The authors of the medical study count on these doctors' good disposition to take care of patients given that the clinic has been tested. Indeed, it is the speaker's hope that this is the case.

In (8), the use of *could* is also dynamic in that there is proof that "lifestyle change programs" exist and are known by Americans. Its use in the first line of the abstract also reflects a hypothetical situation as regards the likelihood that these programmes do reach the population to whom they are aimed at, revealing some wishful thinking on the second speaker's part. However, the use of the remote form of *can* also reveals the value judgement concerning the probability of the proposition to happen, and thus an epistemic interpretation is possible as well.

> (7) We present our experience of launching the adult treatment clinic – a daytime clinic for semiurgent referrals to oral and maxillofacial surgery (OMFS). This has proved to be an effective way in which cross-covering junior doctors ***could*** refer patients for a safe and efficient review in a supervised environment. [DYN]
>
> (8) Lifestyle change programs implemented within healthcare systems ***could*** reach many Americans, but their impact on cardiovascular disease (CVD) remains unclear. [DYN]

4.4 *Should*

Should occurs 8 times in the texts analysed and they tend to be used in the conclusion/implications section:

> (9) Doctors and patients ***should*** pay attention to these "tips" in order to have an effective medical consultation.

(10) The addition of bevacizumab to capecitabine in the adjuvant setting for colorectal cancer yielded no benefit in the treatment of an unselected population and ***should*** not be used.

It is a prototypical case of a modal of obligation, though weaker than *must* as noted by Coates (1983: 60). Huddleston and Pullum (2002: 177, 186) posit that *should* is located in the category of "medium-strength modality". Giltrow (2005: 171) notes that deontic *should* conveys obligation "to pursue knowledge" or to "take action in the world", an interpretation that seems logical to us as they are typically found at the end of the abstract.

4.5 *Will*

Will occurs 6 times in our corpus. According to Collins (2009: 125), the domains of prediction and volition which are typically associated with *will* have received less attention in studies on modality. This may be due to the fact that whenever *will* is taken into account, the notion of futurity is frequently raised. As a matter of fact, there is still a concern about its status as a tense marker, a modal marker, and an ambiguous marker between the two positions (Jaszczolt 2005: 471). It should be noted, however, that "both future time reference and modality [may] coexist" (Sarkar 1998: 93).

(11) Taken together, the integration of metabolomics with other "omics" platforms ***will*** allow us to gain insight into pathophysiological interactions of metabolites, proteins, genes, and disease states, while advancing personalized medicine. [EPI]

(12) Secondary outcomes were overall survival, adverse events, neurocognitive function (***will*** be reported separately), health-related quality of life and neurological function (reported separately). [DYN]

The majority of our examples show an epistemic use of *will*, as in (11). Classifications as for the epistemic sense of this modal normally take into account the time reference factor, and so whenever there is a past or present time reference, *will* is labelled as "central-epistemic" (Huddleston and Pullum 2002: 188). If there is a future time reference, in contrast, then *will* is taken to indicate "predictability" (Coates 1983: 169). In (11), *will* indicates a confident prediction based on the knowledge the authors have in relation to the employment of both metabolomics and omics technologies in the development of medicine. This reading seems to be the most appropriate if we further take into account that the modal appears in the conclusion/implications part of the abstract. In this case, the use of *will* emphasises the writers' confident voice and builds up their authoritative persona. In (12), the modal sense of *will* is dynamic and it is the only dynamic reading we have found in our corpus. It is related to volition as it expresses the writers' intention to provide the report on the neurocognitive function somewhere else. To the authors of this paper, *will* here fulfils a textual function in the fashion of Hyland's (2005: 50) interactive resources.

4.6 *Might*

As regards *might*, there are 4 occurrences in our corpus, all of them with an epistemic interpretation. Perkins (1983: 50) and Palmer (1990: 58) take *might* to be a distal form of *may* expressing a higher degree of tentativeness. Similarly to *may*, its use appears to be mainly restricted to the background/introduction/purpose section and to the findings/results section, and again, that may be interpreted as a solidarity strategy used by the authors so as not to sound imposing their views nor in the opening nor in the closing parts of the abstracts. However, there is an example in which *might* is used in the methodology section:

> (13) Flexible parametric survival models were used to quantify changes in the cause-specific survival inequalities and the number of lives that ***might*** be saved if these inequalities were removed. [EPI]

This example of *might* would fall into what Collins (2009: 106) calls hypothetical use, and more specifically, the unreal use. This is typically found in the apodosis of unreal conditional clauses which express a counterfactual situation. Apart from this, conditional structures themselves have already been acknowledged as indicators of authorial stance in scientific communication as in Puente-Castelo (2017). In this sense, Warchal (2010: 142–142) posits that conditionals are "rhetorical device[s] for gaining acceptance of one's claims" as they allow to establish an "agreement between the writer and the reader of an academic text". In our example and as it is in the methodology section of the abstract, it opens up a path for negotiation in the possible sceneries that scientists may encounter when applying the models referred to.

4.7 *Would*

The remote form *would* has been also found in the corpus, though there are only 2 occurrences, one of them in the background/introduction/purpose section of the abstract and the other in the conclusion/implications section:

> (14) Using a consistent, accurate method ***would*** allow for timely interpretation of HIV trends. The objective of our study was to assess

the recent progress toward reducing HIV infections in the United States overall and among selected population segments with available incidence estimation methods. [EPI]

(15) To comply with NIH communication guidelines, government entities and nongovernment organizations ***would*** benefit from improving the readability of e-cigarettes information and advice. [EPI]

In both (14) and (15), *would* shows an epistemic sense and expresses a prediction based on the deductions made by the writers about the use of certain methods to estimate the incidence of HIV trends and about the action that should be taken so as to increase the readability of information hosted on webpages related to e-cigarettes. The predictions are made with an apparent lack of confidence on the part of the writers.

4.8 Must

This modal verb only appears twice, one in the background section of the abstract and the second in the conclusion. Collins (2009: 34–36) explains that this modal verb usually expresses deontic necessity or obligation, but may also convey epistemic necessity meaning and a minor dynamic necessity meaning. In the case of deontic *must*, he adds that there is no necessary connection between subjectivity and the use of this modal since the source of the obligation can be external to the speaker, as one of the examples below reflects. Collins agrees with Coates (1983: 34–35) that *you* is the subject in the most evident cases of deontic subjective *must*, whereas in deontic objective *must*, there is a third person subject. Deontic modality has been also referred to as root modality which covers both deontic and dynamic modalities. Coates (1983: 20–21) rejects the term deontic because it mainly pertains to the logical notions of obligation and permission, and modals like *must* and *may* possess other interpretations as well. De Haan (2006: 32), for his part, establishes that *must* is used to express necessity on the subject in deontic modality and strong conviction of the speaker in epistemic modality.

As for epistemic *must*, it includes possibility and probability meanings (de Haan 2006: 30). Collins (2009: 38–39) distinguishes between subjective and objective uses of this modal auxiliary. The first use is concerned with variation in the speaker's confidence, whereas the second use is related to logical certainty and logical necessity that is based on what is known. Coates (1983: 177) points out that epistemic *must* expresses the speaker's confidence in the truth of the proposition, and is based on a process of logical inference. In turn, Palmer (2003: 8) explains that epistemic *must* and *will* show some characteristics of evidential modality on the grounds that they allude to conclusions which are based on evidence.

Example (16) is present in the background section of the abstract and is examined as deontic. The author(s) indicate that "an appropriate method of fixation must be chosen" after deciding on surgery. It thus shows the necessity of this event to happen, a derived need after the "decision to treat surgically has been made".

> (16) Controversy continues about the benefits and disadvantages of open reduction and internal fixation of fractures of the condylar head. Once a decision to treat surgically has been made, an appropriate method of fixation ***must*** be chosen. [DEO]

The occurrence of *must* in (17) is mainly epistemic but a further evidential reading is plausible as well. In the example found in the conclusion, *must* illustrates the logical necessity of the proposition to occur. Given the results which have been identified to treat the diseases differently, the author(s) specify that none of these results have survived multiple corrections and, therefore, they "must be considered preliminary". *Must* can also be considered as inferential evidential. The fact that the results of the clinic are not valid enough for now leads them to be necessarily "preliminary". In this vein, Van der Auwera and Plungian (1998: 86) state that inferential evidentiality is a case of epistemic necessity, and specify that "inferential reading amounts to epistemic modality and more particularly to epistemic necessity".

> (17) We performed qPCR analyses of 29 miRNAS previously implicated in psychiatric illness (major depressive disorder (MDD), bipolar disorder (BD) and/or schizophrenia (SZ)) in AnCg of patients with MDD and BD versus controls. miR-132, miR-133a and miR-212 were initially identified as differentially expressed in BP, miR-184 in MDD and miR-34a in both MDD and BP (although none survived multiple correction testing and ***must*** be considered preliminary). [EPI]

5 Conclusion

We can derive some closing remarks as regards the use of modal verb categories in medical abstracts which reveal the authors' stance. In the corpus selected, epistemic modal verbs prevail upon other modal meanings. Epistemic *may* is the most numerous and its occurrence is mainly restricted to the background/introduction/purpose section of the abstract and the findings/results section. The authors' position in these cases is influenced by their audience by moderating their statements expressed by *may*. Hence, they "withhold complete commitment to an accompanying proposition and allow information to be presented as an opinion rather than as a fact" (Facchinetti 2003: 321). Other epistemic modals which can also achieve this goal present a lower incidence in categories like *might*, *would*, *will*, and *should*. While *might* mainly occurs in the background/introduction/purpose section and the results section, *would* is found in the introductory and the conclusion/implications sections, and *will* and *should* usually appear in the conclusion/implications section of the abstract. Similarly to *may*, they represent a more tentative stance on the speakers' part with respect to their attitude to the status of the proposition, which can transmit assumption, possibility, and/or confidence (or lack of it). *Must* only appears twice in the corpus and depicts epistemic and deontic readings.

The second relevant meaning is dynamic, which is mainly encountered in modals *can* and *could* and, to a lesser extent, *may*. *Can* and *could* are mostly located in the background/introduction/purpose and the conclusions/implications sections of the abstract. Contrary to epistemic modality, dynamic modals appear to be more objective in that they seem to convey facts instead of opinions. While this is expected in the introductory part of the abstract with respect to the demonstration of previous research in the form of empirical results, seven examples are also found in the final lines of the abstracts, which suggests the authors' higher confidence about the prospective results and conclusions of their studies. Apart from the predominant epistemic meaning, we have found some inferential evidential qualifications in modals like *can* and *must*. These are related to the authors' deductive reasoning which is manifest in the interpretation of the surrounding utterances. All in all, the authors' stance in medical abstracts reflects the inclusion of epistemic modals in an attempt to show their judgement of the truth of the proposition and thus avoid criticism. In contrast, the fewer significant number of dynamic modals involves a counterpart in the presentation of objective data.

Note

1 This paper is part of the research project "Identification and analysis of metadiscourse strategies in Spanish and English research papers", Grant FFI2016-77941-P (Ministerio de Economía, Industria y Competitividad). This Grant is hereby gratefully acknowledged.

References

Ad Hoc Working Group for Critical Appraisal of the Medical Literature. (1987). A proposal for more informative abstracts of clinical articles. *Annals of Internal Medicine* 106/4, 598–604.

Alonso Almeida, F. (2015). Propositional epistemic and evidential strategies in Spanish and English texts on computing, in Juan Rafael Zamorano-Mansilla et al. (eds.) *Thinking Modally: English and Contrastive Studies in Modality*. Castle upon Tyne: Cambridge Scholars, 383–408.

Berkenkotter, C. and H. Huckin, T. (1995). *Genre knowledge in disciplinary communication: Cognition, culture, power.* Hillsdale, NJ: Lawrence Earlbaum Associates.
Bhatia, V. (1993). *Analysing genre: Language use in professional settings.* London: Longman.
Biber, D. and Finegan, E. (1988). Adverbial stance types in English. *Discourse Processes* 11/1, 1–34.
Biber, D. and Finegan, E. (1989). Styles of stance in English: Lexical and grammatical marking of evidentiality and affect. *Text* 9/1, 93–124.
Biber, D., Johansson S., Leech G., Conrad S. and Finegan E. (1999). *Longman grammar of spoken and written English.* London: Longman.
Brenton, F. (1996). Rhetoric in competition: The formation of organizational discourse in conference on College Composition and Communication abstracts. *Written Communication* 13/3, 355–384.
Carrió-Pastor, M. L. (2012). A contrastive analysis of epistemic modality in scientific English. *Revista de Lenguas para Fines Específicos* 18, 115–132.
Coates, J. (1983). *The semantics of modal auxiliaries.* London/Canberra: Croom Helm.
Collins, P. (2007). Can/could and may/might in British, American and Australian English: A corpus-based account. *World Englishes* 26/4, 474–491.
Collins, P. (2009). *Modals and quasi-modals in English.* Amsterdam/New York: Rodopi.
Conrad, S. and Biber, D. (2000). Adverbial marking of stance in speech and writing, in S. Hunston and G. Thompson (eds.) *Evaluation in text: Authorial stance and the construction of discourse.* New York: Oxford University Press, 56–73.
Cornillie, B. (2009). Evidentiality and epistemic modality: On the close relationship between two different categories. *Functions of Language* 16/1, 44–62.
Cornillie, B. and Pietrandrea P. (2012). Cognitive, interactional and textual functions of modal markers. *Journal of Pragmatics* 44, 2109–2115.
de Haan, F. (1999). Evidentiality and epistemic modality: Setting boundaries. *Southwest Journal of Linguistics* 18, 83–101.
de Haan, F. (2006). Typological approaches to modality, in W. Frawley (ed.) *The expression of modality.* Berlin: Mouton de Gruyter, 27–70.
Downing, A. (2002). 'Surely you knew!': Surely as a marker of evidentiality and stance. *Functions of Language* 8/2, 251–282.
Englebretson, R. (ed.) (2007). *Stancetaking in discourse.* Amsterdam/Philadelphia: John Benjamins.
Facchinetti, R. (2003). Pragmatic and sociological constraints on the functions of *may* in contemporary British English, in R. Facchinetti, M. Krug and F. Palmer (eds.) *Modality in contemporary English.* Berlin: Mouton de Gruyter, 301–327.
Giltrow, J. (2005). Modern conscience: Modalities of obligation in research genres. *Text-Interdisciplinary Journal for the Study of Discourse* 25/2, 171–199.
Gresset, S. (2003). Towards a contextual micro-analysis of the non-equivalence of *might* and *could*, in R. Facchinetti, M. Krug and F. Palmer (eds.) *Modality in contemporary English.* Berlin: Mouton de Gruyter, 81–99.

Huddleston, R. (1971). *The sentence in written English.* Cambridge: Cambridge University Press.
Huddleston, R. and Pullum G. K. (2002). *The Cambridge grammar of the English language.* Cambridge: Cambridge University Press.
Hyland, K. (1998). *Hedging in scientific research articles.* Amsterdam/Philadelphia: John Benjamins.
Hyland, K. (2004). *Disciplinary discourses. Social interactions in academic writing.* Ann Harbor: The University of Michigan Press.
Hyland, K. (2005). *Metadiscourse. Exploring interaction in writing.* London/New York: Continuum.
Jaszczolt, K. M. (2005). Futurity in default semantics, in K. von Heusinger and K. Turner (eds.) *Where semantics meets pragmatics (Current research in the semantics/pragmatics interface).* Amsterdam: Elsevier, 471–492.
Kaplan, R. B., Cantor, S., Hagstrom C., Kamhi-Stein L. D., Shiotani Y., and Boyd Zimmerman, Ch. (1994). On abstract writing. *Text* 14/3, 401–426.
Lyons, J. (1977). *Semantics.* Cambridge: Cambridge University Press.
Lyons, J. (1994). Subjecthood and subjectivity, in M. Yaguello (ed.) *Subjecthood and subjectivity: Proceedings of the colloquium 'The Status of the subject in linguistic theory'.* Paris: Ophrys, 9–17.
Martin, J. R. and White P. R. R. (2005). *The language of evaluation. Appraisal in English.* Hampshire: Palgrave Macmillan.
Nuyts, J. (2006). Modality: Overview and linguistic issues, in W. Frawley (ed.) *The expression of modality.* Berlin: Mouton de Gruyter, 1–26.
Palmer, F. R. (1986). *Mood and modality.* Cambridge: Cambridge University Press.
Palmer, F. R. (1990). *Modality and the English modals* (2nd edition). London: Longman.
Palmer, F. R. (1991). *Mood and modality* (2nd edition). Cambridge: Cambridge University Press.
Palmer, F. R. (2003). Modality in English: Theoretical, descriptive and typological issues, in R. Facchinetti, M. Krug and F. Palmer (eds.) *Modality in contemporary English.* Berlin: Mouton de Gruyter, 1–17.
Perkins, M. (1982). The core meanings of the English modals. *Journal of Linguistics* 18/2, 245–273.
Perkins, M. (1983). *Modal expressions in English.* London: Frances Pinter.
Puente-Castelo, L. (2017). 'If I mistake not.' Conditionals as stance markers in late modern English scientific discourse. *Estudios de Lingüística Aplicada* 2, 111–129.
Salager-Meyer, F. (1990). Discoursal flaws in medical English abstracts: A genre analysis per research and text type. *Text* 10/4, 365–384.
Salager-Meyer, F., Alcaraz Ariza M. A. and Lewin B. A. (2014). Abstract quality in complementary and alternative medicine papers: A structural and cross-generic analysis, in M. Bondi and R. Lorés Sanz (eds.) *Abstracts in academic discourse. Variation and change.* Bern: Peter Lang, 221–356.
Samraj, B. (2005). An exploration of a genre set: Research article abstracts and introductions in two disciplines. *English for Specific Purposes* 24, 141–156.
Sarkar, A. (1998). The conflict between future tense and modality. The case of will in English. *University of Pennsylvania Working Papers in Linguistics* 5/2, 91–117.

Swales, J. (1990). *Genre analysis in academic and research settings.* Cambridge: Cambridge University Press.

Thompson, G. and Hunston, S. (2000). Evaluation: An introduction, in S. Hunston and G. Thompson (eds.) *Evaluation in text: Authorial stance and the construction of discourse.* New York: Oxford University Press, 1–27.

Van der Auwera, J. and Plungian, V. (1998). "On modality's semantic map". *Linguistic Typology* 2, 79–124.

Warchal, K. (2010). Moulding interpersonal relations through conditional clauses: Consensus building strategies in written academic discourse. *Journal of English for Academic Purposes* 9, 140–150.

White, P. R. R. (2003). Beyond modality and hedging: A dialogic view of the language of intersubjective stance. *Text* 23/2, 259–284.

5 A Disciplinary Analysis of *Fairly* in Late Modern English Scientific Writing

Francisco J. Álvarez-Gil

1 Introduction

This chapter focuses on the analysis of the adverb *fairly* as a metadiscourse device in written documents from the Late Modern English period (1700–1900). For this purpose, I will analyse textual material included in the *Coruña Corpus of English Scientific Writing* papers in the two distinct fields of science, namely astronomy and history. These texts are compiled under the names of the *Corpus of History English Texts* and the *Corpus of English Texts on Astronomy*. I shall examine the different pragmatic functions they fulfil in each specific context and check whether genre differences apply, or the uses of this adverbial are otherwise a stylistic rather than a disciplinary feature.

As we are here dealing with stancetaking material, it is inevitable to touch, albeit in passing, on some related features such as mitigation and politeness; all these concepts hold a tight relation to epistemic modality and evidentiality. For some scholars, evidentiality is nothing else than a subdomain of epistemic modality. Others, however, claim for an independent categorial status of evidentiality. Epistemic modality seems to be strongly connected to the idea of truth and the authors' responsibility regarding their statements (Carrió-Pastor, 2012; Traugott, 1989; Sweetser, 1990; Stukker, Sanders and Verhagen, 2009), but I will come to this later in Section 2.

The aim of this chapteris to shed further light on the pragmatic functions of the adverb selected, i.e. *fairly*. Two such functions are mitigating or reinforcing the propositional content it appears. It is also employed to express possibility and to offer perspectivisation concerning the propositional content. To achieve this objective, a corpus-based analysis of this adverb has been carried out by taking into consideration the communicative context of the occurrences. That said, the structure of this chapter is as follows. First, a description of the corpus and the methodology used will be carried out. Then, I shall focus on the theoretical framework within which I shall discuss concepts such as metadiscourse, stance, and hedging (Álvarez-Gil, 2018). After this, the analysis and the discussion of findings will be offered to finally present the conclusions drawn from this study.

2 Theoretical Framework

2.1 Metadiscourse

The term metadiscourse was first mentioned in 1959 by the American linguist Zellig Harris "as a method to understand language in use, representing a writer's or speaker's attempts to guide a receiver's perception of a text" (Hyland, 2005:3). As Hyland (2005:16) himself puts it, we are dealing with a fuzzy term: "Metadiscourse has always been something of a fuzzy term, often characterized as simply 'discourse about discourse' or 'talk about talk'". Currently, there is a broad agreement among scholars that the term metadiscourse makes reference "to material which goes beyond the subject matter to signal the presence of the author" (Hyland, 2005:35), but there is still no agreed definition of what is exactly the scope of the concept. In this chapter, the following Hyland's definition of the term has been adopted: "Metadiscourse is the cover term for the self-reflective expressions used to negotiate interactional meanings in a text, assisting the writer (or speaker) to express a viewpoint and engage with readers as members of a particular community" (Hyland, 2005: 37–38). This definition is clearly related to the ones presented in previous works about the subject, but it clearly differs from them "overlapping with other views of language use which emphasize the interpersonal, such as evaluation, stance and engagement" (Hyland, 2005:37).

The main principles of metadiscourse can be summarised in the following: (a) metadiscourse is distinct from prepositional aspects of discourse, (b) metadiscourse refers to aspects of the text that embody writer–reader interactions, (c) metadiscourse refers only to relations which are internal to the discourse (Hyland and Tse, 2004, in LI Fa-gen, 2012:847). The relevance of metadiscourse in academic texts is undeniable as has been highlighted in Mauranen (1993), Hyland (1998; 2005), Hyland and Tse (2004), Mur-Dueñas (2011), Quintana-Toledo (2009), and Carrió-Pastor (2016), among others. In this chapter, the division of metadiscourse into two dimensions will be followed (Hyland and Tse, 2004:161): the interactive dimension, which includes code glosses, endophoric markers, evidentials, frame markers, and transition markers, and the interactional dimension including attitude markers, boosters, engagement markers, hedges, and self-mention, on the other. Readers are an essential part in academic writing and authors are responsible for promoting and guiding the interaction with them as a consequence; the use of interactive metadiscourse devices is basic for writers to successfully interact with their readers. Mur-Dueñas (2011) describes this division in the following terms:

> Thus, both interactive metadiscourse features (intended to organise and shape the material in the light of the readers' likely needs and expectations) and interactional metadiscourse features (aimed at

> portraying the scholars as authors and at binding writer and reader together) are a response to the interpersonal component of writing.
>
> (Mur-Dueñas, 2011:3069)

All this means that in academic writing, there are expressions, which make reference to the authors and to the potential readers. Those expressions are known as metadiscourse. We can claim that without metadiscourse devices, communication would be less successful due to the lack of contextual information for the readers to understand the message and, therefore, writers would be unable to convey their ideas and engage their readers effectively (Hyland, 2005).

2.2 *Stance*

Stance is a complex linguistic concept whose function is to signal authorial attitudes. Much research has been carried out as to the way in which language is used to express opinion and attitude. The concept has been analysed from different perspectives, but there is no scholarly consensus as to the exact extent of its scope. The large amount of diverse definitions related to this term show this lack of conceptual uniformity; e.g. Biber et al. (1999:966) consider stance is related to the expression of the speakers and writers' "personal feelings, attitudes and value judgements, or assessments". According to Hyland (2005):

> stance can be seen as an attitudinal dimension and includes features which refer to the ways writers present themselves and convey their judgements, opinions and commitments. It is the way that writers intrude to stamp their personal authority onto their arguments or step back and disguise their involvement.
>
> (Hyland, 2005:176)

For Johnstone (2009:30–31), "Stance is generally understood to have to do with the methods, linguistic and other, by which interactants create and signal relationships with the propositions they utter and the people they interact with". Meanwhile, Dzung Pho (2013:3) states that stance has to do with "the writer's identity as well as the writer's expression of attitudes, feelings, or judgements".

These definitions have in common that all of them identify the evaluative dimension of stance. In general terms, stance can be understood as the way in which speakers appraise people, objects, and ideas, but it also covers self-evaluation, as Alonso-Almeida (2015:1) claims. The concept of evaluation is defined by Hunston and Thompson (2000) as follows:

> evaluation is the broad cover term for the expression of the speaker or writer's attitude or stance towards, viewpoint on, or feelings about the entities or propositions that he or she is talking about.

> That attitude may relate to certainty or obligation or desirability or any of a number of other sets of values. When appropriate, we refer specifically to modality as a sub-category of evaluation.
>
> (Hunston and Thompson, 2000:5)

This notion of evaluation leads us to consider other linguistic phenomena, also included within the arena of stance, namely: stance (Gray et al., 2011), epistemic stance (Marín Arrese, 2011), epistemic modality (Alonso-Almeida and Mele-Marrero, 2014; Cornillie, 2009; De Haan, 2009; Kranich, 2009), commitment (De Branbater and Dendale, 2008), mitigation (Caffi, 1999; 2007), reinforcement (Brown, 2011), involvement (Cornillie and Delbecque, 2008), hedging (Hyland, 1998; 2005), politeness (Brown and Levinson, 1987), modality and evidentiality (Chafe, 1986; Diewald et al., 2009), affect (Ochs, 1989), and vagueness in language (Channell, 1994; Myers, 1989). All of these concepts have received scholarly attention as rhetorical devices to convey mitigation and strengthening of claims.

Biber et al. (1999) consider the term stance to be a superordinate, which covers not simply the senses speakers want to convey, but also the propositional content. The term is defined as the expression of "personal feelings, attitudes and value judgements, or assessments", as already mentioned. The linguistic elements, which can convey stance, are numerous but we shall focus on adverbs. Biber et al. (1999) make a distinction between three main groups of adverbs: (i) circumstance adverbs, i.e. here, now; (ii) linking adverbs, i.e. nevertheless, moreover, additionally; and (iii) stance adverbs, which are categorised as and defined, thus.

Epistemic stance adverbials and attitude stance adverbials both comment on the content of a proposition. Epistemic markers express the speaker's judgement about the certainty, reliability, and limitations of the proposition; they can also comment on the source of the information. Attitude stance adverbials convey the speaker's attitude or value judgement about the proposition's content. Epistemic stance adverbials (Biber et al., 1999:59–60) can entail a large number of meanings such as (i) doubt and certainty, i.e. perhaps, probably; (ii) actuality and reality, i.e. actually, in fact, really; (iii) source of knowledge, i.e. apparently, evidently, according to; (iv) limitation, i.e. in most cases, typically, mainly; (v) viewpoint or perspective, i.e. in my opinion, from my perspective; (vi) imprecision, i.e. kind of, roughly.

Stance adverbs can be used to indicate authors' attitude and certainty towards their propositions. The adverb object of this analysis, fairly, falls within this category. Most occurrences of fairly indicate a low level of authorial commitment to text content by presenting information with doubts and hesitancy. As seen in the classification of stance adverbs, there are some adverbs such as evidently which are said to indicate source of knowledge. In fact, for some scholars, evidentiality represents a subdomain of epistemic modality, but there are others who consider evidentiality as an independent category: "Evidentiality is concerned with indicating the information source the speaker is relying on to make a claim. This places this category next to epistemic modality without, however, merging them into one" (Diewald, Kresic and Smirnova, 2009:190). Epistemic modality is frequently associated with the ideas of truth, commitment, reliability, and authorial responsibility with respect to the strength of their claims (Lorés Sanz, 2011; Stukker et al., 2009; Traugott, 1989). As noted by Pic and Furmaniak (2012), discourse-oriented studies of epistemic markers have frequently focused their attention on hedging "of which epistemics are the most common realisation" (2012:19).

As I have indicated previously, the main reason to choose adverbials as the target part of speech of this analysis is that it seems that adverbials stand as one of the grammatical categories that most clearly contribute to the expression of interpersonal meanings (Biber and Finegan, 1988). Most classifications of adverbials establish three main types, specifically adjuncts, conjuncts, and disjuncts. Nonetheless, and as happens with other linguistic concepts, this taxonomy coined by Greenbaum (1969) and adopted, among others, by Quirk et al. (1972; 1985) has not been followed by all linguists. One case in point is Biber et al. (1999:763). They use circumstance, stance, and linking adverbials as the corresponding terms. Within Systemic Functional Linguistics, Halliday and Christian (2004:123ff) propose a similar classification of adverbs comprising three types too: circumstantial or adjuncts, conjunctive, conjuncts, or linking adverbials, and finally modal or disjuncts. Adverbials contributing to referential meaning have been referred to as adjuncts or circumstantial adverbials; those fulfilling connective and text-organising functions are conjuncts, or conjunctive or linking adverbials; and adverbials conveying the speaker's evaluation of the propositional information are disjuncts or modal adverbials. The form fairly can be included into this last category.

Focusing specifically on those adverbials expressing some evaluation of the propositional information, Greenbaum (1969) and Quirk et al. (1985) identify a group of adverbs, which provide a "comment about the truth-value of what is said". Greenbaum (1969) distinguishes between adverbs that "merely express shades of doubt or certainty" and adverbs that "in addition refer to the observation or perception of a state of affairs". Quirk et al. (1985), on their part, distinguish between adverbs that "express conviction" and adverbs that "express some degree of doubt", and similarly, Biber and Finegan (1988; 1989) deal with "surely-adverbials" and "maybe-adverbials". Biber et al. (1999), in contrast, take all of these adverbials to be under the label of epistemic stance adverbs, and these are deployed to convey doubt or certainty. In the same line of Greenbaum's (1969) original distinction, Biber et al. (1999) and Fraser

(1996) further distinguish between adverbials that merely convey degrees of certainty and adverbials that indicate the type of source for making a claim.

In the fashion of Biber et al. (1999), Hyland (2005) classifies fairly as a stance adverb since it expresses possibility or a lack of complete commitment to the truth of a specific proposition, thus exhibiting a hedging function. It clearly indicates the authors' attitude towards their texts, and their use depends on the effect an author is seeking to have on readers.

2.3 Hedging

My understanding of the concept of hedging is based on earlier studies on the topic including Hyland (1994; 1996; 1998), Salager-Meyer (1994), Markkanen and Schröder (1997), Mauranen (1997), Crompton (1997), Caffi (2007), and Fraser (2010), among others. Each of them presents a solid methodology of study and body of data, but, for the purpose of this chapter, I shall follow the definition included in Hyland's work (1998:5), which states that the term *hedge* can be defined as "the means by which writers can present a proposition as an opinion rather than a fact". For his part, Fraser (2010) highlights that although there exist different taxonomies related to hedges, there is

> general agreement today that hedging is a rhetorical strategy, by which a speaker, using a linguistic device, can signal a lack of commitment to either the full semantic membership of an expression (propositional hedging) [...] or the full commitment to the force of the speech act being conveyed (speech act hedging).
>
> (Fraser, 2010: 22)

Regarding their use, Salager-Meyer (1994) claims that hedges are used for two different purposes:

1 The first one: to "present the true state of writers' understanding, namely, the stronger claim a careful researcher can make" (Salager-Meyer, 1994:150) which means that writers use hedging devices to express uncertainty because they are really not sure about the information given or cannot demonstrate it.
2 The second one: to "convey (purposive) vagueness and tentativeness, and to make sentences more acceptable to the hearer/reader, thus increasing their chance of ratification and reducing the risk of negation" (Salager-Meyer, 1994:150).

Hyland's position (1998) is not really in contradiction with Salager-Meyer's (1994). In fact, the analysis of context is unavoidable in this study if one really wants to highlight cases of hedging with any degree of confidence (Alonso-Almeida, 2012). In this chapter, I analyse the use of the adverb *fairly* as a metadiscourse element in astronomy and history texts from the late Modern English period and compare its uses and functions to check whether differences among these two scientific genres exist. Corpus linguistics tools have been used, but manual analyses were also fundamental, as computerised findings require contextual interpretation.

3 Corpus Description and Methodology

The corpora used for the present research are the *Corpus of English Texts on Astronomy* (henceforth CETA) and the *Corpus of History English Texts* (henceforth CHET), one of the subcorpora within the *Coruña Corpus of English Scientific Writing.* Crespo and Moskowich (2015) have offered an extensive description of these subcorpora on their works *A Corpus of History English Texts (CHET) as Part of the Coruña Corpus Project* (2015), and *Astronomy 'playne and simple': The Writing of Science between 1700 and* 1900 (2012). Their description is followed in the present work. The texts compiled in both of them cover the eighteenth and nineteenth centuries.

Several scientific landmarks have been considered in order to limit the time-span represented in the subcorpora. The texts included here cover the period from 1700 to 1900. The end of the sixteenth century and the beginning of the seventeenth century have been recognised by Taavitsainen and Pahta (1997) as the moment at which the medieval scholastic thought-style started to be gradually superseded by new patterns of thought, and new methodological procedures based on observation started to be used. The foundation of the Royal Society in 1660 and the publication of the guidelines for presenting scientific works in a clear and simple way had a greater impact on accentuating the importance of style in scientific communication.

The end of the nineteenth century and the beginning of the twentieth century roughly coincide with some important events in the history of science such as the discovery of the electron (1896), the formulation of Planck's Quantum Theory (1900), and the publication of Einstein's Special Theory of Relativity (1905). Obviously, all of these events brought about the need to change scientific discursive patterns, as put forward by Huxley in the 1897 *International Congress of Mathematics.* As regards the genres represented in CHET and CETA, there are articles, essays, lectures, textbooks, dialogues, dictionaries, and treatises, as can be seen in Figure 5.1, written by both male and female authors. Both corpora cover around 400,000 words.

The relevance of this data lies in the fact that these corpora are multigenre and, moreover, previous studies have shown that 1,000-word samples are not really enough for the study of variation within the scientific register (Biber, 1993), mainly because the scientific register was not as standardised at that time as it is nowadays (Crespo and

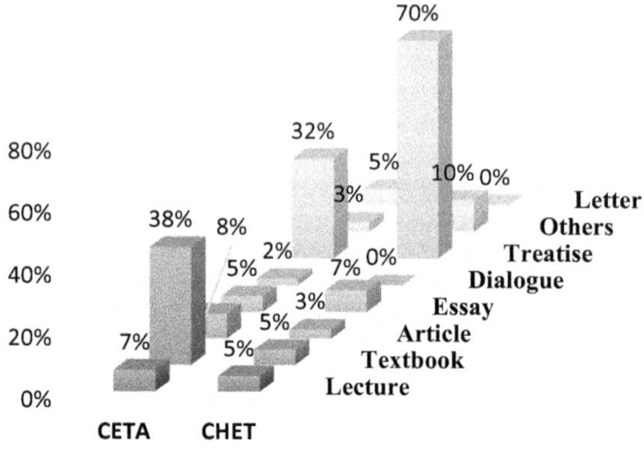

Figure 5.1 Distribution of words per genre in CETA and CHET.

Moskowich, 2015). For the purpose of this study, I have used the *Coruña Corpus Tool* for quantification and text retrieval. Then, manual analyses were also performed in order to check stance adverbs' functions.

4 *Fairly* in CHET and CETA

Fairly is used to indicate that the speaker has inferred some information on the basis of evidence and, as such, it may be considered as an evidential adverb. There are some occurrences of these forms in the corpora analysed, and one thing worth noting is the scarcity of instances given the size of the samples reviewed, i.e. ca. 800,000 words: 19 occurrences of *fairly* in CHET, and only 4 occurrences in CETA. In CHET, we can find 7 occurrences, which belong to the eighteenth century, and 12 occurrences in texts from the nineteenth century. The examples belong to different textual genres: article, essay, textbook, and treatises.

The adverb *fairly* is defined by the *Oxford English Dictionary* as a "submodifier to indicate a moderately high degree". Examples of this meaning, a and b, can be found above these lines, or it can also be used "to emphasize something surprising or extreme" exemplified in c and d:

a 'I am fairly difficult to get along with apparently and we haven't talked in a number of years'.
b 'I've been through a phase of having a fair amount of capital and I was fairly miserable to be honest'.
c 'In the history of empire and colonialism, the voices raised in dissent are fairly few actually'.

d 'So in each case, it tends to be fairly extreme behaviour that's likely to give rise to liability'.

(*Fairly*, OED)

In relation to its position in the sentences, the adverb is generally placed before the verb and in most cases used after the modal verb *may*. In history texts, the examples, which can be found, are the following:

> (1) Becaufe from their knowledge of its great ftrength, and of the many refources its prodigious wealth furnifhed, they judged the conqueft of it impracticable at this time, and before Sicily was fubdued. And that they judged right, one may **fairly** conclude from Polybius's not reproving their policy, and from the difficulties they afterwards met with in that enterprize, even when mafters of Sicily, and of all the iflands between Italy and Africa.
>
> (Hooke, 1745)

> (2) But as the election of fenators, made by the people in the firft inftance, feems to have been made, in confequence of a conftitutional right to chufe all magiftrates without distinction; it was evidently, not the effect of any conceffion of the king's, but of a power which was properly vefted in them; and which, for that reafon, they would be as cautious of parting with, as any other privilege, to which they were intitled, by the conftitution of their ftate: and therefore, unlefs it fhould appear plainly, that the people were excluded from having any fhare, in the enfuing elections of fenators, I think, we may very **fairly** prefume, that they continued to exercife the fame right, in every fubfequent inftance, which we have already fhewn them to have done, in the firft.
>
> (Chapman, 1750)

In example (1), which is a treatise dating back to the eighteenth century, the position of the modal verb *may* before the adverb *fairly* serves to reinforce the moderated nature of the adverb as its semantic meaning in the context given has to do with "expressing possibility" in the pattern *modal verb: may + adverb fairly + cognitive verb: conclude*. Example (2) presents a comparable pattern to example (1): *may + fairly + presume*. The difference with the previous one is that in this specific example, the mitigating function is even stronger than in the previous one due to the presence of the intensifier *very* and the semantic meaning of the verb *presume*, which seems to indicate a reinforcement of the sense of possibility. Other similar examples are the following:

> (3) But the wealth of the province, and the truft of the revenue, were founded on the fair and plentiful produce of trade and

manufactures: and ſome ſymptoms of liberal policy may be traced in a law which exempts from all perſonal taxes the mariners of Peloponeſus, and the workmen in parchment and purple. This denomination may be **fairly** applied or extended to the manufactures of linen, woollen, and more eſpecially of ſilk: the two former of which had flouriſhed in Greece ſince the days of Homer; and the laſt was introduced perhaps as early as the reign of Juſtinian.

(Gibbon, 1788)

(4) At this period neither dignitary could, under the sanction of the law, walk at midday along the streets; and the work now completed — which may be said **fairly** to exhaust the subject— is a singular evidence of what ecclesiastical ambition can accomplish in the face of surrounding discouragements.

(Killen, 1875)

All the cases of *fairly* show a similar pattern, as they co-occur with the epistemic modal *may*. Some of them with the cognitive verbs, namely *conclude* (1) and *presume* (2), as pointed earlier, while (3) and (4) show different verb semantic classes, such as the communicative verb *say*. Generally speaking, the function of the modal *may* as an epistemic marker in all these instances is certainly strengthened by the presence of *fairly* in an attempt to mitigate the claim resulting from the deductive process shown in instances (1) and (2). In the other two examples, the adverb *fairly* comes to indicate perspectivisation concerning the propositional content framed.

In CETA, there are 4 occurrences of *fairly*, all of them in the nineteenth-century texts. These are given below:

(5) Owing to the want of air, however, it seems impossible that any form of life analogous to those on earth can subsist there. No appearance indicating vegetation, or the slightest variation of surface which can **fairly** be ascribed to change of season, can any where be discerned.

(Herschel, 1833)

(6) It is clear that as the joint M is urged home towards the surface, the legs will open, and the ruler will become more nearly straight, but will not attain perfect straightness till M is brought **fairly** up to contact with the surface at m, in which case its whole length will become a tangent to the sphere at m, as is the line xy. This explains what is meant by the dip of the horizon.

(Bradford, 1845)

(7) Still greater uniformity is observable in the different parts of the same line; for each line maintains its individual width throughout. Although at and near the point where it leaves the dark regions, or the

Solis Lacus, —for the same phenomenon appears there, some slight enlargement seems to take place, after it has **fairly** started on its course it remains substantially of the same size from one end to the other.

(Lowell, 1895)

In cases (5)–(7), *fairly* is placed next to a verb and in all the instances, the adverb functions as a mitigator of the propositional content manifested. In case (5), there are other elements reinforcing the attenuating function of the adverb, such as *the slightest variation of surface which can fairly be ascribed*. Note that the same that happens in (5) occurs again in (8):

(8) For the system seems sublimely superior to possible obstructions in the way; the lines running, apparently, not where they may, but where they choose. The Eumenides-Orcus, for example, pursues the even tenor of its unswerving course for nearly 3500 miles. Now, it might be possible so to select one's country that one canal should be able to do this; but that every canal should be straight, and many of them **fairly** comparable with the Eumenides-Orcus in length, seems to be beyond the possibility of contrivance.

(Lowell, 1895)

There are certain parts of speech strengthening the mitigating function of the adverb, e.g. *some, slight slight, seems to take place*. In this case, the adverb *fairly* is placed next to an adjective, and its pragmatic function differs from the other cases, as it works to reinforce the meaning of the adjective next to it rather than a complete proposition.

Regarding the textual genre, there exist some differences in the occurrences analysed previously, as in the use of modal verbs accompanying *fairly*, for instance. In the historical excerpts analysed, modal verbs tend to co-occur frequently, not only in the examples above these lines, but also in other examples shown in a previous study (Álvarez-Gil, 2017), with the adverb *fairly* in order to downtone the propositional content. In the specific examples included in this study, the modal verb deployed is always *may*, although we can find other examples in which modal verbs such as *might, must*, and *could* also co-occur with this adverb to accomplish the pragmatic function of mitigation.

There exist disciplinary differences in the use of *fairly* as a mitigator in the vicinity of a modal verb, and so I have found almost all cases of this pattern in historical texts rather than in the astronomy ones. Despite this evident disciplinary difference, the pattern *modal verb + fairly + verb* is found only once in the corpus of astronomy texts. Here, this pattern recurrent in historical texts has been attested just once in an astronomy treatise, e.g. *can fairly be*. This may be tentatively considered a textual genre rather than a domain-based variation. In any case, the adverb signals mitigation of the claim, and so it might be categorised as an example of positive politeness seeking to avoid future academic criticism.

5 Conclusion

This study presents evidence of the use of adverbs as metadiscourse devices in eighteenth- and nineteenth-century astronomy and history texts. I have examined authorial stance and, more specifically, mitigation as expressed by the use of *fairly* in the *Corpus of Modern English History Texts* (CHET) and *The Corpus of Modern English Astronomy Texts* (CETA). The findings suggest an authorial tendency to use those adverbs with a primary evidential meaning pursuing different pragmatic effects. Among these effects, there are mitigation of truth regarding a particular proposition, negative politeness, and even manifestation of collegiality and solidarity. As also shown in the examples presented, softening a particular claim can imply lack of knowledge on the author's side but that is not always the case. As Alonso-Almeida (2012:218) affirms, it depends on contextual factors, as "writers cannot always fully rely on the methods or the sources available, and hence they safeguard their public self-image by admitting drawbacks or limitations".

In the case of the excerpts analysed, it has been shown that the adverb *fairly* can function as a mitigating element that may serve as a face-saving strategy for the authors as well as an indicator of detachment towards the propositional content presented. However, it has been shown that there exist differences in the syntactic pattern where this adverb is embedded and its pragmatic function concerning the scientific register it appears. Although I have found that these differences do not take place according to the textual genre, since there are treatises in both subcorpora, the CHET and the CETA, evidence shows that the adverb *fairly* occupies the same position and textual pattern, i.e. modal + *fairly* + verb in the examples taken from treatises and, more importantly, it performs exactly the same pragmatic function.

Future research will focus on disciplinary similarities and differences as represented in other subcorpora of the *Coruña Corpus,* namely the *Corpus of English Philosophy Texts* and the *Corpus of English Life Sciences Texts* (CELiST). Apart from that, the number of adverbials under investigation could be enlarged so as to get a more precise and exhaustive picture of the pragmatic functions of stance adverbials as indicators of the authorial presence in scientific texts.

References

Alonso-Almeida, F. (2015). On the mitigating function of modality and evidentiality from English and Spanish medical research papers. *Intercultural Pragmatics* 12/1, 33–57.

Alonso-Almeida, F. & Mele-Marrero, M. (2014). Stancetaking in seventeenth century prefaces on obstetrics. *Journal of Historical Pragmatics* 15/1, 1–35.

Alonso-Almeida, F. (2012). An analysis of hedging in Eighteenth Century English Astronomy Texts, in I. Moskowich & B. Crespo (Eds), *Astronomy 'playne and simple': the writing of science between 1700 and 1900*. Amsterdam: John Benjamin Publishing, 199–220.

Álvarez-Gil, F. J. (2017). Apparently, fairly and possibly in The Corpus of Modern English History Texts (1700–1900), in F. Alonso-Almeida (ed.) *Stance-taking in late Modern English scientific writing. Evidence from the Coruña Corpus*. Valencia: Servicio de Publicaciones de la Universidad Politécnica de Valencia, 93–105.

Álvarez-Gil, F. J. (2018). *Adverbs ending in -ly in late Modern English. Evince from the Coruña Corpus of History English Texts*. Colección Estudios de Lingüística Aplicada, vol. 4. Valencia: Servicio de Publicaciones de la Universidad Politécnica de Valencia.

Biber, D., Johansson, S., Leech, G., Conrad, S. & Finegan, E. (1999). *Longman grammar of spoken and written English*. New York: Longman.

Biber, D. & Finegan, E. (1989). Styles of stance in English: lexical and grammatical marking of evidentiality and affect. *Text*, 9/1, 93–124.

Biber, D. & Finegan, E. (1988). Adverbial stance types in English. *Discourse Processes* 11, 1–34.

Biber, D. (1993). Representativeness in corpus design. *Literary and Linguistic Computing* 19, 219–241.

Brown, P. (2011). Color me bitter: Cross-modal compounding in Tzeltal perception words, in A. Majid & S. C. Levinson (eds.) The senses in language and culture [Special Issue] *Senses and Society* 6/1, 106–116.

Brown, P. & Levinson S. (1987). *Politeness. Some universals in language usage*. Cambridge: Cambridge University Press.

Caffi, C. (1999). On mitigation. *Journal of Pragmatics* 31, 881–909.

Caffi, C. (2007). *Mitigation*. New York: Elsevier.

Carrió-Pastor, M. L. (2012). A contrastive analysis of epistemic modality in scientific English. *Revista de lenguas para fines específicos* 18, 115–132.

Carrió-Pastor, M. L. (2016). A contrastive study of interactive metadiscourse in academic papers written in English and in Spanish, in F. Alonso-Almeida, L. Cruz-García & V. González-Ruiz (eds.) *Corpus-based studies on language varieties*. Bern: Peter Lang, 89–114.

Chafe, W. L. (1986). Evidentiality in English conversation and academic writing, in W. L. Chafe & J. Nichols (eds.) *Evidentiality and the linguistic coding of epistemology*. Norwood, NJ: Ablex, 261–272.

Channell, J. (1994). *Vague language*. Oxford: Oxford University Press.

Cornillie, B. (2009). Evidentiality and epistemic modality. On the close relationship between two different categories. *Functions of Language* 16/1, 44–62.

Cornillie, B. & Delbecque, N. (2008). Speaker commitment: back to the speaker. Evidence from Spanish alternations. *Belgian Journal of Linguistics* 22, 37–62.

Crespo, B. & Moskowich, I. (2015). A corpus of history texts (CHET) as part of the Coruña Corpus Project. *Proceedings of the international scientific conference «Corpus linguistics - 2015»*. St. Petersburgh: St. Petersburgh State University, 14–23.

Crompton, P. (1997). Hedging in academic writing: some theoretical aspects. *English for Specic Purposes* 16/4, 271–289.

De Branbater, P. & Dendale, P. (2008). Commitment: the term and the notions. *Belgian Journal of English Linguistics* 22/1, 1–14.

De Haan, F. (2009). On the status of 'epistemic' must, in A. Tsangalidis and R. Facchinetti, (eds.) *Studies on English modality*. Bern: Peter Lang, 261–284.

Diewald, G., Kresic, M. & Smirnova, E. (2009). The grammaticalization channels of evidentials and modal particles in German: integration in textual structures as a common feature, in M.M. Hansen & J. Visconti (eds.) *Current trends in diachronic semantics and pragmatics*. UK: Emerald, 189–209.

Dzung Pho, P. (2013). *Authorial stance in research articles: examples from applied linguistics and educational technology*. New York: Palgrave Macmillan.

Fairly | Definition of fairly in English by Oxford Dictionaries. *Oxford English Dictionary*, <en.oxforddictionaries.com/definition/fairly>.

Fraser, B. (1996). Pragmatic markers. *Pragmatics Quarterly Publication of the International Pragmatics Association* 6/2, 167–190.

Fraser, B. (2010). Hedging in political discourse. The Bush 2007 press conferences, in U. Okulska & P. Cap (eds.) *Perspectives in politics and discourse*. Amsterdam/New York: JohnBenjamins Publishing, 201–214.

Gray, B., Douglas, B. & T. Hiltunen. (2011). The expression of stance (1665–1712) in early publications of the Philosophical Transactions and other contemporary medical prose: Innovations in a pioneering discourse, in I. Taavitsainen & P. Pahta (eds.) *Medical writing in Early Modern English*. Cambridge: Cambridge University Press, 221–247.

Greenbaum, S. (1969). *Studies in English adverbial usage*. London: Longman.

Halliday, M. & Christian M. (2004). *An introduction to functional grammar*. London: Hodder Arnold.

Hunston, S., & Thompson, G. (eds). (2000). *Evaluation in text*. Oxford: Oxford University Press.

Hyland, K. (1994). Hedging in academic writing and EAP textbooks. *English for Specific Purposes* 13/3, 239–256.

Hyland, K. (1996). Writing without conviction? Hedging in science research articles. *Applied Linguistics* 17/4, 433–454.

Hyland, K. (1998). *Hedging in scientific research articles*. Amsterdam/Philadelphia: John Benjamins.

Hyland, K. & Tse, P. (2004). Metadiscourse in academic writing: a reappraisal. *Applied Linguistics* 25/2, 156–177.

Hyland, K. (2005). *Metadiscourse: exploring interaction in writing*. London: Continuum.

Johnstone, B. (2009). Stance, style, and the linguistic individual, in A. Jaffe (ed.) *Stance: sociolinguistic perspectives*. Oxford: Oxford University Press, 29–71.

Kranich, S. (2009). Epistemic modality in English popular scientific texts and their Germantranslation. *Transkom* 2, 26–41.

Lorés Sanz, R. (2011). The study of authorial voice: using a Spanish-English corpus to explorelinguistic transference. *Corpora* 6, 1–24.

Marín Arrese, J. I. (2011). Epistemic legitimizing strategies, commitment and accountability in discourse. *Discourse Studies* 13, 789–797.

Markkanen, R. & Schröder, H. (eds.) (1997). *Hedging and discourse. Approaches to the analysis of a pragmatic phenomenon in academic texts*. Berlin/New York: Walter de Gruyter.

Mauranen, A. (1997). Hedging in language revisers' hands, in R. Markkanen & H. Schröder (eds.) *Hedging and discourse. Approaches to the analysis of a pragmatic phenomenon in academic texts*. Berlin: Walter de Gruyter, 115–134.

Mauranen, A. (1993). *Cultural differences in academic rhetoric: a textlinguistic study*. Bern: Peter Lang.
Mur-Dueñas, P. (2011). An intercultural analysis of metadiscourse features in research articles written in English and in Spanish. *Journal of Pragmatics* 43, 3068–3079.
Myers, G. (1989). The pragmatics of politeness in scientific articles. *Applied Linguistics*, 10/1, 1–35.
Ochs, E. (ed.) (1989). The pragmatics of affect. *Special issue of Text* 9/1.
Pic, E. & Furmaniak, G. (2012). A study of epistemic modality in academic and popularised discourse: the case of possibility adverbs perhaps, maybe and possibly. *Revista de Lenguas para Fines Específicos* 18, 13–44.
Quintana-Toledo, E. (2009). Middle English medical recipes: a metadiscoursive approach. *Studia Anglica Posnaniensia* 45/2, 21–38.
Quirk, R., Greenbaum, S., Leech, G. L. & Svartvik, J. (1985). *A comprehensive grammar of the English language*. Essex: Longman.
Quirk, R., Greenbaum, S., Leech, G. L. & Svartvik, J. (1972). *A grammar of contemporary English*. Essex: Longman.
Salager-Meyer, F. (1994). Hedges and textual communicative function in medical English written discourse. *English for Specific Purposes* 13/2, 149–70.
Stukker, N., T. Sanders, & Verhagen, A. (2009). Categories of subjectivity in Dutch causal connectives: a usage-based analysis, in T. Sanders and E. Sweetser (eds.) *Causal categories in discourse and cognition*. Berlin: Mouton de Gruyter, 119–172.
Sweetser, E. (1990). *From etymology to pragmatics. Metaphoric and cultural aspects of semantic structure*. Cambridge: Cambridge University Press.
Taavitsainen, I. & Päivi P. (1997). Corpus of early English medical writing 1375–1550. *ICAME Journal* 21, 71–78.
Traugott, E. C. (1989). On the rise of epistemic meanings in English: An example of subjectification in semantic change. *Language* 57, 33–65.

6 An Analysis of Lexical Bundles in Academic Journal Descriptions[1]

Davide Simone Giannoni

1 Introduction

Since the appearance of the first English-language periodicals devoted to the dissemination of scientific knowledge (Gross et al. 2002), academic journals have gradually grown in importance and overtaken books as the preferred venue for scholarly publication in most disciplines. The transition from print to online publishing has only added momentum to this trend, making content distribution/retrieval both faster and simpler across geographical borders. The sheer number of periodicals now available to researchers has intensified competition for visibility and for high-quality contributions, especially in the realm of commercial publishing. This is compounded by the use of such data as citation rates and reader-access metrics for promotional purposes and as tools to gauge academic performance. One underlying reason for the success of journals is to be found in their adaptability to the evolving needs of scientific communities, as scholars seek legitimate research arenas within clearly defined territories (Becher 1981) where access is properly regulated by institutional gatekeepers. In a sense, academic journals are evidence of the intellectual and interactional maps created by disciplinary communities of practice.

Self-definition is the main source of insights into the institutional nature of academic journals. It is typically found in a 'journal description' (henceforth JD) section, where the periodical's scope, aims, and standards are spelled out for readers. In many regards, JDs resemble other forms of online representation observed in academia and in corporate communication, insofar as they provide institutions with "a virtual shop window for communicating their ethos to a global audience" (Isaksson & Jørgensen 2010: 120). As suggested by Hyland and Tse (2009), they serve a diverse audience, ranging from young authors in search of a suitable venue for their manuscript to library subscription services and readers seeking specific types of content. At the same time, by foregrounding a journal's academic credentials, JDs "play an indispensable role in the mechanisms of delivering and promoting knowledge" (Tse & Hyland 2010: 1880).

Despite the well-established nature of such texts, whose origin predates the advent of online publishing, they have been largely neglected by EAP scholars and by the literature on academic writing. Only a few authors have taken interest in JDs. There is some evidence, for example, of convergence across disciplines: Hyland and Tse (2009) found similarities in the rhetorical structure and wording of 200 JDs from print-based academic journals in applied linguistics, sociology, biology, and mechanical engineering. The lexis tended to communicate novelty (e.g. *new, current, original*), ranking (*main, major, best, excellent*), importance (*important, relevant, significant*), and scholarliness (*quality, scholarly, critical*). Tse and Hyland (2010) looked at the function of relative clauses in the same disciplines, with the most frequent being scope (50%), followed by evaluation (35%) and clarity (15%). A comparable sample of JDs analysed more recently by Giannoni (2016) suggests that evaluative items tend to cluster around seven values: orientation (*theoretical, experimental, scientific, empirical*), relevance (*interest, important, significant, relevant*), inclusiveness (*interdisciplinary, broad, wide*), novelty (*new, recent*), globalism (*international, world*), worth (*high, quality, well*), and primacy (*leading, most*).

This kind of empirical work describes how journals draw on specific lexicogrammatical resources to construct an authoritative self-representation or 'persona'. It also points to the need for more holistic analytical approaches capable of capturing the whole range of wordings associated with JDs and their variation – or lack thereof – across academic domains. The present study is an attempt to shed further light on the genre by looking at recurring word sequences.

1.1 Lexical Bundles

The phenomenon of lexical bundles has attracted considerable interest from linguists, starting from Anthony's (1954) pioneering work to recent contrastive investigations of academic writing (cf. Pan et al. 2016; Durrant 2017; Jalali 2017). Despite the adoption of different terminologies (e.g. multi-word sequences, clusters, n-grams, formulaic patterns) and approaches, such research helps to understand the ecology of lexemes whose collocations and co-occurrences follow context-dependent patterns that are highly indicative of generic proclivities.

Like keywords and other measurable features targeted by corpus analysts, lexical bundles are so embedded in academic discourse as to be easily overlooked by users – which makes their investigation all the more interesting. They can be broadly understood as "recurrent expressions, regardless of their idiomaticity, and regardless of their structural status" that have to "occur more than 20 times in a million words to qualify" (Biber et al. 1999: 990) or as "extended collocations, sequences of three or more words that statistically co-occur in a register" (Cortes 2004: 400).

The main choice for an analyst is the size of the unit considered, with most authors focusing on three- to four-word sequences; the result is a set of "structurally incomplete units, but the co-occurrence of two or more items becomes interesting if it seems to happen for a purpose and is repeated across many texts" (Hyland 2008: 43).

Bundles are a rich source of linguistic evidence for EAP scholars due to the highly formulaic construction of academic writing and can be used to analyse the linguistic profile of any type of text. As the present study focuses on the distribution of bundles in JDs, the most frequent occurrences and their functions will be investigated contrastively in a small but representative multidisciplinary corpus.

2 Material and Method

A range of JDs was assembled from the four target domains chosen by Hyland and Tse (2009). To identify representative journals, the top 20 titles ranked by impact factor were selected for each discipline, as listed in *Journal Citation Reports* (JCR 2013). The Social Sciences Edition was consulted for Linguistics and Sociology, the Science Edition for Biology and Mechanical Engineering; since applied linguistics is not allocated a separate section in JCR, the related field of Linguistics was chosen instead. This produced a total of 80 periodicals (for a complete list, see Giannoni 2016), whose homepage is generally hosted by an academic publisher's website. Though not directly relevant to this study, it was noted that each publisher tends to adopt a similar layout and structure in its journal homepages across the disciplinary spectrum.

Each journal homepage and its hyperlinks were then inspected to locate the JD; where an option was available, the more extensive version of the JD was considered. Information about the journal's scope and content was included, but not such accessory information as subscription details, benefits to authors and topic lists. The resulting texts measured on average 139 words – well below the 208 words reported by Hyland and Tse (2009) for JDs in the print editions of journals; this may partly be due to the greater conciseness of digital as opposed to analogue material. The breakdown by discipline shows a limited degree of variation in length: Linguistics totalled 2,544 words; Sociology 2,995; Biology 2,850; Mech Eng 2,736.

The method of investigation combined both n-gram analysis and manual observation of occurrences. More specifically, the n-gram function of AntConc (Anthony 2014) was used to extract a list of three- to five-word bundles with a minimum threshold of five occurrences in the whole corpus – i.e. 449.5 occurrences per million words. After omitting the items that belonged to the journal's name (e.g. <*the journal of*>) or encoded disciplinary specialisms (e.g. <*sociology of religion*>) and those overlapping with shorter sequences (e.g. <*on all aspects of*> under <*all aspects of*>), a total of 24 bundles were identified.

3 Results

Of the 24 bundles extracted from the corpus, 21 were three-word sequences and only three were four-word sequences (<*a wide range of*>, <*state of the art*>, <*in the fields of*>). Their occurrence was then normalised per million words, as is common practice in this type of analysis (cf. Biber et al. 1999; Hyland 2008) in order to compare frequencies in and across the corpus. The following examples illustrate how the top item in each discipline is employed: i.e. <*the journal is*> (1,965 occurrences per million words) for Linguistics; <*all areas of*> (1,669) for Sociology; <*as well as*> (2,456) for Biology; <*of the journal*> (3,289) for Mech Eng:

> The journal is keen to help make connections between fields, theories, research methods, and scholarly discourses (LING#10).
>
> The journal presents pathbreaking work from all areas of sociology, with an emphasis on theory building and innovative methods (SOC#2).
>
> Our audience is the international scientific community as well as educators, policy makers, patient advocacy groups, and interested members of the public (BIO#1).
>
> The mission of the journal is to publish high quality work from experimental, theoretical, and computational investigations (ME#5).

The data was then manually investigated and classified into referential, discourse organising, and stance bundles, using the well-established taxonomy proposed by Biber et al. (1999; 2004). Results are summarised in Table 6.1.

The total count is the highest in Mech Eng – with 20,101 of these bundles per million words – and the lowest in Biology (14,098). Their function is mainly referential in all domains but there is a degree of variation in the proportion of discourse organising bundles (11% in Mech Eng; 22% in Biology) and stance bundles (none in Sociology; 9% Mech Eng).

Table 6.1 Distribution of bundles by type

	LING	*SOC*	*BIO*	*ME*	*Ave.*
Referential	81%	85%	73%	80%	80%
Discourse Organising	12%	15%	22%	11%	14%
Stance	7%	–	5%	9%	6%
Total	16,901	16,026	14,098	20,101	16,781

A detailed description of the results is given in the following subsections, which include a further classification of items based on functional categories adapted from Simpson-Vlach and Ellis (2010) and Hyland (2012).

3.1 *Referential Bundles*

On average, 80% of the bundles were of the referential type, meaning that they "make direct reference to physical or abstract entities, or to the textual context itself, either to identify the entity or to single out some particular attribute of the entity as especially important" (Biber et al. 2004: 384). Normalised occurrences were: 13,757 per million words in Linguistics; 13,689 in Sociology; 10,238 in Biology; 16,081 in Mech Eng. After manual inspection of the co-text, their function was found to fit one of three subcategories: specification, qualification, or quantification.

3.1.1 Specification

Around half of the referential bundles (51%) encode meanings that Simpson-Vlach and Ellis (2010) refer to as 'specification of attributes'. They often do so through the sequence <*a/the* N *of*>, as may be noted in Table 6.2. The figure is the lowest in Biology and peaks in Mech Eng, where the bundle <*of the journal*> is particularly prominent compared to the other disciplines. Two other items that stand out are <*journal of the*> in Sociology (expressing institutional affiliation) and <*the scope of*> in Mech Eng (mapping out the journal's intellectual territory). The varying combination of bundles employed by these disciplines is indicative of their specific goals and concerns.

Table 6.2 Referential bundles: specification

	LING	*SOC*	*BIO*	*ME*	*Av.*
of the journal	393	334	–	3,289	1,004
research in the	1,179	1,336	351	1,096	990
the study of	1,572	668	–	365	651
is devoted to	393	1,002	351	731	619
forum for the	393	–	351	1,462	551
to the editor	393	–	702	1,096	548
the scope of	–	–	351	1,827	544
journal of the	–	1,336	702	–	509
in the fields of	393	334	351	731	452
in the journal	393	334	702	365	448
research on the	393	1,336	–	–	432
ALL	5,503	6,678	3,860	10,964	6,751

3.1.2 Qualification

The second function of referential bundles (27%) is qualification. Here, the focus is not on a journal's attributes but rather on its status. The figure peaks in Linguistics, which has almost three times more bundles of this type than Sociology (see Table 6.3). Interestingly, both disciplines – which Hyland and Tse (2009) rank as 'soft' – share a tendency to use the sequence <*state of the art*>. It is also worth noting that although the journals are all peer-reviewed, the bundle <*peer reviewed journal*> was absent in Sociology.

3.1.3 Quantification

The last function is encoded by 'quantity specifiers' (Simpson-Vlach & Ellis 2010), which account for 22% of referential bundles. They tend to encode the value of Inclusiveness – the third most frequent evaluative parameter identified in the lexis of JDs (cf. Giannoni 2016). As shown in Table 6.4, these bundles were most prominent in Sociology, which is a particularly broad field with many specialisms. The sequences <*a wide range of*> and <*all areas of*> are one of the few instances suggesting a clear-cut distinction between hard and soft sciences.

3.2 Discourse Organising Bundles

The second type of bundles (14% of total) consists of interactional devices that point readers to "relationships between prior and coming discourse"

Table 6.3 Referential bundles: qualification

	LING	*SOC*	*BIO*	*ME*	*Av.*
the journal is	1,965	334	702	1,096	1,024
the journal publishes	1,179	334	1,404	365	820
is an international	1,179	668	702	365	728
state of the art	786	668	351	365	542
peer reviewed journal	786	–	351	731	467
ALL	5,896	2,003	3,922	2,924	3,686

Table 6.4 Referential bundles: quantification

	LING	*SOC*	*BIO*	*ME*	*Av.*
all aspects of	1,179	1,336	1,404	731	1,162
a wide range of	1,179	1,336	351	731	899
all areas of	–	1,669	351	–	760
one of the	–	668	351	731	437
ALL	2,358	5,008	2,456	2,193	3,004

Table 6.5 Discourse organising bundles

	LING	*SOC*	*BIO*	*ME*	*Av.*
as well as	1,179	1,336	2,456	1,096	1,517
in addition to	786	1,002	702	1,096	896
ALL	1,965	2,337	3,158	2,193	2,413

Table 6.6 Stance bundles

	LING	*SOC*	*BIO*	*ME*	*Av.*
will be considered	786	–	–	1,096	470
not be considered	393	–	702	731	456
ALL	1,179	–	702	1,827	927

(Biber et al. 2004: 384). Simpson-Vlach and Ellis (2010: 506–507) class them as Discourse markers, i.e. bundles “signaling or referring to prior or upcoming discourse”. The two items found here (see Table 6.5) occur relatively more often in the hard sciences and are both additive phrases.

3.3 *Stance Bundles*

Stance bundles, which account for only 6% of occurrences, point to “attitudes or assessments of certainty that frame some other proposition” (Biber et al. 2004: 384). The two instances identified in the corpus (Table 6.6) belong to the ability/possibility subcategory, as they “frame or introduce some possible or actual action or proposition” (Simpson-Vlach & Ellis 2010: 506). They are both deontic expressions encoding the gatekeeping function of JDs. Linguistics and Mech Eng are the disciplines that tend to emphasise what kinds of contributions to the journal are acceptable (or not).

4 Conclusions

A number of conclusions might be drawn from this study. First of all, the high frequency of lexical bundles – albeit partly influenced by the dimensions of the corpus (cf. Simpson-Vlach & Ellis 2010) – suggests that JDs are highly formulaic, standardised texts. Top-ranking journals tend to construct self-representations that draw on a common repertoire of lexicogrammatical resources whose meaning is instrumental to the genre’s evaluative orientation. In line with earlier research (Hyland & Tse 2009; Giannoni 2016), it appears that disciplinary variation is on the whole rather limited. This finding may be explained by the relatively diverse audience of JDs and/or by similar concerns influencing editors across academic fields.

The fact that referential bundles account for 80% of occurrences is consistent with other institutional-academic genres: for instance, the figure reported for university brochures, policy statements, and descriptions is 70% (Biber & Barbieri 2007). The impression is one of asymmetry on the communicative plane, considering that "referential bundles are extremely common in classroom teaching and somewhat less common in textbooks and academic prose" (Biber et al. 2004: 396). Half of these bundles express specification, with noun phrases or prepositional phrases drawing attention to the journal and its stakeholders. The soft fields have relatively more qualification (Linguistics) and quantification (Sociology), in line with their stronger promotional flavour. However, the soft/hard distinction is far from being the "primary organizing principle" (Durrant 2017: 190) observed in bundle usage by postgraduate students, which suggests that expert writers converge towards a similar phraseological toolbox.

Despite its limited size and coverage, this corpus suggests various avenues for future research. To start with, it would be interesting to establish whether the same kind of bundles are commonplace in less prestigious and/or peripheral English-language periodicals, where the promotional element has less leverage and editors need to foreground assets other than the journal's current achievements. A comparison of this kind might reveal differences akin to those observed between more or less prestigious institutions in universities' mission statements (Sauntson & Morrish 2011).

A second aspect that deserves attention is the discursive continuum that JDs share with other descriptive texts produced by academics, such as book blurbs (Gesuato 2007; Basturkmen 2009) and universities' 'About us' pages (Giannoni 2018). Finally, the actual reliability of JDs deserves further scrutiny; in other words, how far are a journal's practices consistent with its espoused aims? There is some indication (cf. Kidd 2002) that this is not always the case.

Note

1 Early results of this research were presented at the annual Cutting Edges Conference held at Canterbury Christ Church University, UK, on 3 July 2015.

References

Anthony, L. (2014). *AntConc 3.4.1.* Tokyo: Waseda University.

Anthony, M. (1954). An exploratory inquiry into lexical clusters. *American Speech* 29/3, 175–180.

Basturkmen, H. (2009). Back cover blurbs: puff pieces and windows on cultural values, in K. Hyland & G. Diani (eds.) *Academic Evaluation: Review Genres in University Settings*. Basingstoke: Palgrave, 68–86.

Becher, T. (1981). Towards a definition of disciplinary cultures. *Studies in Higher Education* 6/2, 109–122.

Biber, D. & Barbieri, F. (2007). Lexical bundles in university spoken and written registers. *English for Specific Purposes* 26/3, 263–286.

Biber, D., Conrad, S. & Cortes, V. (2004). *If you look at...*: lexical bundles in university teaching and textbooks. *Applied Linguistics* 25/3, 371–405.

Biber, D., Johansson, S., Leech, G., Conrad, S. & Finegan, E. (1999). *Longman Grammar of Spoken and Written English*. London: Longman.

Cortes, V. (2004). Lexical bundles in published and student disciplinary writing: examples from history and biology. *English for Specific Purposes* 23/4, 397–423.

Durrant, P. (2017). Lexical bundles and disciplinary variation in university students' writing: mapping the territories. *Applied Linguistics* 38/2, 165–193.

Gesuato, S. (2007). Evaluation in back-cover blurbs, in M. Dossena & A.H. Jucker (eds.) *(R)evolutions in Evaluation*, special issue of *Textus* 20/1, 83–101.

Giannoni, D.S. (2016). 'An international journal publishing high quality, original research': self-evaluative categories in journal descriptions, in T. Harrison, U. Lanvers & M. Edwardes (eds.) *Breaking Theory: New Directions in Applied Linguistics. Proceedings of the 48th Annual Meeting of the British Association for Applied Linguistics*. London: Scitsiugnil Press, 213–229. www.baal.org.uk/who-we-are/resources [retrieved 1.12.2017].

Giannoni, D.S. (2018). An investigation of value claims in academic and corporate 'About us' texts. *Applied Linguistics* 39/3, 328–351.

Gross, A.G., Harmon, J.E. & Reidy, M. (2002). *Communicating Science. The Scientific Article from the 17th Century to the Present*. Oxford: Oxford University Press.

Hyland, K. (2008). Academic clusters: text patterning in published and postgraduate writing. *International Journal of Applied Linguistics* 18/1, 41–62.

Hyland, K. (2012). Bundles in academic discourse. *Annual Review of Applied Linguistics* 32, 150–169.

Hyland, K. & Tse, P. (2009). 'The leading journal in its field': evaluation in journal descriptions. *Discourse Studies* 11/6, 703–720.

Isaksson, M. & Jørgensen, P.E.F. (2010). Communicating corporate ethos on the web. The self-presentation of PR agencies. *Journal of Business Communication* 47/2, 119–140.

Jalali, H. (2017). Reflection of stance through *it* bundles in applied linguistics. *Ampersand* 4, 30–39.

JCR (2013). *Journal Citation Reports 2013 Edition*. New York: Thomson Reuters. Online resource.

Kidd, S.A. (2002). The role of qualitative research in psychology journals. *Psychological Methods* 7/1, 126–138.

Pan, F., Reppen, R. & Biber, D. (2016). Comparing patterns of L1 versus L2 English academic professionals: lexical bundles in telecommunications research journals. *Journal of English for Academic Purposes* 21, 60–71.

Sauntson, H. & Morrish, L. (2011). Vision, values and international excellence: the 'products' that university mission statements sell to students, in M. Molesworth, R. Scullion & E. Nixon (eds.) *The Marketisation of Higher Education and the Student as Consumer*. London: Routledge, 73–85.

Simpson-Vlach, R. & Ellis, N.C. (2010). An academic formulas list: new methods in phraseology research. *Applied Linguistics* 31/4, 487–512.

Tse, P. & Hyland, K. (2010). Claiming a territory: relative clauses in journal descriptions. *Journal of Pragmatics* 42/7, 1880–1889.

7 Collaborating with Disciplinary Experts in Corpus Compilation Processes

Isabel Herrando-Rodrigo

1 Introduction

Researchers are nowadays encouraged to meet certain social challenges, posed by national and international institutions and research programmes, in order to increase their reputation, visibility, and, eventually, raise funding. To be internationally competitive, calls favour research projects that disseminate and transfer knowledge to society. In other words, academics should make sure that their findings are transferred, communicated, and disseminated not only among their colleagues and scholars from related disciplines, but also among lay readers since researchers are expected to boost citizens' concern about science.[1] In addition, the advent of the internet and consequent modes of creating and disseminating science are driving researchers to re-contextualise the way they code and, thus, communicate their findings and also the possibilities brought about by the dynamic nature of digital genres (Mur-Dueñas, 2018). Nowadays, platforms such as Wikipedia (Thompson & Hanley, 2017), Twitter, or Facebook (Ciprut et al., 2017) not only provide engagement with the reader but also enhance visibility and reputation, successful knowledge reception, and overall, effective communication among disciplinary members and non-specialised readers.[2]

In the same vein, more sophisticated textual adaptations of the canonical research articles (here-to-after RAs) published on such ungovernable domain as the internet are being produced, disseminated, and consumed by specialised and lay readers. Despite the potential amalgam of scientific RA adaptations or *popularisations* available on the net[3], it is being observed that medical popularisations published on the internet by well-known institutions and specialised mass-media publications are being formulated without any previous agreement on both textual organisations and lexico-grammatical features (Herrando-Rodrigo, 2012). Since little research has been published about these new medical popularisations (here-to-after Med-E-Pops), which are medical RA (Med-RA) instant adaptations published on the net, launched immediately after the Med-RAs publication, this author decided to manually collect authentic corpora that should eventually allow her to identify, classify, and then describe this new genre, and also to assess to what extent this electronic genre, which favours medical knowledge transfer, is shaping the voice, presence, and visibility of medical researchers.

Since language cannot be *context-less* (Blommaert, 2006: 4), an ethnographic perspective seems to be essential to frame and, therefore, describe the nature of this type of texts and their process of production. Concretely, this chapter shares some revealing insights into conducting face-to-face interviews and making observations to identify possible relations between Med-RAs and Med-E-Pops, in an attempt to identify if new genres emerge (Orlikowski & Yates, 1994; Crowston & Williams, 2000; Giltrow & Stein, 2009), evolve (Campagna et al., 2012; Herrando-Rodrigo, 2014), or are simply reconfigured (Herring, 2012) in the medical context in future research. Such an approach could be seen as a point of departure for the design of a survey-based study counting with medical staff expertise, which should illuminate a corpus collection of authentic texts.

Dealing with the *authenticity* and usefulness of a linguistic research, one may wonder whether counting on professionals' expertise might be indispensable to make a complete sense of our contribution as applied linguists and language teachers to society. In other words, if linguists feel the need to study the *academic coding* of medical knowledge and how the medical personnel promote their work in their own field-specific and also in related areas (e.g. urology and gynaecology), should we (language mediators) not turn to their context and experience to select texts for our research and reflect on these texts production processes? Should we not directly ask them about their professional discursive practices (Bhatia, 2004)? As observed in previous research based on ethnographic orientations to explore textual practices in professional domains (Lillis, 2013; Paltridge et al., 2016), academic literacies (Tuck, 2016), students' literacies (Harwood & Petric, 2016), or academics' literacies research (McCulloch, 2017), these methodologies increase the range of data collected and the ways in which it is analysed and combine quantitative with qualitative analysis (face-to-face interviews, talk around the text, think-aloud protocols, observations, questionnaires, etc.), which should have a greater impact on practice. Needless to say, more time needs to be invested if we want our data collection to be contextualised due to the nature of our ultimate research objectives. Nevertheless, ethnographic data will allow applied linguists and ESP teachers (Cerezo, Manchón & Nicolás-Conesa, 2019) to work with production processes and not reified texts and also to critically re-visit assumptions about language use, texts, and genres (Lillis, 2017). In addition, taking a context-dependent bound perspective, our linguistic results should be more transferable, appealing, and representative in the profession. Making English language users/learners reflect on the different types of discourses, practices, registers, or inter-generic translations (Muñoz-Miquel, 2012; García-Izquierdo & Montalt, 2013; Askehave & Zethsen, 2014) could be highly relevant and significant for boosting their discursive enculturation into the discipline.

Regardless of the discrepancy on the conceptualisation of corpus validity, there is still not an agreed definition (Sinclair, 1991; Alvar Ezquerra et al., 1994; Baker, 1995; Kennedy, 1998; Flowerdew, 2002; Meyer, 2002; or Butler, 2004; among others). However, the study of corpora has widely changed the way language is approached and analysed by applied linguists and it has provided more accurate and reliable descriptions of language use, as Mur-Dueñas (2007) argues. The results of discourse analyses based on this type of corpus gathering should be greatly beneficial for ESP (English for Specific Purposes) and EAP (English for Academic Purposes) teachers, students, language mediators, and professionals.

Therefore, this work aims to raise awareness about why linguists, and ESP teachers, should turn to authentic texts and professionals' expertise describing a process of corpora compilation based on an ethnographic approach. The methodology implemented here suggests researchers and language consultants a potential way of corpus gathering which attempts to comprehend the context of specialised texts production, and the nature of field-specific genres evolutions and, thus, of the consequent efficient exploitation of linguistic results for teaching purposes. In this chapter, section 2 describes the three steps taken (phases 1, 2, and 3) in this ethnographically informed corpus compilation. How the corpora were accordingly collected is explained in Section 3 and, consequently, Section 4 describes the corpora. Finally, some final remarks close this chapter (Section 5).

2 Methods

Corpora collection process took almost a year. It consisted in three phases. In phase 1, four semi-structured interviews with the questionnaire included in Appendix 1 were conducted as a way of pilot study. Phase 2 consisted in the reassessment of the potential questionnaire and its delivery to the participants. Once questionnaires were collected, phase 3 was devoted to interpret the ethnographic data and gather the corpora.

2.1 Phase 1: The Semi-structured Interviews

Four well-known medical researchers and lecturers were contacted by this author. Two of them were lecturers and researchers at the Faculty of Medicine (University of Zaragoza) – here-to-after LR1 and LR2, and the other two were practitioners at the two University Hospitals (*Hospital Clínico Universitario Lozano Blesa* and *Hospital Universitario Miguel Servet,* both in Zaragoza, Spain) and part-time lecturers and researchers at the Faculty of Medicine (University of Zaragoza) – here-to-after PL1 and PL2. The four interviewees were first contacted by email. When they agreed to collaborate with the study, we face-to-face had a semi-structured interview.

In the semi-structured interview, LR1 was sceptical with any research related to ESP or EAP, since to begin with, he considered that students should fully master English before entering the Faculty of Medicine. In addition, he affirmed that "one cannot consider him(her)self, researcher or practitioner in the field in Medicine if he or she cannot command [the] English language. Being unable to use a computer or speak English must be associated to basic literacy".[4] That said, he agreed to review and answer the questionnaire. He acknowledged to ignore any medical research different from those findings disseminated by top research journals or *John Hopkins Newsletter*. Unlike their colleague, LR2, PL1, PL2 encouragingly supported this research proposal. They answered the questionnaire and during the semi-structured interview, the three of them suggested that I should carry out the survey-based study among doctors who worked at the two University hospitals and at the University of Zaragoza, since these practitioners lecture in the Degree of Medicine at the Faculty of Medicine as well and they are also used to researching and publishing in English. These three informants pointed out that these colleagues are used to reading not only Med-RAs but also new Med-RAs adaptations that specialised webs are offering medical personnel to keep up-to-date with the latest medical findings. LR2, for instance, showed me some Med-E-Pops he recently read on *Nature on line* and PL1 on *Docguide* and *New York Times Healthguide*. Informants also suggested that I should clarify the notion of *Med-E-Pops*; otherwise, future participants would not understand what I meant by it. Thus, I revised the questionnaire and included that explanation as an end-note. Once the questionnaires were delivered, PL1 and PL2 encouraged me to personally go to every guard and service "tracking" my questionnaires back from time to time, since medical personnel are bombarded with hundreds of surveys every week regarding issues from a varied nature, and these surveys are likely to be ignored.

2.2 Phase 2: The Survey-based Study

In phase 2, one hundred and ten professionals, from 20 different medical specialities, agreed to participate. All the participants worked at the two University hospitals and at the University of Zaragoza, lecturing in the Degree of Medicine at the Faculty of Medicine (part-time lecturers). I personally distributed the questionnaires in all the services or guards of the two hospitals mentioned earlier. In addition, I spoke with, at least, one of the participants of each speciality to ensure that these informants understood what was meant by medical popularisation and what the aim was in this study in particular. The response rate (91% of the potential informants) was higher than expected possibly due to my weekly insistence. As regards the professional background of this study participants, Table 7.1 shows the varied specialities of the practitioners who kindly participated in this survey-based study.

Table 7.1 Number of practitioners classified according to their medical speciality and percentage over the total number of participants

	Number of participants by speciality	*Percentage over total number of medical participants per speciality*
A&E (Accidents and Emergency)	15	13.6
Anaesthesia & Intensive Care	8	7.3
Cardiology	2	1.8
Dermatology	3	2.7
Haematology	1	0.9
Internal Medicine	8	7.3
Microbiology	4	3.6
Neurology	9	8.2
Obstetrics & Gynaecology	12	10.9
Ophthalmology	10	9.1
Otorhinolaryngology	2	1.8
Paediatrics	4	3.6
Paediatric surgery	2	1.8
Pharmacology	1	0.9
Physical Medicine & Rehabilitation	5	4.5
Pneumonology	5	4.5
Radiology	6	5.5
Surgery	5	4.5
Traumatology	2	1.8
Urology	6	5.5
Total	110	100.0

Table 7.2 summarises the distribution of junior/senior participants. Their medical speciality and range of year of experience were the only variables considered. The average working experience of these medical participants was 17.8 years (with five years being the minimum and 40 years of experience the maximum).

Table 7.2 Percentage of junior/senior medical participants

Medical informants' years of experience	*Number of participants per age range*	*Percentage over the total number of participants*
1–10 years	30	27.27
10–20 years	35	31.81
20–30 years	26	23.63
30–40 years	19	17.27

They were asked to indicate their years of experience in an attempt to observe whether it should influence somehow their reading of different medical texts disseminated in different modes and channels. It is apparent from this table that informants with fewer years of experience were more willing to participate than senior doctors.

2.3 *Phase 3: The Interpretation of the Ethnographic Data*

All these professionals who participated in this survey-based study acknowledged reading Med-RAs written in English very often. They also acknowledged seeking to publish their research results in English. As regards results related to Med-E-Pops status among practitioners obtained from the questionnaires, 71 (64.5%) out of 110 participants affirmed that they read Med-E-Pops either to be up-to-date with their discipline-related topics or because they lacked time to keep up-to-date with the number of Med-RAs which are published every day. The remaining 39 participants (35.5%) openly stated that they did not read Med-E-Pops, as summarised in Figure 7.1.

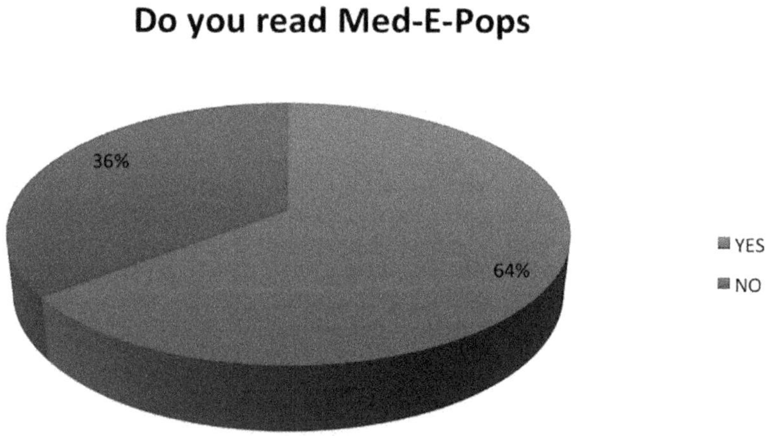

Figure 7.1 Graphical distribution of participants' answers to question number 2, "Do you read Med-E-Pops?".

A remarkable percentage of participants acknowledged reading Med-E-Pops. The participants who answered positively to the previous question were also asked to name which e-journals they read. These electronic publications were: *Doctor's Guide, New York Times Health Guide, Johns Hopkins News Release, Health Day News, Medical News Today, Science Daily*, and *Nature*. Figure 7.2 illustrates the distribution of informants' answers according the e-journals they read. Section 3 explains how forty pairs (each pair including a Med-RA and its corresponding electronic popularisation) were selected.

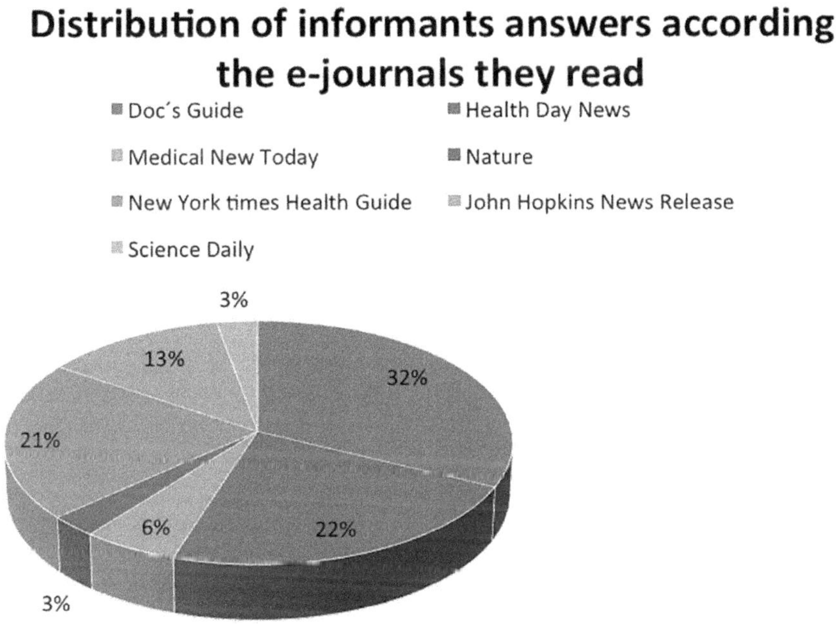

Figure 7.2 Distribution of informants' answers according the e-journals they read.

3 Corpora Compilation

These data were used to select an equivalent number of textual samples based on the results from the survey-based study. Therefore, I took participants' answers as a reference to select the number of Med-E-Pops, and their Med-RAs counterparts, to be taken from each e-journal in order to compile my Med-E-Pops corpus and my Med-RAs corpus. Table 7.3 summarises the data related to the number of answers and the correspondent number of Med-E-Pops chosen to select the Med-E-Pops corpus.

Table 7.3 E-journals suggested by medical informants, number of answers, and the correspondent number of Med-E-Pops chosen to select the Med-E-Pops corpus

Med-E-Pop journal	*Raw counts*	*Percentage*	*Med-E-Pops selected*
Doc's Guide	23	32.39%	13
New York Times Health Guide	15	21.13%	9
Health Day News	16	22.54%	9
Johns Hopkins News Release	9	12.68%	5
Medical News Today	4	5.63%	2
Science Daily	2	2.82%	1
Nature	2	2.82%	1
TOTAL	71	100%	40

In the collection process, I accessed the home page of these Med-E-Pops publications suggested by my informants and read the Med-E-Pops. Over 80 Med-E-Pops were first studied to identify the most recurrent features. Then, I explored whether all those texts fulfilled a number of criteria I devised as the most frequent as displayed in Table 7.4.

Table 7.4 Criteria for selecting Med-E-Pops out of their e-journals

Criteria for selecting Med-E-Pops	*Realisation of criteria*
Number of words	400–500 words because it seemed to be their usual average number of words
Med-E-Pops mention Med-RAs source	The name of the Med-RA journal was mentioned and hyperlinked to the Med-RA abstract
Med-E-Pops includes the date of the Med-RAs publication, researchers' name and affiliation	The date of publication of the Med-RAs details about researchers' research and affiliation
Medical issue is not repeated in the corpus (Diversification)	I chose different research medical topics
Direct interpellation from the Med-E-Pops writers	Direct and indirect reporting sequences from the Med-RAs researchers which always reflected the same information gathered in the Med-RAs
Med-E-Pops do not change the scientific information displayed in the corresponding Med-E-RAs	Med-E-Pop adapted the scientific information but they did not manipulate such information
The corresponding Med-RAs had to: • display IMRAD generic structure • be co-authored • be published in a JCR journal	

If a Med-E-Pop met the first criterion mentioned earlier, I traced the corresponding Med-RA and if that RA met the last criterion, namely, it followed the Introduction Methods Results and Discussion (IMRAD) generic conventions, was co-authored, and published in a JCR journal (Q1), I established a pair.

These corpora can then be defined as a diachronic comparable specialised collection of a Med-E-Pops corpus and a Med-RAs corpus. It was comprised by a total amount of 203,905 words – 40 Med-E-Pops (21,840 words) and their source texts, 40 Med-RAs (182,065 words) – a size that can be considered to afford some representativeness and also offer reliable results. The data related to these texts (titles, dates, source of publication, and writers) can be found in Appendix 3, and Table 7.5 displays the names of the e-journals and the research journals these Med-E-Pops reported on:

Table 7.5 Names of the e-journals and the research journals these Med-E-Pops reported on

Med-E-Pop journal	*Medical research journals*
Doc's Guide (13 Med-E-Pops)	American College of Surgeons
	Gynecologic Oncology
	The Lancet (3)
	Journal of the National Medical Association
	Journal of Clinical Endocrinology Metabolism
	The British Journal of Medicine
	Journal of the American Medical Association (3)
	Clinical Cancer Research
	Archives of Internal Medicine
New York Times Health Guide (9 Med-E-Pops)	An International Journal of Obstetrics and Gynaecology
	Human Reproduction
	British Medical Journal
	The Lancet (2)
	Journal of Allergy and Clinical Immunology
	Journal of the American Medical Association
	American Journal of Epidemiology
	New England Journal of Medicine
Health Day News (9 Med-E-Pops)	Archives of Neurology
	Autism
	Plos Genetics
	Journal of Palliative Medicine
	Pediatrics (2)
	Clinical Journal of the American Society of Nephrology
	Journal of Epidemiology and Community Health
	Neurology
Johns Hopkins News Release (5 Med-E-Pops)	Archives of Internal Medicine
	Journal of Consulting and Clinical Psychology
	Journal of Allergy and Clinical Immunology
	The Journal of Urology
	New England Journal of Medicine
Medical News Today (2 Med-E-Pops)	The Lancet
	Annals of Internal Medicine
Science Daily (1 Med-E-Pops)	International Journal of Cancer
Nature (1 Med-E-Pops)	PlosPathogens

4 Brief Description of the Corpora

Having introduced the process of corpus compilation, the following subsections (4.1 and 4.2) provide a brief description of both the non-academic and the academic corpora.

4.1 Brief Description of the Med-E-Pops Corpus

The 40 Med-E-Pops were published in seven different American and British electronic journals and were written in English. They were numbered from 1 to 40 following the date of publication in the electronic journal. As mentioned earlier, the corpus of Med-E-Pops amounts to a total of 21,840 words. The average number of words per Med-E-Pop was 546.

All the texts were single authored. Regarding the source of publication, one of them, *DocGuide*, is specially designed for doctors since internet readers need to register and select their profile as health professionals. Nonetheless, any internet user can enter the website and sign up. The reporters who write these versions are said to be doctors. *The New York Times Health Guide* is a special section that one of the main newspapers in the world devotes to health issues. The reporters are said to be specialised journalists. As for the rest of the publications – *Johns Hopkins News Release, Health Day News, Medical News Today, Science Daily*, and *Nature* – it can be read on their home page that health specialists (doctors, nurses, researchers, the RA researchers, or students) are in charge of writing these Med-E-Pops. These publications can be said to offer a reader-friendly interpretation of science. However, the survey-based approach carried out among practitioners validates these publications as highly reliable texts which disseminate medical knowledge outside the academia. All of them belong to the same kind of popular medical texts, and thus, there are no different levels of informality since all these Med-E-Pops aim at building trust around the research they report on. Table 7.6 shows an excerpt from the table that schematically describes these electronic publications (see Appendix 2 for the complete table).

Table 7.6 Excerpt from the general characteristics of each e-journal publication

Med-E-Pop journal	*Characteristics*
Doc's Guide (13 Med-E-Pops)	It does not name the Med-E-Pops writers. It does not mention how to reach Med-E-Pops writers. It does not mention the background of the Med-E-Pops writers in the home page. It does not advertise medical products. It does not include hyperlinks to other related Med-E-Pops. It includes informal interviews with the Med-E-RAs researchers. It does not explicitly state the nationality of the publication. The potential audience is defined by doctors or medical personnel.

The potential readership comprises a wide range of readers who should be competent in English – either native speakers or not – and who are regular internet users. Different characteristics of this emergent genre make readers, and medical personnel, trust not only these publications but also the research they report. The readers can be medical personnel, regular consumers of medical information who enjoy keeping up-to-date with the most recent health research, or readers who sporadically seek medical information. Hence, this amalgam of readers can be considered to be discourse community members of the Med-E-Pop genre.[5]

4.2. Brief Description of the Med-RAs Corpus

The corpus of Med-RAs amounts to a total of 182,065 words. The average number of words per article is 4,452, once the abstract, footnotes, acknowledgements, and bibliography were removed. The 40 Med-RAs published in international journals had a high impact factor classified in the first quartile of their category JCR (Q1) and, therefore, they were addressed to members of the same discourse community. The Med-RAs were downloaded from the internet in PDF format (see Appendix 3 to know more about these publications).

All the Med-RAs selected in the corpus were co-authored and all the researchers were mentioned by name. The number of authors varied and the Med-RAs were first published on line. To create a pair (Med-RA and Med-E-Pop), the Med-RAs were selected because their corresponding Med-E-Pops fulfilled in the first place the criteria mentioned in section 3 (see Table 7.4). As regards language, not all the authors shared English as their first language. Non-Anglophone scholars have written some of the articles studied, and all of them were published in prestigious American and British journals (see Appendix 3). These Med-RAs were studied as final products disregarding potential language mediation. Not surprisingly, as regards formal features, every Med-RA included in the corpus displayed a conventionalised structure based on moves (Swales, 1990; Nwogu, 1997; Bhatia, 2004). As in any canonical RA, the discourse community of these Med-RAs was expected to be composed by field-specialised doctors or field-related colleagues.

5 Final Remarks

The chapter has considered the need to look into a way of collecting authentic comparable corpora, describing the adopted steps and criteria. The self-compiled corpora will be the materials for the future study of the researchers' and writers' visibility in the medical RA genre and the consequent and emergent medical genre, the Med-E-Pop genre. To conduct textual and discursive analysis, this work posed a reflection regarding the extent to which linguists should turn to authentic academic knowledge dissemination channels to reflect on linguistic practices when dealing and transferring medical knowledge. I hereby presented a potential method to take an ethnographic approach to the collection of such corpora.

This piece of research attempts to show that to study real-life communication situations for research and teaching purposes, linguists and teachers should turn to the authentic texts users who produce and 'consume' these texts, in order to have access to representative samples and sources in their field – since these informants, or professionals, are constantly involved in their own discursive practices (Bhatia, 2004). Otherwise, language researchers may depict texts following sensible variables, yet distant from authentic and real communicative situations. If results failed to be obtained from representative types of discourses – being those oral or written – in EAP or ESP settings, our knowledge transfer to the academia and to the (future) professionals would have a timid visibility. Thus, the advantage of compiling authentic corpora counting on professionals' expertise is that the texts selected and, concretely, the medical context displayed, are meaningful to both EAP and ESP users and language mediators, and teachers. In addition, ethnographically informed research provides an insider perspective, complements the interpretation of results, raises users' awareness and reflexivity on lexico-grammatical aspects potentially unexplored by these specialised informants, and, above all, may allow prolonged collaboration among us (scholars/researchers and linguists/teachers). In that vein, our research could make a greater impact on society basing our studies, teaching practices and materials on our learners' authentic linguistic practices. Thus, taking an ethnographic approach to a corpus compilation for research and teaching purposes drives us from context to text, and back to context (Lillis, 2017), allowing us to effectively frame our linguistic research and outcomes.

In the same line, many researchers (Sinclair, 2004; O'Keeffe, McCarthy & Carter, 2007; Campoy, Bellés-Fortuño, & Gea-Valor, 2010 or Breeze, 2015; among others) suggest that a further advantage of this kind of corpus is that it can help EAP and ESP users and learners to 'enculturate' in the discursive practices of the professional communities of which they will become members. The use of such a corpus in EAP and ESP contexts not only integrates learning but also boosts learners' interest and effectiveness in consolidating their command of language throughout all their career as professionals of any discipline, as a considerable amount of literature recognises (Harrop, 2012; Herrando-Rodrigo & Yebra-Pertusa, 2014; Muñoz-Miquel, 2014; Di Pardo, 2015, etc.).

Acknowledging that there is not a single framework of corpus analysis to fit it all and that different ways of conducting trustworthy research are required, this chapter has described a potential methodology to manually compile corpora and to further discuss their application. Hence, researchers who aim at collecting their own corpus to raise awareness about potential factors affecting the texts production process may find this work transferable and applicable. This author believes that the nature of the research to be conducted deserved such an ethnographic approach, which could be seen as potentially laborious, yet meticulous and appropriate for its ultimate research aims. Hence, in line with the research objectives and strategies proposed by international institutions and strategies concerning the social impact of research (ONU, OMS, European Council, among others), which state that research must be *fair*, *findable*, *interoperable*, and *reusable* (see Horizon, 2020), this work offers a replicable research process for EAP and ESP researchers, teachers, and language mediators who may aim to explore new dimensions emerging from our new knowledge transfer scenarios and who may be interested in going down similar research paths.

Acknowledgement

This research has been supported by the Spanish *Ministerio de Economía, Industria y Competitividad* (FFI2017–84205-P) and by the *Fundación Ibercaja* together with the University of Zaragoza (JIUZ-2018-HUM-03). The author would also like to thank Dr. Silvia Murillo Ornat (University of Zaragoza, Spain) for her insightful comments on this paper.

References

Alvar-Ezquerra, M., Blanco-Rodríguez M.J. & Lagos, F. (1994). Diseño de un corpus español en el marco de un corpus europeo, in M. Alvar Ezquerra & J.A. Villena Ponsoda (eds.) *Estudios para un Corpus del Español*. Málaga: Servicio de Publicaciones de la Universidad de Málaga, 9–29.

Askehave I. & Zethsen, K. (2014). Gendered Construction of Leadership in Danish Job Advertisement. *Gender, Work & Organization* 21/6, 531–545.

Baker, M. (1995). Corpora in Translation Studies: An Overview and some Suggestions for Future Research. *Target* 7/2, 223–243.

Bergenholtz, H. & Tarp, S. (1995). *Manual of Specialised Lexicography*. Amsterdam/Philadelphia: John Benjamins.

Bhatia, V. K. (2004). *Worlds of Written Discourse: A Genre-based View*. London: Continuum.

Blommaert, J. (2006). *Discourse*. Cambridge. Cambridge University Press.

Breeze, R. (2015). Teaching the Vocabulary of Legal Documents: A Corpus-driven Approach. *ESP Today* 3/1, 44–63.

Butler, C. S. (2004). Corpus Studies and Functional Linguistic Theories. *Functions of Language* 11/2, 147–186.

Cabré, M.T. (2000). Elements for a Theory of Terminology: Towards an Alternative Paradigm. *Terminology* 6/1, 35–57.

Campagna, S., Garzone, G., Ilie, C. & Rowley-Jolivet, E. (2012). *Evolving Genres in Web-Mediated Communication.* Bern/Berlin/Frankfurt am Main/New York/Wien: Peter Lang.

Campoy, Mg., Bellés-Fortuño, B. & Gea-Valor, M. L. (2010). *Corpus Based Approaches to English Language Teaching.* London/New York: Continuum.

Cerezo, L., Manchón, R. & Nicolás-Conesa, F. (2019). What Do Learners Notice While Processing Written Corrective Feedback? A Look at Depth of Processing via Written Languaging, in Ronald P. Leow (ed.) *The Routledge Handbook of Second Language Research in Classroom Learning.* London/New York: Routledge

Ciprut, S. Curnyn, C., Davuluri, M., Sternberg, K. & Loeb, S. (2017). Twitter Activity Associated with U.S. News and World Report Reputation Scores for Urology Departments. *Urology* 108, 11–16.

Crowston, K. & Williams, M. (2000). Reproduced and Emergent Genres of Communication on the World Wide Web. *Information Society* 16, 201–216.

Di Pardo, D. (2015). CLIL in the Business English Classroom: From Language Learning to the Development of Professional Communication and Metacognitive Skills. *ELTWorldOnline.com.* http://blog.nus.edu.sg/eltwo/?p=4850 [retrieved 17.7.2016].

Evans, W. & Hornig-Priest, S. (1997). Science Content and Social Context. *Public Understanding of Science* 4, 327–340.

Flowerdew, J. (2002). Corpus-based Analyses in EAP, in Flowerdew, J. (ed.) *Academic Discourse.* Harlow: Longman, 95–114.

García-Izquierdo, I. & Montalt, V. (2013). Equigeneric and Intergeneric Translation in Patient-centred Care. *Hermes - Journal of Language and Communication in Business* 51, 39–54.

Giannoni, D. S. (2008). Popularizing Features in English Journals Editorials. *English for Specific Purposes* 27/2, 212–232.

Giltrow, J. & Stein, D. (2009). Genres in the Internet: Innovation, Evolution and Genre Theory, in J. Giltrow & D. Stein (eds) *Genres in the Internet.* Amsterdam: John Benjamins, 1–26.

Gotti, M. (2014). Reformulation and Recontextualization in Popularization Discourse. *Iberica* 27, 15–34.

Gotti, M. (2015). Insights into Medical Discourse: Diachronic and Sinchronic Perspectives. *ESP Today* 3/1, 5–24.

Harrop, E. (2012). Content and Language Integrated Learning (CLIL): Limitations and Possibilities. *Encuentro* 21, 57–70.

Harwood, N. & Petric, B. (2016). *Experiencing Master's Supervision. Perspectivo of International Students and Their Supervisors.* Oxford: Taylor & Francis.

Herrando-Rodrigo, I. (2012). Blurred Genres: Hybrid Functions in the Medical Field, in Berkenkotter, C., V. K. Bhatia & M. Gotti (eds.) *Insights into Academic Genre.* Bern: Peter Lang, 257–279.

Herrando-Rodrigo, I. (2014). Genre Evolution in Research Communication in English. *Revista Canaria de Estudios Ingleses* 69, 35–49.

Herrando-Rodrigo, I. & Yebra-Pertusa, JM. (2014). LFE y la necesidad de trabajar destrezas profesionales en Grados técnicos. *Revista de Lenguas para Fines Específicos* 20, 82–100.

Herring, S. C. (2012). Grammar and Electronic Communication, in C. Chapelle (ed.), *Encyclopedia of Applied linguistics.*
Horizon. (2020). European Commission Funding Research Programmes. https://ec.europa.eu/programmes/horizon2020/en [retrieved 1.3.2020].
Kennedy, G. (1998). *An Introduction to Corpus Linguistics.* London and New York: Routledge.
Lillis, T. (2013). *The Sociolinguistics of Writing.* Edinburgh Sociolinguistics. Edinburgh: Edinburgh University Press.
Lillis, T. (2017). Working with Ethnography to Explore Textual Practices. Seminar, University of Zaragoza, Spain, September 26th, 2017.
McCulloch, S. (2017). Hobson's Choice: The Effects of Research Evaluation on Academics' Writing Practices in England. *ASLIB Journal of Information Management* 69/5, 503–515.
Meyer, C. F. (2002). *English Corpus Linguistics.* Cambridge: Cambridge University Press.
Muñoz-Miquel, A. (2012). From the Original Article to the Summary for Patients: Reformulation Procedures in Intralingual Translation. *Linguistica Antverpiensia NS,* 153–162.
Muñoz-Miquel, A. (2014). El perfil y las competencias del traductor médico desde el punto de vista de los profesionales: una aproximación cualitativa. *TREC* 18, 163–181.
Mur-Dueñas, P. (2007). *A Contribution to the Intercultural Analysis of Metadiscourse in Business Management Research Articles in English and Spanish: A Corpus-driven Approach.* (Unpublished doctoral dissertation). University of Zaragoza, Zaragoza, Spain.
Mur-Dueñas, P. (2018). Disseminating and Constructing Academic Knowledge in Online Scholarly Journals: An Analysis of Virtual Special Issue Introductions. *Discourse, Context & Media* 24, 43–52.
Myers, G. (1989). Science for Women and Children: The Dialogue of Popular Science in the Nineteenth Century, in Christie, J. & S. Shuttleworth (eds.) *Nature Transfigured: Science and Literature.* Manchester: Manchester University Press, 171–200.
Nwogu, K. N. (1991). Structure of Science Popularizations: A Genre-analysis Approach to the Schema of Popularized Medical Texts. *English Specific Purposes* 10, 111–123.
Nwogu, K.N. (1997). The Medical Research Paper: Structure and Functions. *English* for *Specific Purposes* 16/2, 119–138.
O'Keeffe, A., McCarthy, M. & Carter, R. (2007). *From Corpus to Classroom: Language Use and Language Teaching.* Cambridge: Cambridge.
Orlikowski, W. & Yates, J. (1994). Genre Repertoire: The Structuring of Communicative Practices in Organizations. *Administrative Science Quarterly* 39, 541–574.
Paltridge, B., Starfield, S. & Tardy, C. M. (2016). *Ethnographic Perspectives on Academic Writing.* Oxford: Oxford University Press.
Sinclair, J. (1991). *Corpus, Concordance, Collocation.* Oxford: Oxford University Press.
Sinclair, J. (2004). *How to Use Corpora in Language Teaching.* The Netherlands: John Benjamins.
Swales, J. M. (1990). *Genre Analysis: English in Academic and Research Settings.* Cambridge: Cambridge University Press.

Thompson, N. & Hanley, D. (2017). Science Is Shaped by Wikipedia: Evidence from a Randomized Control Trial. *MIT Sloan Research Paper* 5238-17. https://ssrn.com/abstract=3039505 [retrieved 5.1.2018].

Tuck, J. (2016). 'That Ain't Going to Get You a Professorship': Discourses of Writing and the Positioning of Academics' Work with Student Writers in UK Higher Education. *Studies in Higher Education* 41/9, 1612–1626.

Appendices

Appendix 1: Questionnaire distributed among practitioners for the corpus survey-based study.

Appendix 2: General characteristics of each e-journal publication.

Med-E-Pop Journal	*Characteristics*
Health Day News (9 Med-E-Pops)	It names the Med-E-Pops writers. It mentions how to reach Med-E-Pops writers. It mentions the background of the Med-E-Pops writers in the home page. It mentions the background and prestige of the Med-E-Pops publication. It does not advertise medical products. It does not include hyperlinks to other related Med-E-Pops. It includes informal interviews with the Med-E-RAs researchers. It explicitly states that it is an American publication. The potential audience is conformed by Internet readers who search reliable medical Med-RA adaptations.
Johns Hopkins News Release (5 Med-E-Pops)	It names the Med-E-Pops writers. It mentions how to reach Med-E-Pops writers. It mentions the background and prestige of the Med-E-Pops writers in the home page. It mentions the background and prestige of the Med-E-Pops publication. It does not advertise medical products. It does not include hyperlinks to other related Med-E-Pops. It includes informal interviews with the Med-E-RAs researchers. It explicitly states that it is an American publication. The potential audience is conformed by Internet readers and medical personnel.

(*Continued*)

Med-E-Pop Journal	*Characteristics*
Medical News Today (2 Med-E-Pops)	It does not name the Med-E-Pops writers. It does not mention how to reach Med-E-Pops writers but you can tweet the editors. It does not mention the background and prestige of the Med-E-Pops writers in the home page. It does not mention the background and prestige of the Med-E-Pops publication. It does not advertise medical products. It does not include hyperlinks to other related Med-E-Pops. It includes informal interviews with the Med-E-RAs researchers. It explicitly states that it is a British publication.
Science Daily (1 Med-E-Pops)	It does not name the Med-E-Pops writers. It does not mention how to reach Med-E-Pops writers. It does not mention the background and prestige of the Med-E-Pops writers in the home page. It does not mention the background and prestige of the Med-E-Pops publication. It advertises medical insurances. It does not include hyperlinks to other related Med-E-Pops. It includes informal interviews with the Med-E-RAs researchers. It does not explicitly state the nationality of the publication. The potential audience is conformed by Internet readers who search reliable medical Med-RAs adaptations.
Nature (1 Med-E-Pops)	It names the Med-E-Pops writers. It mentions how to reach Med-E-Pops writers. It mentions the background and prestige of the Med-E-Pops writers in the home page. It mentions the background and prestige of the Med-E-Pops publication. It does not advertise medical products. It includes hyperlinks to other related Med-E-Pops. It does not include informal interviews with the Med-E-RAs researchers. It explicitly states that it is an American publication. The potential audience is conformed by readers who aim to stay up-to-date with the latest scientific news.

Appendix 3: Corpora titles, dates and source of publication, and writers.

Before beginning, please write your Field/Speciality________ and years of experience as practitioner______

1 How often do you read medical articles written in English?
2 Do you read medical popularisations published in English on the Internet (New Your Times Health guide, Doc Guide, etc.?[6] (If so, please mention the electronic journal you usually read) Why?
3 If you read a medical popularisation and you are interested in the topic covered in it, do you read the corresponding research article?
4 If you think that research articles differ from popularisations, what do you think the differences are?

- USE OF LANGUAGE. Have you observed any differences? Tick the ones you have observed:
    - Passive voice
    - Reported speech
    - Pronouns
    - Nouns
    - Others
- PURPOSE. Is the content expressed differently in medical research articles and in electronic popularisations? If so, could you identify the reasons by ticking the ones you have observed:
    - Different audience (different readers)
    - Different means of publications
    - Others:...................
- STRUCTURE. Experimental medical research articles are generally structured following the so-called IMRAD pattern (Introduction, Methods, Results And Discussion)

5 Do medical popularisations follow the same *IMRAD* pattern as experimental research articles do?

Thank you very much indeed for your contribution
Isabel Herrando-Rodrigo (herrando@unizar.es)

Pair	*Med-RAs titles*	*Sources*	*Date of publication*	*Med-E-Pops titles*	*Source*	*Date of publication*
1	Fetal exposure to herpesviruses may be associated with pregnancy-induced hypertensive disorders and preterm birth in a Caucasian population	*BJOG An International Journal of Obstetrics and Gynaecology*	2008	Having a Baby: Blood Pressure Troubles Linked to a Virus Infection	*New York Times Health*	March 4th, 2008
2	Presence of depressive symptoms during early pregnancy and the risk of preterm delivery: a prospective cohort study	*Human Reproduction, Vol. 24, No. 1 pp. 146–153.*	2009	Having a Baby: Depression Linked to Premature Deliveries	*New York Times Health*	November 4th, 2008
3	Identification of Tuberculosis Susceptibility Genes with Human Macrophage Gene Expression Profiles	*PlosPathogens*	December 2008	Opening the door to TB	*Nature*	February 2009
4	Predictors of driving safety in early Alzheimer disease	*Neurology*	Vol 72, February 10th, 2009	Tests May Predict Driving Safety in People with Alzheimer's Disease	*HealthNews*	February 2009

5	*Predicting risk of type 2 diabetes in England and Wales: prospective derivation and validation of QDScore*	*British? Medical Journal*	March 25th, 2009	Awareness: Calculator Gives Risk of Type 2 Diabetes	*New York Times Health*	March 24th, 2009
6	Comparing the Quality of the Suture Anastomosis and the Learning Curves Associated with Performing Open, Freehand, and Robotic-Assisted Laparoscopic Pyeloplasty in a Swine Animal Model	*American College of Surgeons*	April 4th, 2009	Robot Improves Suture Proficiency More Rapidly for Surgeons Inexperienced in Laparoscopic Techniques	*Doctor's Guide*	April 20th, 2009
7	Timing of initiation of antiretroviral therapy in AIDS-free HIV-1-infected patients: a collaborative analysis of 18 HIV cohort studies	*www.thelancet.com Published online DOI:10.1016/S0140–6736(09)60612-7*	April 9th, 2009	AIDS: Earlier Drug Treatment for AIDS Saves More Lives, Study Finds	*New York Times Health*	April 13th, 2009
8	Effectiveness of haemodialysis access with an autologous tissue-engineered vascular graft: a multicentre cohort study	*The Lancet*	Vol 373 April 25th, 2009	The First Completely Autologous Tissue-Engineered Vascular Grafts For Dialysis Patients - 'A Revolutionary Milestone'	*Medical News Today*	April 28th, 2009

(Continued)

Pair	*Med-RAs titles*	*Sources*	*Date of publication*	*Med-E-Pops titles*	*Source*	*Date of publication*
9	A phase II study of weekly topotecan and docetaxel in heavily treated patients with recurrent uterine and ovarian cancers	*Gynecologic Oncology (2009), doi:10.1016/j. ygyno.2009.02.018*	April 26th, 2009	New Treatment Shows Promise Against Recurrent Gynecologic Cancers	*Doctor's Guide*	July 21st, 2009
10	Disorders of Balance and Vestibular Function in US Adults	*Archives of Internal Medicine*	Vol 169(10): 938–944, May 25th, 2009	Survey Suggests Higher Risks of Falls Due To Dizziness In Middle-Aged And Older Americans	*Johns Hopkins News Release*	May 20th, 2009
11	The Child Anxiety Prevention Study: Intervention Model and Primary Outcomes	*Journal of Consulting and Clinical Psychology*	2009, Vol 77(3), 580–587	Children of Adults with Anxiety Disorder May Need Help Too	*Johns Hopkins News Release*	June 1st, 2009
12	Aspirin in the primary and secondary prevention of vascular disease: collaborative meta-analysis of individual participant data from randomised trials	*The Lancet*	Vol 373 May 30, 2009	Benefits of Aspirin as Primary Prevention of Vascular Events Do Not Outweigh Risks	*Doctor's Guide*	May 29th, 2009

13	Perinatal Outcomes in Nutritionally Monitored Obese Pregnant Women: A Randomized Clinical Trial	*Journal of the National Medical Association*	Vol 101(6), June 2009 569	Study Suggests Obese Women Should Not Gain Weight During Pregnancy	*Doctor's Guide*	June 2nd, 2009
14	Higher serum folate levels are associated with a lower risk of atopy and wheeze	*The Journal of Allergy and Clinical Immunology*	Vol 123(6): 1253–1259, June 2009	Folic Acid May Help Treat Allergies, Asthma	*Johns Hopkins News Release*	April 30th, 2009
15	Prevalence, treatment, and associated disability of mental disorders in four provinces in China during 2001–05: an epidemiological survey	*The Lancet*	Vol 373(9680): 2041–2053, June 13, 2009	Mental Illness: Far More Chinese Have Mental Disorders Than Previously Reported, Study Finds	*New York Times Health*	June 16th, 2009
16	Mediterranean Diet, Alzheimer Disease, and Vascular Mediation	*Archives of Neurology*	June 16th, 2009	Mediterranean Diet Aids the Aging Brain: Study Eating plan seems to reduce the risk of cognitive impairment, dementia	*Health Day News*	February 2009
17	Interaction Between the Serotonin Transporter Gene (*5-HTTLPR*), Stressful Life Events, and Risk of Depression	*JAMA*	Vol 301(23), June 17, 2009	Report on Gene for Depression Is Now Faulted	*New York Times Health*	June 17th, 2009

(*Continued*)

Pair	*Med-RAs titles*	*Sources*	*Date of publication*	*Med-E-Pops titles*	*Source*	*Date of publication*
18	Venom immunotherapy reduces large local reactions to insect stings	*The Journal of Allergy and Clinical Immunology Available online May 14, 2009*	Vol 123(6): 1371–1375, June 2009	Insect Venom Shots Work For Severe "Local" Sting Reactions, Too	*Johns Hopkins News Release*	June 29th, 2009
19	Effect of Gastric Bypass Surgery on Kidney Stone Disease	*The Journal of Urology*	Vol 181: 2573–2577, June 2009	ROUX-EN-Y Weight Loss Surgery Raises Kidney Stone Risk	*Johns Hopkins News Release*	June 17th, 2009
20	Contact With Beach Sand Among Beachgoers and Risk of Illness	*American Journal of Epidemiology*	Vol 170(2): 164–172, June 18th, 2009	Hazards: At the Beach, Watch Out for Dirty Sand, Too	*New York Times Health*	July 21st, 2009
21	Changes in case fatality of aneurysmal subarachnoid haemorrhage over time, according to age, sex, and region: a meta-analysis	*The Lancet*	Vol 8 (7): 635–642, July 2009	Improvements in Diagnosis, Treatment Linked to Reduced Risk of Death in Patients With Brain Haemorrhage	*Doctor's Guide*	June 3rd, 2009

22	Bone Mineral Density in Estrogen-Deficient Young Women	*The Journal of Clinical Endocrinology and Metabolism*	94(7): 2277–2283, July 2009	Study Defines Strategy to Protect Bones in Women, Girls With Primary Ovarian Insufficiency	*Doctor's Guide*	June19th, 2009
23	Rates of Serious Infection after Changes in Regimens for Medical Abortion	*New England Journal of Medicine*	Vol 361;2, July 9th, 2009	Abortion Pill Study Suggests Way to Limit Infection	*New York Times Health*	July 9th, 2009
24	Prevalence and Repair of Intraoperatively Diagnosed Patent Foramen Ovale and Association With Perioperative Outcomes and Long-term Survival	*JAMA*	Vol 302(3): 290–297, July 2009	Not Clear Benefit Seen for Incidentally Repairing Patent Foramen Ovale	*Doctor's Guide*	July 14th, 2009
25	A Pooled Analysis of the Effect of Condoms in Preventing HSV-2 Acquisition	*Archives of Internal Medicine*	Vol 169(13): 1233–1240, July 13, 2009	Condoms Associated With Moderate Protection Against Herpes Simplex Virus 2	*Doctor's Guide*	July 15th, 2009

(Continued)

Pair	*Med-RAs titles*	*Sources*	*Date of publication*	*Med-E-Pops titles*	*Source*	*Date of publication*
26	Use of fertility drugs and risk of ovarian cancer: Danish population based cohort study	*BJM*	2009;338; b249, July 15th, 2009	Fertility Drugs and Ovarian Cancer Not Linked, Study Says	*New York Times Health*	July 15th, 2009
27	Hormone Therapy and Ovarian Cancer	*JAMA*	302(3): 298–305, July 15th, 2009	Hormone Therapy Use Associated With Increased Risk of Ovarian Cancer	*Doctor's Guide*	July 15th, 2009
28	High Levels of CirculatingVEGFR2+ Bone Marrow -Derived Progenitor Cells Correlate with Metastatic Disease in Patients with Pediatric Solid Malignancies	*Clinical Cancer Research*	Vol, 15(14) 4561–4571, July 15, 2009	Circulating Blood Cells Are Important Predictors of Cancer Spread in Children	*Doctor's Guide*	July 15th, 2009
29	Parenting stress and psychological functioning among mothers of preschool children with autism and developmental delay	*Autism*	Vol 13(4); 375–387, 2009	Parents of Children With Autism Report High Stress Levels	*Health Day News*	July 17th, 2009

30	Evolution and Survival on Eutherian Sex Chromosomes	*Plos Genetics Published on line July 2009*	Vol 5(7): e1000568	Male Sex Chromosome on Its Way Out: Study	*Health Day News*	July 17th, 2009
31	Positive and Negative Religious Coping and Well-Being in Women with Breast Cancer	*Journal of Palliative Medicine*	Vol 12(6):537–545, July 2009	Spiritual Outlook Can Affect Mental Health in Breast Cancer	*Health Day News*	July 17th, 2009
32	Prenatal Airborne Polycyclic Aromatic Hydrocarbon Exposure and Child IQ at Age 5 Years	*Pediatrics published online July 20, 2009*	Vol 124(2): e195–e202, August 2009	Exposure to Common Pollutant in Womb Might Lower IQ	*HealthDay News*	July 20th, 2009
33	Exposure to Tobacco on the Internet: Content Analysis of Adolescents' Internet Use	*Pediatrics published online July 20, 2009*	Vol 124(2): e180–e186, August 2009	Internet May Be Newest Venue for Teen Tobacco Exposure	*HealthDay News*	July 20th, 2009
34	Phosphorus and Potassium Content of Enhanced Meat and Poultry Products: Implications for Patients Who Receive Dialysis	*Clinical Journal of the American Society of Nephrology Draft available on July 23rd, 2009*	Vol 4: 1370–1373, August' 2009	Fresh-Meat Additives May Be Dangerous for Kidney Patients	*HealthDay News*	July 23rd, 2009

(*Continued*)

Pair	Med-RAs titles	Sources	Date of publication	Med-E-Pops titles	Source	Date of publication
35	Repeated measures of serum glucose and insulin in relation to postmenopausal breast cancer	*International Journal of Cancer International Union Against Cancer available online July 23rd, 2009 as a draft for the Medical School of the University of Sheffield*	Available on line in August. 2009 in press: Dec 1; 125(11): 2704–2710	Einstein Scientists Link Elevated Insulin to Increased Breast Cancer Risk	*Science Daliy*	July 9th, 2009
36	When to Start Antiretroviral Therapy in Resource-Limited Settings	*Annals of Internal Medicine*	Vol 151(3):157–166 August 4, 2009	Treatment For HIV In South Africa Would Be More Effective If Started Earlier	*Medical News Today*	July 21st, 2009
37	Peginterferon Alfa-2b or Alfa-2a with Ribavirin for Treatment of Hepatitis C Infection	*The New England Journal of Medicine*	361: 580–93, August 6th, 2009	Top Hepatitis C Treatments Equally Effective	*Johns Hopkins News Release*	July 22nd, 2009
38	Surgical Mask vs N95 Respirator for Preventing Influenza Among Health Care Workers	*JAMA Journal of American Medical Association*	October 10th 2009	Surgical Masks Non-Inferior to N95 Respirators for Preventing Influenza Among Health Care Workers	*Docguide*	October 10th, 2009

39	Exposure to Fine Particulate Matter and Acute Effects on Blood Pressure: Effect Modification by Measures of Obesity and Location	*Journal of Epidemiology and Community Health*	October 15th 2009	Smog Tougher on the Obese	*HealthDay*	October 15th, 2009
40	Critically Ill Patients With 2009 Influenza A(H1N1) Infection in Canada	*JAMA Journal of American Medical Association*	October 21st 2009	Influenza A(H1N1) Critical Illness Can Occur Rapidly; Predominantly in Young Patients	*DocGuide*	October 21st, 2009

Notes

1 See for Horizon 2020 societal objectives (https://ec.europa.eu/programmes/horizon2020/en/h2020-section/societal-challenges).

2 This research is a contribution to the project "*Hacia una mayor visibilidad y diseminación de la investigación científica: estudio lingüístico, retorico y pragmático de géneros digitales en inglés como lengua internacional*" funded by Plan Nacional I+D+i (FFI2017-84205) and to the project JIUZ-2018-HUM-03.

3 The study of the complex nature of the popularisation genre, its discourse, and its realisations have received a lot of attention in applied linguistics for decades (c.f. Myers, 1989; Nwogu, 1991; Bergenholtz & Tarp, 1995; Evans & Hornig-Priest, 1997; Cabré, 2000; Giannoni, 2008; Gotti, 2014, 2015). This study further aimed to study a phenomenon that has been greatly influenced by the medium of publication: the internet.

4 Direct translation from Spanish into English, made by the author of this piece of research.

5 It should not be overlooked that the high demand of this broad readership spectrum, which displays a potential wide variety of cultural, professional, and personal backgrounds, has inspired e-journals to come to a sort of generic agreement. In other words, the medium and the discourse community (writers and readers) have construed and, therefore, accepted a valid generic evolution of the medical dissemination article or medical popularisation.

6 By Medical popularisations, I mean medical research articles versions designed for the lay or general public different from the medical personnel.

8 Researching Academic Genres, Language, and Discourse with Computer-Assisted Qualitative Data Analysis Software

Ana Bocanegra-Valle

1 Introduction

Qualitative research is growing considerably across Applied Linguistics, either as a field of inquiry on its own or as a supplement to quantitative research. This approach makes use of unstructured or non-numerical data obtained from diverse forms of data gathering (such as interviews, case studies, participant observations, open-ended survey responses, memos, diaries, social media, or web content) to retrieve results and discuss them critically. These data collection procedures are common when researching the genre, linguistic, and discourse features in academic settings because qualitative studies are numerous, and researchers more often aim at identifying tendencies, behaviours, relationships, and multiple realities rather than counting data, obtaining averages, and examining frequencies.

Coding, organising, interpreting, and understanding the resulting mass of qualitative data are cumbersome and time-consuming. However, these tasks may be alleviated and the data fine-grained by the use of computer-assisted qualitative data analysis software (CAQDAS). The reduction of manual tasks and the obtainment of more professional results by facilitating data management, ensuring rigour, and supporting findings with evidence are among the most prominent advantages of CAQDAS (Smit, 2002; Dörnyei, 2007; Bazeley & Jackson, 2013; Hilal & Alabri, 2013).

Even though current literature offers much theoretically based guidance to using computers for a qualitative data analysis (Richards & Richards, 1987; Fielding & Lee, 1998; Weitzman, 2000; Silverman, 2005; Lewins & Silver, 2007; Davidson & di Gregorio, 2011; Bazeley & Jackson, 2013; among others), very few empirical studies have investigated how qualitative researchers actually use computer technology to support their research (a notable exception is Woods et al., 2015 – see a discussion in section 2.2). Moreover, no attention has so far been paid to the fact of using computers for the qualitative analysis of the language and discourse that occur in academic settings. This study, thus, is an initial approach to this issue and contributes to partially fill this gap.

This chapter has been organised into three main sections. First, I introduce the construct of qualitative research and briefly discuss its potential to conduct research on language use and discourse in academic settings. I then explore the role that CAQDAS can play in qualitative research and focus on ATLAS.ti and NVivo – two popular software packages that are increasingly being used in English for specific and academic purposes-related research. The next section contains the study itself. First, I provide the study aims, describe the dataset, and explain the methodology carried out to gather and analyse the data. Results are then profiled to conclude with a discussion of the main findings.

2 Qualitative Research and Data Analysis Software

2.1 *Why Qualitative Research When Investigating the Language, Genres, and Discourse that Prevail in Academic Settings?*

Current research in the field of Applied Linguistics can be enhanced by means of qualitative data analysis. Adopting a qualitative approach to a piece of research helps to enrich the collection, management, and in terpretation of data because, as Denzin and Lincoln (2011: 8) observed, emphasis is placed on "the qualities of entities and on processes and meanings that are not experimentally examined or measured (if measured at all) in terms of quantity, amount, intensity, or frequency". Thanks to this, it is possible to stress "the socially constructed nature of reality, the intimate relationship between the researcher and what is studied, and the situational constraints that shape inquiry".

Qualitative research is on the rise among the Social Sciences and Humanities. It explores unstructured or non-numerical data to yield results and discuss findings. Such data may be obtained from various data collection instruments, from "more traditional" (like interviews, surveys, diaries, or essays) to the latest communication modes featuring in social media and web content (like blogs or Facebook posts). As Fielding and Lee (1998: 1) pointed out after the outbreak of CAQDAS, "[t]he rapid development and diffusion of the Internet has revolutionized scholarly communication, and provides ready access to large volumes of widely dispersed information". Today, qualitative research sources do not only comprise written artefacts and text collections of any kind, but other forms of audio-visual material (such as photographs, paintings, illustrations, audio and video recordings) originally developed and gathered *ad hoc* by the researcher, or still widely dispersed on the Internet.

Qualitative data analysis "emphasize[s] words rather than quantification in the collection and analysis of data" (Bryman, 2008: 366); therefore, "coding" is at the heart of qualitative research. Coding is the process of subdividing data and assigning tags or labels to stretches of text (chunks of words, sentences, or entire paragraphs) from a collection of documents. Non-text documents, like graphics, video, and audio files, can also be labelled, so that units of meaning are allocated to the explicit and implicit information they contain. Labels entail units of meaning ("codes") that can be organised and combined together (into categories called "nodes") with a view to making connections, interpreting, and understanding the resulting mass of collected data. Saldaña (2009: 3) defines a code in a qualitative inquiry as, most often, "a word or short phrase that symbolically assigns a summative, salient, essence-capturing, and/or evocative attribute for a portion of language-based or visual data". By establishing these codes, the collected data is categorised in terms of commonalities, differences, patterns, and structures, thus creating a conceptual scheme that "helps the researcher to ask questions, to compare across data, to change or drop categories and to make a hierarchical order of them" (Basit, 2003: 144).

Two main coding styles or procedures prevail in qualitative research: "deductive coding" and "inductive coding". Deductive (also "a priori") coding is a top-down process which begins with pre-set themes, codes, or categories that have been previously suggested in the literature. A list of deductive codes emerges from the literature review previously carried out by the researcher and data is coded in line with these pre-established themes or categories. Inductive (also "emerging" or "grounded") is a bottom-up and iterative process which is initiated with a set of themes, codes, or categories that the researcher has anticipated and brings to the study – that is, "a provisional 'start list' of codes prior to fieldwork" (Basit, 2003: 145). S/he may have gathered them prior to the data collection event or by reading and familiarising with data once collected. Initial codes will be reformulated as the investigation proceeds. In both inductive and deductive coding, the analysis procedure may be open or axial. The process of "open coding" comes in the first stage, and implies reading the data several times and annotating the texts line by line, sentence by sentence, or paragraph by paragraph with key words, observations, or ideas so that data is segmented or disentangled and expressed in the form of concepts, categories, or codes (Flick, 1998). "Axial coding" is the next step and helps to refine the categories and assemble the data in many ways. It implies the identification of primary and secondary themes/sub-themes (also categories and sub-categories) in the data and then their arrangement so that themes are connected to and harmonised with the salient findings.

Fielding and Lee (1998: 87) further explain that qualitative coding aims at stimulating "the identification of analytic themes", organising "the data so that the strength of its support for those themes can be determined", illustrating "those themes by providing quotable material", and supporting "data reduction by representing its key features and identifying redundant peripheral or irrelevant data". For Maxwell (2009: 236), coding is "the main categorizing strategy in qualitative research" and, unlike coding in quantitative research, it does not contribute to generating frequency counts of items, but to breaking down and rearranging data into categories "that facilitate comparison between things in the same category and between categories".

Coding is a rather slow and cumbersome process. If done by hand, it may also turn out to be rather inefficient and inaccurate. Exploration of the methodology sections of many qualitative studies in the field of academic discourse shows that manual or traditional coding is, still today, a common practice: researchers use coloured markers or pencils to mark the data, write down notes on the text sides, use sticky notes to annotate codes, photocopy texts on coloured paper according to sources (e.g. interviewees' transcripts), use word processors to highlight different sections of a text in different ways, cut and paste highlighted text onto cards or separate documents, etc. As shall be discussed in the next subsection, computer technology and specific software, however, help to alleviate this task by assisting researchers with "the mechanization of the clerical aspects of data management" (Dörnyei, 2007: 263).

2.2 *The Role of CAQDAS*

The first generation of CAQDAS, also referred to as qualitative data analysis software (QDAS), dates back to the early 1980s. CAQDAS may be defined as those stand-alone software packages that were designed "to bring the power of computing to the often labor-intensive work of qualitative research" (Davidson & di Gregorio, 2011: 627) and to increase the effectiveness and efficiency of learning from research-purposeful data (Bazeley & Jackson, 2013). In order to facilitate the qualitative analysis of texts, graphics, audio, or video, CAQDAS includes a number of tools which may vary across packages (e.g. coding tools, query tools, annotation tools, linking tools, text searching tools, or mapping and visualising tools – see Figure 8.1 for a sample NVivo screen shot).[1] It should be noted, however, that unlike statistical or quantitative data software, CAQDAS are data management packages and they do not analyse data; instead, they support the researcher during the data analysis process (Dörnyei, 2007; Bazeley & Jackson, 2013; Zamawe, 2015). In this line, García-Horta and Guerra-Ramos (2009: 151) observed that CAQDAS capabilities "must not be overestimated, since computers are still unable to perform an independent rational process or substitute the analyst's capacities".

The benefits offered by CAQDAS outweigh the two most immediate drawbacks of first purchasing the package and then gaining the required expertise to run that software. The use of CAQDAS requires an economic investment that not all researchers can afford. This is particularly evident among the Social Sciences and Humanities disciplines, in which poorly funded research groups abound. Contrary to the case of quantitative research, and to the best of my knowledge, there are no open-source

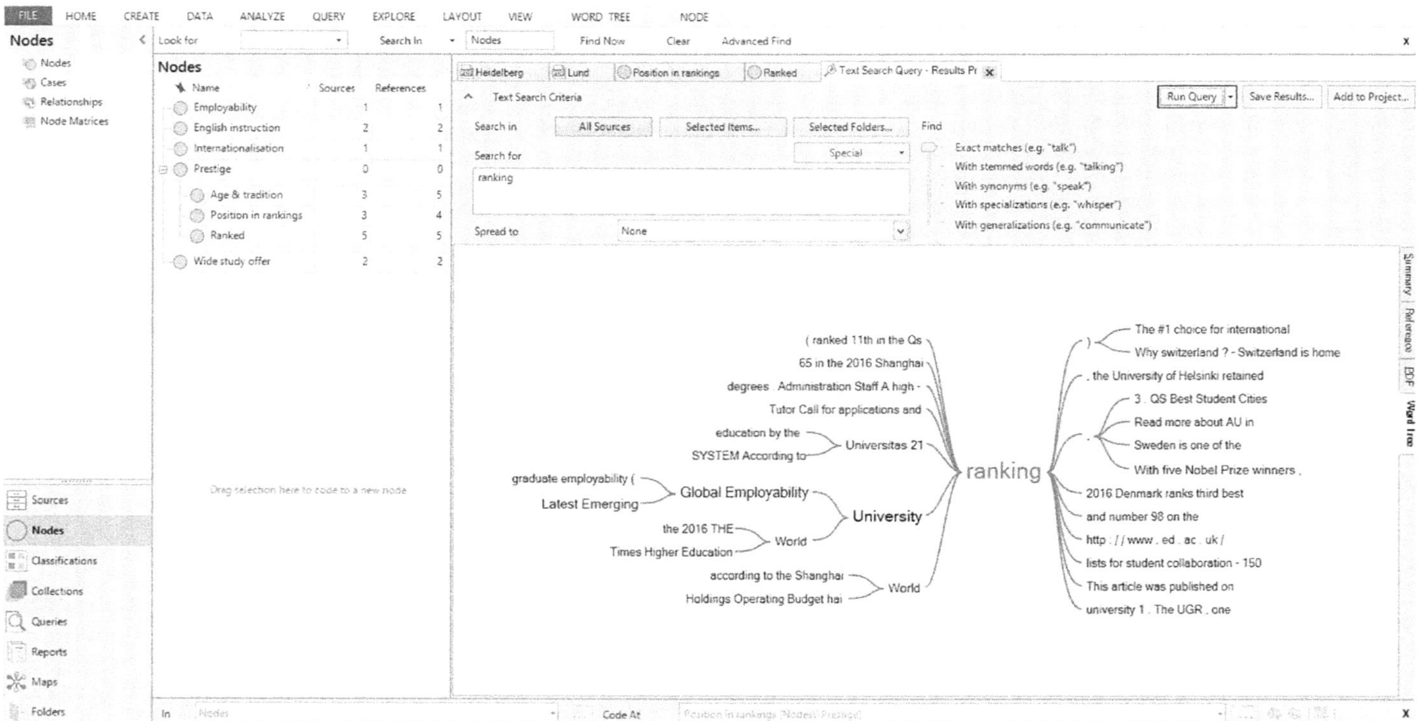

Figure 8.1 NVivo visualizing tool showing connections for the code “ranking” by means of a word tree.

shareware or freeware software solutions currently available for implementation in qualitative research. Also, the mastery of a software package requires time, training, and effort, and CAQDAS is no exception. To succeed in their endeavour, researchers not only need to have easy and funded access to dedicated training (classroom courses, online workshops, or consultancy services) but also be ready to spend long time periods gaining control over the software and developing the necessary skills before expecting to apply it in an ongoing research project – at least the data-handling basic functions of the package like how to import, organise, analyse, and visualise text-based research data, how to use coding queries and find connections, or how to display data. As Basit (2003: 153) claimed, "it may take several weeks to get acquainted with a software package to code qualitative data electronically"; therefore, this should be taken into account by the research community and "those who have not done it [electronic coding] already should build it into their development plans to allow time for training to use packages for analysing qualitative data".

Regardless of the aforementioned two disadvantages, current literature (Smit, 2002; Silverman, 2005; Dörnyei, 2007; Hwang, 2008; Bazeley & Jackson, 2013; Hilal & Alabri, 2013; Woods et al., 2015) lists the advantages of CAQDAS programmes as follows:

- They help to organise a number of muddled data documents so that they can be easily accessible. Data as a whole is more organised and can be analysed more effectively; in fact, it allows for analyses that could not be carried out otherwise (i.e. manually).
- They facilitate data management – particularly, large data becomes more manageable. Any kind of material under analysis (e.g. text, photographs) can be searched and located more quickly and easily.
- They reduce manual tasks because processes are automated and electronically performed. More particularly, they speed up and simplify the tasks of coding and retrieving data, and ensure rigour to the whole coding process. Also, coded data can be more easily, efficiently, and accurately retrieved for analysis.
- The transcription of video and audio files into text is not required; graphics, video, and audio files can be coded directly. Also, text and non-text materials can be linked, jointly coded, and analysed.
- They help to establish relationships between data (ideas, themes) by creating links among data chunks, codes, and memos. The resulting codes and networks can be displayed visually in a number of formats to suit the goals and requirements of a particular discipline (e.g. comparison diagrams, project maps, mind maps, word clouds, word trees, cluster analysis, hierarchical charts, or geovisualisations).
- The whole research process can be more effective in terms of project management and teamwork. Collaborative research is facilitated by

combining individual projects and facilitating access to group projects that have been developed by researchers at various institutions or even at distant locations in any part of the world.
- They lead to more professional results. CAQDAS helps to support and better test findings with evidence. The processes can be more transparent and replicable – hence more credible. CAQDAS also ensures more methodical, thorough, and attentive work at the same time it adds validity, rigour, transparency, and trustworthiness to the whole analytical process and the research outcomes.

Empirical studies that investigate how researchers use CAQDAS to support research are rare. A notable exception is Woods et al. (2015), who investigated how researchers used two particular packages (ATLAS.ti and NVivo) to learn about the scholars themselves and how software was used to support their research. Woods et al. (2015) explored 763 empirical research articles published in the Scopus database between 1994 and 2013 and found, among others, that the number of CAQDAS articles published was rising each year, that researchers using these packages came from a wide range of geographic and disciplinary areas (the majority of studies published in health sciences journals), and that scholars were not "leveraging QDAS to analyze new forms of data or adapting their research practices to leverage new program features" (page 611). As shall be seen in section 3, this study concurs with some of the findings revealed in Woods et al. (2015) but they cannot be fully compared given the wider scope, the variety of disciplines addressed, and the higher number of articles these scholars used for their analysis.

2.3 ATLAS.ti and NVivo as Examples of CAQDAS

Today, a number of CAQDAS programmes are widely used for qualitative research within the Social Sciences and Humanities. They include: Annotations, AQUAD, askSam, ATLAS.ti, Datagrav, Dedoose, Ethno, ETHNOGRAPH, f4analyse, FilemakerPro, Focuss On, HyperResearch, HyperSoft, Info Select, Martin, MAXQDA, NVivo, NUD*IST, QDAMiner, Qippa, Qualrus, Quirkos, Raven's Eye, SaturateApp, Textanalyser, Transana, weftQDA, or XSight.

Fielding and Lee (1998: 6–11), and Weitzman (2000) classified CAQDAS into two broad types and three subtypes each. A first group comprises "generic software", and includes:

- i Word processors: the usual software used to manipulate text;
- ii Text retrievers: they find specific terms or phrases in one or several files; and
- iii Textbase managers: they are similar to database software programmes that store text in an organised fashion.

A second group comprises "dedicated qualitative analysis packages". These have been developed exclusively for use by qualitative researchers and include the following sup-types:

- i Code-and-retrieve programmes: codes are assigned to segments of text and later on the text passages are retrieved and displayed according to the coding;
- ii Code-based theory builders: codes may turn into categories which suggest relevant themes in the data to support a researcher's theory; and
- iii Conceptual network builders (also textual mapping software): they bring to the surface the underlying structure of a text by interconnecting nodes into semantic networks.

For this study purposes, I will focus on two software packages, ATLAS.ti and NVivo. The reasons for choosing these particular packages are (i) because they are "among the best available and potentially most useful qualitative data analysis (QDA) tools" (Lewis, 2004: 439); and (ii) because they have attained greater name recognition among researchers publishing academic discourse-related studies. As current literature attests and shall be seen in this study, ATLAS.ti and NVivo have become two powerful computer programmes for qualitative data analysis that assist linguists when working with unstructured, non-numerical data. Following Fielding and Lee's (1998) and Weitzman's (2000) classification of CAQDAS mentioned earlier, ATLAS.ti and NVivo are examples of "code-based theory builders".[2]

ATLAS.ti (<http://atlasti.com/product/what-is-atlas-ti/>) was the outcome of a research project titled "Archive for Technology, the Lifeworld, and Everyday Language", developed at the Technical University Berlin in 1989 by Thomas Muhr (Muhr, 1991). The first commercial version was released in 1993 as ATLAS/ti under the company name "Scientific Software Development", and later became ATLAS.ti GmbH. This software was initially designed to help researchers when interpreting and dealing with large amounts of texts as well as with annotations, concepts, and complex structures (Muhr, 1991). ATLAS.ti 8 is the latest version to date available for Windows and Mac.

NVivo (<http://www.qsrinternational.com/nvivo/nvivo-products>) is produced by QSR International and dates back to 1999 when the first NVivo software products were developed by Tom Richards. To date, the latest version is NVivo 11 (for Windows and Mac), released in 2015, and comes in three editions: NVivo Starter (basic), NVivo Pro (which allows for working with ordinary text, images, video, audio, emails, spreadsheets, online surveys, web content, and social media), and NVivo Plus (which is more robust and allows for social network and big data analysis).

To the best of my knowledge, the first study in the field of academic discourse that used a CAQDAS package was John Flowerdew's study published in the *Journal of Second Language Writing* in 1999 on the problems faced by Hong Kong researchers when writing for scholarly publication in English.[3] This scholar used ATLAS.ti to analyse the data resulting from (i) the interviews to 26 Hong Kong scholars from a number of disciplines, and (ii) a questionnaire survey. Data was loaded onto ATLAS.ti and sorted and resorted into categories. The aim of this qualitative analysis was to look for both commonalities and differences within the group of participants.

3 ATLAS.ti and NVivo in Academic Genre-, Language-, and Discourse-Related Research

3.1 Study Aims

This study explored the use of CAQDAS, and more precisely, the use of ATLAS.ti and NVivo by researchers dealing with academic discourse, genres, and language. My final aim was to (i) ascertain if researchers around the world used CAQDAS for the advancement of knowledge in the field, and (ii) shed some light on the main features of such use.

As explained earlier, these two software packages were the object of this study for two reasons: (i) they have proved to be among the best available and potentially most useful CAQDAS in the market; and (ii) these are the packages that academic language researchers are most familiarised with (or at least, they have often heard of) because they recurrently appear in renowned journals and the latest publications in the field.

3.2 Data and Methodology

The dataset for my analysis comprised all the research articles published in the lifetime of five mainstream top-tier journals that disseminate research pertaining to the study of academic discourse (see Table 8.1). Four of these journals (ESP, JEAP, JoP, and JSLW) were published by Elsevier and only one (WC) by Sage; consequently, they were accessed via their corresponding online platforms (ScienceDirect for Elsevier journals and Sage Premier for the Sage journal). All the journals were indexed in Scopus' SCImago Journal Rank and the Web of Science's Arts and Humanities Citation Index and Social Sciences Citation Index, JSLW showing the highest and JoP the lowest impact factors (3.324 and 1.039, respectively). The publication periods under analysis were in line with the lifetime of the journal (JoP and WC, ESP, JSLW, and JEAP in order of seniority). The target volumes comprised all the articles published from the year the journal first came out to the end of 2018. Issues "in progress" (containing articles that were final and fully citable) as well as "articles in press" for the year 2019 were not included in this study because this kind of information was not available across all journals.

Table 8.1 Target journals in this study

Journal	*Acronym*	*Publisher*	*Publication periods*	*Impact factor*	*Accessed via*
English for Specific Purposes	ESP	Elsevier	1986–2018	1.362	ScienceDirect
Journal of English for Academic Purposes	JEAP	Elsevier	2002–2018	1.420	ScienceDirect
Journal of Pragmatics	JoP	Elsevier	1977–2018	1.039	ScienceDirect
Journal of Second Language Writing	JSLW	Elsevier	1992–2018	3.324	ScienceDirect
Written Communication	WC	Sage	1977–2018	1.267	Sage Premier

For the selection of target articles in the dataset, I accessed the online versions of the five journals and via their corresponding platforms. Then, I searched each journal for the key words "ATLAS.ti" and "NVivo" in the main fields (abstract, key words, main text, references). This yielded an initial group of articles per journal. After this, I looked at each article closely trying to identify those works that, first, were characterised solely or primarily as qualitative (they might also use a quantitative approach) and, second, employed either ATLAS.ti or NVivo for the analysis of qualitative data. The resulting articles (63 in all, see next subsection) were then saved as .pdf files for further exploration.

3.3 Results

During the lifetime of these five journals, 63 qualitative research articles which used either ATLAS.ti or NVivo to analyse data were published. The number and distribution of articles per journal are shown in Table 8.2. JEAP and JSLW contain the highest and lowest number of articles, respectively (22 and 9). Thus, JEAP has published the majority of CAQDAS-based articles (34.9%) followed by JoP and WC (17.5%, respectively), ESP (15.9%), and JSLW (14.3%). NVivo was the preferred option in these target studies as it was used in 51 articles (81%) against 12 articles (18%) that employed ATLAS.ti.

The use of CAQDAS in academic discourse and genre-related studies is fairly recent. As can be observed in Figure 8.2, the first articles using ATLAS.ti and NVivo were published in 1999 and 2007, respectively, but it is only recently, along the 2010s, that their use has gradually increased and become more popular in the field. In this decade, an average of 6.4

Table 8.2 Distribution of articles (number and percentage) using ATLAS.ti and NVivo

Journal package	*ESP*	*JEAP*	*JoP*	*JSLW*	*WC*	*Total*
ATLAS.ti	1	2	4	3	2	12 (19%)
NVivo	9	20	7	6	9	51 (81%)
Total	10 (15.9%)	22 (34.9%)	11 (17.5%)	9 (14.3%)	11 (17.5%)	63 (100%)

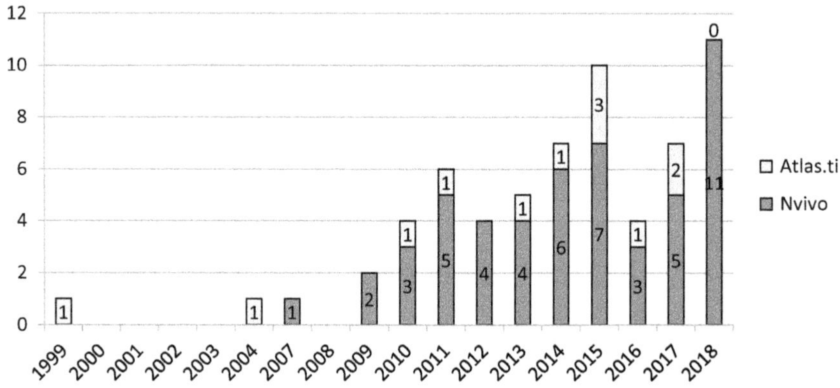

Figure 8.2 Number of articles using ATLAS.ti and NVivo published per year in the lifetime of target journals.

CAQDAS-based articles was published each year, which is significantly low if compared with the total number of articles published by all the journals along these years. By way of example, in 2017, 27 research articles were published by ESP, 33 by JEAP, 134 by JoP, 13 by JSLW, and 17 by WC; if a total of 224 articles were published in these journals in 2017, and only seven of them used CAQDAS for the analysis of their qualitative data, it may be concluded that the percentage of ATLAS.ti- and NVivo-related articles was just 3.1% of the total number of research articles published in that year. In the last year under study (2018), only NVivo articles (11 in all) were published.

A close look at the origin of authors[4] showed that the popularity of CAQDAS was not evenly distributed across the world (see Table 8.3). Anglophone countries led the number of research articles that employed these two software packages so that the United Kingdom, United States (USA), Canada, Australia, New Zealand, South Africa, and Hong Kong[5] all together amounted to 92% of published works (58 articles in all). The remaining 8% (5 articles) were mainly authored by European multilingual scholars[6] in four particular countries – i.e. Austria, Denmark, Spain, and Sweden. There is also one article from a non-European

Table 8.3 Distribution of articles (number and percentage) per country using ATLAS.ti and NVivo

Package country		*ATLAS.ti (no. articles)*	*NVivo (no. articles)*	*Subtotal*	*Total*
Anglophone	Australia	0	8	8 (12.7%)	58 articles (92%)
	Canada	0	4	4 (6.3%)	
	Hong Kong	1	11	12 (19%)	
	New Zealand	0	2	2 (3.2%)	
	South Africa	1	0	1 (1.6%)	
	USA	5	7	12 (19%)	
	United Kingdom	3	16	19 (30.2%)	
Non-Anglophone	Austria	1	0	1 (1.6%)	5 articles (8%)
	Denmark	0	1	1 (1.6%)	
	Spain	0	1	1 (1.6%)	
	Sweden	1	0	1 (1.6%)	
	Taiwan	0	1	1 (1.6%)	

multilingual scholar (i.e. Taiwanese). NVivo was the most popular option among both groups, but particularly among Anglophone scholars who used it in almost 80% of the published works (NVivo was used in 48 Anglophone-authored articles, whereas ATLAS.ti was used in just 10 of them).

Both ATLAS.ti and NVivo handled data from various collection instruments (see Table 8.4). The most popular data collection instrument was interviews (31.9%), followed by questionnaire surveys (10.1%) and essays (9.2%). Nevertheless, even though interview-based studies predominated, qualitative researchers reported using a rich array of collection instruments – all of them matching CAQDAS capabilities. In particular, up to ten different instruments were used (see Table 8.4, left), and each of these comprised a number of particular data gathering tools (see Table 8.4, right) that enhanced the data collection procedure. By way of example, the collection instrument "oral interactions" entailed ordinary interactions taking place in a classroom, notes taken from conversations, oral interactions occurring in any setting, face-to-face discussions, focus groups, tutoring sessions, think-aloud sessions, talking aloud while performing a particular task, stimulated recalls, or phone calls at work involving three or more people (conference calls).

Data revealed that, very often, studies were not purely based on a single collection instrument (15.9% articles) but on a collection of different instruments deriving from multiple sources (see Table 8.5). Thus, the use of two (52.4% articles), three (20.6% articles), four (7.9% articles), and even five (3.2% articles) data collection instruments successfully matched CAQDAS capabilities and was also a common practice.

Table 8.4 Data collection instruments and distribution according to number and percentage of articles

Main data collection instrument	*No. and % of articles*	*Specific data gathering tools*
Interviews	38 articles (31.9%)	Structured interviews Semi-structured interviews
Surveys	12 articles (10.1%)	Online surveys Email surveys Classroom questionnaires
Essays	9 articles (7.6%)	Student writings (Hand-)Written assignments Written narratives Written opinions Essays
Digital genres	8 articles (6.7%)	Social media posts and conversations Discussion forum Email interviews Email messages On-line discussions Academic homepages Researcher blogs
Documents	11 articles (9.2%)	Literature review Medical information sheets Forensic letters University prospectuses Language banks Meeting-related books Doctoral texts Opinion pieces Research articles
Observation	10 articles (8.4%)	Classroom observation Classroom observation field notes Lesson observations Notes based on observations Field notes
Oral interactions	10 articles (8.4%)	Classroom recordings Notes on conversations Recorded interactions Face-to-face discussions Videotapes of tutoring sessions Think-aloud sessions Talk aloud during task Focus groups Stimulated recalls Conference calls
Diaries	6 articles (5.0%)	Diary entries Reflection journals Students' diaries Students' personal statements
Press	3 articles (2.5%)	Apology press uptakes Newspaper commentaries Press reports

Main data collection instrument	*No. and % of articles*	*Specific data gathering tools*
Others	12 articles (10.1%)	Scoring rubrics Test Role-play instructions Grade definitions from writing programs Tutor feedback Masters' feedback texts Corpora of spoken and written English Class materials Proofreading tasks Concept maps

Table 8.5 Number of data collection instruments per article

No. of data collection instruments	*One*	*Two*	*Three*	*Four*	*Five*	*Total*
No. and % of articles	10 (15.9%)	33 (52.4%)	13 (20.6%)	5 (7.9%)	2 (3.2%)	63 (100%)

No article reported using ATLAS.ti or NVivo for functions other than coding – that is, to theorise conceptual relationships or to visually display data showing connections between data and codes. Table 8.6a shows that the majority of articles (60.3%) did not provide details about the analysis procedure – that is, they did not explain if they used any particular form of coding and which. In the remaining 25 articles (39.7%), authors reported having conducted some kind of coding (see Table 8.6b and excerpts 1–4). Of these, an ample majority (60%) reported open-axial coding; the remaining 40% reported the use of three equally distributed types of coding: inductive, deductive, and open coding were implemented by ten articles in all (12% of articles used inductive and deductive coding each, and 16% reported open coding use).

Some scholars clearly named their coding procedure and explicitly explained the ways coding was conducted (see excerpts 1 and 2); some others, however, described it in terms of how they arranged and conducted coding to organise their data, and did not define a particular coding style (see excerpts 3 and 4):

Excerpt 1: Beginning with *open coding* [...] one of the authors coded chunks of text into 673 codes, and then grouped these preliminary codes thematically into 23 families or themes. (Article published in JEAP – *italics added*)

Table 8.6a Distribution of articles (number and percentage) conducting coding by means of ATLAS.ti and NVivo

Coding Package	*Inductive*	*Deductive*	*Open*	*Open-axial*	*Not mentioned*	*Total*
ATLAS.ti	0	1	0	4	7	12 (19%)
NVivo	3	2	4	11	31	51 (81%)
Total	3 (4.8%)	3 (4.8%)	4 (6.3%)	15 (23.8%)	38 (60.3%)	63 (100%)

Table 8.6b Types of coding per article (number and percentage)

Coding package	*Inductive*	*Deductive*	*Open*	*Open-axial*	*Total*
ATLAS.ti	0	1	0	4	5 (20%)
NVivo	3	2	4	11	20 (80%)
Total	3 (12%)	3 (12%)	4 (16%)	15 (60%)	25 (100%)

Excerpt 2: ... the analysis of the interviews involved both *open coding* and *axial coding* [...] The former consisted of annotating the transcripts (totalling 224,073 words) based on key words, observations and ideas, and *axial coding* was the identification of primary and secondary themes in the data. (Article published in ESP – *italics added*)

Excerpt 3: NVivo was used in *extracting and coding* the discourse markers. (Article published in JoP – *italics added*)

Excerpt 4: We *coded* the articles for themes of contexts and participants, research focus and theoretical orientation, and research methodology and data sources. To establish reliability, we conducted *intercoder analyses* of 25 randomly-selected articles (about 10% of the sample). We *coded* this sample in two separate rounds. (Article published in JSLW – *italics added*)

An illustrative example is excerpt 5 because it provides good detail of the whole procedure followed to code the target data previously elicited from think-aloud sessions – that is, oral data was first recorded and turned into text; then, it was deductively coded and entered into ATLAS.ti:

Excerpt 5: The think-aloud sessions were audio-recorded and I also observed and made notes regarding specifically what the participants were reading (e.g. notes, books, the computer screen, etc.) at any given time. The think-aloud sessions were then transcribed and coded using ATLAS.ti software [...] The think-aloud protocols were closely examined and each individual "act" in the transcripts assigned a code. This process was repeated and adjustments made, with some codes being subdivided as the system was refined, and others being collapsed under a single code in cases where duplication occurred or where the original coding system did not reflect a useful distinction between codes. Multiple coding was used where one event in the protocols seemed to serve more than one function. The coding was then checked using what Johnson (2003, p. 49) calls a "top-down" approach to ensure that acts were seen within the context of the larger units that might contribute to their meaning. Finally, to check the reliability of the coding system over time, a sample of the protocols was re-coded by the same rater after a three-week interval. (Article published in JEAP)[7]

4 Findings

This analysis reveals that the qualitative analysis of academic language, genre, and discourse data can be efficiently supported by computer-assisted tools. However, even though CAQDAS has been around for a couple of decades, very few studies report using it. Moreover, the latest literature contains little or no suggestion for researchers in the field to resort to qualitative analysis software (Paltridge & Phakiti, 2015; Hyland & Shaw, 2016; McKinley & Rose, 2017).

Among the wide variety of qualitative analysis packages currently available, ATLAS.ti and NVivo stand out as the most popular for the investigation of language, discourse, and genre in academic settings. NVivo, however, is gradually exceeding ATLAS.ti as the most popular package in the field. These findings are in line with Dörnyei (2007: 264) who foresaw that the popularity of NVivo was "on the increase". They also concur with Woods et al. (2015) who, for the particular case of health sciences, claimed that more studies used NVivo than ATLAS.ti.

This study has profiled the trend of CAQDAS presence in academic discourse-related articles. It has been shown that the use of ATLAS.ti and NVivo has risen during the present decade, and particularly shot up in the past five years (2014–2018). The increased use of both packages reveals that CAQDAS has a major role to play in the field of academic language-related studies and can contribute significantly to enhance our knowledge of the discourse and genres produced in academic settings.

Results have also revealed that the vast majority of articles have originated in English-speaking countries and that the use of CAQDAS for the study of academic discourse is still rare across non-Anglophone areas (although gaining some popularity in Europe). Anglophone scholars feature prominently in qualitative articles using CAQDAS and this may lead multilingual qualitative researchers in the discipline to fall behind a methodological trend that is gradually being defined and shaped by mainstream (Anglophone) scholars. To what extent this situation impacts upon qualitative research cultures (will Anglophone scholars set the guidelines for CAQDAS use in the field?) is an issue to be elucidated in the future, when the use of computer-aided research becomes an established practice among academic language qualitative researchers around the world.

Both ATLAS.ti and NVivo have many capabilities that can be taken to the best advantage of qualitative research studies pertaining to the language, discourse, and genre that prevail in academic settings. A wide number of data collection instruments can be employed (e.g. observations, interviews, surveys, diaries), social media and other non-textual sources (videos, audios, photographs) can be analysed directly, and language-based, audio and visual data may be easily entered into CAQDAS. Still, findings in this study reveal that only interviews and texts (essays, diaries, and documents of various kinds) are referred as the most frequently data-gathering instruments. These instruments (together with observation) have been very favourably supported in the qualitative research literature (Hilal & Alabri, 2013) and cited as the most commonly employed (Harklau, 2011) regardless of CAQDAS use.

As far as audio and video materials are concerned, researchers prefer to transcribe audio material or convert it into text rather than analysing or coding it directly. Similarly to previous literature, this study has found no evidence of these packages being used to analyse new forms of data.[8] In this same vein, this study has attested that the collection of digital genres is emerging and that the computer-assisted analysis of large digital genre data might hopefully lead to a deeper understanding of the language, discourse, and genres occurring in academic settings.

Most articles do not explicitly explain in what ways CAQDAS use has contributed to enhance their qualitative data analysis, nor do they seem to have served to support collaborative team-based analyses. Most articles report using these packages just for coding data (that is, to assign codes and then revise such coding) and none of them report more complex analytical tasks – for example, to structure ideas or concepts at various stages of the interpretive process and visually represent their relationships. This concurs with Bazeley and Jackson's (2013: 2) claim that "the average use of any software program typically accesses only a small portion of its capabilities" and leads to the conclusion that researchers in the field are not (at least apparently) taking CAQDAS to their best advantage. By way of illustration, just one article (out of 63) coded photographs on websites as a supplement to text: with the aim of discovering how academics used various semiotic resources to construct an identity online in the context of the university as a workplace, this article author[9] first examined 100 academic homepages from scholars working at 25 top universities and then email-interviewed five webpage subjects. Homepages were analysed by looking at their text choices, visual design, and hyperlinks. The text was coded by what was mentioned, and also the position, size, and content of photographs together with the hypertext links were categorised by means of NVivo.

The use of more than one instrument prevails when collecting data (usually two or three instruments). This means that qualitative researchers need to place a greater effort when collecting target data, need more time to efficiently conduct coding from a variety of sources, and are faced with more elaborated tasks when designing the correct methodology to follow throughout their research. Following Denzin and Lincoln (2011: 5), the use of multiple collection methods suggests here that qualitative researchers are like "quilt makers", "bricoleurs", or "jazz improvisers" because they stitch, edit, and put "slices of reality together" in an attempt to "secure an in-depth understanding of the phenomenon in question".

5 Concluding Remarks

This study aimed to shed some light on the use of CAQDAS when researching the language, genres, and discourse that occur in academic settings. It may seem paradoxical to carry out a study on qualitative research such as this one by making use of numerical data but, as this study attests, qualitative and quantitative research approaches are not conflicting or contradictory. In fact, they may function as supplements to each other, enhancing results or serving different purposes that, in some instances, cannot be addressed individually by just any of them. Qualitatively oriented studies should thus be more attuned to quantitative research, and vice versa.

Unlike computer-aided quantitative research, computer-aided qualitative research is fairly recent in Applied Linguistics and, particularly in the field of English for specific and academic purposes. In order to develop the necessary skills that CAQDAS demands to use it to its best efficiency, researchers working in the field of academic discourse would highly benefit from specific training on qualitative research and coding procedures; more particularly, on the use of dedicated software tools such as ATLAS.ti and NVivo and on how to apply the software strategically to the data collected in academic contexts. Hopefully, access to online courses, workshops, and hands-on training focused on how to master these packages may contribute to gaining a better understanding of the language, discourse, and genres that recur in academic settings and the underlying rationale for their use.

Acknowledgements

This work is a contribution to national research project FFI2015-68638-R MINECO/FEDER, EU, funded by the Spanish Ministry of Economy and Competitiveness.

Notes

1 To learn about the common tools that CAQDAS offers and the research activities they support, see Lewins and Silver (2007).
2 For an examination of major features and a thorough comparative review of NVivo and ATLAS.ti, see Lewis (2004). For a review of ATLAS.ti with cases of actual research examples, see Hwang (2008). For a step-by-step guide to NVivo software, see Bazeley and Jackson (2013). For a large-scale review of empirical studies showing how ATLAS.ti and NVivo are used and reported by qualitative researchers, see Woods et al. (2015).
3 Flowerdew, J. (1999). "Problems in writing for scholarly publication. The Case of Hong Kong". *Journal of Second Language Writing* 8/3, 243–264.
4 In the case of multi-authored papers, only corresponding authors were taken into consideration for the head count.
5 I am including Hong Kong in this list of Anglophone countries because in this former British colony, English is today one of the two official languages and many academics working at Hong Kong universities are either Anglophone scholars or have been educated in the Anglophone academia.
6 I am using the term "multilingual" (Uzuner, 2008) to refer to non-Anglophone scholars who use English as an additional language for international publication or any other academic and professional purposes.
7 Given the length of this excerpt, I find it advisable to provide the whole citation source: McCullogh, S. (2013). "Investigating the reading-to-write processes and source use of L2 postgraduate students in real-life academic tasks: An exploratory study". *Journal of English for Academic Purposes* 12, page 139.
8 An exception is Woods et al. (2015), who found two studies only (out of 763) that coded directly against audio or video files. In both cases, ATLAS.ti was the package used for the task.
9 Hyland, K. (2011). "The presentation of self in scholarly life: Identity and marginalization in academic homepages". *English for Specific Purposes* 30/4, 286–297.

References

Basit, T.N. (2003). "Manual or electronic? The role of coding in qualitative data analysis". *Educational Research* 45/2, 143–54.

Bazeley, P. & Jackson, K. (2013). *Qualitative Data Analysis with NVivo*. 2nd ed. London: Sage Publications.

Bryman, A. (2008). *Social Research Methods*. Oxford: Oxford University Press.

Davidson, J. & di Gregorio, S. (2011). "Qualitative research and technology. In the midst of a revolution", in N.K. Denzin & Y.S. Lincoln (eds.) *The SAGE Handbook of Qualitative Research*. Thousand Oaks, CA: Sage, 627–643.

Denzin, N.K. & Lincoln, Y.S. (2011). "Introduction: The discipline and practice of qualitative research", in N.K. Denzin & Y.S. Lincoln (eds.) *The SAGE Handbook of Qualitative Research*. Thousand Oaks, CA: Sage, 1–19.

Dörnyei, Z. (2007). *Research Methods in Applied Linguistics*. Oxford: Oxford University Press.

Fielding, N.G. & Lee, R.M. (1998). *Computer Analysis and Qualitative Research*. London: Sage.

Flick, U. (1998). *An Introduction to Qualitative Research*. London: Sage.

García-Horta, J.B. & Guerra-Ramos, M.T. (2009). "The use of CAQDAS in educational research: some advantages, limitations and potential risks". *International Journal of Research & Methods in Education* 32/2, 151–165.

Harklau, L. (2011). "Approaches and methods in recent qualitative research", in E. Hinkel (ed.) *Handbook of Research in Second Language Teaching and Learning, Vol. 2*. London: Routledge, 175–189.

Hilal, A.H. & Alabri, S.S. (2013). "Using NVivo for data analysis in qualitative research". *International Interdisciplinary Journal of Education* 2/2, 181–186.

Hyland, K. & Shaw, P. (eds.) (2016). *The Routledge Handbook of English for Academic Purposes*. New York: Routledge.

Hwang, S. (2008). "Utilizing qualitative data analysis software. A review of ATLAS.ti". *Social Science Computer Review* 26/4, 519–527.

Lewins, A. & Silver, C. (2007). *Using Software in Qualitative Research: A Step-by-Step Guide*. Thousand Oaks, CA: Sage.

Lewis, R.B. (2004). "NVivo 2.0 and ATLAS.ti 5.0: A comparative review of two popular qualitative data-analysis programs". *Field Methods* 16/4, 439–469.

Maxwell, J.A. (2009). "Designing a qualitative study", in L. Bickman & D.J. Rog (eds.) *The SAGE Handbook of Applied Social Research Methods*. Thousand Oaks, CA: Sage, 214–253.

McKinley, J. & Rose, H. (eds.) (2017). *Doing Research in Applied Linguistics. Realities, Dilemmas, and Solutions*. New York: Routledge.

Muhr, T. (1991). "ATLAS/ti: A prototype for the support of text interpretation". *Qualitative Sociology* 14/4, 349–371.

Paltridge, B. & Phakiti, A. (eds.) (2015). *Research Methods in Applied Linguistics. A Practical Resource*. London: Bloomsbury.

Richards, L. & Richards, T. (1987). "Qualitative data analysis: Can computers do it?" *Journal of Sociology* 23, 23–35.

Saldaña, J. (2009). *The Coding Manual for Qualitative Researchers*. London: Sage.

Silverman, D. (2005). *Doing Qualitative Research*. London: Sage.

Smit, B. (2002). "ATLAS.ti for qualitative data analysis". *Perspectives in Education* 20/3, 65–75.

Uzuner, S. (2008). "Multilingual scholars' participation in core/global academic communities: A literature review". *Journal of English for Academic Purposes* 7/4, 250–263.

Weitzman, E.A. (2000). "Software and qualitative research", in N.K. Denzin & Y.S. Lincoln (eds.) *Handbook of Qualitative Research*, 803–820. Thousand Oaks, CA: Sage.

Woods, M., Paulus, T., Atkins, D.P. & Macklin, R. (2015). "Advancing qualitative research using qualitative data analysis software (QDAS)? Reviewing potential versus practice in published studies using ATLAS.ti and NVivo, 1994–2013". *Social Science Computer Review* 34/5, 597–617.

Zamawe, F.C. (2015). "The implication of using NVivo software in qualitative data analysis: Evidence-based reflections". *Malawi Medical Journal* 27/1, 13–15.

Section 2

Studies on Learner Corpora

9 A Corpus-Driven Exploration of Discourse Markers in L2 Academic Texts

Višnja Pavičić Takač, Barbara Kružić and Sanja Vakanjac Ivezić

1 Theoretical Underpinnings

The concept of 'communicative competence', introduced into the linguistic research by Dell Hymes (1972), has often been described mainly in terms of grammatical and sociolinguistic or pragmatic knowledge. However, any model of communicative competence has to encompass not only a second language user's knowledge but also his/her knowledge about how to form a written (or oral) text which will be both accurate and adequate in terms of the use of language in given linguistic and situational contexts (Bagarić Medve & Pavičić Takač, 2013a:169). Although this ability has been differently labelled or described in many theoretical models of communicative competence (cf. Canale, 1983; Bachman, 1990; Celce-Murcia, Dörnyei, & Thurrell, 1995; Bachman & Palmer, 1996; Common European Framework of Reference [hereafter: CEFR], 2001; Celce-Murcia, 2007), its features seem to fall generally under the term discourse competence. In some communicative competence models, discourse competence is positioned similarly as other components (i.e. strategic, grammatical, and sociolinguistic competence), which are all interrelated (Canale, 1983; Savignon, 1983), whereas in others it is considered to be a part of grammatical dimension of communicative competence (Bachman, 1990; Bachman & Palmer, 1996) or a part of pragmatic competence (CEFR, 2001). However, Celce-Murcia (2007:45) places discourse competence as the core and central competence, which interacts with other competences in the model, i.e. socio-cultural, linguistic, interactional, and formulaic competence as well as with strategic competence (i.e. learning and communication strategies), which supports the use of language competences. This inconsistency in the definition of discourse competence is the result of a lack of agreement among applied linguists as to what discourse competence entails and what its position should be with regard to other components in communicative competence models, making it an issue in need of further exploration in applied linguistic research (Bagarić Medve & Pavičić Takač, 2013a:186).

According to a number of communicative competence models (cf. Canale, 1983; Bachman, 1990; Celce-Murcia et al., 1995; Bachman & Palmer, 1996; Celce-Murcia, 2007; CEFR, 2001), discourse competence includes knowledge about cohesion and coherence. Although the above-mentioned models mostly agree on the definition of cohesion, a review of relevant literature (e.g. Halliday & Hasan, 1976; Van Dijk, 1977; Widdowson, 1978; Carrell, 1982; Brown & Yule, 1983; Canale, 1983; Savignon, 1983; Dastjerdi & Talebinezhada, 2006) suggests that there is no general agreement regarding the concept of coherence. However, most applied linguists agree that cohesion does not spawn coherence but that it can help improve text coherence. Thus, usage of appropriate cohesive devices can be a useful indicator of coherence, which becomes of particular interest in the teaching and evaluation of second language writing skills.

The study of discourse markers, as an aspect of the study of coherence and cohesion, has preoccupied scholars since the late 1980s and 1990s (cf. Schiffrin, 1987; Fraser & Malamud-Makowski, 1996). Although nowadays the term discourse marker (Schiffrin, 1987) is most widely used, it is still possible to find a wide range of different labels for this notion, such as pragmatic marker, discourse particle, pragmatic particle, pragmatic expression, or connective (cf. Jucker & Ziv, 1998: 1). The variety in labels is a reflection of not only different approaches and theories, but also of the complexity of the notion and variability of elements covered by one umbrella term. In this chapter, we have opted for the term *discourse marker,* following Jucker and Ziv (1998: 2), because "[...] it seems to be the one with the widest currency and with the least restricted range of application; one that enables us to include a broad variety of elements under a single conceptual umbrella".

Discourse markers have been investigated within a variety of frameworks. Different approaches have resulted in disagreement regarding their classification and function, especially since discourse markers have "come to be seen not only as an underexplored facet of language behaviour but as a testing ground for hypotheses concerning the boundary between pragmatics and semantics and for theories of discourse structure and utterance interpretation" (Schourup, 1999: 228).

In the field of second language acquisition, studies that aim at analysing the use of discourse markers in written texts are scarce (cf. Milton & Tsang, 1993; Grote, Lenke & Stede, 1995; Granger & Tyson 1996; Chen, 2006; Shea, 2009; Bagarić Medve & Pavičić Takač, 2013b). Although the number of such studies has been boosted by technological advances of computer text-processing tools that enable investigation of large samples of learner writing, it is still too early to draw any conclusions. What seems to emerge as a common phenomenon is the tendency of non-native language users to overuse or misuse and underuse particular connectors (cf. Milton & Tsang, 1993; Granger & Tyson, 1996; Bolton, Nelson, & Hung, 2002; Tankó, 2004; Chen, 2006; Bagarić Medve & Čelebić, 2012; Bagarić Medve & Pavičić Takač, 2013b; Carrió-Pastor, 2013).

2 The Present Study

Having in mind previous research done in this field, the present study sets out to explore patterns in the use of discourse markers of contrast, i.e. words and phrases used to introduce counter-arguments in academic argumentative essays written by non-native users of two foreign languages, English and German. It also aims at exploring the possibilities of using corpus-analytic tools to investigate coherence and cohesion. In summary, the analysis focuses on two aspects: (1) frequency of use of individual discourse markers, which is expected to be indicative of preference, underuse, overuse, and variety, followed by a more detailed qualitative analysis of discourse markers used; and (2) erroneous use of discourse markers.

3 Methodology

3.1 The Corpus

The corpus compiled for the study consists of two subcorpora, English and German, each containing 10 texts written by non-native users of English or German. Participants were all humanities and social sciences students at the B2 proficiency level (CEFR, 2001). Students were given a task to write a 200–230 words argumentative essay in which they had to present two points of view, express their opinion, and give supporting arguments. The writing task was designed to elicit comparable argumentative essays but the topics varied in order to avoid topic bias. In total, the English subcorpus consisted of 9,657 tokens and the German subcorpus contained 11,435 tokens.

3.2 Corpus Analysis

We completed our corpus analysis of the discourse markers using Sketch Engine. It is a user-friendly multifunctional concordance tool and has the tool (corpus architect) for creating own corpora. A simple lexical search was conducted.

Before the analysis, three issues had to be considered. The first was the definition of discourse markers. As a result of a variety of approaches to discourse markers research, there are many definitions of discourse markers. Schiffrin (1987:31) defines discourse markers as "[…] sequentially dependent elements which bracket units of talk", emphasising thus their use in spoken language, but also defining them too broadly. Fraser (1990:387) uses the term pragmatic markers and defines them as "[…] a class of expressions, each of which signals how the speaker intends the basic message that follows to relate to the prior discourse". In Siepmann Dirk's view (2005:43), discourse markers are "[…] linguistic expressions of varying length which carry pragmatic and/or propositional meaning, occur in both speech and writing, and facilitate rather than disrupt discourse". This definition highlights the facilitating use of discourse markers in both spoken and written discourses. These few exemplary definitions point to at least two common features of discourse markers: they are a broad class of expressions of varying length and are crucial to establishing relations between parts of message.

For the purposes of this chapter, we have adopted Grote et al.'s (1997) definition which states that discourse markers are textual elements used to organise and mark boundaries in the text and cue words used to signal the relations holding between text segments to the reader. The focus on discourse markers of contrast, typical for argumentative essays, required a generation of a comprehensive list of words and phrases expressing contrast. To this end, a number of linguistic grammars and dictionaries were consulted (Quirk, Greenbaum, Leech & Svartvik, 1985; Thompson & Martinet, 1985; Greenbaum & Quirk, 1990; Swan, 1995; Buscha & Helbig, 2000; Duden, 2003; Buscha, Szit & Raven, 2013). These were selected because they are the most commonly used reference books in English and German foreign language classes at both secondary and tertiary education levels. In addition, relevant papers covering the topic of contrastive discourse markers were consulted (Grote et al., 1997; Bell, 1998; Fraser, 1998; Stede, 2004; Fraser, 2013).

The second issue we had to address was a potential classification of English and German contrastive discourse markers. The notion of contrast in English, and likely other languages such as German, is not well defined and as a result, there is no "agreement on what constitutes the class of contrastive discourse markers, if in a fact a class exists" (Fraser & Malamud-Makowski, 1996:865). According to Fraser, definitions of contrast in the literature range across the semantic, logical, pragmatic, functional, and discourse domains, and some of these definitions overlap and intersect. Ideally, different functions of discourse markers would be differentiated on the basis of precise semantic criteria that could keep them apart (Malchukov, 2004). Although some attempts are available in semantics to account for some of the relevant uses of discourse markers of contrast (Lang, 1984; König, 1988; Winter & Rimon, 1994; Karagjosova, 2001), there are no generally accepted definitions for the whole range of their functions. On the basis of their analysis of both English and German, Grote et al. (1997:99) group discourse markers of contrast into three groups according to the cohesive bond they create between the constituents: (1) conjunctive adjuncts (mostly realised by means of an adverb or a prepositional phrase) and coordinating conjunctions (when they occur in sentence-initial position) which form a relation between a clause and the preceding text; (2) markers that form an interdependency relation, i.e. coordinating conjunctions forming intra-clausal relations and conjunctive adjuncts which can occur within a clause complex, but that do not create any kind of independency relation; and (3) markers that create dependency, i.e. subordinating conjunctions which "[...] relate two clauses and prepositions forming a relation within, and not between the processes" (Grote et al., 1997:99). We have decided to base the data analysis data on three formal-syntactic categories, viz. conjuncts (type of adverbial), coordinating conjunctions, and subordinating conjunctions following Quirk et al. (1985) for one important reason. Namely, the exact inventory and the categorial vs. subcategorial status of some of the semantic types involving contrast are not certain. For instance, Quirk et al. present "contrast" and "concession" (1985:1087ff) as two semantic types of adverbial clauses (albeit featuring a considerable overlap as far as the interpretation of particular examples (p. 1102, also 1098) and the choice of subordinators is concerned (*whereas*, *while*, *whilst*). However, their semantic classification of conjuncts features 'contrast' as a category superordinate to, among others, concessive conjuncts (others being reformulatory, replacive, antithetic (p 635–636)).

To avoid commitment to the categorial vs. subcategorial status of these semantic distinctions or to any particular taxonomy of semantic subtypes under a putative umbrella term "contrast", we have decided to base our classification on the syntactic categories, viz. conjuncts, coordinating conjunctions, and subordinating conjunctions from Quirk et al. (1985). Although they are far from completely discrete (cf. the coordination–subordination gradient featuring some conjuncts in Quirk et al. (1985:927–928)), these categories provide a better handle on the data, since they are based on explicit syntactic criteria like (im)mobility in front of the clause, sequential fixedness between the linked clauses, combinability with a preceding conjunction, subject ellipsis, etc. (cf. Quirk et al., 1985:927–928). Finally, this approach to data analysis is applicable to both English and German examples of contrastive discourse markers.

The final issue to be dealt with was the treatment of errors in the texts. Learner-produced texts are typically "[...] spiced with deviant uses of language" (Thomas, 2015:12) but any intervention in the text compromises the authenticity of the texts and may result in the loss of valuable information (such as the nature of deviation from standard language). To minimise these risks, only spelling mistakes which would interfere with automatic computer searches were corrected (e.g. **nevertheles* → *nevertheless*).

4 Results

4.1 Frequency Analysis

Tables 9.1 and 9.2 show the raw and relative frequency (representing hits per 1,000 tokens), as well as dispersion of discourse markers of contrast

Table 9.1 List of discourse markers of contrast in the English subcorpus: frequency and dispersion

	Frequency		*Dispersion*				
	Raw	*Relative (per 1,000)*	*Mean*	*SD*	*Range %*	*CV*	*Juilland's D*
but	68	7.04	1.7	1.36	83	0.8	0.87
on the other hand	22	2.28	0.55	0.59	50	1.07	0.83
however	9	0.93	0.26	0.47	20	1.81	0.29
while	7	0.72	0.18	0.44	18	2.44	0.61
and	6	0.62	0.15	0.36	15	2.4	0.62
although	4	0.41	0.1	0.37	7.5	3.7	0.41
instead	4	0.41	0.1	0.3	10	3	0.52
even though	3	0.31	0.075	0.35	7.5	4.67	0.25
nevertheless	2	0.21	0.05	0.22	5	4.4	0.29
even if	1	0.1	0.025	0.16	2.5	–	–
whereas	1	0.1	0.025	0.16	2.5	–	–

Table 9.2 List of discourse markers of contrast in the German subcorpus: frequency and dispersion

	Frequency		*Dispersion*				
	Raw	*Relative (per 1,000)*	*Mean*	*SD*	*Range %*	*CV*	*Juilland's D*
aber	51	4.46	1.28	1.14	68	0.89	0.86
doch	18	1.57	0.45	0.99	23	2.2	0.65
obwohl	18	1.57	0.45	0.77	17.5	1.7	0.73
auf der anderen Seite	8	0.7	0.2	0.4	20	2	0.68
andererseits	7	0.61	0.18	0.38	17.5	2.11	0.66
trotzdem	7	0.61	0.18	0.44	15	2.44	0.61
sondern	6	0.52	0.15	0.42	12.5	2.8	0.55
allerdings	4	0.35	0.1	0.37	7.5	3.7	0.41
anderseits	2	0.17	0.05	0.22	5	4.4	0.3

in English and German subcorpora. A relatively small number of different discourse markers as well as the fact that the marker *but* in English and *aber* in German appeared almost as often as all others put together point to the lack of variability. This is further supported by dispersion indices which show that the most frequently used markers appear in a large number of individual texts. Although there was a slight difference in the number of various discourse markers between English and German essays, users of both languages seem to prefer a few particular discourse markers[1].

4.2 *Qualitative Analysis of Corpus-Attested Discourse Markers*

The next step in the analysis included a qualitative analysis of the use of discourse markers used in the English and German essays.

4.2.1 *Classification of English Contrastive Discourse Markers Found in the Corpus*

4.2.1.1 CONJUNCTS

The following examples of conjuncts were found in the English subcorpus: *however*, *nevertheless*, *instead*, and *on the other hand*. The latter was the most frequently used of the four. All the expressions are

> "[...] used in a three-part structure: (1) the speaker/writer mentions facts that point in a certain direction; (2) it is agreed that a particular contradictory fact points the other way; (3) but the speaker/writer dismisses that and returns to the original direction of argument"
>
> (Swan, 1995:152)

On the other hand, categorised as a split particle by Grote et al. (1997:101), and as a conjunct by Quirk et al. (1985:635–636), was used 22 times in the English subcorpus, out of which six times as a second member of the phrase *on the one hand... on the other hand* (1).

1 *<On the one hand>, it is easier to access anything here; a pharmacist's, hospital, different kinds of shops...* [...] *<On the other hand>, I suppose you don't have that much freedom and peace* [...]

Halliday and Hasan (1976) describe *on the other hand* as contrastive, adversative, and corrective. Swan (1995) notes that *on the other hand* is used to balance two facts of ideas that contrast, but not contradict each other. The expression *on the other hand* prompts readers to regard the second clause as more important (Grote et al., 1997). In our subcorpus, *on the other hand* appears 20 times at the beginning of a new sentence, introducing the new argument, contrasted to the previous sentence, i.e. balancing between two ideas presented by the author (example 2; cf. Halliday & Hasan, 1976; Swan, 1995). But the phrase does not necessarily introduce the second clause/sentence as more important. It simply introduces another or an opposing point of view, especially in examples which are a continuation of *on the one hand*.

2 [...] *pets notice everything, and they can often save their owner's life by pointing that something is wrong with their health. <On the other hand>, it can be very difficult to keep a pet in an apartment.*

Similarly to *on the other hand, however* is used to introduce a more important argument (Grote et al., 1997:96; Fraser, 1998:313). Interestingly, in our corpus, nine out of ten arguments introduced by *however* were negative (3), which could imply that the writers considered negative experience as more important and thus attempted to emphasise it with *however. Nevertheless* is considered more restrictive than *however,* which could be related to the fact that it was used only once in the English subcorpus. It signals that second sentence is to be interpreted as a denial of a proposition associated with the first sentence. Furthermore, there is also a sense of unexpectedness of that denial (cf. Fraser & Malamud-Markowski, 1996; Fraser, 1998). This was corroborated by example (4) found in the subcorpus. *Instead* is most commonly used to signal that one speaker intends to correct a message conveyed by the other, which the other accepts (cf. Fraser, 1998:307). The way it is used in the examples found in the corpus confirms Quirk et al.'s (1985:636) view that it is a blend of antithetic and replacive conjunct.

3 *people with pets are happier, live longer, are healthier and have better immune systems. <However>, not everything about living with pets in an apartment is great.*
4 [...] *to be aware of the possible disadvantages such as being fooled by faulty sellers and supposedly free shipping. <Nevertheless>, it is the way to go in the future for people who like diversity...*

Based on Quirk et al.'s (1985:638–639) differentiation of contrastive conjuncts, we could conclude that examples of replacive (*on the other hand*), antithetic (*instead*), and concessive (*however, nevertheless, on the other hand*) conjuncts were found in the English subcorpus. No examples of reformulatory conjuncts were found.

4.2.1.2 COORDINATING CONJUNCTIONS

This group of discourse markers is represented by one example in the English subcorpus: *but.* However, this conjunction is the most commonly used contrastive discourse marker in the subcorpus: as the results in Table 9.1 show, it was used more than twice as many times as all the other discourse markers together. In Roschean representation of the prototype theory, *but* would be the prototype example of contrastive discourse markers. This "overuse" leads to quite a few erroneous examples, which will be discussed later in this chapter as well.

Linguists have analysed and discussed different meaning and function aspects of this conjunction, such as "denial of expectation *but*" (Lakoff, 1971), internal and external *but* (Halliday & Hasan, 1976), three types of *but* corresponding to *aber, sondern*, and *dafür* in German (Abraham, 1979), denial of expectation and contrast *but* (Blakemore, 1987), and referential, functional, and contrastive *but* (Schiffrin, 1987), to name but a few. It seems that the fact that *but* was the most frequently used discourse marker and that it appeared in over 80% of the texts in the subcorpus can be explained by Fraser's (1998:310) observation that the one core meaning of *but* is to signal simple contrast. In other words, *but* expresses contrast and repudiation of what has been said or implied by negation in the first clause (cf. Quirk et al., 1985). Both Thompson and Martinet (1985:288–299) and Fraser (1988:313) point out that *but* can occur instead of *however* in all contexts, but not vice versa. Thus, since the usage of *but* is not as constrained as some other expressions, it represents a "safe choice" for non-native language users.

The contrast expressed by *but* could alternatively be expressed by *and* followed by a conjunct *yet*. There were six examples of contrastive use of *and* in the English subcorpus, but without *yet*. *And* is a neutral coordinating conjunction, but can be used with adversative meaning "contrary to expectations" (Bell, 1988:520). In the English subcorpus, examples involving *and* consist of the first clause which introduces an idea or thought (i.e. 'expectation') and the second clause which introduces unexpected contrast to the first-mentioned idea (5).

5 [...] unless it is a book that I really want to read <and> it still hasn't been published.

4.2.1.3 SUBORDINATING CONJUNCTIONS

In the English subcorpus, the following subordinating conjunctions were identified: *while*, *although*, *even though*, *even if*, and *whereas*. *While* can mean 'but' and it is used to emphasise contrast. It can also mean 'although', and is then usually placed at the beginning of a sentence (Thompson & Martinet, 1985:293). This is corroborated by the examples in the English subcorpus – *while* is placed at the beginning of a sentence and means 'although' (6). *Although*, *even though*, and *even if* are interchangeable having almost exactly the same meaning, that of concession, i.e. unexpected denial of what has been mentioned before. According to Thompson and Martinet (1985:289), they usually appear at the beginning of a clause. In the English subcorpus, *although* and *even though* are used relatively rarely, whereas *even if* is a hapax. *Although* is found in the sentence-initial position in 3 out of 4 examples (7), and *even though* is also used in the mid-sentence position. The sentence position could be related to a degree of emphasis the author wants to express. Interestingly, *even if* was used in the sequence *but even if*, where *but* could be interpreted as denoting additional emphasis of the contrast, i.e. denial presented by the speaker (8). Another hapax in this group of discourse markers is *whereas*, which is not originally classified as a subordinating conjunction by Grote et al. (1997), but is characterised as a contrast subordinator along with *while* by Quirk et al. (1985). It was found in the initial position in a sentence representing the opinion of others, while the opinion of the speaker was given later on, in the second clause (9). This might also be the result of the attempted emphasis.

6 *<While> many people, especially women are delighted with this new brand, others say that shopping online is unnecessary and useless.*
7 *In my opinion online shopping is good <although> it has some bad sides.*
8 *But <even> if it is fast to order something, it takes time for it to arrive.*
9 *<Whereas> some claim keeping pets in apartments should be forbidden by law, others have a completely different opinion on that subject.*

4.2.2 *Classification of German Contrastive Discourse Markers Found in the Corpus*

Semantic classes of contrastive discourse markers in German have been described by, among others, Helbig and Buscha (1990), Breindl (2004), Di Meola (2004), Pasch, Brauße, Breindl & Hermann Waßner (2009); Breindl, Volodina, Hermann Waßner (2014). To maintain the same structure of data presentation, Quirk et al.'s (1985) classification will be used because it is applicable to contrastive discourse markers found in both subcorpora.

4.2.2.1 CONJUNCTS

Contrastive conjuncts found in the German subcorpus are concessive *doch, trotzdem*, and *allerdings*, and antithetic *ander(er)seits / auf der anderen Seite*.

The most frequently used discourse marker found in the German subcorpus belonging to the group of concessive conjuncts is *doch*. According to Grote et al. (1997:100), *doch* introduces a comment or remark that is surprising, contrary to what is normally expected. In Duden (2003:387), *doch* and *aber* are described as substitutable synonyms. Stede (2004:264) studied different contexts in which German contrastive discourse markers are substitutable and claim that *doch*, *aber*, and *jedoch* can almost always be substituted without the change in meaning, which holds for the most instances of *doch* found in the German subcorpus (10). The choice between them depends on syntax configuration. The conjunct *doch* is only one of a number of different uses of the German discourse marker *doch*. In general, *doch* can also be used as an adverb, where it is accented and placed in the middle field of the German sentence, as an unaccented modal particle or as a response particle (Karagjosova, 2001).

10 *Natürlich ist Onlineshopping sehr leicht und man muss nicht einmal aus dem Haus gehen, <doch> manchmal kann das auch teuer werden.*

The second most frequently used discourse marker in the German subcorpus is concessive *trotzdem*. It expresses restriction (Buscha et al., 2013:173). It is usually substitutable with *obgleich* / *obwohl*, but *trotzdem* is more colloquial (Duden, 2003:1611). According to Karagjosova (2001), *trotzdem* is a proper unambiguous concessive marker whose concessive meaning is lexically encoded, i.e. lexically transparent (cf. *trotzdem*: *trotz* = 'despite', *dem* = 'that DATIV'). The meaning of concessive marker *trotzdem* is usually explicated in terms of denied expectation (Karagjosova, 2001:15), which is the case of the examples found in the German subcorpus.

11 *Schließlich geht es auch um die Ruhe, die man mit Singleleben kriegt. Es gibt hier weniger Streiten und Stress, die eine große Familie mit sich unbedingt bringt. <Trotzdem> gibt es auch die Nachteile.*

Another discourse marker attested in the German subcorpus belonging to this group is concessive *allerdings*. It expresses restriction (Duden, 2003:116) or a contrastive comparison in which two propositions are directly contrasted (Breindl, 2004) and can be placed within a clause in front of the finite verb, or at the beginning of the clause (Buscha & Helbig, 2000:155). According to Grote et al. (1997:100), *allerdings* is used in dialogues, introducing counter-arguments phrased by the speaker as a concession. It is usually substitutable with *trotzdem* / *dennoch* / *gleichwohl* (Buscha et al. (2013:174). Of these, only *trotzdem* was found in the German subcorpus. In our German subcorpus, *allerdings* was used both to express restriction (12) and to introduce counter-arguments (13).

12 [...] *dass jede Wahl, Single- oder Familienleben, einige Kosten hat. <Allerdings>, wurde ich mich für das Familienleben entscheiden.*
13 [...] *man hat zugleich eine sportliche Aktivität. <Allerdings> gibt es auch Nachteile dabei.*

Items can be contrasted with a preceding one by introducing a direct antithesis, which is realised by means of antithetic conjunct. One discourse marker belonging to this group found in the German subcorpus is *andererseits* together with its variants *anderseits* and *auf der anderen Seite*. Antithetic conjuncts *andererseits*, *anderseits*, *andrerseits* meaning 'auf der anderen Seite, zum andern' can be used as a part of a correlation *einerseits…andererseits* (Duden, 2003; Buscha et al., 2013), to state 'the opposite' (Duden, 2003:429), implying that *andererseits, anderseits, anderseits* are used to balance two facts or ideas that contrast, but do not necessarily contradict each other. The examples of all variants of *andererseits* found in our corpus were used to state the opposite, as well as to balance ideas that do not necessarily contradict each other (14).

14 *Für ihnen ist leichter wenn die Eltern Geld verdienen, damit sie Taschengeld bekommen oder auf ein Essen, dass die Mutter macht, zu warten. <Anderseits> müssten sie selbst kochen* […]

4.2.2.2 COORDINATING CONJUNCTIONS

The frequency analysis showed that the coordinating conjunct *aber* is the most frequently used discourse marker in the German subcorpus. According to Grote et al. (1997:100), *aber* denotes a contrast, which can have a concessive meaning aspect to it when the contrast arises from the unexpectedness of what is being said in the second clause. The unexpectedness depends on our presuppositions. According to Duden (2003:77), in addition to contrast and unexpectedness, *aber* expresses contradiction or elimination. *Aber* is not necessarily placed between the two propositions; it can take various positions within a clause (Buscha et al., 2013:171). Stede (2004) outlined how contrasting relations for description of coherence in a discourse can be formed, with definitions of relations of the discourse marker *aber* corresponding to communicative goals (for a more detailed account, see Stede, 2004:282): (1) to overrule a counter-argument – proposition 1 potentially contradicts proposition 2, but proposition 2 is argumentatively stronger; (2) to reject an obvious conclusion – a proposition which the reader will not accept indirectly arises from proposition 1; (3) to inform about a surprising correlation – a reader is informed that propositions 1 and 2 normally do not go together; (4) to compare neutral contrast of two situations; (5) to balance different evaluations – propositions are not potentially contrastive (as in 1), but give rise to counter evaluation of an underlying proposition; (6) to question the validity of a statement; (7) to inform about a failure of a plan; (8) to hint to a change in *event – consequence* (similar to 7) but without an intentional act. The analysis of the use of *aber* in our German subcorpus showed that it was mostly used to compare neutral contrast of two situations (15). The second most common use of *aber* was to balance different evaluations. This result may be attributed to the text type, i.e. argumentative essay, in which arguments of both sides of an issue are to be presented. *Aber* was also often used by students to overrule a counter-argument and to question the validity of a statement

(16), but there were also few instances of other uses of *aber* corresponding to Stede's (2004) definitions of relations.

15 [...] *ist das Stadtleben sehr reich in Möglichkeiten <aber> manchmal fehlt diese menschliche Komponente.*

16 *Das Leben in der Stadt In der heutigen Welt leben immer mehr Leute in einer Stadt, <aber> man muss sich fragen, ist dass eine gute Sache?*

Another marker found in the German subcorpus that was classified to this group is *sondern*. Although not mentioned by Grote et al. (1997), it is characterised as a contrast coordinator by Buscha et al. (2013:171). According to Duden (2003:1469), it can have a concessive meaning aspect after a negative statement to express and emphasise improvement, justification of another contradictory statement; meaning 'instead', 'on the contrary'. *Sondern* is placed after a negative proposition and it corrects the information in the previous proposition (Buscha et al., 2013:171). In our German subcorpus, *sondern* was used only with concessive meaning following a negative statement to correct the earlier information (17).

17 *Nicht nur könnte dass Schwierigkeiten für Tierbesitzer bedeuten, <sondern> könnte es auch problematisch für manche Hundesorten sein.*

4.2.2.3 SUBORDINATING CONJUNCTIONS

One example of subordinating conjunct in the German subcorpus is *obwohl*. Realisation with *obwohl* can be observed as a typical representative of concession relation, i.e. when contrast arises from unexpectedness (Grote et al., 1997; Buscha & Helbig, 2000; Stede, 2004). It introduces a concessive subordinate clause with the meaning 'despite the fact that' (Duden, 2003:1155), which was, in fact, the case with all instances of *obwohl* in our German subcorpus (18), except in the instances of its erroneous use. *Obwohl* can be substituted with *obgleich*, *obzwar*, and *obschon* differing in formality and archaicness, *obgleich*, and *obschon* are today rarely used (Buscha et al., 2013:177). Similarly as *obwohl*, the preposition *trotz* serves as the general-purpose preposition in concessions (Grote et al., 1997:101). According to Stede (2004:257), other *obwohl* can be replaced by other connectors with appropriate syntactic modifications (noun phrase – subordinate clause – main clause): *obgleich / obschon / trotz / dennoch / trotzdem / nichtdestoweniger.*

18 *<Obwohl> man sich problemloser fühlt, fühlt man sich auch einsam.*

4.3 Error Analysis

4.3.1 Analysis of Errors in the English Subcorpus

The error analysis was informed by the semantic analysis of the discourse markers described earlier. The inspection of examples in the English subcorpus revealed several examples of the misuse of the discourse marker. Most of the sentences (19–22) exemplify a wrong choice in terms of the function of the discourse marker.

19 *Every day was special <but> I will now explain why Thursday was the best day.*
20 *Long day at work <but> you need a new pair of pants or groceries?*
21 *In my opinion, I would rather stay on village and travel to city every day (err), <but> at least I would breathe fresh air and have silence.*
22 (...) *case that the food in the city is not home-made, <but> it has really questionable origin.*

The meaning of the two clauses is not contrasted so that a contrastively used *but* is considered erroneous. This is confirmed by the substitution test which includes the insertion of *and yet* instead of *but* in examples (19) and (22). If *but* is substituted with *and* in examples (19) and (20), the entire sentence is understandable, while cohesion remains almost intact.

Example (20) illustrates the argument that the coherence and cohesion of the essay as a whole may be disrupted not only because of the wrong choice of the discourse marker, but also because two nonrelated facts were connected into one sentence. This, however, requires referring to bigger chunks of the text.

The connector in example (21) might even be redundant: the thought expressed by the author would have been much clearer without any connectors. *In my opinion, I would rather stay on village and travel to city every day, at least I would breathe fresh air and have silence.* Examples (21) and (22) are a clear representation of addition, i.e. they require an additive logical connector, if any, not a contrastive one (Milton & Tsang, 1993:223).

23 [...] *the baby from the earliest age will learn emotions like empathy, compassion, love and friendship, because the pet will be its first friend. <Nevertheless>, the baby will develop some skills much faster if accompanied by a pet, which is scientifically proved.*

Similarly, example (23) contains two facts that are in relation of addition, not contrast. A substitution test with *but* and *however* can be used to prove this (cf. Thompson & Martinet, 1985:289). However, the coherence of the thought seems disrupted. *Nevertheless*, as mentioned in Fraser and Malamud-Markowski (1996), signals the denial of what has been said in the first sentence, which is obviously not the case here. An additive connector such as *furthermore* or *also* would function much better in this context and would not disrupt the text cohesion.

4.3.2 Analysis of Errors in the German Subcorpus

The error analysis of German essays revealed that most of the erroneous uses of discourse markers are the wrong choice in terms of their function.

24 *Ob sich die Familie um einen Teil der Familie nicht kümmert kann man das an seinem behalten sehen. <Obwohl> die Meisten ihre Familie als schlecht bezeichnen nur weil sie im Mittelpunkt stehen wollen.*

The use of *obwohl* to link the two clauses in example (24) interferes with reader's understanding of the text and disrupts coherence. The meaning of two clauses is not contrasted and *obwohl* in its contrastive use is redundant. The logical relationship between the clauses without the contrastive *obwohl* is quite clear and the entire sentence is understandable: the clause in which *obwohl* was used is supposed to be the main clause with regard to the second subordinating clause containing the subordinating conjunction *weil*. A possible alternative would be to use *wohl*, which would not disrupt the cohesion of the text: *Die Meisten bezeichnen ihre Familie wohl als schlecht, nur weil sie im Mittelpunkt stehen wollen.*

25 *Ich hatte den Glück in der Stadt zu leben, auch <doch > am Dorf bei meine Großeltern.*
26 *Zu den Stereotypen gehört die Aussage, dass die Leute die im Dorf leben, weniger ausgebildet, <aber> "primitiver" sind.*

Examples (25) and (26) are similar because the clauses in both examples are not in contrast. They are a clear representation of addition. In both examples, the misuse of the connector implying concessive relation could be attributed to learners' opinion that there is a logical contrast between the two facts (the city and the country in example (25) and being educated and being primitive in example (26)) and an attempt to emphasise it. In both examples, a possible alternative to correct this error would be to use an additive logical connector, such as *sowohl...als auch,* which would not disrupt the coherence of the text.

Example (25) could be corrected by substituting *doch* with *aber* (with appropriate modification in word order): *Ich hatte das Glück in der Stadt zu leben, aber auch am Dorf bei meinen Großeltern. Aber,* as mentioned by Stede (2004: 282), can be used to compare a neutral contrast of two situations. According to Milton and Tsang (1993:232), this type of error could be attributed to exposure to simplistic lists of connectors categorised only by a particular function, misleading the learner to choose, in this case, either one from the list of contrastive discourse markers in an attempt to emphasise the contrast of two situations.

5 Discussion

The results of the present study have corroborated three different and most prominent features of non-native speakers' use of discourse markers observed in previous studies (cf. Milton & Tsang, 1993; Granger & Tyson, 1996; Hinkel, 2001; Bolton et al., 2002; Chen, 2006, Bagarić Medve & Pavičić Takač, 2013b) which have shown that non-native English and German users tend to overuse or misuse certain connectors as well as use them with limited variability. The comparison between the two languages in the present study showed an even lower variability in the German texts, because the second element of a split particle *anderseits* and *auf der anderen Seite* are variants of the linguistic form *andererseits.*

The phenomena of limited variability and overuse are closely connected because language learners are often taught lists of mutually interchangeable connectors (Bagarić Medve & Pavičić Takač, 2013b) without a detailed analysis of nuances of meaning or usage constraints. Learners often choose to learn one or two examples from each of the groups of discourse markers and use them indiscriminately. This leads to overuse of a small number of discourse markers.

An inspection of variability and dispersion of connectors in the two subcorpora revealed that non-native English and German users use one dominant, i.e. prototypical contrastive marker: *but* in English and *aber* in German. These, along with *on the other hand* in English, and *doch* in German, are typical for lower levels of communicative language competence and were used most frequently in our subcorpora. As has already been indicated, it seems that learners opt for "safe choices", i.e. those discourse markers that have fewer constraints and consequently a wider coverage.

The error analysis pointed to the conclusion that erroneous or imprecise use of discourse markers can disrupt cohesive ties and coherence of the text. To use connectors appropriately, "students must possess, beyond semantic and syntactic knowledge of the language, a sensitivity to register as well" (Milton & Tsang, 1993:216). The present analysis showed that foreign language users have insufficient knowledge about the distinction between formal and informal connectors. Next, by using a wrong discourse marker, or using it in the wrong place in the text, the writer misleads the reader. Finally, in both corpora, we found examples of redundant use of discourse markers which, according to Milton and Tsang (1993: 228), "does not contribute to the coherence of the text" (Milton & Tsang, 1993:228).

The observed misuse, overuse, and lack of variability in the use of discourse markers in our subcorpora can be attributed to an intensive exposure of learners to explicit teaching which usually takes the form of relatively extensive lists of mutually interchangeable connectors. Textbook analyses have also shown that learners are exposed not only to a limited repertoire of connectors but also to simplistic lists which ignore their semantic, syntactic, and stylistic differences (cf. Milton & Tsang, 1993; Granger & Tyson, 1996; Hinkel, 2001; Bolton et al., 2002). According to Milton and Tsang (1993:232), learners are exposed to lists of connectors categorised by a particular function, with an example sentence provided for only one or two of the items without being taught about the subtle differences. The effects of discourse markers instruction on second language users' production have not yet been confirmed, but there have been a few studies whose results suggest that the explicit approach to teaching discourse markers may be effective (Håukas & Hoheisel, 2013; Sadeghi & Kargar, 2014; Al-Qahtani, 2015; DavatgariAsl & Moradinejad, 2016). However, the present findings suggest that teaching discourse markers has to be more systematic and elaborate, if limited variability, misuse, or overuse of discourse markers is to be avoided. Explicit teaching should encompass more detailed analyses and illustrative examples of discourse markers use. It should also aim at raising learners' awareness of the fact that one connector cannot always be replaced by any other connector listed in the same category. Granger and Tyson (1996) propose that more emphasis be placed on how to use connectors by studying their semantic and syntactic differences in authentic contexts. They also agree that "learning when not to use them (connectors) is as important as learning when to do so" (Granger & Tyson, 1996:25).

It seems to be safe to conclude that explicit teaching of the use of cohesive device has to avoid exposing learners to simplistic lists of connectors and focus on details of discourse functions of cohesive devices. This can be achieved through data-driven learning by using authentic materials in which students can "[...] discover for themselves the patterns of occurrence of logical connectors" (Milton & Tsang, 1993:238). We suggest that learner corpora, such as ours, and their comparison with (comparable) native-speaker corpora can also serve as a starting point for analysis in second language classes. Such comparisons may reveal patterns of transfer from first to second language, or from second to third language.

Moreover, the potential washback effect must be taken into account. Although it can be positive if learners expand their repertoire of discourse markers and start using them more often, it can also result in discourse markers overuse: learners may use discourse markers just to meet the evaluation criteria, without having a clear idea about the constraints regarding their use and nuances of meaning. This further implies that learners' use of discourse markers is not automated, but that they consciously choose discourse markers from lists based on what they have learned about them.

There seems to be an agreement that proper use of cohesive devices can improve coherence of learners' writing. But teaching discourse markers is not enough. Learners have to explore longer stretches of meaningful context in order to narrow down the meaning of a particular discourse marker, restrictions on its location in the discourse structure and clause ordering, as well as analysis of 'strength' of arguments that follow (such is the case of *but* vs. *however*). Development of cohesion also requires an analysis of typical academic moves, for example, how and where in the text one might introduce counter-arguments.

6 Conclusion

In this study, we presented the results of a corpus-based analysis of the use of discourse markers of contrast in the writing of non-native users of English and German. The issues addressed included the similarities and differences in discourse markers use between English and German texts, and the extent to which erroneous use of discourse markers causes coherence disruption. In spite of the relatively small sizes of the two subcorpora, which prevent us from drawing any general conclusions, marked trends emerged. The results demonstrated that non-native language users encounter a number of problems when using discourse markers, which leads to coherence breaks. A closer inspection of patterns in the use of discourse markers revealed inappropriate use and limited variability with one prototypical contrastive marker in both languages. Our analysis revealed some critical problems regarding the teaching of discourse markers, which is often limited to presenting simplistic lists of connectors from which language users consciously, but arbitrarily, choose discourse markers from those lists, often in order to meet evaluation criteria.

A path to be followed in further research is a detailed comparison of comparable corpora of non-native and native-speaker essays which would provide a better understanding of types and sources of differences. Corpus-analytic tools are invaluable in such endeavours. What the present study showed is that corpus analysis can be used in the exploration of the role of cohesive devices in establishing coherence. A simple lexical search can uncover some patterns which can then be further analysed. This, however, would require mixed-method approach, specially designed corpus tools, and last but not least, larger corpora.

Acknowledgement

This work has been supported by Croatian Science Foundation under the project (IP-2016-06-5736).

Note

1 Although not the aim of the present study, and with due caution as to the limitations of comparing different corpora, we conducted an ad-hoc comparison of discourse marker occurrence in learner corpora with native-speaker corpora available in the Sketch Engine. The analysis showed that the HPMs for all discourse markers were much larger in learner corpora than in native-speaker corpora, signalling limited variability and overuse of connectors by non-native users of English and German.

References

Abraham, W. (1979). But. *Stadia Linguistica* 33, 89–119.

Al-Qahtani, A. A. (2015). The effect of explicit instruction of textual discourse markers on Saudi EFL Learners' Reading Comprehension. *English Language Teaching*, 8/4, 57–66.

Bachman L. F. (1990). *Fundamental Considerations in Language Testing*. Oxford: Oxford University Press.

Bachman, L. & Palmer, A. (1996). *Language Testing in Practice: Designing and Developing Useful Language Tests*. Oxford: Oxford University Press.

Bagarić Medve, V. & Čelebić, I. (2012). Bewertung der Diskurskompetenz: holistischer vs. analytischer Ansatz, in L. Pon, V. Karablić & S. Cimer (eds.) *Applied Linguistics Today: Research and Perspectives – Angewandte Linguistik heute: Forschung und Perspektiven*. Frankfurt a/M: Peter Lang, pp. 33–49.

Bagarić Medve, V. & Pavičić Takač, V. (2013a). *Jezična i strategijska kompetencija u stranome jeziku*. Osijek: Filozofski fakultet.

Bagarić Medve, V. & Pavičić Takač, V. (2013b). The influence of cohesion and coherence on text quality: A cross-linguistic study of foreign language learners' written production, in E. Piechurska-Kuciel & E. Szymanska-Czaplak (eds.) *Language in Cognition and Affect*. Berlin-Heidelberg: Springer, pp. 111–131.

Bell, D., M. (1998). Cancellative discourse markers: a core/periphery approach. *Pragmatics*, 8/4, 515–541.

Bolton, K., Nelson, G. & Hung, J. (2002). A corpus-based study of connectors in student writing: Research from The International Corpus of English in Hong Kong (ICE-HK). *International Journal of Corpus Linguistics*, 7/2, 165–182.

Blakemore, D. (1987). *Semantic Constraints on Relevance*. Oxford: Blackwell.

Breindl, E. (2004). Polysemie und Invarianz bei Konnektoren: allerdings und andere Kontrastmarker, in Pohl, I., Konerding, K.-P. (Hrsg.), *Stabilität und Flexibilität in der Semantik. Strukturelle, kognitive, pragmatische und historische Perspektiven (Sprache - System und Tätigkeit)*. Frankfurt am Main/ Berlin/Bern/Bruxelles/New York/Oxford/Wien: Lang, pp. 171–197.

Breindl, E., Volodina, A. & Hermann Waßner, U. (2014). *Handbuch der deutschen Konnektoren 2: Semantik der deutschen Satzverknüpfer*. Walter de Gruyter GmbH & Co.

Brown, G. & Yule, G. (1983). *Discourse Analysis*. Cambridge: Cambridge University Press.

Buscha, J. & Helbig. G. (2000). *Leitfaden der deutschen Grammatik*. Berlin und München: Langenscheidt KG.

Buscha A., Szita S. & Raven S. (2013). *Übungsgrammatik, Deutsch als Fremdsprache, Sprachniveau C1, C2*. Leipzig: Schubert Verlag.

Canale, M. (1983). From communicative competence to communicative language pedagogy, in J.C. Richards, R.W. Schmidt (eds.) *Language and Communication*. London: Longman, pp. 2–27.

Canale, M. & Swain, M. (1980) Theoretical bases of communicative approaches to second language teaching and testing. *Applied Linguistics*, 1/1, 1–47.

Carrell, P. (1982). Cohesion is not coherence. *TESOL Quarterly*, 16, 479–488.

Carrió-Pastor, M. L. (2013) A contrastive study of the variation of sentence connectors in academic English. *Journal of English for Academic Purposes*, 12, 192–202.

Celce-Murcia, M. (2007). Rethinking the role of communicative competence in language teaching, in E. Alcón Soler & M.P. Safont Jordà (eds.), *Intercultural Language Use and Language Learning*. Dordrecht: Springer, pp. 41–57.

Celce-Murcia, M., Dörnyei, Z. & Thurrell, S. (1995). Communicative competence: a pedagogically motivated model with content specifications. *Issues in Applied Linguistics*, 6/2, 5–35.

Chen, Ch. W. (2006). The use of conjunctive adverbials in the academic papers of advanced Taiwanese EFL learners. *International Journal of Corpus Linguistics*, 11/1, 113–130.

Council of Europe (2001). *Common European Framework of Reference: Learning, Teaching, Assessment*. Cambridge: Cambridge University Press.

Dastjerdi, H. V. & Talebinezhad, R. M. (2006). Chain-preserving deletion procedure in cloze: a discoursal perspective. *Language Testing*, 23/1, 58–72.

DavatgariAsl, H. & Moradinejad, A. (2016). The effect of explicit instruction of discourse markers on Iranian EFL Learners' Speaking Ability. *Journal of Applied Linguistics and Language Research*, Vol. 3/5, 190–202.

Di Meola, C. (2004). Kontrast im Diskurs, in H. Blühdorn, E. Breindl and U. Hermann Wassner (eds.) *Brücken schlagen: Grundlagen der Konnektorensemantik Volume 5 of Linguistik – Impulse & Tendenzen*. Walter de Gruyter, pp. 255–284.

Dirk, S. (2005). *Discourse Markers Across Languages. A Contrastive Study of Second-level Discourse Markers in Native and Non-native Text with Implications for General and Pedagogic Lexicography*. London and New York: Routledge.

Duden (2003). *Deutsches Universalwörterbuch, 5. Auflage*. Manheim: Dudenverlag.

Fraser, B. (1990). An approach to discourse markers. *Journal of Pragmatics*, 14, 383–395.

Fraser, B. (1998). Contrastive discourse markers in English, in Andreas H. Jucker and Yael Ziv (eds.) *Discourse markers. Descriptions and Theory*. Amsterdam/Philadelphia: John Benjamins Publishing Company, pp. 301–326.

Fraser, B. (2013). Combinations of Contrastive Discourse Markers in English. *International Review of Pragmatics*, 5, 318–340.

Fraser, B. & Malamud-Makowski, M. (1996). English and Spanish contrastive discourse markers. *Language Sciences*, 18/3–4, 863–881.

Granger, S. & Tyson, S. (1996). Connector usage in the English essay writing of native and non-native EFL speakers of English. *World Englishes*, 15/1, 17–27.

Greenbaum, S. & Quirk R. (1990). *A student's grammar of the English language*. Harlow: Longman.

Grote, B., Lenke, N. & Stede, M. (1997). Ma(r)king Concessions in English and German, in A. Graesser (ed.) *Discourse Processes. A Multidisciplinary Journal 24/1*. Greenwich, Connecticut, pp. 87–117.

Halliday, M. A. K. & Hasan, R. (1976). *Cohesion in English*. London: Longman Pub Group.

Håukas, Å. & Hoheisel, M. (2013). "Vermittlung der Textstruktur im fremdsprachlichen Deutschunterricht – eine Interventionsstudie". *Zeitschrift für Interkulturellen Fremdsprachenunterricht*, 18/1, 76–92.

Helbig, G. & Buscha, J. (1990). *Deutsche Grammatik: Ein Handbuch für den Ausländerunterricht*. Berlin, Leipzig: Langenscheidt, Verlag Enzyklopädie.

Hinkel, E. (2001). Matters of Cohesion in L2 Academic Texts. *Applied Language Learning*, 12/2, 111–132

Hymes, D. (1972). On communicative competence, in J.B. Pride & J. Holmes (eds.) *Sociolnguistcs: Selected readings*. Harmondsworth: Penguin, pp. 269–293.

Jucker, A. H. & Ziv, Y. (1998). Discourse markers: Introduction, in Andreas H. Jucker and Yael Ziv (eds.) *Discourse Markers. Descriptions and Theory*. Amsterdam/Philadelphia: John Benjamins Publishing Company, pp. 1–13.

Karagjosova, E. (2001). Towards a comprehensive meaning of German *doch*, *Proceedings of the ESSLLI 2001*. Helsinki.

König, E. (1988). Concessive connectives and concessive sentences, in J. Hawkins (ed.), *Explaining Language Universals*. Oxford: Oxford University Press, pp. 145–166.

Lang, E. (1984). *The Semantics of Coordination*. Amsterdam: John Benjamins.

Lakoff, R. (1971). If/s and/s and but/s about conjunction, in Charles J. Fillmore, and D. Terence Langendoen (eds.), *Studies in Linguistic Semantics. Papers presented at a conference sponsored by the Dept. of Linguistics, Ohio State University*, April 14–15, 1969. New York: Holt, Rinehart and Winston.

Malchukov, A. (2004). Towards a semantic typology of adversative and contrast marking article. *Journal of Semantics 21*, 177–198.

Milton, J. C., & Tsang, E. S. C. (1993). A corpus-based study of logical connectors in EFL students' writing: directions for future research, in R. Pemberton & E.S.C. Tsang (eds.) *Studies in Lexis*. Hong Kong: The Hong Kong University of Science and Technology Language Center, pp. 215–246.

Pasch, R., Brauße U., Breindl E. & Hermann Waßner U. (2009). *Handbuch der deutschen Konnektoren 1: Linguistische Grundlagen der Beschreibung und syntaktische Merkmale der deutschen Satzverknüpfer (Konjunktionen, Satzadverbien und Partikeln)*. Berlin, New York: Walter de Gruyter.

Quirk, R., Greenbaum, S., Leech, G. & Svartvik, J. (1985). *A Comprehensive Grammar of the English Language*. London and New York: Longman.

Sadeghi, B & Kargar, A. (2014). The effect of explicit instruction of discourse markers on EFL learners' writing ability. *International Journal of Educational Investigations* 1/1, 328–338.

Savignon, S. J. (1983). *Communicative Competence: Theory and Classroom Practice. Texts and Contexts in Second Language Learning.* Reading, Massachusetts: Addison-Wesley Publishing Company.

Schiffrin, D. (1987). *Discourse Markers.* Cambridge: Cambridge University Press.

Schourup, L. (1999). Tutorial overview discourse markers. *Lingua 107,* 227–265

Shea, M. (2009) "A Corpus-Based Study of Adverbial Connectors in Learner Text". *MSU Working Papers in SLS 2009 Vol. 1, No. 1 Adverbial Connectors in Learner Texts*; pp. 1–13.

Stede, M. (2004). Kontrast im Diskurs, in H. Blühdorn, E. Breindl and H. Hermann Wassner (eds.) *Brücken schlagen: Grundlagen der Konnektorensemantik Volume 5 of Linguistik – Impulse & Tendenzen.* Walter de Gruyter, pp. 255–284.

Swan, M. (1995). *Practical English Usage Second Edition.* Oxford: Oxford University Press.

Tankó, G. (2004). The use of adverbial connectors in Hungarian university students' argumentative essays, in J. McH. Sinclair (ed.) *How to Use Corpora in Language Teaching.* Amsterdam: John Benjamins, pp. 157–181.

Thomas, J. (2015). *Discovering English with Sketch Engine.* Brno: Laptop Languages.

Thompson A. J. & Martinet A. V. (1985). *A Practical English Grammar. Fourth Edition.* Oxford: Oxford University Press.

van Dijk, T. A. (1977). *Text and Context. Explorations in the Semantics and Pragmatics of Discourse.* New York: Longman.

Widdowson, H. G. (1978). *Teaching Language as Communication.* Oxford: Oxford University Press.

Winter, Y. & Rimon, M. (1994) 'Contrast and implication in natural language'. *Journal of Semantics* 11, 365–406.

10 Personal Metadiscourse Markers in a Corpus of Final Degree Dissertations in Education Sciences

Francisco Núñez-Román

1 Introduction

Since the seminal works of Vande Kopple (1985) and Crismore (1989) about metadiscoursivity, an important development of this concept has been provided by the contributions of Markkanen, Steffensen, and Crismore (1993), Mauranen (1993), Hyland (1998; 2005; 2017), and Ädel (2006), among others. Metadiscoursivity has become a productive issue and it has been studied from different perspectives. As part of this drive, metadiscourse markers in academic writing have been among the main lines of research, primarily in English contexts (Dahl, 2004; Gillaerts & Van de Velde, 2010; Hu & Cao, 2011; Kuhi & Behnam, 2011). Thus, Mauranen (1993) analysed the cultural difference among diverse types of academic texts, along the lines of contrastive rhetoric studies (Candarli, Bayyurt & Marti, 2015; Crismore, Markkanen & Steffensen, 1993; Mur Dueñas, 2011; Perales-Escudero & Swales, 2011). A new research field focused on the Disciplines has emerged from these works, and offers detailed analyses on academic texts from diverse areas (Bolívar, Beke & Shiro, 2010; Ezeiza Ramos & Alberdi Larizgoitia, 2015; Figueras, 2000; Piqué-Noguera & Camaño-Puig, 2015; Saz Rubio, 2011). The concern about the acquisition of research skills, such as academic writing, has led to describe how researchers acquire the discursive elements of their disciplines, especially in Final Degree Dissertations, masters and doctoral theses (Ädel, 2012; Hyland & Tse, 2004; Kawase, 2015).

Another line of research is addressed to investigate the metadiscursive elements in different genres in the context of undergraduate studies, such as essays (Beke, 2005; Bruce, 2010, Steffensen & Cheng, 1996) or literature reviews (Núñez, Muñoz & Mihovilovic, 2006). However, despite the increasing interest in academic texts produced in Higher Education contexts, the Final Degree Dissertation has been of little interest to scholars, particularly among Spanish researchers, because this academic genre did not become widespread in Spanish Higher Education until the implementation of the European Higher Education Area (EHEA) in the late 1990s. Greater efforts in this area are focused on filling the gaps that students have when they face their Final Degree Dissertations, by focusing on improving writing skills (Corcelles, Cano, Mayoral &

Castelló, 2017) or collecting data about students' perceptions, practices, and opinions on this genre (Todd, Bannister & Clegg, 2004). Researches from a linguistic perspective are less common (Cano Vela, 2016; López-Cózar, Priede & Benito, 2013).

This work, therefore, belongs to a recent research line in Spanish language and aims to analyse what kinds of personal metadiscourse markers (PMM) are used in a Corpus of Final Degree Dissertations and which functions they perform. This study will provide, firstly, a deeper knowledge of the PMM used in this academic genre in Spanish, and secondly, new data that will facilitate the development of training initiatives intended to improve writing skills as well as the author's awareness of the students (Castelló, Bañales, Corcelles, Iñesta, Vega, 2011; Lorés-Sanz, 2011).

For this purpose, this work attempts to answer these questions: are the discursive functions determined by the typology of FDD? Which are the main discursive functions of PMD in an FDD in Education Sciences? In order to answer these questions, the first part of this article offers the theoretical foundations of our research and the analysis criteria. The second part describes the corpus and the methodology in detail. The third part presents the results of the analysis. Finally, the last section draws the conclusions, limitations, and implications of the findings for research and pedagogy.

2 Theoretical Framework

2.1 The Reflexive Model of Metadiscursivity

Metadiscourse, broadly speaking, refers to the relation that language has with itself and the instruments used by the speaker/writer and recognised by the listener/reader to organise, interpret, and evaluate the discourse within a determined communication context which allows the speaker to modulate the text depending on the recipient and the conventions of the genre in order to achieve a communicative purpose (Hyland, 2005). Given these basic premises, Ädel and Mauranen (2010) distinguish two approaches to the study of metadiscoursivity, the "integrative" (Mauranen, 1993) or "interactive model" (Ädel, 2010) and the "non-integrative" (Mauranen, 1993) or "reflexive model" (Ädel, 2010). In the integrative or interactive model (Hyland, 2005), metadiscoursivity involves the devices showing how the text is organised or referring to the text itself (textual functions), indeed the linguistics elements reflecting the speaker's point of view about what is said in the text (interpersonal function). The metadiscursivity categories of the interactive model include textual markers (*in addition*, *on the other hand*, *to begin with*, *in this chapter*, etc.), and a set of interactive and interactional resources that make the speaker's attitude towards the content of the text explicit, such as evidentiality markers (*maybe*, *as one might expect*, *certainly*, etc.), attitude markers (*unfortunately*, *I agree*, etc.), or relational markers (note that, consider that, etc.). The non-integrative or reflexive model (Mauranen, 1993) excludes the interpersonal resources and any external reference, since it is focused on the linguistics devices that show how the text is organised or refers to the text itself or the writing process (*as will be presented below*, *as we have mentioned before*, *in other words*, etc.). As we can see, it is strictly a textual approach.

To save this dichotomy, Ädel (2006) takes as a starting point the text itself, core element of the discourse, and considers the visibility of writer and reader *qua* writer and reader of the text. Ädel, therefore, excludes any category referring to the writer's attitude towards the content of the texts because these references go beyond the text and refer to the writer or the reader as individuals in the real world. From Ädel's point of view, metadiscourse refers to the "text about the evolving text, or the writer's explicit commentary on her own ongoing discourse" (Ädel, 2006:20). As Salas Valdebenito points out, Ädel's reflexive model "logra un alto grado de rigor científico al circunscribir una categoría difusa como el metadiscurso, delimitando su alcance y deslindándola de otros fenómenos como la evaluación (o actitud), la mitigación, la intertextualidad y la atribución". Our research is based on Ädel's reflexive model approach to personal metadiscourse.

In Ädel's model, there is a functional distinction between two types of metadiscourse: the *metatext* and the *writer–reader interaction*. The metatext guides the reader through the text, by using expressions like *as it has seen before*, *in this work*, *in sum*, etc. The writer–reader interaction makes it possible to establish and maintain the writer–reader relationship, so that the writer can influence the reader directly. This function uses linguistic expressions like *as we can see*, *the reader could imagine*, *I would like to add that*, etc. It is important to remind ourselves that in this model, metadiscourse markers always refer to the text itself, and any reference to the writer or reader is restricted to the writer or the reader of the "world of discourse" (Ädel, 2006:28), not to the writer or the reader as entities of the real world.

We can also draw a distinction between the personal and impersonal dimension of metadiscourse. Personal metadiscourse makes explicit references to the writer or the reader of the text, and impersonal metadiscourse does not. In personal metadiscourse, thus, the writer–reader relationship with the text or between themselves inside the text is emphasised. Metadiscourse markers used in this case are personal pronouns (*I*, *you*, *me*, *your*, *us*, etc.), the preference for the first person (*I consider that…*, *I would like to say…*), the imperative (*Imagine that…*, *Note that…*), and the references to the participants in the text (*The reader could think…*, *It's not the author's intention to…*, etc.). Meanwhile, impersonal metadiscourse does not make explicit references to the participants of the communicative event and prefers the use of passive or impersonal structures (*A questionnaire has been designed to..., It has to be noted that..., It is important to observe that...*, etc.).

As Ädel says, the distinction between personal and impersonal metadiscourse is not a theoretical division, but "a way of labelling different surface types" (2006:16) of the texts. Furthermore, this distinction is fundamental in academic and scientific writing, since it allows the author to choose, first, his level of visibility and explicitness and, consequently, show his relationship with the content of the discourse.

From this perspective, the study of metadiscourse can be approached in four different ways (Ädel, 2006:20):

1 Metadiscourse oriented to the text: references to the text or the use of language.
2 Metadiscourse oriented to the writer: references to the writer *qua* writer of the text.
3 Metadiscourse oriented to the reader: references to the reader *qua* reader of the text.
4 Metadiscourse oriented to the participants: references to the writer and the reader *qua* writer and reader of the text.

Table 10.1 shows these configurations and some examples from our corpus.

Our study will be focused on all the possibilities of personal dimension (oriented to the writer, oriented to the reader, oriented to the participants) in the metatext and the writer–reader interaction surfaces.

Table 10.1 Personal and impersonal dimensions of metatext and writer–reader interaction (Ädel 2006:38)

Metadiscourse	Metatext	*Impersonal*	oriented to the text	*Así, este trabajo se estructura...* *En segundo lugar...* *En relación a lo mencionado anteriormente sobre...*
		Personal	oriented to the writer	*Como he mostrado en este trabajo...* *Con esto quiero decir que...*
			oriented to the reader	*...pudiesen ser comprendidas por el lector de este trabajo fin de grado...*
			oriented to the participants	*Como hemos visto en...* *Si tomamos el juego como...*
	Writer–reader interaction	*Personal*	oriented to the reader	*No les suena, siempre al cuidado de las demás, para eso me educaron ¿no?*
			oriented to the participants	*Sé que para algunas personas...*

2.2 *Functions of Personal Metadiscoursivity*

Metadiscursive structures can develop different functions that can be classified according to the text or to the dimension of the participants (reader, writer, reader-writer). Table 10.2 illustrates the discursive functions used in our analysis (Ädel, 2006):

Table 10.2 Discursive functions (Ädel, 2006:60)

Dimension	*Discursive functions*
Text	**Defining:** explicitly comments on how to interpret terminology.
	Saying: the fact that something is being communicated is foregrounded.
	Introducing the Topic: gives explicit proclamations of what the text is going to be about, which facilitates the processing of the subsequent text for the reader.
	Focusing: refers to a topic that has already been introduced in the text: announces that the topic is being focused on again, or it narrows it down.
	Concluding: is used to conclude a topic.
	Exemplifying: explicitly introduces an example.
	Reminding: points backwards in the discourse to something that has been said before.
	Adding: overtly states that a piece of information or an argument is being added to existing one(s).
	Arguing: emphasises the discourse act being performed in addition to expressing an opinion or viewpoint.
	Contextualising: contains traces of the production of the text or comments on (the conditions of) the situation of writing.
Participants	**Anticipating the reader's reaction:** pays special attention to predicting the reader's reaction to what is said, e.g. by explicitly attributing statements to the reader as possible objections or counterarguments conceived by him.
	Clarifying: marks a desire to clarify matters for the reader; motivated by a wish to avoid misinterpretation. Negative statements are common.
	Aligning perspectives: takes it for granted that the reader takes the writer's perspective. The reader's agreement is presupposed.
	Imagining scenarios: is a 'picture this' type of encouragement that (often politely) asks the reader to see something from a specific perspective. It allows writers to make examples vivid and pertinent to the reader.
	Hypothesising about the Reader: makes guesses about the reader and his knowledge or attitudes.
	Appealing to the Reader: attempts to influence the reader by emotional appeal. The writer persona conveys her attitude with the aim of correcting or entreating the reader.

3 Methodology

3.1 Corpus Description

The corpus used in this work, named TFE-Prim, contains 130 FDD belonging to the Undergraduate degree in Primary Education from 16 Spanish universities (Annex I). TFE-Prim Corpus is composed of three sub-corpora according to the typology of FDD: TFE-Did (Pedagogic Proposals), TFE-Inv (Research), and TFE-Rev (Literary Review). All the typologies share the core characteristics of an FDD in Primary Education, such as front page, index, abstract, key words, or bibliography, although each typology has specific features:

1 TFE-Did presents an original Pedagogic proposal, generally based on the students' experience during their traineeship. It contains an introduction, theoretical framework, pedagogic proposal, critical reflection on the proposal (extent, analysis, proposal for improvements), and conclusions.
2 TFE-Inv aims to answer a research question in Education and it is structured as a paper: introduction, theoretical framework, methodology, results, discussion, and conclusions.
3 FTE-Rev is a literature review of a topic related to Education. Commonly, after the introduction or justification, the author develops the topic from a historical or theoretical point of view. It shows the state of the art.

Corpus selection has been made according to two criteria (Biber & Jones, 2009): the date (from 2014 to 2017) and availability in institutional open-access repository with quality criteria. The length of the FDD is between 10,000 and 15,000 words, but we can find some examples with around 22,000 words. Front pages, index, bibliography, and references to the names of real persons have been deleted. The number of tokens according to the sub-corpora is presented in Table 10.3.

3.2 Procedure

There are two approaches to the study of metadiscursivity called by Ädel and Mauranen (2010:2) "the thin approach" and "the thick approach". The thin approach is a quantitative one. It is limited to collecting the number of occurrences of an item from a preset list. The thin approach doesn't consider the relevance of each item. However, the thick approach is based on a qualitative methodology. Once the items have been gathered, their metadiscursive relevance is established by a contextual analysis. In this case, the results are not intended to provide a frequency list, but to show the formal expressions of metadiscursive units longer than

Table 10.3 Corpus TFE-Prim data

Sub-corpus	Number of FDD	Number de tokens
TFE-Did	60	829,810
TFE-Inv	43	499,987
TFE-Rev	27	283,487
TFE-Prim total	**130**	**1,613,284**

a simple word and to explain their metadiscursive functions (Ädel & Mauranen, 2010). This work has followed this procedure. Firstly, we have established a list of metadiscursive elements from the taxonomies proposed by Salas Valdebenito (2015), Ädel (2006), and Hyland (2005); secondly, we have searched the metadiscursive elements in the TFE-Prim Corpus with AntConc 8.5 software; finally, once we have verified the metadiscursive function of each item obtained during the corpus scan using a contextual analysis, we have analysed their functions according to the Text and Participant dimensions exposed in Table 10.2.

In the next section, we will present the results of our analysis. Firstly, we will show the quantitative results, presenting the normalised frequency (1/1,000,000) of PMM in each sub-corpora. Secondly, we will expose the qualitative data, analysing the discursive functions used in TFE-Prim Corpus.

4 Results

The quantitative analysis shows, as we can see in Figure 10.1, that TFE-Inv has a higher normalised frequency of PMM; meanwhile, TFE-Did and TFE-Rev present a similar number of occurrences.

If we look inside the sub-corpora, we can observe that the correlation of the two dimensions is fairly uneven (Figure 10.2). TFE-Inv has the highest normalised frequency both in Text and Participant dimensions (86 and 15,4, respectively), but as long as TFE-Did and TFE-Rev show a similar normalised frequency of PMM in the Text dimension, this distribution clearly changes in the Participant dimension, where the normalised frequency of PMM in TFE-Rev (9,4) is nearly twice that of TFE-Did (5,1).

If we now turn to a qualitative analysis, regarding the discursive functions of PMM, Table 10.4 shows that the trends shown in Figures 10.1 and 10.2 are maintained.

Regarding the discursive functions oriented to the Text, the most used function is Say. This function is usually expressed by the verbs *decir* 'say', *señalar* 'point out', and *afirmar* 'afirm'. This function is more frequent in TFE-Inv (32) than in TFE-Did (22.1) and TFE-Rev (18.6). The latter, however, shows a broader range of *verba dicendi*. The most

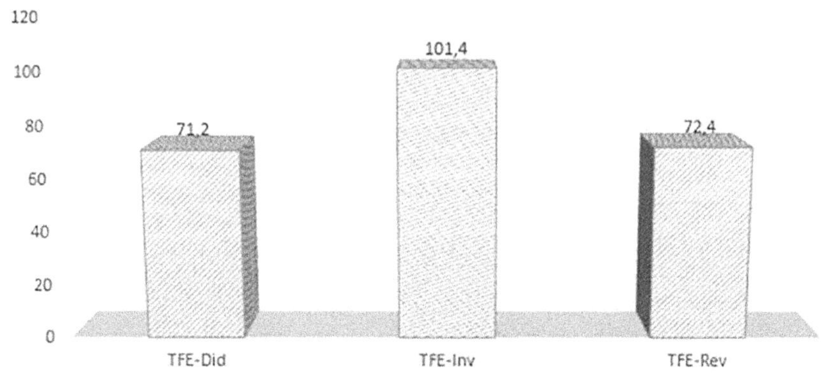

Figure 10.1 Normalised frequency (1/100,000) of PMM by typology of FDD.

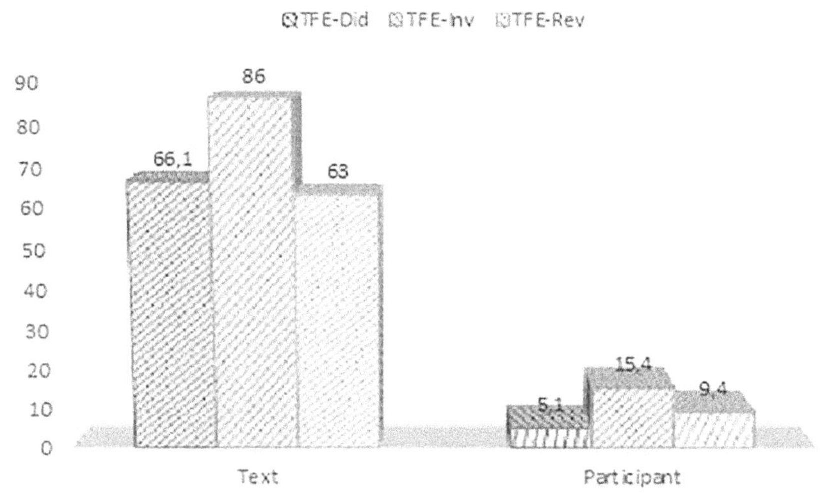

Figure 10.2 Normalised frequency of PMM by dimensions in each sub-corpora.

frequent structure used to express this metadiscursive function is *podemos decir* 'we can say':

1 Por último, **me gustaría señalar** la importancia que el principio "Dime cómo evalúas y te diré cómo enseñas" ha tenido en mi trabajo. (TFE-Did)
2 **He expuesto** este banco de recursos por el hecho de que hay muchos estudios para trabajar sobre la promoción de la autoestima pero se nota una actual tendencia de los educadores a fomentar el constructo autonomía [...] (TFE-Rev)

Table 10.4 Normalised frequency (1/100,000) of discursive functions of PMM by sub-corpora

Discursive functions		*TFE-DID*	*TFE-INV*	*TFE-REV*	Total
Text: product structure-oriented	Defining	2.4	3	3.5	8.9
	Say	22.1	32	18.6	72.7
	Introducing the topic	9.6	11	9.5	30.1
	Focusing the topic	1.4	2.8	1	5.2
	Concluding	3.8	4	2.4	10.2
	Exemplifying	2.7	4.8	3.1	10.6
	Reminding	13	18.6	14.1	45.7
	Adding	3.3	1.4	2.1	6.8
	Arguing	0.1	0.6	0.3	1
	Contextualising	7.7	7.8	8.4	23.9
	Total	**66.1**	**86**	**63**	**215.1**
Participant: writer or reader-oriented	Anticipating the reader's reaction	–	–	–	0
	Clarifying	2.2	2	4.9	6.9
	Aligning perspectives	2.6	12.6	4.2	19.4
	Imagining scenarios	–	0.6	–	0.6
	Hypothesising about the reader	–	–	–	0
	Appealing to the reader	0.3	0.2	0.3	0.8
	Total	**5.1**	**15.4**	9.4	29.9
		71.2	101.4	72.4	245

Sometimes, the writer wants to highlight the information. In this case, commonly used verbs are *destacar* 'emphasize' or *resaltar* 'highlight':

3 En primer lugar, **podríamos destacar que** la psicología hasta hace pocas décadas ha estado exclusivamente dedicada al estudio de los cambios conductuales. (TFE-Did)

4 **Quiero resaltar que** con la realización de este trabajo no acaban mis ganas de seguir aprendiendo cosas nuevas sino que gracias a lo que he podido conseguir me puede servir para mi formación continua como futura docente. (TFE-Inv)

Following the Say function, we find the Reminding, Introducing the topic, and Contextualising functions. Reminding uses some usual metadiscursive frameworks like *como (ya) hemos dicho/mencionado/visto (anteriormente/en el capítulo X, etc.)* 'as we have (already) said/mentioned/ seen (before/in chapter X, etc.)'. This function is slightly more frequent in TFE-Inv (18.6) compared with FTE-Rev (14.1) and TFE-Did (13):

5 Es decir, del mismo modo que **anteriormente señalábamos que** no es lo mismo el plurilingüismo que el multilingüismo, sin embargo, no

es igual el enfoque multicultural que el intercultural en la enseñanza. (TFE-Inv)

6 La intervención de esta propuesta pedagógica va dirigida, pensado en los profesores como programa de ayuda, pero **como hemos indicado en nuestra fundamentación**, su labor revierte en el desarrollo integral del alumnado del primer curso de Educación Primaria (6–7 años). (TFE-Did)

Introducing the topic usually includes a direct reference to the process of writing, mostly through structures like *a continuación* 'next' or *en este apartado* 'in this chapter'. *Tratar* 'discuss' is the most usual verb used in this function, followed by *exponer* 'set out' and *describir* 'describe', normally in inchoative periphrasis (*vamos a* 'let's...', *pasaremos a* o *nos disponemos a* 'going to...'):

7 **En este apartado me voy a centrar en** explicar cuales son los objetivos, el ámbito de actuación, y las fases a seguir dentro de un programa de Atención Temprana dirigido a niños sordos. (TFE-Rev)

8 Una vez definida la muestra y explicado el instrumento utilizado para el estudio, **pasamos a detallar** los pasos que hemos seguido para el correcto análisis de los datos obtenidos. (TFE-Inv)

Contextualising is slightly more frequent in TFE-Rev (8.4) than in TFE-Inv (7.8) and TFE-Did (7.7). The most recurrent construction is *como veremos* 'as we will see', but we can also find examples with *profundizar* 'delve into' or *tratar* 'discuss' followed by an endophoric marker (*más adelante* 'forward', *en el próximo capítulo* 'in the next chapter'). The future tense is most commonly used:

9 Estas nuevas modificaciones las podemos observar en la Escuela Nueva, diferente a la llevada a cabo en la escuela clásica y que **trataré con mayor profundidad en apartados posteriores.** (TFE-Did)

10 Para ello, **comenzaremos explicando** la metodología que vamos a utilizar, **continuaremos analizando** los participantes que han tomado parte en este informe y en sus investigaciones así como las técnicas e instrumentos de investigación utilizados. (TFE-Inv)

Except Say, which has a closer relation with the transmission of ideas, the other most commonly used functions in TFE-Prim aim to make the structure of the text and the process of writing more explicit.

In the Text dimension, the low frequency of occurrences of Focusing the topic (TFE-Did: 1.4; TFE-Inv: 2.8; TFE-Rev: 1; example 11) and Arguing (TFE-Did: 0.1; TFE-Inv: 0.6; TFE-Rev: 0.3; example 12) should be noted:

11 **La pregunta que debemos plantear aquí es:** ¿por qué es necesario que la música clásica forme parte de los contenidos culturales que existen en la televisión? (TFE-Rev)

12 Por ello, es por lo que a continuación de dicho resumen aparecen motivos y referencias clave a autores y autoras que reflejan en su mayoría de los argumentos que **sostengo y defiendo** de cara a la acción docente en ambos ámbitos, Plástica y EVA, y su enlace para conformar una apuesta potente por ambos ámbitos. (TFE-Did)

Moving on now to the Participant dimension, which establishes the interaction between the writer and the reader, we can observe that it is by far the least used dimension in TFE-Prim. There are no examples of Anticipating the reader's reaction or Hypothesising about the reader's functions in the TFE-Prim Corpus. This fact shows that the recipient of the text is not in reader's mind during the process of writing, at least from the point of view of the use of PMM. The PMM obtained in the TFE-Prim Corpus serve to express functions such as Aligning perspectives (19.4; example 13) or Clarifying (6.9; example 14). The functions aimed at reflection or appealing to the reader are practically non-existent (examples 15 and 16).

13 **No debemos ver** la ciencia **como** un campo dedicado únicamente a los expertos, ni tampoco creer que no está al alcance de todos. (TFE-Inv)

14 **Con esto quiero decir, que** se hace necesaria la inclusión de todas las personas en el ámbito educativo, siendo necesario para ello, el apoyo de la comunidad educativa al completo, así como otros agentes externos (TFE-Inv)

15 En segundo lugar, **para que el lector comprenda mejor** la importancia de dicha Atención Temprana es necesario exponer brevemente cuales son las características y niveles de actuación de la Atención Temprana en general (TFE-Rev)

16 El trabajo por tanto, se va a estructurar **de tal modo que el lector pueda hacerse**, de forma visual y gráfica, **una idea global** de todos los aspectos más importantes tratados

As we have mentioned before, the presence of the reader of the text is not explicitly marked in TFE-Prim Corpus. The absence of one of the main participants in the communicative process is definitely one of the key features of FDD in Primary Education Undergraduate degrees in Spanish Higher Education.

5 Conclusions

This work has allowed us to analyse the use of PMM in a corpus of FDD in Education Sciences from a quantitative and qualitative perspective. From a quantitative approach, the current study found that PMM are more frequent in the sub-corpus TFE-Inv than in the other sub-corpora. In TFE-Did and TFE-Rev, the normalised frequencies are similar. According to this data, we can infer that the typology of FDD could determine the use of PMM. This result may be explained by the fact that this typology of FDD, TFE-Inv, is closer to a well-defined academic genre with a well-defined set of rules: the research article. It is possible that research articles may be used as a model by Research FDD writers.

From a qualitative approach, we can observe that PMM are mainly used referring to Text dimension; in other words, the main function of PMM in our corpus is addressing the recipient during the reading process. PMM normalised frequencies in Text dimension are visibly higher than the Participant dimension frequency. These findings suggest that TFE-Prim authors aren't aware of the role of the writer and reader as participants in the writing process do not take notice of the author's voice as a member of a discursive community. The TFE-Prim authors seem not to be interested in influencing the reader. Regarding the typology of TFE, what is surprising is that the TFE-Rev sub-corpus presents a higher normalised frequency of PMM in the Participant dimension in relation to the TFE-Inv sub-corpus. A possible explanation for this might be that TFE-Rev sub-corpus is focused on providing information that has to be understood by the reader, so the writer tries to engage the reader in the topic under discussion.

Concerning specific discursive functions, the results of this study show that there is a strong preference for some discursive functions, such as Say and Reminding, which are usually used for the transmission of knowledge (Say) and organisation of ideas (Reminding). However, the TFE-Prim corpus is lacking PMM devoted to reflecting on the subject, like Arguing. In line with the low normalised frequency of the Participant dimension in the corpus, the discursive functions related to this dimension are restricted to inviting the reader to share the author's point of view, through the Aligning perspectives or the Clarifying functions. No significant examples of appealing to the reader or hypothesising about the subject were found in our corpus.

In summary, the present results are significant in at least two major respects. One of the issues that emerges from these findings is that the typology of FDD has an influence on the use of PMM. FDD concerning research are more likely to present a higher rate of PMM, compared with FDD concerning pedagogic proposals or literature reviews. Secondly, much work needs to be done in order to develop the author's awareness in FDD in Education Sciences. TFE-Prim authors show a lack of critical thinking and prefer a "knowledge telling" approach (Scardamalia & Bereiter, 1992). It is necessary, therefore, to work deeply with FDD writers in developing their own voice as authors inside a discursive community, enhancing the linguistic structures that reflect the discursive functions related to the Participant dimension.

These results therefore need to be interpreted with caution, since a wider sample of FDD could affect these findings. Thus, further research should be undertaken to confirm the trends that have been shown in this work.

References

Ädel, A. (2006). *Metadiscourse in L1 and L2 English*. Amsterdam-Philadelphia: John Benjamins.

Ädel, A. (2010). Just to give you kind of a map of where we are going: a taxonomy of metadiscourse in spoken and written academic English. *Nordic Journal of English Studies* 9/2, 69–97.

Ädel, A. & Mauranen, A. (2010). Metadiscourse: diverse and divided perspectives. *Nordic Journal of English Studies* 9/2, 1–11. http://ojs.ub.gu.se/ojs/index.php/njes/article/view/412 [retrieved: 25.5.2017].

Ädel, A. (2012). 'What I want you to remember is.': audience orientation in monologic academic genres. *English Text Construction* 5/1, 101–117.

Beke, R. (2005). El metadiscurso interpersonal en artículos de investigación. *Revista Signos. Estudios de Lingüística* 38/57, 7–18. https://scielo.conicyt.cl/scielo.php?script=sci_arttext&pid=S0718-09342005000100001 [retrieved: 22.06.2017].

Biber, D. & Jones, J. K. (2009). Quantitative methods in corpus linguistics, in A. Lüdeling & M. Kytö (eds.) *Corpus Linguistics: An International Handbook*. Berlín: Mouton de Gruyter, pp. 1286–1304.

Bolívar, A., Beke, R. & Shiro, M. (2010). Las marcas lingüísticas del posicionamiento en las disciplinas: Estructura, voces y perspectivas discursivas, in G. Parodi (ed.) *Alfabetización académica y profesional en el siglo XXI: Leer y escribir desde las disciplinas*, Santiago: Ariel, pp. 95–125.

Bruce, I. (2010). Textual and discoursal resources used in the essay genre in sociology and English. *Journal of English for Academic Purposes* 9/3, 153–166.

Candarli, D., Bayyurt, Y. & Marti, L. (2015). Authorial presence in L1 and L2 novice academic writing: cross-linguistic and cross-cultural perspectives. *Journal of English for Academic Purposes* 20, 192–202.

Cano Vela, A. G. (2016). El uso de marcadores del discurso en textos escritos por estudiantes del grado de maestro y de la especialidad de lengua castellana y literatura del MUFPS, in A. E. Díez Mediavilla, V. Brotons Rico, D. Escandell & J. Rovira Collado (eds.) *Aprendizajes plurilingües y literarios: Nuevos enfoques didácticos*, Alicante: Universitat d'Alacant, pp. 419–427.

Castelló, M. Bañales, G., Corcelles, M., Iñesta, A. & Vega, N. (2011). La voz del autor en los textos académicos: construyendo la identidad como escritor, in C. Monereo & J. I. Pozo (eds.) *La identidad en Psicología de la Educación: enfoques actuales, utilidad y límites*, Barcelona: Edebé, pp. 153–168.

Corcelles, M., Cano, M., Mayoral, P. & Castelló, M. (2017). Enseñar a escribir un artículo de investigación mediante la revisión colaborativa: Percepciones de los estudiantes. *Revista signos* 50/95, 337–360.

Crismore, A. (1989). *Talking with Readers: Metadiscourse as a Rhetorical Act*. New York, NY: Peter Lang.

Crismore, A., Markkanen, R., Steffensen, M. (1993). Metadiscourse in persuasive writing: a study of texts written by American and Finnish university students. *Written Communication* 10, 39–71.

Dahl, T. (2004). Textual metadiscourse in research articles: a marker of national culture or of academic discipline? *Journal of Pragmatics* 36/10, 1807–1825.

Ezeiza Ramos, J. & Alberdi Larizgoitia, X. (2015). Los marcadores discursivos como rasgo distintivo de los textos del ámbito de las ciencias jurídicas en lengua vasca: Aproximación estadística con proyección jurilingüística. *Revista signos* 48/87, 3–29.

Figueras, C. (2000). Las expresiones referenciales en el texto académico, in E. Montolío (coord.) *Manual práctico de escritura académica*, v. III, Barcelona: Ariel, 17–75.

Gillaerts, P. & Van de Velde, F. (2010). Interactional metadiscourse in research article abstracts. *Journal of English for Academic Purposes* 9/2, 128–139.

Hu, G. & Cao, F. (2011). Hedging and boosting in abstracts of applied linguistics articles: a comparative study of English- and Chinese-medium journals. *Journal of Pragmatics* 43/11, 2795–2809.

Hyland, K. (1998). Disciplinary identity in research writing: metadiscourse and academic communities, in L. Lundqvist, H. Picht, & J. Qvistgaard (eds.) *LSP Identity and Interface Research, Knowledge and Society. Vol. II. Proceedings of the 11th European Symposium on LSP. Copenhagen, August 1997.* Copenhagen: CBS, 648–655.

Hyland, K. (2005). *Metadiscourse: Exploring Interaction in Writing.* London: Continuum.

Hyland, K. (2017). Metadiscourse: what is it and where is it going? *Journal of Pragmatics* 113, 16–29.

Hyland, K. & Tse, P. (2004). Metadiscourse in academic writing: a reappraisal. *Applied Linguistics* 25/2, 156–177.

Kawase, T. (2015). Metadiscourse in the introductions of PhD theses and research articles. *Journal of English for Academic Purposes* 20, 114–124.

Kuhi, D. & Behnam, B. (2011). Generic variations and metadiscourse use in the writing of applied linguists: a comparative study and preliminary framework. *Written Communication* 28/1, 97–141.

López-Cózar, C., Priede, T. & Benito, S. (2013). Análisis de la expresión escrita en las Universidades de Madrid a través de la asignatura Trabajo Fin de Grado en los estudios de ADE. *Revista de Docencia Universitaria. REDU* 11/3, 279–299.

Lorés-Sanz, R. (2011). The construction of the author's voice in academic writing: the interplay of cultural and disciplinary factors. *Text and Talk* 31/2, 173–193.

Markkanen, R, Steffensen, M. & Crismore, A. (1993). Quantitative contrastive study of metadiscourse: problems in design and analysis of data. *Papers and Studies in Contrastive Linguistics* 28, 137–152.

Mauranen, A. (1993). *Cultural Differences in Academic Rhetoric: A Textlinguistic Study.* Frankfurt am Main: Peter Lang.

Mur Dueñas, P. (2011). An intercultural analysis of metadiscourse features in research articles written in English and in Spanish. *Journal of Pragmatics* 43/12, 3068–3079.

Núñez, P., Muñoz, A. & Mihovilovic, E. (2006). Las funciones de los marcadores de reformulación en el discurso académico en formación. *Revista Signos* 39/62, 471–492.

Perales-Escudero, M. & Swales, J. (2011). Tracing convergence and divergence in pairs of Spanish and English research article abstracts: the case of Iberica. *Iberica* 21, 49–70.

Piqué-Noguera, C. & Camaño-Puig, R. (2015). El resumen del artículo de investigación: Análisis del género en un corpus de textos de Enfermería. *Revista Signos* 48/87, 77–94.

Saz Rubio, M. del (2011). A pragmatic approach to the macro-structure and metadiscoursal features of research article introductions in the field of agricultural sciences. *English for Specific Purposes* 30/4, 258–271.

Scardamalia, M. & Bereiter, C. (1992). Dos modelos explicativos de los procesos de composición escrita. *Infancia y aprendizaje* 15/58, 43–64.

Salas Valdebenito, M. (2015). Una propuesta de taxonomía de marcadores metadiscursivos para el discurso académico-científico escrito en español. *Revista Signos* 48/87, 95–120.

Steffensen, M. & Cheng, X. (1996). Metadiscourse and text pragmatics: how students write after learning about metadiscourse, in L. Bouton (ed.) *Pragmatics and Language Learning. Monograph Series* 7, 153–170.

Todd, M., Bannister, P. & Clegg, S. (2004). Independent inquiry and the undergraduate dissertation: perceptions and experiences of final-year social science students. *Assessment & Evaluation in Higher Education* 29/3, 335–355.

Vande Kopple, W. (1985). Some exploratory discourse on metadiscourse. *College Composition and Communication* 36/1, 82–93.

11 Interactional Metadiscourse Features in the Written Production Made by Spanish EFL Learners

Chiara Tasso

1 Introduction

In recent decades, the analysis of metadiscourse features in non-native English learners has been examined by a large number of authors, such as Crismore, Markkanen, & Steffensen (1993), Intaraprawat and Steffensen (1995), Thompson (2001), Hyland (2004), Ädel, (2006), Ying (2007), Simin, and Tavangar, (2009), Hong and Cao (2014), and Sesek (2016), among others, who have analysed the different metadiscourse resources used by EFL/ESL learners in written texts. Conversely, lack of studies on metadiscourse use in English texts written by Spanish EFL learners, in areas different from English for specific purposes, was detected and it was for this reason that the present study was undertaken.

Once the subject of this study has been presented, we consider it important to specify what the term metadiscourse refers to. The term metadiscourse was used for the first time by Harrig in 1959, to refer to the writer or speaker attempts to guide the perception that recipients develop from a written or oral message. Successively, the metadiscourse concept was developed by Williams (1981), Vande Kopple (1985), and Crismore (1989) who included in this term the study of different elements of discourse such as discourse connectors and other textual elements, through which writers or speakers express their presence in the text, influencing the way in which recipients receive the message. According to Hyland (2005:3), the concept of metadiscourse is based on the idea that "communication is more than just the exchange of information, good or services, but also involves the personalities, attitudes and assumptions of those who are communicating". Metadiscourse is based on the concept of communication not only as an exchange of information but also as an interaction between the message senders both with the message itself and with their recipients. In any type of discourse, there are two participating parts, both of them bringing to the communicative act their experiences, aptitudes, and previous knowledge. The set of these interpersonal elements affects the way in which the participants interpret the message and how they interact in the communication. Whenever speakers or writers produce a message, they always take into consideration their potential recipients. Metadiscourse consists of linguistic options that the writer or speaker chooses to establish a contact and influence his/her recipient. Metadiscourse elements are defined by Hyland (2005:5), as "[...] various ways that these understandings of context and audience are realized in texts, the forms we use to transform what may otherwise be a lifeless text into discourse that meets the needs of participants". The message senders can either share their point of view with their receivers, using, for example, the pronoun *we*, or express distance through the pronoun *you*. Through metadiscourse strategies, writers or speakers bring their voice into the text and build a relation with their recipients. Metadiscourse also expresses the sender's attitude towards the content of the message. For all these reasons, thanks to metadiscourse elements, the message not only becomes a (Hyland, 2005:4) "reader-coherent and reader-friendly prose but also relate it to a given context and convey his or her personality, credibility, audience-sensitivity and relationship to the message". Sending messages, either orally or written, cannot be considered as a neutral act, as they are always embedded in a situational context, communication being the purpose of any message. Every act of communication is strongly related to the subjects who produce it, their recipients and the situation in which the message transmission takes place. Therefore, taking into account the potential recipient and context characteristics will help to achieve effective communication. Regarding metadiscourse taxonomies, the present study uses Hyland's (2005) classification which recognises two main categories of metadiscourse elements: interactive and interactional elements. Interactive elements express the author's awareness of the audience by structuring texts using cohesion and coherence devices. However, interactional elements bring the author's voice into the text expressing his/her viewpoint towards a proposition and establishing a dialogue with the potential readers. Hyland emphasises the importance of metadiscourse elements in students' writing as follows:

> Students are often told that successful writing in English is reader-friendly. It must fit together logically, be sign posted to guide readers and take their likely responses and processing difficulties into account. But it also needs to work for the writer too, as we communicate for a reason. We use language to persuade, inform, entertain or perhaps just engage an audience, and this means conveying an attitude to what we say and to our readers.
>
> (Hyland, 2005:11)

The ability to correctly employ metadiscourse strategies improves the quality of any type of written text, providing it with internal coherence and cohesion and expressing the authors' relationship with both the text itself and their potential reader. This chapter focuses on the identification and analysis of interactional strategies in the written production of Spanish C1 EFL learners. It was hypothesised that by analysing the written production of Spanish students with a C1 (CEFR, 2001) English level, it is possible to determine which interactional elements are included in their metadiscourse competence and identify the specific characteristics of the knowledge of these elements at a C1 level. It might also be possible to identify interactional elements not included in Hyland's (2005) taxonomy which could be considered as a specific expression of Spanish EFL writers' communication with their potential readers. The decision to focus on the C1 level of the CEFR was made after finding that, it is just at this linguistic level that discourse markers start gaining importance and are considered as one of the core contents within the process of teaching English as a non-native language. This decision is based on the document "A core inventory for general English" (North, Ortega & Sheehan, 2010) and on the information published on the website of the English Profile project (2017) carried out by the University of Cambridge, Cambridge University Press, and the Cambridge English Language Assessment. The aim of this chapter is to examine the use and distribution of metadiscourse interactional features in Spanish EFL learners with a C1 level of the CEFR (2001). An additional objective of this study is to increase knowledge that Spanish teachers of English as a foreign language possess of the metadiscourse competence of their students. We intend to provide them with detailed information on the elements that must be taken into account when teaching metadiscourse strategies to Spanish EFL learners. Consequently, the research questions of this study are as follows:

1 What categories of interactional metadiscourse strategies included in Hyland's taxonomy (Hyland, 2005) have been applied in English texts written by Spanish EFL learners with a C1 level of the CEFR (2001)?
2 To what extent and how have interactional metadiscourse features been used?
3 What is the predominant characteristic of Spanish C1 EFL writers' relation with their potential readers?

2 Method

In this study, a corpus of 55 explanatory essays, a total of 13,499 words, written by Spanish EFL learners were manually compiled. The texts included in the corpus were all produced in exam sessions to obtain the C1 (CEFR, 2001) English certificate at the Language Center of the Catholic University of Valencia San Vicente Mártir between 2012 and 2018. All texts were assessed positively by the official exam assessor board, thus ensuring a C1 level of analysis. The written texts compiled were between 200 and 250 words. Corpus data can be seen in Table 11.1.

Table 11.1 Description of the corpus

Corpus	*N°. Text*	*N°. Writers*	*N°. Words*	*N°. Words per text*
Texts written by C1 Spanish EFL learners	55	55	13.499	between 200 y 250

Once selected and compiled, each text was transformed into a digital format in order to carry out an automatic counting, thus limiting the number of inaccuracies derived from manual counts. This study uses Hyland's (2005) metadiscourse markers taxonomy displayed in Table 11.2.

Table 11.2 Interactional metadiscourse taxonomy according to Hyland (2005)

Category	*Function*	*Examples*
Interactional	Expresses writer's relation both with his text and his potential reader.	
Attitude markers	Show writer attitude about a proposition	Unfortunately, hopefully.
Boosters	Indicate certainty and conviction about a proposition	Definitely, of course.
Engagement markers	Show explicit communication between author and his potential readers	Consider, note that, should.
Hedges	Hold back author's commitment towards a proposition	Might, possibly.
Self-mentions	Explicit signal to authorial persona	I, we, me, my, our.

Using the corpus-digitalised version, each text was carefully read and all interactional metadiscourse features listed by Hyland (2005:218–224) were manually searched for. In addition, following Hyland's classification, other interactional features not included in the above-mentioned Hyland's list were detected in the learner corpus and ascribed to their respective categories. Once identified, each occurrence was analysed in context to make sure that it performed a metadiscourse function and could be included in the Excel spreadsheets for automatic counting. Interactional features identified in the C1 learner's corpus organised by category were quantitatively and qualitatively analysed providing both frequency of use and examples extracted from the corpus. Results and discussion are described in the next section.

3 Results

Before displaying and discussing the results obtained, specific information about the different types of interactional strategies will be provided. Following Hyland (2005), the main characteristics and functions of each interactional category will be given starting with a general definition of what interactional features are and which their main function in a text is. Interactional strategies are responsible for expressing the relationship between the participants of a communicative act. When dealing with a written discourse, they are concerned with manifesting writers' presence in the text and show their relationship with readers. Interactional strategies include all those words or expressions the authors of a text use to express their voice and communicate with their readers. Following Hyland (2005), there are five types of interpersonal strategies:

1 Hedges
2 Boosters
3 Attitude markers
4 Engagement markers
5 Self-mentions

Hedges include all the linguistic resources that the writer uses to mitigate his/her point of view towards a proposition. Through hedges, the author decides to provide an affirmation as an opinion opening it to other points of view. These metadiscourse strategies give the reader the possibility of dissenting by maintaining a different viewpoint. In opposition to this type, we find the intensifiers, whose function is just the opposite: they are used to emphasise the veracity of an affirmation by eliminating any other possible point of view. Through intensifiers, writers aim to convince their reader that their point of view is the only one acceptable leaving no room for different interpretations. Although the writer recognises the existence of other alternatives, he/she decides to ignore them and tries to convince the reader to do the same. However, attitude markers express the writer's affective evaluation of an idea presented in the text. These elements can be used to transmit surprise, agreement or disagreement, obligation, necessity, and frustration. In order to carry out these discourse functions, the writer can choose among three types of resources: attitude verbs, adverbs, and adjectives. Engagement markers are those resources used by the writers to directly address their readers in order to draw their attention and include them into their discourse. The personal pronoun *you* and the inclusive *we*, together with the possessive adjective *your* and the inclusive *our* are in charge of establishing a dialogue with the reader, recognising him/her as a separate entity, as in the case of the first example, or merging with the author, as in the case of inclusive pronouns and adjectives. Another type of engagement marker consists of using questions, through which the writer requests an explicit participation of the reader, and in using verbs in imperative forms. Self-mentions are all those elements the writer uses to express his/her presence in the text. They include the use of the personal pronouns *I* and *we* (used to refer to the writer) and the possessive adjectives and pronouns *my / mine, our / ours*. Once provided information about each interactional category, the results obtained for metadiscourse interactional features in Spanish C1 EFL learners will be shown in the following tables, starting with the overall results displayed in Table 11.3.

Table 11.3 Data extracted from the corpus

Corpus	*N° of text*	*N° of words*	*Occurrences of interactional features*	*Average per text*
Spanish C1 EFL learners	55	13.619	1211	25.91

Analysing in detail each interactional category, the results obtained can be seen in Table 11.4.

Table 11.4 Use and distribution of interactional features in Spanish C1 EFL learners

Category of interactual features	*Number of occurrences*	*Percentage over total occurrences*
Hedges	176	14.53
Self-mentions	115	9.50
Boosters	138	11.40
Attitude markers	206	17.01
Engagement markers	576	**47.56**
Total occurrences	1.211	100

As shown in Table 11.4, for each category, occurrences used by writers were calculated as well as their percentage of use. Engagement markers, highlighted in bold, are the most frequent, representing almost 50% of total occurrence. Once the overall results are displayed, a detailed description of the results obtained in each interpersonal subcategory will be provided as well as examples extracted from the learners' corpus, starting with engagement markers whose results are shown in Table 11.5.

Table 11.5. Occurrences and examples of engagement markers identified in the corpus

	Engagement markers (occurrences) / frequency *Total occurrences: 576*
1	() (1) / 0.17%
2	? (63) / 10.93%
3	**Ask** medieval countrymen (4) / 0.69%
4	**Believe** me (1) / 0.17%
5	**Broaden** your (2) / 0.34%
6	But don't let your health (2) / 0.34%
7	**Change** it (1) / 0.17%
8	**Cook** your own (1) / 0.17%
9	Do not forget (1) / 0.17%
10	Do things right for you (2) / 0.34%
11	Don't **be** (2) / 0.34%
12	**Don't Give Up** (1) / 0.17%
13	**Don't misunderstand me** (1) / 0.17%
14	**Keep** cooking (1) / 0.17%
15	Let's face (3) / 0.52%
16	Ourselves (inclusive) (2) / 0.34%
17	Our (inclusive) (123) / 21.35%
18	Remember (1) / 0.17%
19	Think about yourselves (6) / 1.04%
20	**Treat** yourself. (1) / 0.17%
21	**Turn off** (1) / 0.17%
22	Us (inclusive) (21) / 3.64%
23	We (inclusive) (208) / 36.11%
24	We don't have to complain (11) / 1.90%
25	We have to (2) / 0.34%
26	We should (16) / 2.77%
27	We must (5) / 0.86%
28	You (71) / 12.32%
29	You need to (16) / 2.77%
30	**Yourself** (5)
31	You ought to be (1) / 0.17%

Note: Boosters not included in Hyland's list (2005:218–224) are highlighted in bold.

As it can be observed in Table 11.5, the three most frequent engagement markers were the inclusive personal pronoun *we*, followed by the possessive inclusive adjective *our* and the personal pronoun *you*. The greater use of the inclusive pronoun *we* and possessive adjective *our* rather than *you* and *your* implies the writers' tendency to merge with the reader. Questions and exhortative verbs also registered a high frequency. However, the engagement markers found in this corpus show that Spanish C1 EFL writers only know 31 types of engagement markers out of the 81 included in Hyland's list (2005:218–224). In terms of self-mentions, the corpus writers used the strategies shown in Table 11.6.

Table 11.6 Occurrences and examples of self-mentions identified in the corpus

	Self-mentions (occurrences) / frequency *Total occurrences: 115*
1	I (71) / 61.73%
2	Me (4) / 3.47%
3	My (25) / 21.73%
4	Our (1) / 0.86%
5	Us (1) / 0.86%
6	We (12) / 10.43%
7	Mine (2) / %

As displayed in Table 11.6, the personal pronoun *I* was the most used self-mention. However, other types of strategies included in Hyland's list (2005, pp. 218–224), such as *the author* or *the writer*, are missing. Using those types of self-mentions expressions would provide the learners' text with a more academic approach. As far as boosters are concerned, occurrences and examples are described in Table 11.7.

Table 11.7 Occurrences and examples of boosters identified in the corpus

Boosters (occurrences) / frequency *Total occurrences: 138*					
1	! (4) / 2.89%	16	I think it always (18) / 13.04%	26	It is undoubtedly effective (1) / 0.72%
2	**Absolutely** (2) / 1.44%	17	I want to emphasise (1) / 0.72%	27	It's always a good (2) / 1.44%
3	Actually (2) / 1.44%	18	In fact (2) / 1.44%	28	Must be (4) / 2.89%
4	Certainly (2) / 1.44%	19	Indeed, (2) / 1.44%	29	Obviously (3) / 2.17%
5	Conclusively (1) / 0.72%	20	It is an obvious fact (2) / 1.44%	30	Of course (9) / 6.52%
6	Completely (2) / 1.44%	21	It is believed that (2) / 1.44%	31	Really (9) / 6.52%
7	Definitely (2) / 1.44%	22	It is true that (9) / 6.52%	32	Surely (1) / 0.72%
8	Known (17) / 12.31%	23	It is clear that (4) / 2.89%	33	**There is no doubt that** (1) / 0.72%
9	Evidently (1) / 0.72%	24	It is demonstrated that (1) / 0.72%	34	Truly (1) / 0.72%
10	**Highly** (3) / 2.17%	25	It is proved that (1) / 0.72%	35	Under no circumstances (1) / 0.72%
11	I am also **convinced** that (1) / 0.72%				
12	I am bound (1) / 0.72%				
13	Believe (17) / 12.31%				
14	I **fully** agree (2) / 1.44%				
15	I **strongly** (5) / 3.62%				

Note: Boosters not included in Hyland's list (2005:218–224) are highlighted in bold.

The occurrences and examples of boosters showed in Table 11.7 indicate Spanish C1 EFL writers used 35 types of boosters being the verbs *think* and *believe*, the most frequent of all. Further analysis in the use of the aforementioned verbs revealed that both of them were used always together with adverbs such as *fully*, *strongly*, or *really* which increase the writers' commitment towards a proposition. In contrast, stronger booster phrases such as *There is no doubt that*, *Under no circumstances*, or *It is demonstrated that*, which block any other reader's interpretation of a proposition, were found only once, thus expressing the writers' tendency to avoid a strong commitment. As it can be seen in Table 11.8, attitude markers, as previously stated, obtained the highest frequency of use and were also the richest interactional markers in terms of variety.

Table 11.8 Occurrences and examples of attitude markers identified in the corpus

Attitude markers (occurrences) / frequency *Total occurrences 206*			
1 **Absurd** (2) / 0.97%	20 **Easier** (4) / 1.94%	38 Interesting (6) / 2.91%	56 Quite shocking (1) / 0.48%
2 Agree (5) / 2.42%	21 **Effective** (2) / 0.97%	39 **Key** (1) / 0.48%	57 Really worth trying (1) / 0.48%
3 **Alarming** (2) / 0.97%	22 **Essential** (4) / 1.94%	40 **Luckily** (1) / 0.48%	58 **Reasonable** (1) / 0.48%
4 Appropriately (3) / 1.45%	23 **Even worse** (4) / 1.94%	41 **Main** (8) / 3.88%	59 **Risky** (1) / 0.48%
5 **Awful** (2) / 0.97%	24 **Fortunately** (1) / 0.48%	42 **Necessary** (1) / 0.48%	60 **Sadly** (1) / 0.48%
6 **Bad** (2) / 0.97%	25 **Fundamental** (4) / 1.94%	43 **Need** (2) / 0.97%	61 **Serious** (1) / 0.48%
7 **Beloved** (2) / 0.97%	26 **Good** (4) / 1.94%	44 **Not advisable** (1) / 0.48%	62 Shocked (1) / 0.48%
8 **Benefits** (3) / 1.45%	27 **Great** (3) / 1.45%	45 **Not difficult** (1) / 0.48%	63 **Significant** (1) / 0.48%
9 **Best** (6) / 2.91%	28 **Hard** (3) / 1.45%	46 **Not easy** (1) / 0.48%	64 **Simple** (1) / 0.48%
10 **Better** (10) / 2.85%	29 **Harmful** (1) / 0.48%	47 **Not impossible** (1) / 0.48%	65 So understandably (1) / 0.48%
11 **Biggest** (3) / 1.45%	30 Hated (1) / 0.48%	48 **Not necessary** (1) / 0.48%	66 **Stressful** (2) / 0.97%
12 **Brilliant** (2) / 0.97%	31 **High time** (1) / 0.48%	49 **Not recommendable** (1) / 0.48%	67 **Useful** (2) / 0.97%
13 **Complex** (3) / 1.45%	32 Hopefully (1) / 0.48%	50 Not usual (1) / 0.48%	68 Terrible (1) / 0.48%
14 **Complicated** (2) / 0.97%	33 **Horrible** (1) / 0.48%	51 **Not worthy!** (1) / 0.48%	69 Unfortunately, (1) / 0.48%
15 **Considerable** (3) / 1.45%	34 I agree (7) / 3.39%	52 **Paradoxically** (1) / 0.48%	70 **Unthinkable** (1) / 0.48%
16 **Controversial** (3) / 1.45%	35 I can't fully agree (2) / 0.97%	53 **Poor** (1) / 0.48%	71 **Urgent** (1) / 0.48%
17 **Crucial** (2) / 0.97%	36 I don't agree (3) / 1. 45%	54 **Prejudicial** (1) / 0.48%	72 **Well developed** (1) / 0.48%
18 **Decisive** (2) / 0.97%	37 Important (31) / 15.04%	55 **Properly** (1) / 0.48%	73 **Worringly** (1) / 0.48%
19 **Drawback** (1) / 0.48%			

Note: Attitude markers not included in Hyland's list (2005:218–224) are highlighted in bold.

Corpus writers showed their attitude mainly by using adjectives, whose frequency of use was much higher than the one registered for other types of attitude markers such as the adverbs *luckily* or *hopefully*, with just one occurrence identified, or the opinion verbs *agree*, with just 7 tokens. Regarding the opinion, the verb *agree* was always used in combination with boosters such as *fully* or *strongly*. An in-depth adjective use analysis showed that adjectives expressing a negative meaning, for example, *terrible*, *shocking*, or *alarming* were always used together with hedges, such as the verb *sound*, showing writers' tendency to reduce a negative meaning allowing readers to dissent from the writer's attitude. Although corpus writers showed to know only some of the attitude markers included in Hyland's list (2005:218–224), it is important to highlight that they used a great variety of new attitude markers not included in Hyland's list. As far as hedges are concerned, occurrences and variety are shown in Table 11.9.

Table 11.9 Occurrences and examples of hedges identified in the corpus

Hedges (occurrences) / frequency *Total of occurrences: 176*		
1 Almost (2) / 1.13%	15 **In some cases** (2) / 1.13%	30 **Occasionally** (1) / 0.56%
2 Approximately (2) / 1.13%	16 **Not always** (4) / 2.27%	31 On the whole (1) / 0.56%
3 **As far as I am concerned** (3) / 1.70%	17 It could be (13) / 7.38%	32 Tend to think (3) / 1.70%
4 **As far as I can see** (3) / 1.70%	18 It is **commonly** believed that (4) / 2.27%	33 Perhaps (1) / 0.56%
5 **Commonly** (2) / 1.13%	19 It is generally believed that (3) / 1.70%	34 **Personally** (1) / 0.56%
6 **Doesn't necessarily** (2) / 1.13%	20 It is generally known that (2) / 1.13%	35 Probably (2) / 1.13%
7 **From my own professional experience** (2) / 1.13%	21 It is more likely to have (1) / 0.56%	36 Seems to (4) / 2.27%
8 **From my point of view** (8) / 4.54%	22 It is often claimed that (7) / 3.97%	37 Should be (17) / 9.65%
9 **From this point of view** (2) / 1.13%	23 It sometimes (5) / 2.84%	38 **Somehow** 'bad' (1) / 0.56%
10 Generally speaking (3) / 1.70%	24 **It sounds** (6) / 3.40%	39 **Suggestions** (2) / 1.13%
11 I also suggest (6) / 3.40%	25 Would (15) / 8.52%	40 **That's not completely true** (1) / 0.56%
12 **In general terms** (2) / 1.13%	26 May (10) / 5.68%	41 **There is little likelihood** (1) / 0.56%
13 In my opinion (8) / 4.54%	27 May be (4) / 2.27%	42 **To some extent** (1) / 0.56%
14 In my view (2) / 1.13%	28 Might be (5) / 2.84%	43 To suggest that (1) / 0.56%
	29 **Most of** (5) / 2.84%	44 Usually (3) / 1.70%

Note: Hedges not included in Hyland's list (2005:218–224) are highlighted in bold.

As shown in Table 11.9, the most used hedging strategies were the modal verbs *could* and *should*, and the auxiliary verb *would* was always used with opinion verbs such as *recommend* or *suggest*. Further analysis of results displayed in Table 11.9 indicates that Spanish C1 EFL learners only know 31 types of hedging strategies out of 101 listed by Hyland (2005:218–224). After having provided an in-depth result analysis, conclusions drawn from this study will be described in the next section.

4 Conclusions

The results obtained have allowed us to identify the use and distribution of interactional metadiscourse features in a Spanish C1 EFL learner corpus of written texts. The research questions posed in the introduction section of this chapter were answered in the following way.

The quantitative analysis of the data collected showed that Spanish C1 EFL learners use and consequently know all interactional metadiscourse categories included in Hyland's taxonomy (2005). Regarding the extent of interactional features use, results from this study revealed that engagement markers were the most frequent interactional metadiscourse features. These strategies were responsible for 47.56% of the total occurrences, while self-mentions and boosters were the least used, with only 9.50% and 11.40% frequency of use, respectively. As stated in the result section, engagement markers are strategies used to establish a dialogue with potential readers, bringing them into the text. Greater use of these types of interactional features underlines that Spanish C1 EFL learners want their reader to take part in their discourse. The high frequency registered for the inclusive pronoun *we* and possessive adjective *our* reveals that our writers involve readers in their discourse by merging with them. It may also be noted that Spanish C1 EFL learners show a need to create a dialogue with their readers by making the readers' participation in the text the most important type of interactional function for Spanish C1 EFL writers. In terms of qualitative analysis, the results obtained from the comparison between Hyland's interactional list of features (2005:218–224) and the interactional features found in the present corpus (see Appendix A) showed that Spanish C1 EFL writers used and consequently knew only a very small amount of all the interactional devices included in Hyland's list. However, although our corpus writers tend to use only a limited range of the existing interactional metadiscourse features, it is important to emphasise that this study found interactional features not included in Hyland's list (2005:218–224). Regarding the use of different interactional features, attitude markers stand out among the other categories as the richest category in terms of variety (see Appendix A). The new interactional devices identified in this corpus can be considered as specific interactional metadiscourse devices of Spanish C1 EFL learners.

Further studies based on the same corpus could be carried out on interactive metadiscourse features in order to provide a complete description of the use and distribution of metadiscourse devices in Spanish C1 EFL learners.

References

Ädel, A. (2006). *Metadiscourse in L1 and L2 English.* Amsterdam: John Benjamin. Publishing.

Council of Europe. (2001). *Common European Framework of Reference for Languages: Learning, Teaching, Assessment (CEFR).* Cambridge: Press Syndicate of the University of Cambridge.

Crismore, A. (1989). *Talking with Readers: Metadiscourse as Rhetorical Act.* New York: Peter Lang.

Crismore, A., Markkanen, R., & Steffensen, M. (1993). Metadiscourse in persuasive writing: a study of texts written by American and Finnish university students. *Written Communication* 10/1, 39–71.

Hyland, K. & Tse, P. (2004). Metadiscourse in academic writing: a reappraisal. *Applied Linguistics* 25/2, 156–177.

Hyland, K. (2004). Disciplinary interactions: metadiscourse in L2 postgraduate writing. *Journal of Second Language Writing* 13, 133–51.

Hyland, K. (2005). *Metadiscourse: Exploring Interaction in Writing.* London: Continuum.

Hong, H. & Cao. F. (2014). Interactional metadiscourse in young EFL learner writing: a corpus-based study. *International Journal of Corpus Linguistics* 19/2, 201–224.

Intaraprawat M. & Steffensen, S. (1995) The use of metadiscourse in good and poor ESL essays. *Journal of Second Language Writing* 4/3, 253–272.

North, B., Ortega, A., & Sheehan, S. (2010). *A Core Inventory for General English. British Council.* EAQUALS (European Association for Quality Language Services).

Sesek, U. (2016). Revising and metadiscourse in advanced EFL/ESL writing. *International Journal of Applied Linguistics & English Literature* 5/3, 35–45.

Simin, S. & Tavangar, M. (2009). Metadiscourse knowledge and use in Iranian EFL Writing. *Asian EFL Journal*, 11/1, 230–255.

Thompson, G. (2001). Interaction in academic writing: learning to argue with the reader. *Applied Linguistics* 22/1, 58–78.

Vande Kopple, W. (1985). Some exploratory discourse on metadiscourse. *College Composition and Communication*, 36/1, 82–93.

Williams, J. (1981). *Style: Ten Lessons in Clarity and Grace.* Boston: Scott Foresman.

Ying, S. (2007). An analysis of discourse markers used by non-native English learners: its implication for teaching English as a foreign language. *Intercultural Communication Studies*, 19, 51–83.

Appendix A

Interactional features found in this corpus and not included in Hyland's list (2005:218–224).

Engagement markers: ask; believe; broaden; change; cook; be; give up; misunderstand; keep; treat; turn off; yourself.

Boosters: absolutely; highly; convinced; fully; strongly; there is no doubt that.

Attitude markers: absurd; alarming; awful; bad; beloved; benefit; best; better; biggest; brilliant; complex; complicated; considerable; controversial; crucial; decisive, drawback; easier; effective; essential; worse; fortunately; fundamental; good; great; hard; harmful; hated; high time; horrible; key; luckily; main; necessary; need;, worthy; paradoxically; not advisable; difficult; easy; impossible; necessary; recommendable; worthy; paradoxically; poor; prejudicial; properly; reasonable; risky; sadly; serious; significant; simple; stressful; useful; unthinkable, urgent, well developed; worryingly.

Hedges: as far as I am concerned; as far as I can see; commonly; it doesn't necessarily; from my own experience; from my point of view; from this point of view; in general terms; in some cases, not always; commonly; it sounds; most of; occasionally; personally; somehow; suggestion; not completely true; there is little likelihood; to some extent.

12 Intercultural Rhetoric in the Written Academic Discourse

The Rhetorical Functions of Citations in English and Spanish by College Students and Expert Writers[1]

David Sánchez-Jiménez

1 Introduction

The primary goal of this research is to compare the rhetorical functions of citations used by Spanish students and American students in their master's theses written in their native languages – Spanish and English – in the field of Applied Linguistics, and study whether there are any significant differences. The results are then compared from the analysis of articles written by expert scholars in both the same languages in the same discipline.

A master's thesis illustrates a lopsided communicative exchange between a novice writer and an expert reader, in which the latter assesses the novice whether he/she adapts to social norms (not only of writing but also of the level of accumulated knowledge in the subject, application of specific terms, content organisation, politeness, etc.) agreed upon by the scientific community. The outcome of this interaction will be either to accept or reject the writer as a member of the academic community by the panel (Hyland, 1999; Soler-Monreal & Gil-Salom, 2011). In this regard, the postgraduate students must compare different sources in their discourse in a polyphonic communication situation (Bakhtin, 1979; Fløttum, Dhal & Kinn, 2006; Bondi, 2012) in which they must adjust the content and the rhetorical demands of the communicative context. In this knowledge transformation process, they will organise, shape, and analyse the bibliographic knowledge, and indicate with their own voice the research limitations previously done in their field of study to claim their new knowledge (Arnoux *et al.*, 2005). Similarly, the students must also meet the linguistic, rhetorical, and discursive conventions governing the disciplinary community of their specialisation. However, it is within this intertextual network where writers construct their identity as authors through the dialogic connections they establish with the others' voices in the research. It is, therefore, necessary to consider the rhetorical functions of citations in its relation to the writer's position in the text (Breivega, Dahl & Fløttum, 2002; Bazerman, 2003; P. Thompson, 2005; Petrić, 2007; Harwood, 2009; Castelló *et al.*, 2011; Sánchez-Jiménez, 2013; Soler-Monreal & Gil-Salom, 2014). In the case of the expert scholars, they recognise their firsthand knowledge of the subject matter and the rhetorical conventions of writing; they are not compelled to demonstrate their scholarship to the discourse community which they are already part of. Through publications, they interact with their peers by establishing a dialogic communication with other members of the discipline.

This study fills the epistemological vacuum on citation in Applied Linguistics. The bibliography remains scarce in terms of cross-cultural comparison of citation use in master's thesis, in comparison to works by expert scholars (For review, see Sánchez-Jiménez, 2011, 2018a). Despite the large extent of the branches of Intercultural Rhetoric, even to other fields of study (*cf.* Kaplan, 1988; Connor, 1996, 2011) and has been researched in this field and in Genre Analysis, I am unaware of any existing contrastive studies on two different linguistic cultures and rhetorical functions of citations in the genres of research articles, theses, and dissertations. There is a need for academic training in this element because of the growing demand of foreign students in the universities and language studies in the postgraduate programmes in recent decades (Vázquez, 2001a; Swales, 2004; Hyland, 2009). Globalisation has restructured the needs of society and the main characteristics of teaching and learning, which have become increasingly internationalised through exchange programmes, scholarships to study abroad, or through joint postgraduate studies (e.g. Fulbright, Andrew W. Mellon, Erasmus Socrates, MAEC-AECID, ALBAN, FUNIBER, Fundación Carolina) promoted by various government and academic institutions from different countries and taught in different languages (e.g. Coemius, Leonardo da Vinci, European Master in Learning and Teaching of Spanish in Multilingual and International Contexts).

To sum up, this research aims to provide an intercultural overview on the use of rhetorical functions of citations in texts written in English and Spanish by postgraduate students and professional authors in Applied Linguistics, discover the differences arising from the discipline, culture, language, and level of expertise (both expert and novice), and determine how these variables contribute to constructing the writer's identity.

2 Theoretical Framework

Citation processes are shaped in a textual context that characterises the academic discourse within each genre, disciplinary community, or culture framework. In other words, the explicit reference to theoretical background is a hugely important indicator of the relationship between the academic text and the context of knowledge, which thus constitutes a collaborative construction of new knowledge between writers and readers (Hyland, 2000; Parodi, 2007). Citations are, therefore, to be considered as disseminators of knowledge that is radially transmitted, moving across the author's discourse community from which it expands to other neighbouring areas that could operate through its discipline. This element is, undoubtedly, an essential part of any academic work, and its proper use through the adoption of effective rhetorical strategies of communication should be interpreted as a quality indicator of a text. It is likewise one of the main identifier elements of academic writing that marks its own specificity within each discipline and the author's personal style (Hyland, 1999, 2000; P. Thompson & Tribble, 2001; P. Thompson, 2005; Samraj, 2008). Thus, its significance is far beyond its functionality as a source, given the writer communicates with the discourse community with not only the range of information on specific topics and the regular update of data, but also with the adoption of the rhetorical purposes shown in the functions of citations in texts. In this regard, many studies in Linguistics have highlighted its rhetorical importance in academic writing organisation and in knowledge construction (Swales, 1990, 2004; Hyland, 1999, 2000, 2005; Thompson & Tribble, 2001; Petrić, 2007; Samraj, 2008, 2013; Sánchez-Jiménez, 2012; Dontcheva-Navratilova, 2015).

The linguistics studies of citation started in the 1980s, twenty years after it became a subject of research among information scientists and sociologists. The original concept of citations as the main catalyst of objectivity in scientific writing – the theoretical roots of which started from Information Science – has evolved over recent decades, and in the late 1970s, some sociologists began to publish persuasive papers involving the use of this textual resource (Gilbert, 1977; Brooks, 1986; Latour, 1987; Vinkler, 1998; Wang & White, 1999; Case & Higgins, 2000), followed later by other linguists (Swales, 1986; Hyland, 1999, 2000, 2002, 2005, 2011; P. Thompson, 2005; Petrić, 2007; Samraj, 2008; Harwood, 2009; Mansourizadeh & Ahmad, 2011). Citation use by the writer implies his/her knowledge claims on topics, which are reinforced by alluding to the expert voices of his/her sources in order to persuade the audience of the validity of his/her research. Once the writer places his/her work next to the other authors', he/she wants to establish a dialogue with the members of the disciplinary community. Moreover, the position of the voice in constructing the network of intertextual references (Bazerman, 2003) enables the writer to build a credible representation of him/herself within the scientific text by the varied use of different rhetorical functions of citations (Ivanič, 1998; Hyland, 2002, 2005, 2011; P. Thompson, 2005; Charles, 2006; Soler-Monreal & Gil-Salom, 2014; Dontcheva-Navratilova, 2015).

However, this stance varies based on the writer's academic rank and the use of the language. Two previous studies analysed the differences between the expert writers' and the novice writers' citations. In the case of Mansourizadeh and Ahmad (2011), the results showed how, through citation, the expert writers generally made contrastive viewpoints on topics indicated by the cited sources, which they annotated and paraphrased to consolidate their voice in the text. Their stance thus clearly intended to persuade the readers on the validity of their opinions based on their in-depth knowledge of pertinent topics in their writings. In addition, they exhibited greater control over the discursive conventions of the discipline and strategically used information gathered from the sources through citations, using a greater number of non-integral citations in order to put emphasis on the message. Such a category, in comparison to the integral (Swales, 1990), includes the author's name between parentheses. The students, however, would generate a smaller number of citations in their work, most preferably the integral type. They are limited to collecting ideas taken from sources in order to show their knowledge through citations in isolation without sustaining their voice or transmitting their personal opinions. Relying on referred texts is a characteristic shared among postgraduate students in their academic writings (Dong, 1996; Hyland, 2002; Petrić, 2007; Mansourizadeh & Ahmad, 2011; Soler-Monreal & Gil-Salom, 2011; Jalilifar, 2012; Sánchez-Jiménez, 2013) since as novice researchers, in general, they still lack a formed opinion on the subject of their research.

Jalilifar (2012), for his part, analysed the differences in citation use by both postgraduates and authors of research articles written in L1 and L2. The results indicated that the non-expert writers exceeded in their citation practices than those who are experts in research writing despite the fact that both sides use citations in concordance with the conclusions presented by Mansourizadeh and Ahmad (2011). This makes us then reflect the relevance of cultural and academic variations in the use of citations.

With respect to the linguistic variation in the studies conducted in English and Spanish, Mayor Serrano (2006) analysed three medical genres (research article, popular article, and textbook) and discovered that there was a variation in citation use in both languages. Like Mayor Serrano (2006), Mur Dueñas (2009) also found corroborating evidence of a cultural variation in the use of English and Spanish in knowledge transfer through the use of citations by expert writers. The author concluded in her study that writers in English, in comparison to Spanish writers, used a more assertive style in their citation use and even generated a significant large number of citations.

As to the non-expert postgraduate authors' writings, Soler-Monreal and Gil-Salom (2011) found variation in citation use in English and Spanish after comparing the data from twenty (20) doctoral theses. Based on this study, the English postgraduate students often resort to using literal and integral citations (48.85%). The Spanish group, however, tend to paraphrase words from the author and use non-integral citations (61.98%). To sum up, the native writers of English are more assertive than the Spanish, a result that corroborates Mur Dueñas' (2009) study on expert writers. The authors confirmed these findings in a further research (Soler-Monreal & Gil-Salom, 2014), in which they made an in-depth qualitative analysis of politeness strategies in citation and the implications of the reporting verbs selection in the text's dialogicity.

These studies have been fundamental to this research because thematic areas and different disciplinary conventions are addressed from an intercultural perspective. This solidifies the relevance of my study for those readers interested in determining how these variables interact in texts written by experts and postgraduate students in English and Spanish in the field of Applied Linguistics.

3 Typology of Rhetorical Functions of Citations

The typology of the rhetorical functions of citations used in this research is based on Petrić's 2007 study, which was carried out with Central European students in the Gender Studies discipline. Nine (9) types of rhetorical functions of citations were identified, which I adapted in the context of my research. For example, the category "statement of use" was not applied due to the difficulty of distinguishing "statement of use" from "application" and "attribution" because the researcher does not have any knowledge of the author's intentions when citing. However, the difference between attribution and application can also be at times complex. Therefore, a new section was created in my typology for the "declaration of use" category, which refers to citations on borrowed materials or instrument from the cited source.

Another significant change in my study in relation to Petrić's typology (2007) is the "establishing links between sources" category. In my proposal, I divided this category into two: first, the uses of comparison and contrast between or among different sources (Petrić, 2007:246–247) and second, "competence" which refers to the statement that is attributed to a group of studies or authors.

Finally, I include a new category called "self-citation". It was not included in Petrić's typology (2007) because she focused on the analysis of texts written by master's degree students. This type of function alludes to the author's citation of his/her own prior works, and this can often be observed in expert authors' writings.

In the following pages, we find the ten (10) functions of citations and its corresponding description. This typology can be found in Sánchez-Jiménez (2013), in which it is explained exhaustively.

In the typology presented below, I include text samples from master's theses analysed in this research, which are coded in parentheses. There is a label that refers to the author of the text with the capitalised initial of his/her nationality (E: Spanish; A: American), a lowercase is used to mark the discursive genre (a: article; m: master's thesis), and numbers are assigned to each student (1, 2, 3, 4, 5, 6, 7, 8, 9, 10, 11, 12).

1 ATTRIBUTION (AT): This rhetorical function of citation is merely descriptive and gives citation an informative value which states that the opinion, idea, or proposition included in the text is in line with that of another author making a previous reference to it.

> The role of speaking in ESL writing classrooms has unfortunately been less researched than the focus on writing itself, with the pervasive assumption that writing and speaking are on opposite sides of a "great divide" of the language learning spectrum(Hyland, 2002, p. 52). (**Am1**)

2 EXEMPLIFICATION (EX): The researcher's statement is clarified by citing examples from the author.

> For example, Ashby reports an overall rate of use of 20% following forms of'être' (to be), which rises to 37% for the third person singular form of this verb, 'est', and 0% following forms of "avoir" (to have) (**Aa5**)

3 REFERENCE (REF): It redirects the reader to the source, which facilitates him/her in text consultation. It usually appears in parentheses and is normally preceded by abbreviations such as "vid.", "v.", "cf." in Spanish and primarily "see" in English, or verb forms such as "ver" or "véase" in Spanish and "for a review" or "refer to" in English.

> But see White and Juffs (1998), who found evidence that Chinese-speaking learners can acquire this feature. (**Am6**)

4 DECLARATION OF USE (DE): It is used to refer to citations on borrowed materials or instruments from the cited source.

> In each case, the data collection was based on Labov's (1984) sociolinguistic interview format, which aims to elicit natural, spontaneous speech. (**Aa5**)

5 APPLICATION (AP): It refers to an idea or concept that the researcher borrows from the source in order to incorporate it into his/her study.

> Similarly, CS3's citations to other literature justify the topic of research, but in this case by helping to create a research space (Swales, 1990). (**Aa2**)

6 EVALUATION (EV): This function refers to the researcher assessing the work of another author.

As Granger rightfully points out, this method—although not particularly time-consuming—is inherently limiting the research to those pre-selected linguistic features **(Am3)**

7 ESTABLISHING LINKS BETWEEN SOURCES (EN): The function underscores the links, comparisons, and contrasts between the used sources. It may highlight the different standpoints on a particular topic, as well as emphasise that the researcher can identify debatable issues by differentiating the opinions of cited authors that have opposing views (Petrić, 2007:245).

While Krashen (1985) thought comprehensible input was the major condition necessitating SLA, Swain (1995) hypothesized that in the production of language a learner must consider Syntax. **(Am4)**

8 COMPARISON OF ONE'S OWN FINDINGS OR INTERPRETATION WITH OTHER SOURCES (CO): It is used to indicate similarities or differences between the researcher's works and those of the source (Petrić, 2007:246).

Research question 3 posited the question of whether sensitivity to specific L2 structures would be modulated by verbal aptitude. Based on the results of previous studies (DeKeyser, 2000; Abrahamsson and Hyltenstam, 2008; Harley and Hart, 1997), it was hypothesized that sensitivity to agreement violations (here, d' scores) would be correlated with MLAT scores. **(Am6)**

9 COMPETENCE (COMP): This function highlights the relevance of a concept, term, or idea by citing several authors in a research statement. This type of information is considered general knowledge in the discipline. Each multiple citation in this category is counted as a single citation.

Research question 3 posited the question of whether sensitivity to specific L2 structures would be modulated by verbal aptitude. Based on the results of previous studies (DeKeyser, 2000; Abrahamsson and Hyltenstam, 2008; Harley and Hart, 1997), it was hypothesized that sensitivity to agreement violations (here, d' scores) would be correlated with MLAT scores. **(Am6)**

10 SELF-CITATION (SE): The researcher cites his/her own previous works in order to prove his/her knowledge claims and thus his/her proficiency on the subject.

When I turn to citation patterns themselves, a long-standing basic distinction is the division into integral and nonintegral citations (Swales, 1990) **(Aa6)**

4 The Corpus and the Method

The corpus consists of a total of twenty-four (24) master's theses in Applied Linguistics – twelve (12) by native Spanish postgraduate writers in Spanish (Ee) and twelve (12) in English by American (Ai) postgraduate researchers. These were selected based on internal criteria to ensure comparability. Moreover, I compare these results from the analysis of twenty-four (24) articles in Applied Linguistics – twelve (12) in English and twelve (12) in Spanish by professional scholars. To have a comparable corpus, some variables are controlled, such as the date in which these theses were written (2005–2016), the discipline, the topics, the country of publication, and the number of words in each text. The theses in English were downloaded from the repositories *ProQuest Dissertations and Theses Database*, and those in Spanish from the *Biblioteca Virtual de la Red Electrónica de Didáctica del Español como Lengua Extranjera (RedEle)*. The articles, however, were obtained from twenty (20) different journals published in the U.S.A. and Spain. While the theses' authors are all American and Spanish, the experts' origins vary among different English- and Spanish-speaking countries.

In the initial stages of the analysis, I used the citation categories from Petrić's typology that are based on functional criteria. Citations are then manually coded in terms of their rhetorical functions, considering the linguistic context, such as reporting verbs or key words (e.g. see, for example, *vid.*, ej.) that allow me to determine the type of function involved in the citation. After six months, I reviewed the analysis to revise the most complicated cases identified in its initial stages. Thus, a quantitative methodology was used to study this phenomenon based on the computational text analysis (Anthony, 2011) of the rhetorical functions of citations arranged in typological classification. Through the Antconc 3.2.4w program, I was able to make a more accurate calculation of citations. Additionally, it allowed me to reexamine the concordance lines in which the citations were found. Finally, the aggregate data were calculated by multiplying the number of citations per 1,000 words and dividing the product by the total number of words in each master's thesis.

5 Results and Discussion

5.1 General Findings

From the analysis of 48 master's theses and articles, there are 5,702 citations recorded, 2,687 of which are generated by the Spanish group and 3,015 by the American group, even though the Spanish theses (289,132) are longer than the American theses (263,358). The novice writers produce a greater number of citations in their works with 4,012 in comparison to expert authors with only 1,690 occurrences. This can be explained by the number of words in their texts (Em + Am: 552,490; Ea + Aa: 186,810). In this respect, if we consider the density of citations shown in Table 12.1 in the general findings, we can verify that the use of this feature is more common in the subcorpus written by expert writers (Ea: 7.56; Aa: 10.37) compared to the number of words in the texts.

In terms of nationality, the writers in English are those who cite their sources more frequently (Aa + Am: 8.32; Ea + Em: 7.12). This data aligns with the previous studies carried out in this field in both languages (Mayor Serrano, 2006; Mur Dueñas, 2009; Soler-Monreal & Gil-Salom, 2011, 2014). However, some studies (Mansourizadeh & Ahmad, 2011; Soler-Monreal & Gil-Salom, 2011) do not work with the density of citations per 1,000 words, which impedes our data comparison with their research findings. Their quantitative findings are open to question, since the length of the texts was not considered in the study because the researchers only worked on the total number of citations computed in the analysis and its resulting percentage.

5.2 Results of the Citations by Rhetorical Function and Group

As observed in Table 12.2, the results show that the most frequently used rhetorical functions of citations in the corpus are AT (Am: 2.85; Em: 2.88; Aa: 1.29; Ea: 1.80) and EN (Am: 3.14; Em: 2.04; Aa: 4.58; Ea: 2.99), which outweighed all the other categories.

Notwithstanding, the differences between the groups in these functions are significant to this research. The frequent use of EN citation appears to be common among researchers writing in English; even the group of American students largely uses this type of complex citation in comparison to the group of experts who write in Spanish. I consider this citation to be complex because it shows advanced disciplinary knowledge on content and exceptional reference authors in the discourse community (Mansourizadeh & Ahmad, 2011:158). In the excerpt below,

Table 12.1 Number of citations, length, and density in the four sub-corpora

	No. of Citations	*Length (words)*	*Average per paper*	*Density per 1.000 words*
Group Ea	667	88,222	132.26	7.56
Group Em	2,020	289,132	143.13	6.98
Groups Ea+Em	2,687	377,354	140.43	7.12
Group Aa	1,023	98,588	96.37	10.37
Group Am	1,992	263,358	132.21	7.56
Groups Aa+Am	3,015	361,946	120.04	8.32
Totals	5,702	739,300	129.65	7.71

Table 12.2 Frequency and density of the rhetorical functions of citations by expert and novice writers in English and Spanish

	Ea	*Den.*	*Aa*	*Den.*	*Em*	*Den.*	*Am*	*Den.*	*Ea+ Em*	*Aa+ Am*	*Am+ Em*	*Aa+ Ea*
SE	34	0.38	64	0.65	32	0.11	6	0.02	0.17	0.19	0.06	0.52
EN	264	2.99	452	4.58	592	2.04	829	3.14	2.26	3.56	2.57	3.83
EV	2	0.02	17	0.17	19	0.06	34	0.13	0.05	0.14	0.09	0.11
EX	18	0.20	74	0.75	49	0.16	76	0.28	0.17	0.41	0.22	0.49
REF	46	0.52	87	0.88	74	0.25	21	0.08	0.31	0.29	0.17	0.71
CO	9	0.10	36	0.36	15	0.05	50	0.19	0.06	0.23	0.11	0.24
COMP	83	0.94	106	1.07	103	0.35	128	0.48	0.49	0.64	0.58	1.01
DE	13	0.14	17	0.17	143	0.49	44	0.16	0.41	0.16	0.33	0.16
AP	39	0.44	42	0.42	158	0.54	53	0.21	0.52	0.26	0.38	0.43
AT	159	1.80	128	1.29	835	2.88	751	2.85	2.63	2.42	2.87	1.53

the writer reviews the inadequate definition of the concept of voice in the pedagogical context by firstly showing the studies conducted in the United States and comparing them afterwards with those conducted in Europe.

> Jeffery's (2011) interview of secondary school teachers reveals that a majority of them still hold an expressivist orientation to voice despite the theoretical dominance of social and dialogical models. Matsuda and Jeffery's (2012) textual study of assessment rubrics (in tests such as TOEFL, IELTS, and SAT) shows that voice is inadequately operationalized, even though statements of writing outcomes (such as those of Writing Program Administrators) increasingly make a place for voice. Outside the United States, I find a similar inconsistency. Through interviews with master's degree students in Central Europe, Petrić´ (2010) found that the most frequent conceptions of voice are individualistic, based on expression of opinion, authorial presence, and personal experience. **(Aa9)**

The AT citation, however, appears to be isolated in the text throughout the paragraph, without contrasting ideas or authors, as it occurs with EN. AT is a category that denotes the use of a more expository style in the discourse; the writer compiles information on the subject in a more descriptive manner.

> Heift and Schultz (In press) draw attention to the fact that the notion of error is not by any means objective (i.e., there appears to be considerable variation in results among the grammaticality judgment tasks conducted even on native speakers). These differences can be attributed to dialectal differences and partially to the variation in socioeconomic and educational backgrounds among the native

> speakers performing the grammaticality judgment tasks; the same holds true when it comes to parsers that often overlook pragmatic and semantic errors.
>
> Corder (1974) makes a distinction between errors, mistakes, and lapses—errors being the central category since, according to Corder's classification, only [...] (**Am3**)

The EX and EV categories appear to distinguish the group of writers by the language used in their texts. This can be largely observed among writers in English who provide examples of other authors in order to show concepts or ideas included in their works. As I discussed about the EN category, this citation requires a broader knowledge of the researchers of their discourse community. The same happens to EV, through which writers evaluate the works of other colleagues. In this study, the texts that were analysed generated only positive evaluations, which were determined by the use of factual verbs in citation introduction, or by the inclusion of an adjective or an adverb in the sentence that contain references, such as in the following:

> Howard (2007, pp. 11–12) offers perhaps the most powerful statement against electronic anti-plagiarism services in a reaction to Turnitin's claim that its service helps students better understand intellectual property while saving teachers' time. (**Am4**)

As Hyland (1999) points out, this function is particularly common in the Humanities compared to the Sciences due to its more controversial nature. My research corroborates the English-Spanish contrastive study of Soler-Monreal and Gil-Salom (2011) on this subject, in which it is maintained that:

> In the Spanish corpus, the option of challenging and criticising is avoided, as the writer assumes she/he must show modesty and prudence. He is aware that she/he is placed in an unequal situation to that of the other participants and criticism of the work of others can constitute a face-threatening activity. Textual and mental verbs are used to mitigate this threat.
>
> (Soler-Monreal & Gil-Salom, 2011:70)

Although the conclusion from Soler-Monreal and Gil-Salom's work (2011) is relevant to groups Am (EV = 0.13) and Em (EV = 0.06) in my study, this finding on expert–novice comparison must be explained to some extent. The group with the least use of EV was the expert group Ea (EV = 0.02), even below Em. This is not the case between Aa (EV = 0.17) and Am, in which the former uses this function more frequently. The writers in English incline to make a clear stance in the text in order to convince the audience of how their views are valued when they assess the cited works in their research development, as previously noted by other authors (see Moreno, 2010).

In the case of DE and AP, the authors who write in Spanish, particularly master's degree students, produce a greater number of occurrences. This is due to the frequent use of references to sources in the Didactic Proposal section that include more than half of the master's theses in Spanish (58.33%), unlike the American group whose theses do not have this section. The following example shows a citation in which the author borrows three (3) materials to create a didactic unit:

> Cinco tiras cómicas: tres páginas (28, 29 y 37) del manga de Hebizo y Nagiko (2009) 日人の知らない日本語 (que hacen referencia al lenguaje asociado a los yakuza japoneses, a un lenguaje japonés arcaico), una viñeta de Uno más en la familia. Diario de un gato recién adoptado (que permite introducir contenidos relacionados con la pragmática), de Fonollosa (2014), y una viñeta de Moderna de Pueblo (que trabaja todo lo estudiado durante la unidad didáctica y, especialmente, lo relativo a las referencias culturales), de Córcoles et al. (2014) **(Em5)**

When it comes to identifying expert from novice writers, AT is by far the most frequently used citation among novice writers, and the one that is most used by Spanish students, as shown in Figure 12.1. The American writers, however, combine this function with EN in similar frequency. With the predominant use of AT, the novice writers generally summarise the information from the sources without contrasting the different views on the subject matter. This type of behaviour in citation is expected at the postgraduate level, as many researchers have previously indicated (Dong, 1996; Hyland, 2002; Petrić, 2007; Mansourizadeh & Ahmad, 2011; Jalilifar, 2012; Sánchez-Jiménez, 2013). All of them concur in pointing out that the postgraduate student is primarily limited to attributing the knowledge borrowed from consulted sources.

Other notable differences relative to the writer's level of expertise between the groups have to do with complex categories such as REF, COMP, AP, and AU. The mastery of the first three functions requires the writer to be an expert in the field and has knowledge base on the topics needed for his/her research in a specific academic discipline. That is why oftentimes he/she can make references that will facilitate the reader to widen his/her knowledge through REF. The need for bibliographical knowledge is evident in the use of several citations with COMP, which is common knowledge in the field. Likewise, the use of AP demonstrates expertise in the discipline, through which the researcher makes a connection with the origin of concept or idea. Due to the degree of complexity involved in mastering these rhetorical functions, its common use is expected among professional writers, as proven by this research's findings.

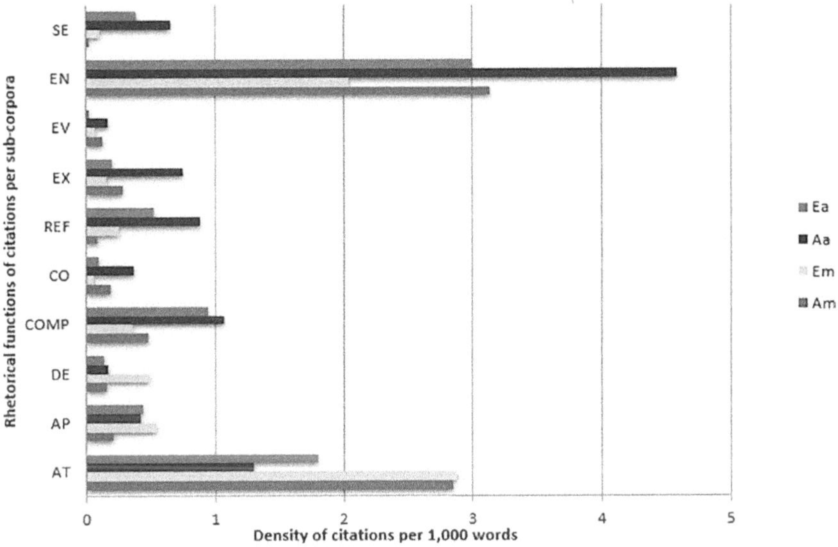

Figure 12.1 Density of rhetorical functions of citations per sub-corpora.

The SE function must be highlighted as it is used to promote the line of research of the text's author and to show the line of previous works that over the years have been cemented in his/her paper. As shown in Table 12.2, this citation is more common among expert writers of both languages, but is evidently not common among students because they are in their initial stages of research writing, i.e. master's thesis writing, and they normally do not have prior publications. However, I have a case of a student who constantly makes references to a master's thesis he/she previously completed. This unique case undermines the study's findings, since the result from a single writer with a large number of citation uses raises the overall number of SE citations found in Em subcorpus despite its rarity among the group.

In this respect, both the number in Table 12.2 and the result shown in the graph can deceive the reader who does not have access to the study's data. This makes us question the reliability of the data from a quantitative analysis. It, therefore, requires an exhaustive qualitative analysis, especially if it involves pragmatic elements in written discourse.

6 Conclusions

Both the language of communication and the cultural rhetorical patterns acquired during the formative years can alter the way we organise the content and how we present them in an academic research paper. This study explores this variation in the use of the rhetorical functions of citation by Spanish and American postgraduate students who write in their native language and by experts in English and Spanish.

After the corpus analysis, it is verified that the authors who write in English use a large number of citations, among which are complex rhetorical functions EN, EV, or EX. This may be due to a higher degree of training that American students receive in academic writing both in undergraduate and postgraduate levels. Spanish universities, however, lack compulsory subjects related to academic writing that enable students to follow criteria and effectively elaborate texts for research (Sánchez-Jiménez, 2013, 2018b). However, texts written in Spanish include a high number of occurrences in DE and AP categories with respect to those written in English. This is due to the idiosyncrasies found in the master's theses written in Spanish. These citations are included in the Didactic Proposal section, which American authors do not have in their works. Moreover, the section includes photographs, text fragments, didactic activities, and borrowed concepts from other authors, which are represented in citation as DE and AP.

As to the corresponding findings on the differences between expert and novice writers, the novice adopts an expository style in which he/she examines the attributed sources from other authors in his/her paper (AT). By doing so, his/her voice remains more objective and impersonal because of his/her inclination to avoid criticism and personal confrontation considering his/her low status in the discourse community (AT, DE). The expert scholars, on the contrary, use a more conventional dialogic style to communicate with their peers in the discipline with EN, REF, and COMP.

In this regard, as P. Thompson (2005:321) points out, one of the most important qualities of an academic professional writer is the capacity to transform knowledge from sources and find his/her own voice and identity as an author with respect to the cited references, thus encouraging the writer to show his/her proficiency on the various rhetorical functions that involve more complex citation uses (EN, COMP, REF, AP). This practice implies a defining element that separates the two groups, that is, the novice prefers to conceal his/her voice by not taking a stance with respect to the cited sources (Dong, 1996; Hyland, 2002; Charles, 2006; Pecorari, 2006; Petrić, 2007; Wette, 2010; Mansourizadeh & Ahmad, 2011; Jalilifar, 2012). The writer, being a novice, develops his/her work by heavily depending on cited texts. He/she still lacks the necessary skills to transform knowledge due to the early stages of academic writing (Pecorari, 2006). The expert, however, demonstrates a greater command of disciplinary conventions and strategically uses citation to support or validate the results of his/her studies.

The findings in my research will enable us to create a didactic proposal that will help college students adapt themselves to the rhetorical-discursive and pragma-linguistic characteristics of the Spanish or the

English language in Applied Linguistics in the genre of master's thesis and research article. In short, this study helps scholars better understand the language and culture in their research development in a new academic community in a foreign country. It facilitates to easily and quickly integrate themselves in these communities and social groups. This study will thus prove to be instrumental in perceiving and reducing cross-cultural differences through the development of writing conventions acquired in a new learning context. In conclusion, the results from this research can contribute pedagogically to academic writing courses, most specifically related to research writing. However, despite the absence of a didactic proposal in this paper, other authors (G. Thompson & Ye, 1991; Swales & Feak, 1994; P. Thompson & Tribble, 2001; Vázquez, 2001a, 2001b; Petrić, 2007; Wette, 2010; Sánchez-Jiménez, 2018b) have already specified materials for such purposes. The importance of the rhetorical functions of citations in academic writing, which if incorporated in course syllabi on academic writing, may prove to be beneficial and necessary. As college students become trained and familiarised, they will be better equipped, organised, and effective in their postgraduate writings and in their subsequent research projects.

Note

1 Support for This Project Was Provided by a PSC-CUNY Award, Jointly Funded by The Professional Staff Congress and The City University of New York.

References

Anthony, L. (2011). Antconc 3.2.4w. Software. www.laurenceanthony.net/software/antconc/ [retrieved: 6.4.2014].

Arnoux, E. Borsinger, A., Carlino, P., Di Stefano, M., Pereira, C. & Silvestre, A. (2005). La intervención pedagógica en el proceso de escritura de tesis de posgrado. *Revista de la Maestría en Salud Pública* 3/6, 1–18.

Bakhtin, M. (1979). The problem of speech genres, in C. Emerson & M. Holquist (eds.) *Speech Genres and Other Late Essays* [1986]. Austin, TX: University of Texas Press, pp. 60–102.

Bazerman, C. (2003). Intertextuality: how texts rely on other texts, in C. Bazerman & P. Prior (eds.) *What Writing Does and How It Does It: An Introduction to Analyzing Texts and Textual Practices*. New Jersey: Lawrence Erlbaum Associates Publishers, pp. 83–96.

Bondi, M. (2012). Voice in textbooks: between exposition and argument, in K. Hyland & C. Sancho-Guinda (eds.) *Stance and Voice in Written Academic Genres*. London: Palgrave-MacMillan, pp. 101–118.

Breivega, K.R., T. Dahl. & K. Fløttum (2002). Traces of self and others in research articles. A comparative pilot study of English, French and NorIgian research articles in medicine, economics and linguistics. *International Journal of Applied Linguistics* 12/2, 218–239.

Brooks, T.A. (1986). Evidence of complex citer motivations. *Journal of the American Society for Information Science (1986–1998)* 37/1, 34–36.

Case, D.O.& Higgins, G.M. (2000). How can I investigate citation behavior? A study of reasons for citing literature in communication. *Journal of the American Society for Information Science* 51, 635–45.

Castelló, M. Bañales, G., Corcelles, M., Iñesta, A. & Vega, N. (2011). La voz del autor en los textos académicos: construyendo la identidad como escritor, in C Monereo & J.I. Pozo (eds.) *La identidad en Psicología de la Educación: enfoques actuales, utilidad y límites.* Barcelona: Edebé.

Charles, M. (2006). The construction of stance in reporting clauses: a cross-disciplinary study of theses. *Applied Linguistics* 27/3, 492–518.

Connor, U. (1996). *Contrastive Rhetoric. Cross-Cultural Aspects of Second Language Writing.* Cambridge: Cambridge University Press.

Connor, U. (2011). *Intercultural Rhetoric in the Writing Classroom.* Ann Arbor, MI: The University of Michigan Press.

Dong, Y.R. (1996). Learning how to use citations for knowledge transformation: non-native doctoral student´s dissertation writing in science. *Research in the Teaching of English* 30/4, 428–457.

Dontcheva-Navratilova, O. (2015). Rhetorical functions of citations in linguistics research articles: a contrastive (English-Czech) study. *Discourse and Interaction* 9/2, 51–74.

Fløttum, K., Dahl, T. & Kinn, T. (2006). *Academic Voices: Across Languages and Disciplines.* Amsterdam/Philadelphia: John Benjamins.

Gilbert, N.G. (1977). Referencing as persuasion. *Social Studies of Science* 7, 113–122.

Harwood, N. (2009). An interview-based study of the functions of citations in academic writing across two disciplines. *Journal of Pragmatics* 41/3, 497–518.

Hyland, K. (1999). Academic attribution: citation and the construction of disciplinary knowledge. *Applied Linguistics* 20/3, 341–367.

Hyland, K. (2000). *Disciplinary Discourses: Social Interactions in Academic Writing.* Harlow, UK: Longman.

Hyland, K. (2002). Authority and invisibility: authorial identity in academic writing. *Journal of Pragmatics* 34, 1091–1112.

Hyland, K. (2005). Stance and engagement: a model of interaction in academic discourse. *Discourse Studies* 7/2, 173–192.

Hyland, K. (2009). *Academic Discourse.* London: Continuum.

Hyland, K. (2011). Projecting an academic identity in some reflective genres. *Ibérica* 21, 9–30.

Ivanič, R. (1998). *Writing and Identity: The Discoursal Construction of Identity in Academic Writing.* Amsterdam: Benjamins.

Jalilifar, A. (2012). Academic attribution: citation analysis in master's theses and research articles in applied linguistics. *International Journal of Applied Linguistics* 22/1, 23–41.

Kaplan, R. B. (1988). Contrastive rhetoric and second language learning: notes toward a theory of contrastive rhetoric, in A. C. Purves (ed.) *Writing Across Languages and Cultures: Issues in Contrastive Rhetoric.* Newbury Park, California: Sage Publications, pp. 275–304.

Latour, B. (1987). *Science in Action.* Cambridge, Massachusetts: Harvard University Press.

Mansourizadeh, K. & Ahmad, U.K. (2011). Citation practices among non-native expert and novice scientific writers. *Journal of English for Academic Purposes* 10, 152–161.
Mayor Serrano, M.B. (2006). La citación en la comunicación médica escrita (inglés-español): funciones y tipos. *Lebende Sprachen* 51/2, 72–78.
Moreno, A.I. (2010). Researching into English for research publication purposes from an applied intercultural perspective, in M. F. Ruiz-Garrido, J. C. Palmer-Silveira & I. Fortanet-Gómez (eds.) *English for Professional and Academic Purposes*. Amsterdam: Rodopi, pp. 57–71.
Mur Dueñas, P. (2009). Citation in business management research articles: a contrastive (English-Spanish) corpus-based analysis, in E. Suomela-Salmi & F. Dervin (eds.) *Cross-Linguistic and Cross-Cultural Perspectives on Academic Discourse*. Amsterdam: John Benjamins, pp. 49–60.
Parodi, G. (2007). El discurso especializado escrito en el ámbito universitario y profesional. *Revista Signos* 40/63, 147–178.
Pecorari, D. (2006). Visible and occluded citation features in postgraduate second-language writing. *English for Specific Purposes* 25, 4–29.
Petrić, B. (2007). Rhetorical functions of citations in high and low rated master´s thesis. *Journal of English for Academic Purposes* 6, 238–253.
Samraj, B. (2008). A discourse analysis of master´s theses across disciplines with a focus on introductions. *Journal of English for Academic Purposes* 7, 55–67.
Samraj, B. (2013). Form and function of citations in discussion sections of master's theses and research articles. *Journal of English for Academic Purposes* 12, 299–310.
Sánchez-Jiménez, D. (2011). Revisión de estudios sobre las funciones de las citas en textos académicos escritos por estudiantes de posgrado nativos y no nativos que aprenden una lengua extranjera. *Marcoele* 13, 1–22.
Sánchez-Jiménez, D. (2012). El uso de las funciones de las citas en la estructura retórica de las Introducciones de memorias de máster escritas en español por estudiantes nativos españoles y filipinos no nativos. *Revista Nebrija de Lingüística Aplicada a la Enseñanza de Lenguas* 12, 137–187.
Sánchez-Jiménez, D. (2013). Aplicabilidad de la tipología de las funciones retóricas de las citas al género de la memoria de máster en un contexto transcultural de enseñanza universitaria. *Revista Signos* 46/81, 82–104.
Sánchez-Jiménez, D. (2018a). Estudio contrastivo intercultural de las funciones retóricas de las citas: la producción de textos académicos en el nivel de posgrado escritos en español e inglés. *Pragmalingüística* 26, 373–393.
Sánchez-Jiménez, D. (2018b). Aproximación didáctica al aprendizaje de las funciones retóricas de las citas en el discurso académico universitario. *Actas del VI Congreso Internacional de español para Fines Específicos*. Brussels, Netherlands: Ministerio de Educación, Consejería de Educación en Bélgica, Países Bajos y Luxemburgo.
Soler-Monreal, C & Gil-Salom, L. (2011). A cross-language study on citation practice in PhD thesis. *International Journal of English Studies* 11/2, 53–75.
Soler-Monreal, C & Gil-Salom, L. (2014). Academic voices and claims: reviewing practices in research writing, in L. Gil-Salom & C. Soler-Monreal (eds.) *Dialogicity in Written Specialised Genres*. Amsterdam/Philadelphia: John Benjamins, 23–52.
Swales, J. (1986). Citation analysis and discourse analysis. *Applied Linguistics* 7/1, 39–56.

Swales, J. (1990). *Genre Analysis: English in Academic and Research Settings.* Cambridge. England and New York: Cambridge University Press.

Swales, J. (2004). *Research Genres: Explorations and Applications.* Cambridge: Cambridge University Press.

Swales, J. & Feak, C. (1994). *Academic Writing for Graduate Students.* Ann Arbor: University of Michigan Press.

Thompson, G. & Ye, Y. (1991). Evaluation in the reporting verbs used in academic papers. *Applied Linguistics* 12/4, 365–382.

Thompson, P. (2005). Points of focus and position intertextual reference in PhD theses. *Journal of English for Academic Purposes* 4, 307–323.

Thompson, P. & Tribble, C. (2001). Looking at citations: using corpora in English for academic purposes. *Language Learning & Technology* 5/3, 91–105.

Vázquez, G., (Coord.) (2001a). *Actividades para la escritura académica.* Madrid: Edinumen.

Vázquez, G., (Coord.) (2001b). *Guía didáctica del discurso académico escrito: ¿cómo se escribe una monografía?* Madrid: Edinumen.

Vinkler, P. (1998). Comparative investigation of frequency and strength of motives toward referencing: the reference threshold model. *Scientometrics* 43, 107–127.

Wang, P. & White, M.D. (1999). A cognitive model of document use during a research project. Study II. Decisions at the reading and citing stages. *Journal of the American Society for Information Science* 50/2, 98–114.

Wette, R. (2010). Evaluating student learning in a university-level EAP unit on writing using sources. *Journal of Second Language Writing* 19, 158–177.

13 Measuring Linguistic Complexity and Proficiency in Learner and Native Academic English[1]

Javier Pérez-Guerra

1 Introduction

This chapter investigates linguistic complexity in learner and native academic English. Under the assumption that learner academic language deviates from native academic language[2] in terms of linguistic complexity, I will test the hypothesis that 'language proficiency involves greater linguistic complexity', specifically in learner language. This hypothesis is checked out in well-known small-scale studies such as Reid (1986) and Frase et al. (1999). As regards the former, the Writer's Workbench was used to investigate native and non-native writing elicited by the Test of Written English (TWE). Reid concluded that metrics such as the average number of words, word length, and traditional readability indexes correlated significantly with proficiency. Frase et al. (1999) also used the Writer's Workbench tool to analyse essays from the TWE. Their study showed a significant increase in the frequency of, among other features, nouns and nominalisations, passive constructions and complex sentences, as well as the average number of words and word length, in proficient academic writing as compared to other genres.

The notion of complexity will be approached in this study by operationalising a number of lexical, structural, and syntactic features (*à la* Bulté & Housen, 2012) as generated by computational tools. The empirical data consist of academic essays written by native-speaking students and by learners ranging from waystage/elementary to proficient students, according to the *Common European Framework of Reference for Languages: Learning, Teaching, Assessment* (CEFR; Council of Europe, 2001).[3] The frequencies of the linguistic features resulting from the computational analysis of the texts will lead to multidimensional scales of the measures, which will be taken as indicators of lexical, structural, and syntactic complexity. Such scales will be used to answer the research question: do linguistic complexity and academic language proficiency go hand in hand?

This chapter is organised as follows. Section 2 deals with the notion of linguistic complexity. In Section 3, I refine the goal of the study and account for the selection of the quantitative measures which will serve as proxies for complexity, as well as for the methodology and the data which serve as the basis of the statistical analysis in Section 4. Finally, Section 5 summarises the results, presents the conclusions, and suggests avenues for further research.

2 Linguistic Complexity

The concept of linguistic (in many respects, restricted to syntactic) complexity,[4] as understood here, is in line with that of Ortega (2003:492), who argues that "[s]yntactic complexity (also called syntactic maturity or linguistic complexity) refers to the range of *forms that surface in language production* and the degree of sophistication of such forms" (my italics). According to this definition, complexity is approached by analysing overt shallow linguistic realisations, rather than undisclosed levels of structural and/or syntactic linguistic analysis. In this vein, the assessment of linguistic productions and their scaling as more/less complex will be undertaken here through the analysis of a number of features identified through computational techniques which do not require the recognition of unveiled levels of syntactic parsing. This approach is in line with a long tradition of studies which have operationalised complexity through the identification and exploration of closed sets of features or metrics.

With the aim of contextualising the theoretical context which frames the current research, it seems in order to touch on Michel's (2017) comprehensive account of complexity metrics which have been recognised in first- and second-language research. In Second Language Acquisition, Michel recognises three types of feature-driven studies addressing the concept of linguistic complexity: (i) developmental studies, based on the recognition of patterns of syntactic development and the frequency of occurrence of these constructions in natural speech (see Lu, 2009 for a review); (ii) cognitive studies, exploring the subjective difficulty of a language feature/item/construction, that is, the way in which a learner perceives the difficulty of an item as it is processed and learned; and (iii) purely linguistic surveys, with/without implications for processing demands. The analysis carried out in the present work will focus on Michel's third category since, as in Ortega (2003), complexity is understood as a measure of sophistication of discourse.

Specifically, my understanding of complexity is very close to Bulté and Housen's (2012: 23) lexical and syntactic levels of the so-called linguistic complexity, as shown in Figure 13.1.

On the one hand, lexical complexity, as understood by Bulté and Housen (2012), involves the study of metrics such as lexical diversity (e.g. type-token ratio), lexical sophistication (e.g. frequency of words beyond the 1,000 most common words), and lexical density (e.g. ratio of lexical words per function words), which measure lexical size, depth, and information packaging, respectively. On the other hand, syntactic (and

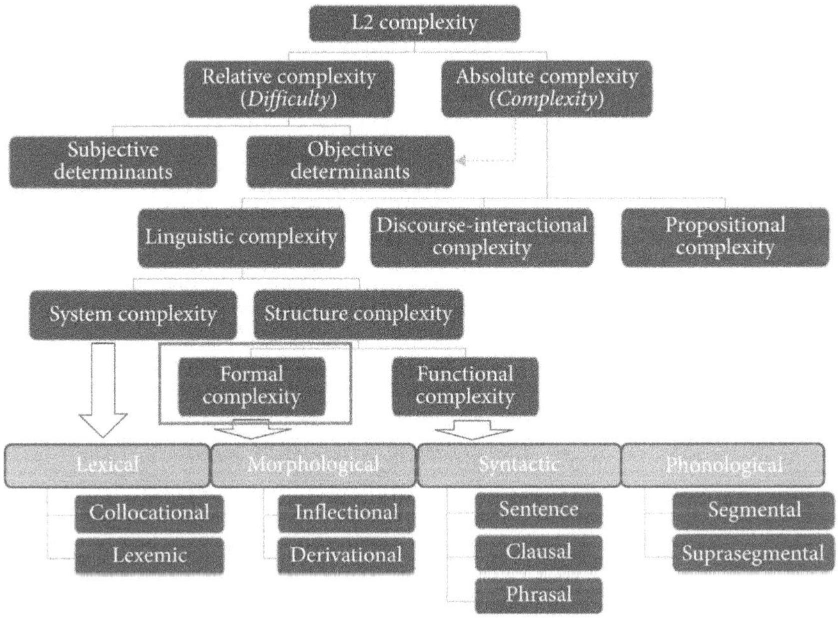

Figure 13.1 Bulté and Housen's (2012:23) linguistic complexity.

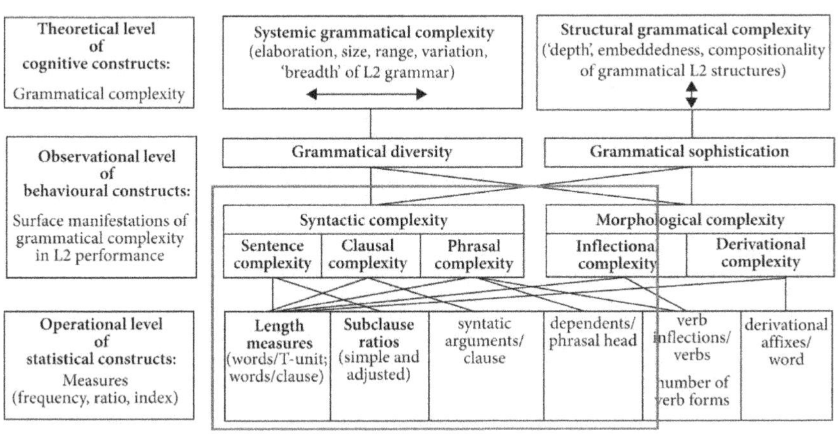

Figure 13.2 Bulté and Housen's (2012:27) grammatical complexity.

morphological) complexity are subsumed under the notion of grammatical complexity, as reflected in Figure 13.2.

Their level of syntactic complexity, as a reflex of grammatical diversity and sophistication, entails the analysis of features such as the following:

mean length of units (T-/c-/AS-units,[5] turns, utterances), number of S-nodes and T-/AS-units, metrics of sentential/clausal syntactic complexity (ratio of coordinated clauses per number of clauses, of clauses per AS-/T-/c-units, of subordinate/relative clauses per clauses/T-units, mean length of clauses, ratio of syntactic arguments per clause), phrasal complexity (ratio of dependents per phrases), and syntactic sophistication (number of passives, infinitivals, conjoined units, *wh*-, imperative, conditional clauses, auxiliaries, comparatives) (see Bulté & Housen, 2012:30–31).

3 Case Study, Data and Methodology

As pointed out in Section 1, the goal of this study is to assess linguistic complexity both in academic English as a Second Language (L2) produced by Spanish learners, and in academic writing produced by native-speaking students, with the aim of testing the hypothesis that 'more proficient writing is syntactically more complex'. Since the concept of complexity, as pointed out in Section 2, relies on the linguistic structure of syntactic units such as phrases, clauses, and sentences, its measurement will draw upon an inventory of features or metrics identified in the relevant literature as proxies for linguistic complexity. Methodologically, this study requires the selection of corpus data of learner and native academic English illustrating different proficiency levels, a set of formal indexes of linguistic (lexical, structural, syntactic) complexity, and an appropriate statistical approach which can reveal the significance of the results. After the application of Principal Component Analysis (PCA) and an ordered logistic regression model to the data, and consequently also following the identification of the dimensions of complexity that are strongly explanatory in the model, I will undertake a quantitative and a qualitative analysis of the set of relevant variables (Section 4).

A survey of previous studies measuring complexity is in order so as to ascertain the features that can be taken as proxies for linguistic complexity.[6] In what follows, I will summarise the main references that have provided valuable measures for this investigation:

i STUDIES FOCUSING ON ERROR- AND CAF- (Complexity, Accuracy – error-free use – and Fluency – ease, eloquence, smoothness of speech/writing –) METRICS. First, Larsen-Freeman's (1978) analysis of proficiency in ESL compositions, using measures based on Hunt's (1964) T-units, led to the conclusion that the best measures of L2 complexity are the percentage of error-free T-units (a measure of accuracy) and the average length of error-free T-units. Second, Ishikawa's (1995) study on low-proficiency L2 students revealed the inadequacy of investigating T-units with low-proficiency students, since many of their utterances contain neither T-units nor even clauses, and favoured measures such as the number of words in error-free clauses and the number of error-free clauses per composition. Third, Norris and Ortega's (2009) "organic" model of measuring CAF involved previously mentioned traditional metrics as well as other task-based features,[7] whose consideration lies beyond the scope of complexity as understood in the present study. Finally, Collentine (2011) investigated Interlanguage complexity and accuracy in learner productions with CALL input through metrics such as type-token ratio, lexical density, clauses per c-unit, and the proportion of error-free clauses.

ii STUDIES USING ANALYSERS. Many studies on linguistic complexity rely on indexes provided by analysers, and several such indexes have been taken into account in this investigation and have been incorporated into the statistical model described in Section 4. That said, the objective of the present study differs substantially from the goals of some of those quantitative feature-driven approaches. To give a few examples, first, Norrby and Håkansson (2007) analysed indexes such as sentence length, ratio of subordination strategies, and the nominal versus verbal style in learners' production, in an attempt to identify characterising models of learners such as risk-taker, recycler, careful and thorough, etc. Second, Crossley and McNamara (2012) examined L2 English writing produced by four groups of different L1 speakers and concluded that there are significant between-group differences regarding metrics such as average number of words before the main verb, interpreted as indicators of working-memory disparity. Third, Casanave (1994) undertook a qualitative student-per-student account of L2 complexity in students' journals, based on features such as frequencies involving T-units (ratio of words per T-unit, of clauses per T-unit, proportion of error-free T-units, length of error-free T-units), and attested striking differences among learners. Fourth, Lu (2011) analysed, in qualitative terms, linguistic differences among learners per institution, genre, timing conditions, proficiency level, and also correlations among traditional complexity measures. He found, on the one hand, that institution, genre, and timing constraints affect the relationship between syntactic complexity and proficiency in a significant way, and, on the other hand, that the best measures of complexity are the proportion of complex nominals per clause – this claim will be discussed below – and the mean length of clauses, the ratio of nominals per T-unit, the mean length of sentences, and the mean length of T-units. Even though they share with the present investigation the need for an inventory of objective features which can be identified and retrieved (semi-)automatically from the data, the studies just mentioned are intended to obtain qualitative characterisations of learners and groups of learners as regards attitudes, mental ability, and the influence of context. Finally, Ai and Lu (2013), who provide an assessment of syntactic complexity in university students' written production by native English speakers and Chinese L1 learners of L2 English, have been influential in the present research, in particular its methodology, despite Ai and Lu's clearly contrastive objectives. In short, they show that non-native students produce shorter units, less subordination and coordination, and a smaller proportion of complex nominals in English than speakers of L1 English.[8,9]

After a brief account of the state of the art regarding the quantification of complexity through specific linguistic features, in what follows, I will describe the analysers and the indexes or features that the former can identify automatically. The software tools used in this study are the L2 Syntactic Complexity Analyzer (L2SCA) (Lu, 2012) and Coh-Metrix (Graesser et al., 2004; McNamara et al., 2014). The L2SCA automates the analysis of complexity by using different measures of lexical density, taken from the first- and second-language acquisition literature, and Coh-Metrix provides basic cohesion, lexical, syntactic, and semantic-discoursive features, as well as other metrics of textual lexical diversity and readability.

Lu's L2SCA (http://aihaiyang.com/software) provides the features listed in Table 13.1, that is, 14 syntactic complexity indexes, selected from those reviewed in Wolfe-Quintero et al. (1998) and Ortega (2003). This analyser pre-processes the texts, analyses the syntactic structures in the samples with the use of the Stanford parser (Klein & Manning, 2003), identifies sentences, clauses, T-units, phrases, etc., using Tregex (Levy & Andrew, 2006), and delivers the frequencies and ratios of the features listed in Table 13.1. According to Lu (2010), when one compares its results with those provided by manual annotators, the analyser's precision, recall, and F-score are optimal, with accuracies of 0.83–1 for specifically structural unit identification.

Coh-Metrix (http://tool.cohmetrix.com) detects over 50 types of cohesion relations and approximately 200 measures of cohesion, language, and readability, 13 of these being primary measures. Since this analyser is particularly relevant to research in cohesion, on top of the syntactic indexes it obtains through the application of Charniak's (2000) parser,[10] Coh-Metrix provides measures resulting from both the cross-checking of the data with lexical, semantic, and cognitive electronic inventories and repositories like WordNet, the MRC Psycholinguistic Database, the CELEX Lexical Database, etc., and the application of models such as Latent Semantic Analysis. Coh-Metrix's output has proved very useful for the identification of significant indexes revealing linguistic complexity and for the validation of the results obtained through the L2SCA.

Table 13.2 shows the indexes which will be used in this chapter and their equivalence with the metrics in the L2SCA (under the 'Lu' column) and Coh-Metrix.

Table 13.1 L2 Syntactic Complexity Analyzer: features (Lu, 2010:479)

Measure	*Code*	*Definition*
Type 1: Length of production unit		
Mean length of clause	MLC	# of words/# of clauses
Mean length of sentence	MLS	# of words/# of sentences
Mean length of T-unit	MLT	# of words/# of T-units
Type 2: Sentence complexity		
Sentence complexity ratio	C/S	# of clauses/# of sentences
Type 3: Subordination		
T-unit complexity ratio	C/T	# of clauses /# of T-units
Complex T-unit ratio	CT/T	# of complex T-units/# of T-units
Dependent clause ratio	DC/C	# of dependent clauses/# of clauses
Dependent clauses per T-unit	DC/T	# of dependent clauses/# of T-units
Type 4: Coordination		
Coordinate phrases per clause	CP/C	# of coordinate phrases/# of clauses
Coordinate phrases per T-unit	CP/T	# of coordinate phrases/# of T-units
Sentence coordination ratio	T/S	# of T-units/# of sentences
Type 4: Particular structures		
Complex nominals per clause	CN/C	# of complex nominals/# of clauses
Complex nominals per T-unit	CN/T	# of complex nominals/# of T-units
Verb phrases per T-unit	VP/T	# of verb phrases/# of T-units

The indexes in Table 13.2 reveal information about the length of linguistic units, their syntactic complexity, and the statistical prominence of subordination strategies in the texts, as well as easiness metrics involving syntactic and lexical features.[11] First, MLC, MLS/DESSL, and MLT provide the mean length values of, respectively, clauses, sentences, and T-units in number of words. Second, the following category contains (positive or negative) sentence complexity indexes. C/S (CS onwards) gauges the ratio of clauses per sentences. SYNLE counts the number of words before the main verb of the clause – high values identify texts with sentences containing long subjects and/or several constituents before the matrix verbs, which have been understood as proxies for high syntactic and cognitive complexity. The SYNSTRUT metrics reflect structural similarity among different categories: SYNSTRUTa compares the

Table 13.2 Indexes of complexity

Type of measure	*Index*	*Lu*	*Coh-Metrix*
Length of production unit	Mean length of clause	MLC	
	Mean length of sentence	MLS	DESSL
	Mean length of T-unit	MLT	
Sentence complexity	Sentence complexity ratio	C/S	
	Words before the main verb		SYNLE
	Syntactic structure similarity in adjacent sentences		SYNSTRUTa
	Syntactic structure similarity between all sentences		SYNSTRUTt
	Editorial distance score for part of speech tags		SYNMEDpos
Connectives	All connectives		CNCAll
	Subordination: T-unit complexity ratio	C/T	
	Subordination: complex T-unit ratio	CT/T	
	Subordination: dependent clause ratio	DC/C	
	Subordination: dependent clauses per T-unit	DC/T	
	Subordination: modifiers per noun phrase		SYNNP
	Coordination: coordinate phrases per clause	CP/C	
	Coordination: coordinate phrases per T-unit	CP/T	
	Coordination: sentence coordination ratio	T/S	
Text easibility/ readability	Syntactic simplicity I		PCSYNz
	Syntactic simplicity II		PCSYNp
	Flesch Reading Ease (average 6–70)		RDFRE
	Flesch-Kincaid Grade Level		RDFKGL
	Editorial distance score for words		SYNMEDwrd
	Editorial distance score for lemmas		SYNMEDlem

structure of tree nodes in adjacent units and provides an index of syntactic similarity in adjacent sentences (basically, within the same paragraph), whereas SYNSTRUTt, which is similar to SYNSTRUTa, pays attention to the degree of syntactic similarity between all sentences by comparing tree nodes across paragraphs. SYNMEDpos is the editorial distance score for part of speech tags, where positive values imply morphosyntactic dissimilarity among sentences – for example, the index will be 0 if one compares *The parser provided correct results* and *The boy bought expensive books* since both sentences are parsed alike. Third, I have explored an additional group of indexes based on the number of connectives. CNCAll counts all the (coordinating and subordinating) connectives in the texts and provides an incidence score per 1,000 words. Some metrics in this category rely on exclusively subordinating connectives: C/T (CT onwards) provides the proportion of clauses per T-units; CT/T (CTT) shows the ratio of complex T-units per T-units; DC/C (DCC henceforth) reflects the proportion of dependent clauses per the overall number of clauses; DC/T (DCT) evinces the ratio of dependent clauses per T-units; and SYNNP counts the number of modifiers in noun phrases. Other measures provide indicators involving coordinating indexes: CP/C (CPC) and CP/T (CPT) give the ratio of coordinated phrases per clauses and T-units, and T/S (TS) the ratio of T-units per sentences. Fourth, the last category of indexes groups those which measure easiness/difficulty as far as readability is concerned. This category includes: PCSYNz (the lower, the more 'familiar' the words) and PCSYNp (the lower, the simpler the syntactic structures) as metrics of syntactic simplicity, and readability indexes like Flesch Reading Ease in RDFRE (easibility: scores 0–30 are associated with texts best understood by university graduates, and 31–100 by younger students) and Flesch-Kincaid Grade Level in RDFKGL (difficulty: e.g. the score 7 implies that text is understood by an average 7th-grade school student in the USA), as well as SYNMEDwrd and SYNMEDlem, which measure the so-called editorial distance scores for, respectively, words and lemmas, that is, the lexical dissimilarity of word variants (technically 'words') and invariable lexical bases (or 'lemmas'). Table 13.3 groups the features in Table 13.2 into two categories: indexes of increasing difficulty and those of increasing easiness.

The use of the previous indexes as proxies for complexity and/or proficiency is not free of controversy in the literature. First, the balance between the feasibility of automated analyses of complexity and the need for a more fine-grained treatment of the indexes has been discussed by a number of scholars. To give a few examples, Lambert and Kormos (2014:2) contend that different types of subordination (e.g. complement clauses controlled by verbs, complement clauses controlled by nouns and adverbial clauses) "emerge at different points in the developmental process (…) [so,] the use of measures that conceptualize subordination as a *unitary* process can mask, rather than illuminate, developmental variation during task performance" (my italics). They also point out that, for example, subordination can be biased by specific lexical controllers, that is, certain verbs prefer specific types of subordinate clauses or even none, so overall frequencies of subordination may be distorted by item-specific lexical factors. Wijers (2018) investigated measures of subordination in Dutch-speaking learners of Swedish as a foreign language and native

Table 13.3 Features of increasing difficulty versus easiness

	Increasing difficulty	*Increasing easiness*
Length	MLC	
	MLS	
	DESSL	
	MLT	
Syntax: phrasal	SYNNP	
Syntax: clausal	SYNLE	
	SYNMEDpos (0–1)	
	CPC	
Syntax: above clausal	CNCAll	SYNSTRUTa (0–1)
	CS	SYNSTRUTt (0–1)
	CT	
	CTT	
	DCC	
	DCT	
	CPT	
	TS	
	SYNMEDpos	
Lexical	SYNMEDwrd	
	SYNMEDlem	
Readability	RDFKGL (0–12)	RDFRE (1-[6–70]-100)
		PCSYNz
		PCSYNp

speakers. Her study revealed significant differences not between the subordination ratios (i.e. number of subordinate clauses divided by the total number of clause of T-units) of learners' and native speakers' writing, but between the subordinate clause types. Similarly, the main conclusion in Kyle and Crossley's (2018) study of TOEFL exams is that, although the measures of phrasal complexity are better predictors of writing quality than clausal indexes, the more fine-grained the taxonomies of phrasal and clausal complexity per dependency/subordination type, the more explanatory the statistical model.

Second, as already pointed out, it has been suggested that mode[12] and task[13] rank higher than proficiency as predictors of complexity. In this vein, Biber et al.'s (2016:662) study on complexity in spoken and written TOEFL exams concluded that "task-type differences on standardized language exams – associated with both speech versus writing and with different communicative purposes – are systematically associated with linguistic differences, especially with the use of grammatical complexity features", a finding which is in keeping with previous research by the same team. In particular, Biber et al. (2011:29; similarly, Biber & Gray, 2011) contended that "complexity is not a single unified construct, and it is therefore not reasonable to suppose that any single measure will adequately represent this construct". They found that T-unit- and subordination-based (i.e. clausal) measures are not typical of academic writing but of conversational discourse, whereas nominal/prepositional (i.e. phrasal) measures are good indicators of academic writing.[14] Michel et al.'s (2019:142) study of the influence of task types on morphosyntactic complexity and proficiency through a battery of indexes revealed that "the task-related factors tend to have a strong influence on what language learners will use, while towards higher levels of proficiency learners are less restricted".

Third, in connection with the influence of mode on the preference for the complexification strategies computed by the analysers, proficiency has been claimed not to run necessarily parallel to complexity, at least in the way the latter is measured by the analysers. In an influential study, Crossley et al. (2014) undertook a multifactorial analysis of L1 academic writing (argumentative essays), with variables such as score/grade, topic, writer's geographical area, timing, and (handwritten or typed) production, as well as with the indexes provided by Coh-Metrix. They concluded that the variable reflecting the grade assigned to the essays explained only 5% of the total variance. However, Biber and colleagues' claim that proficiency involves an increase of phrasal, and not clausal, complexity in academic writing was tested in Parkinson and Musgrave (2014) through the evaluation of EAP (English for Academic Purposes) writing by undergraduate and MA TESOL international students. They concluded that Biber's findings are developmentally confirmed by their data, since the more proficient students used modifying strategies in their writing significantly more frequently than the undergraduate participants. By contrast, Struc and Wood (2011) reached opposite results in their study on sentence variety in L2 writing. They devised an index which reflects sentence variety, ranging from texts with sentences of the same type (simple, complex, compound, and compound-complex) to sentences involving the four types. They reported a "decrease in the use of simple sentences, with corresponding increases in the use of complex and compound sentences" (70) as students advanced to higher levels of proficiency. Thus, their findings disfavoured the trend towards reduced clausal complexity in advanced students. Similarly, in a recent study that explores written argumentative texts by L2 (A2–B1) learners and by native writers of Dutch, Italian, and Spanish, and that calculates a number of objective complexity measures, Folkert and Vedder (2019:197) contend that no conclusive judgements can be reached as regards the connection between phrasal complexity and proficiency level in either L1 or L2 writers. By contrast, Staples et al. (2016) investigated L1 academic writing by undergraduates, taking into account variables reflecting phrasal (e.g. frequencies of nouns, attributive adjectives, nouns as nominal premodifiers, nominalisations, genitives modifying nouns, postmodifying prepositional phrases) and clausal (e.g. finite adverbial clauses, *that-* and *wh*-complement clauses controlled by verbs, clausal coordinating conjunctions) complexity, as well as other so-called 'intermediate' structures (e.g. finite clauses embedded in noun or adjective phrases, phrasal constituents in clauses, nonfinite clauses as complements of verbs, adjectives, and nouns). They concluded that "[c]lausal features (...) are used more predominantly in lower level texts while phrasal features are increasingly used as academic level increases" (179). We might bear in mind that Crossley et al.'s (2014) study on L1 academic writing cannot be straightforwardly extrapolated to L2 research, since grading differences are radically greater in the non-native language. In fact, Lu (2011), Parkinson and Musgrave (2014), and, very recently, Casal and Leeb (2019) have provided empirical support in favour of the increase of, specifically, phrasal complexity as L2 writers develop academic (writing) skills (see also Staples et al., 2016:153). Other studies give support to a certain parallelism between phrasal and clausal complexity. To give an example, with the objective of testing the measures provided by his analyser, Lu (2017:505) operationalised syntactic complexity in L2 writing and concluded that "[a] large subset of the measures incorporated in L2SCA has been found to be predictive of holistic measures of writing quality as well. (...) [T]he following measures significantly correlated with writing scores: mean length of sentence, mean length of T-unit, mean length of clause, dependent clauses per clause, and complex nominals per clause", that is, indexes of phrasal and clausal complexit. By contrast, Lambert and Nakamura's (2019) study compares productions by L2 English produced by Japanese learners and native speakers through variables such as the proportion of simple, compound (coordination), and complex (nominal, adverbial, and relative subordination) utterances, and phrasal-complexity measures like the ratio of words and modifiers per noun phrase. They demonstrate the negative relationship between phrasal and clausal syntax: "[a]s the (...) measures of clausal complexity increase, the (...) measures of phrasal complexity tended to decrease and vice versa" (10), which is in keeping with the claims of Biber and colleagues. However, and this actually contradicts Biber's previous findings, they also observe a "negative relationship between proficiency and all [the] measures of phrasal syntax (words, modifier types, modifier tokens, and subordinated nouns per NP)": as proficiency increased, NPs became syntactically simpler, at least in the intermediate level of students' proficiency.

In an attempt to model the connection between proficiency and complexity, a number of studies have analysed complexity measures according to learners' CEFR levels. Hawkins and Filipović (2012) found that sentence length, not necessarily triggered by a greater degree of complexity at the phrasal level, increased between adjacent levels from CEFR A2 to C2. Verspoor et al. (2012) reported that the proportion of simple versus complex sentences, which is a proxy for clausal and not phrasal complexity, was a good separator of level between A1 and B1.2. Gyllstad et al. (2014) found that the variables length of T-units, length of clauses, and ratio of clauses per T-unit increased from A to B CEFR levels. Alexopoulou et al. (2017) observed a clear increase in both the mean length of clauses and the number of subordinate clauses from A2 to B2, that is, of clausal complexity. Lahuerta Martínez (2018) concluded that indexes of not only clausal complexity such as sentence length, compound- and complex-sentence ratios, and the proportion of coordinate clauses, but also of phrasal complexity, like dependent clause ratios and number of noun phrases per clause, distinguished the CEFR A2 and B1 levels significantly. Michel et al. (2019) carried out a large-scale study of the interaction of task type, morphosyntactic complexity, and learners' proficiency. They computed 571 measures of linguistic (clausal and phrasal) complexity and modelled the results via sophisticated statistical techniques. As a conclusion, "the trajectories from A1 to C2 revealed growth in terms of sentence length and complexity; that is, learners seemed to develop over time when looking at syntactic measures (e.g. subordination)" (140). Finally, Khushik and Huhta (2019) claimed that most of the 30 complexity indexes provided by Lu's and the Coh-Metrix analysers differentiated CEFR levels in their study of Sindhi and Finnish EFL learners.

Even within academic writing, substantial differences among disciplines and sub-registers or sub-genres have been reported in the literature as regards the use of complexity measures. Thus, Gardner et al. (2019:670) analyse L1 university assignments and find that "the writing situation – disciplinary group [Arts and Humanities, Life Sciences, Physical Sciences and Social Sciences], genre family, discipline, and level of study – is key to interpreting each dimension" resulting from the application of the multidimensional analysis of 39 lexico-grammatical features associated with different aspects of linguistic complexity – see also Staples et al. (2016) in this respect.

This section has served as a critical introduction to the methodology which will be followed in the remainder of this chapter. The literature review has highlighted both advantages and drawbacks in the study of linguistic complexity by means of automatic indexes. In what follows, I will describe the data which will be analysed here with the purpose of obtaining sets of linguistic determinants of complexity in learner and native academic language. The L2 data comprise examples of academic writing retrieved from the Written Corpus of Learner English (WRICLE; Rollinson & Mendikoetxea, 2010), specifically essays written in English by students in the Universidad Autónoma de Madrid, whose L1 is Spanish. Placement tests were performed in order to categorise the essays according to the CEFR levels – the data sample includes learner academic language from the A2 to the C2 levels.[15]

In this study, the data sample consists of essays classified in terms of linguistic proficiency, in the ranges A2, B1, B2, C1, and C2. Data for L1 academic writing were retrieved from the Louvain Corpus of Native English Essays (LOCNESS; Granger, 1998), which contains essays written by British A-level pupils, plus British and American university students. The sample used in this study belongs to the British A-level category.

Table 13.4 sets out the texts selected in this study, their mean length, word (sub)totals, and the standard deviation in the number of words.

Table 13.4 WRICLE and LOCNESS texts

Level	*A2*	*B1*	*B2*	*C1*	*C2*	*Locness*
Texts	A120-1	A1-1	A11-1	A30-1	A91-1ed	alevels1_transport01
	A120-2	A1-2	A11-2	A30-2	A91-2ed	alevels1_transport02
	A131-1	A2-1	A16-1	A67-1	A206-1ed	alevels1_transport03
	A131-2	A2-2	A16-2	A67-2	A206-2ed	alevels1_transport04
	A146-1	A4-1	A17-1	A85-1	A252-1ed	alevels1_transport05
	A146-2	A4-2	A19-1	A85-2	A252-2ed	alevels1_transport06
	A148-1	A6-1	A19-2	A99-1	A277-1ed	alevels1_transport07
	A148-2	A6-2	A36-1	A99-2	A277-2ed	alevels1_transport08
	A149-1	A7-1	A36-2	A137-1	A364-1ed	alevels1_transport08
	A149-2	A7-2	A38-1	A140-1	A364-2ed	alevels1_transport10
	A150-1	A10-1	A39-1	A140-2	C15-1ed	alevels1_transport11
	A150-2	A10-2	A39-2	A240-1	C15-2ed	alevels1_transport12
	A18-1	A12-1	A48-1	A243-1	C15-3ed	alevels1_transport13
	A18-2	A12-2	A48-2	A243-2	C46-1ed	alevels1_transport14
	A28-1	A13-1	A62-1	A256-1	C46-2ed	alevels1_transport15
	A28-2	A13-2	A62-2	A258-1	C46-3ed	alevels1_transport16
	A35-1	A14-1	A66-1	A258-2	C108-1ed	alevels2_parliament01
	A35-2	A14-2	A66-2	A260-1		alevels2_parliament02
	A90-1	A29-1	A68-1	A260-2		alevels3_fox01
	A9-1	A29-2	A68-2	A262-1		alevels3_fox02
	A9-2	A31-1	A75-1	A262-2		alevels3_fox03
	A93-1	A31-2		A272-1		alevels3_fox04
	A93-2	A32-1		A272-2		alevels3_fox05
		A32-2				alevels3_fox06
						alevels4_boxing01
						alevels4_boxing02
						alevels4_boxing03
						alevels4_boxing04
						alevels4_boxing05
						alevels4_boxing06
Mean	663.43	641.58	723.76	655.09	930.18	526.53
SD	203.24	125.69	144.40	151.14	353.18	212.81
Word subtotals	15588	15633	15356	15906	16013	15867
Word total	94363					

4 Analysis of the Data

Section 3 described the indexes which will be used to assess linguistic complexity in the learner and native database or, more exactly, to determine the complexity dimensions that are potentially connected with language proficiency. As also pointed out in that section, the database consists of a selection of texts from WRICLE and LOCNESS. The input texts from the corpora were automatically POS-tagged and parsed by the analysers so that the latter could provide the different measures. Since all the metrics are ratios, means, normalised values, or continuum indexes, there is no need to normalise the results using text lengths as baselines. As already mentioned, the sample contains texts produced by learners of English who have been classified according to CEFR levels (A2, B1, B2, C1, and C2) and A-levels native (L1) students. The variable reflecting such a proficiency taxonomy, 'level', will act as the ordinal response variable in the regression analysis which will scale, according to their statistical significance, the potential linguistic dimensions of features resulting from the application of PCA to the data. The 24 measures which have been computed by means of the automatic analysers (see Section 3) will serve as the independent quantitative variables in the statistical model.

In what follows, I will describe the statistical modelling of the data. In an attempt to, first, reduce the number of independent variables and, second, to avoid collinearity among them, I have applied PCA to the numeric measures. Downsizing the database proved to be desirable as a consequence of the inviable ratio of independent variables (24) and the number of observations (138 texts or essays). PCA reduces the dimensionality of a dataset consisting of variables that correlate with each other, while it retains the variation to the maximum extent by providing a set of values of linearly uncorrelated variables. Third, in her account of relevant syntax-based indexes of complexity variation, Ortega (2003:498) asks "'how different is different enough' in terms of magnitudes". In this vein, PCA will help relativise measures by providing a unique joint value per text per component, calculated on the basis of a set of correlating variables, that is, of magnitudes that evince similar complexity strategies.

PCA requires that the variables should be intercorrelated and that the correlations should not be exceedingly high. In this respect, to test correlation among variables, I applied Bartlett's Test of Sphericity to the complexity measures (function 'cortest.bartlett', package 'psych' in R; R Core Team, 2018). With a *p*-value of 2.077331e-192, well below the significance level, this test's null hypothesis that the variables are not correlated can be rejected. In consequence, my numeric variables intercorrelate and PCA can be applied to the data.

PCA has been carried out via the function 'princomp' in R (package 'FactoMineR'). This function undertakes the grouping of the numeric variables and provides as many groupings or components as variables, that is, 24 components (Comp.1–24). The results are reflected in Table 13.5.

Table 13.5 shows that the cumulative proportion of variance (in italics) explained through components 1–4 is 76.5%. Since 70%–80% is usually taken as the operational cut-off point of the cumulate percentage of variance in PCA (and in, for example, Factor Analysis), I will consider only 4 of the components provided by PCA in my analysis. The fact that components 5 onwards do not contribute to the modelling of the measures in a significant way is shown in the scree plot in Figure 13.3 (function 'fviz_eig', package 'factoextra' in R).

Once PCA has revealed that 4 components are sufficiently explicative statistically, the study of the loading coefficients of each variable (or measure) per component will identify, first, those variables that are most explanatory within the component and, second, whether their contribution to the latter is positive or negative. Table 13.6 displays the coefficients or loadings of each measure within each of the four components.

The stronger a variable loads onto a component, the more strongly this variable defines the latter. Since in this study I opted for discarding loadings with absolute (positive or negative) values lower than 0.2, I was left with the explicative measures and coefficients in Table 13.7.

The qualitative interpretation of these components is revealed through the analysis of the variables that contribute either positively or negatively to the component. Accordingly, the grouping of positive measures in component 1 has been associated with the length of major grammatical units (DESSL, MLT), sentential/clausal embedding/recursion (CL, CT, DCC, DCT, CTT), and greater reading difficulty (RDFKGL). The negative loadings correspond to variables that reflect familiarity (PCSYNz, PCSYNp) and similarity (SYNSTRUTa, SYNSTRUTt) of syntactic structures. In short, the variables grouped within component 1 favour the so-called 'productive' complexity (length and internal subordination), as in Vercellotti (2019).

Component 2 contains variables which, on the one hand, operationalise complexity within phrases by means of either stacked modification (SYNNP) or coordinated units (CPT, CPC) and thus lead to greater unit length (MLC), and, on the other hand, disfavour complex clausal (DCC) and T-units (CT, DCT). In sum, component 2 constitutes the grouping of variables which captures phrasal complexity and disfavours clausal complexity. As pointed out in Section 3, Biber and colleagues have shown that high(er) phrasal complexity and low(er) clausal complexity are characteristic features of academic English.

The positive loadings in component 3 have been associated with lexical dissimilarity (SYNMEDwrd, SYNMEDlem) and with different word-unit grammatical status (SYNMEDpos). At the opposite end, variables

Table 13.5 PCA (24 components)

	Comp.1	*Comp.2*	*Comp.3*	*Comp.4*	*Comp.5*	*Comp.6*	*Comp.7*
SD	3.3062534	1.901286	1.42343763	1.33986981	1.1205681	1.00592196	0.88872725
Proportion of variance	0.4554713	0.1506204	0.08442395	0.07480213	0.0523197	0.04216162	0.03290984
Cumulative proportion	*0.4554713*	*0.6060917*	*0.69051561*	*0.76531774*	0.8176374	0.85979907	0.8927089
	Comp.8	*Comp.9*	*Comp.10*	*Comp.11*	*Comp.12*	*Comp.13*	*Comp.14*
SD	0.71501571	0.67457175	0.62742472	0.56261235	0.53161907	0.44531311	0.36041078
Proportion of Variance	0.02130198	0.01896029	0.01640257	0.01318886	0.01177578	0.00826266	0.00541233
Cumulative proportion	0.91401088	0.93297118	0.94937375	0.96256261	0.97433839	0.98260105	0.98801338
	Comp.15	*Comp.16*	*Comp.17*	*Comp.18*	*Comp.19*	*Comp.20*	*Comp.21*
SD	0.30171233	0.25521495	0.24333821	0.16359928	0.13406503	0.11770879	0.08718365
Proportion of variance	0.00379293	0.00271395	0.00246723	0.0011152	0.00074889	0.00057731	0.00031671
Cumulative proportion	0.99180631	0.99452026	0.99698749	0.99810268	0.99885158	0.99942888	0.99974559
	Comp.22	*Comp.23*	*Comp.24*				
SD	0.05715521	0.05080111	1.61E-02				
Proportion of variance	0.00013611	0.00010753	1.08E-05				
Cumulative proportion	0.9998817	0.99998923	1.00E+00				

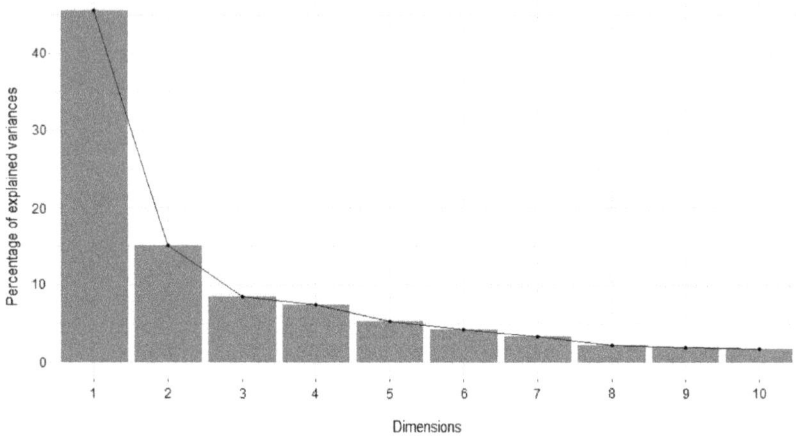

Figure 13.3 Scree plot of cumulative explained variance (x-axis: components).

Table 13.6 PCA coefficients per variable per component

	Comp.1	*Comp.2*	*Comp.3*	*Comp.4*
DESSL	0.28692732	0.09848679	0.04900051	0.09532821
PCSYNz	-0.2719551	-0.0639295	-0.0217606	-0.1532113
PCSYNp	-0.2720566	-0.0629308	-0.0199656	-0.1541264
CNCAll	0.02149892	0.05104171	0.14574345	-0.2893551
SYNLE	0.09488621	0.13668952	-0.0341049	0.02540433
SYNNP	-0.0504643	0.37840505	-0.0785494	0.00703892
SYNMEDpos	-0.1008842	-0.0947181	0.5249908	0.01764014
SYNMEDwrd	-0.1811369	-0.0517537	0.46454341	0.03461546
SYNMEDlem	-0.1686284	-0.0159968	0.45847901	0.0193707
SYNSTRUTa	-0.2366906	-0.0197536	-0.240516	-0.1547779
SYNSTRUTt	-0.2390219	-0.0591385	-0.2575392	-0.1909335
RDFRE	-0.1982473	-0.1874452	0.09647748	0.04373251
RDFKGL	0.26938222	0.15498124	-0.0135761	0.0421681
MLS	0.28427153	0.10496665	0.05839471	0.10824605
MLT	0.26137922	0.16258603	-0.0042061	-0.090006
MLC	0.02219487	0.47078015	-0.0006187	0.11055118
CS	0.26669055	-0.1931742	0.08872311	0.01530185
CT	0.2472675	-0.2183376	0.02452263	-0.2239107
DCC	0.22593088	-0.2017209	0.03319482	-0.3050896
DCT	0.24429459	-0.2156598	0.03065999	-0.2781189
TS	0.13638227	-0.0839652	0.18034426	0.44488431
CTT	0.20873513	-0.18906	0.01381374	-0.2688353
CPT	0.05579477	0.32534509	0.2259897	-0.4259431
CPC	-0.0578318	0.40361818	0.18745038	-0.2980162

Table 13.7 PCA coefficients per variable per component (coefficients' absolute values > 0.2)

	Comp.1	*Comp.2*	*Comp.3*	*Comp.4*
DESSL	0.28692732			
PCSYNz	-0.2719551			
PCSYNp	-0.2720566			
CNCAll				-0.2893551
SYNLE				
SYNNP		0.37840505		
SYNMEDpos			0.5249908	
SYNMEDwrd			0.46454341	
SYNMEDlem			0.45847901	
SYNSTRUTa	-0.2366906		-0.240516	
SYNSTRUTt	-0.2390219		-0.2575392	
RDFRE				
RDFKGL	0.26938222			
MLS	0.28427153			
MLT	0.26137922			
MLC		0.47078015		
CS	0.26669055			
CT	0.2472675	-0.2183376		-0.2239107
DCC	0.22593088	-0.2017209		-0.3050896
DCT	0.24429459	-0.2156598		-0.2781189
TS				0.44488431
CTT	0.20873513			-0.2688353
CPT		0.32534509	0.2259897	-0.4259431
CPC		0.40361818		-0.2980162

such as SYNSTRUTa and SYNSTRUTt, which measure syntactic node similarity, contribute negatively to the interpretation of the component. In sum, the variables grouped by PCA in component 3 favour dissimilarity of words and syntactic nodes.[16]

Finally, in component 4, we find measures implying higher sentential complexity (TS) and lower clausal (and T-unit) complexity (CT, DCC, DCT, CTT, CPC, CPT). CNCAll, which reflects the frequency of connectives, has a negative loading in this grouping of variables as an effect of the lower proportion of independent, dependent, complex, and coordinated clauses embedded within other clauses or T-units, as marshalled by the measures with negative loadings.

To recap, PCA has suggested, through the cumulative percentage coefficient, the number of components which explain more than 75% of variance. It also provides the (positive or negative) loadings of each variable within each component, and this has led to a qualitative interpretation of the four groupings or components summarised in Table 13.8.

The next step is, first, to make all the measures with significant loadings (>0.2) in each component proportional to the corresponding loadings, and, second, to add the resulting values of all the significant

Table 13.8 Dimensional interpretation of components

Component	*Positive contributors*	*Negative contributors*
1	Length of major units Reading difficulty Sentential/clausal embedding	Structural familiarity Syntactic similarity
2	Phrasal complexity and length	Clausal complexity
3	Lexical and grammatical dissimilarity	Syntactic node similarity
4	Sentential complexity	Clausal complexity

variables in each component together in order to reduce the model to only 4 independent variables, that is, one per component. In other words, the new database will consist of one value per observation (or text) per component, that is, four values per essay. Then, I applied an ordered logistic regression analysis to the values of each of the texts per component, with the purpose of determining the components (or groupings of the 24 original independent variables) that contribute most significantly to a model which now includes the response variable 'level', that is, proficiency. Specifically, the ordered logistic regression analysis, with Hessian optimisation, was carried out through the R function 'polr' (package 'MASS'; Venables & Ripley, 2002). Table 13.9 shows the results of the logistic regression (Standard Error, *t*- and *p*-values). The (significance) *p*-values, not provided by 'polr', were calculated by comparing the *t*-values against the standard normal distribution.

The ordered logistic regression analysis has revealed that only components 1 and 2 contribute significantly to a model with the proficiency level acting as the dependent variable. Such a conclusion is in keeping with the comparison of the significance of the models by using ANOVA. The *p*-values of the comparison of the models with 3 and 4 components, and of the models with 2 and 3 components are 0.19865 and 0.17442, respectively. Since ANOVA proves that the differences between the models with 2, 3, and 4 components are not statistically significant, opting for the reduced model with components 1 and 2 is perfectly feasible.

The boxplots in Figures 13.4 and 13.5 show the (median and) mean values and the significance levels of the variables resulting from PCA in each of the proficiency levels.

As regards component 1, Figure 13.4 shows that the only statistically significant difference between proficiency levels is that between the texts written by native students and by learners ($p = 0.00047$). According to these results, learners use more complex language, longer major units, and more diverging structures than native writers, which leads to greater degrees of reading difficulty in the learners' texts.

Table 13.9 Ordered logistic regression analysis (significance codes: 0 '***' 0.001 '**' 0.01 '*' 0.05 '.' 0.1 ' ' 1)

	Value	*Std. Error*	*t-value*	*p-value*	
Component 1	-0.0612502	0.01426987	-4.292274	1.77E-05	***
Component 2	0.3781048	0.13525989	2.795395	5.18E-03	**
Component 3	5.22428303	3.13708697	1.665329	9.58E-02	.
Component 4	0.05341727	0.04152882	1.28627	1.98E-01	

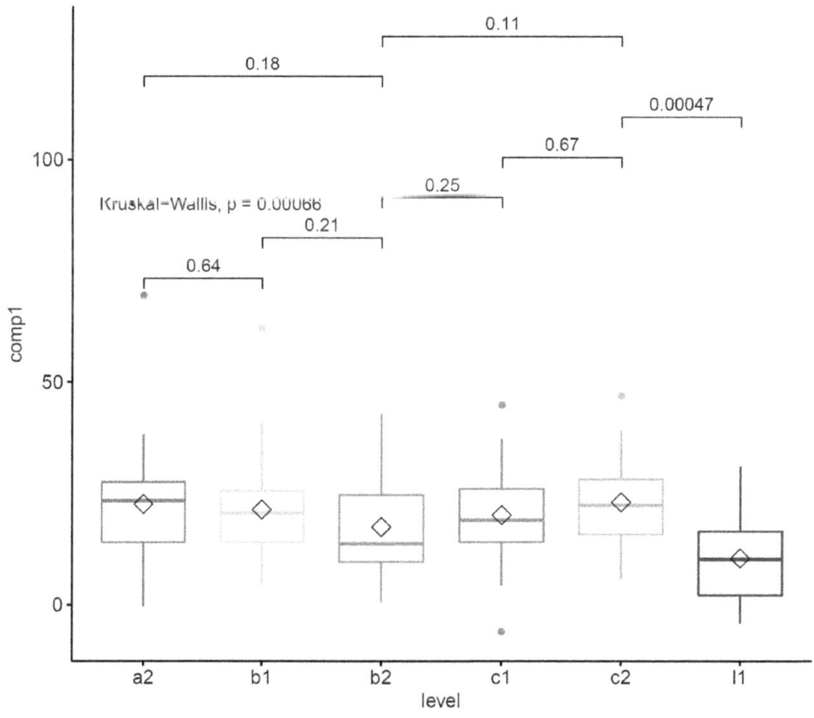

Figure 13.4 Boxplot: proficiency and component 1.

As far as component 2 is concerned, two differences sketched in Figure 13.5 reach statistical significance: first, that between A2 and B1 ($p = 0.01$), and, second, between B2/C1 and C2 ($p < 0.05$). Specifically, the texts written by A2 learners evince greater phrasal complexity and longer phrases than the texts produced by B1 students. The boxplot also reflects intermediate proficiency levels with lower phrasal complexity and length, while they increase their complexity at the level of the clause (negative measure in component 2). Finally, the academic texts by the

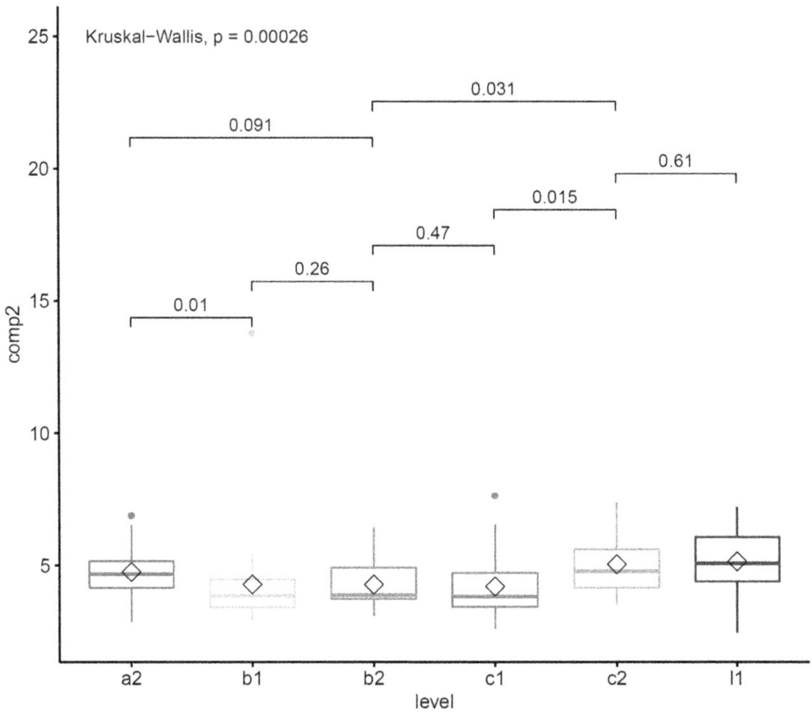

Figure 13.5 Boxplot: proficiency and component 2.

most proficient (C2) learners show higher levels of phrasal complexity, close to those evinced by the native writing.

5 Summary and Conclusions

Sections 1 and 2 showed that the literature is unanimous in viewing complexity as heterogeneous in nature. Of the many dimensions of complexity, this study has tackled those which are reflexes of linguistic aspects associated with length, syntactic design, and in-text divergence among grammatical units. Specifically, this chapter has explored linguistic complexity in L1 and L2 academic English through an inventory of 24 numeric measures, provided by automatic analysers. To this end, I analysed a sample of approximately 95,000 words of academic essays, including those written by native (A-level) students and by university students of ESL. Such a selection criterion has avoided significant task and/or sub-genre distinctions, which, as mentioned in Section 4, may bias the indicators of complexity (see Pallotti, 2009, in this respect).

The corpus is balanced as regards the weight of each CEFR proficiency level (approximately 15,000 words per level) and participants' backgrounds (advanced pre-university and university levels).[17]

The 24 measures per text or essay reflect indexes of syntactic and so-called productive complexity (length, internal embedding), syntactic and lexical divergence, and readability degrees. In order to avoid redundancy or collinearity among such indexes and to reduce the number of significant variables, given that the number of essays or observations is 138, the original database was reduced to 4 components or groups of correlating variables by means of PCA. Of the 4 components, an ordered logistic regression analysis of the downsized database revealed the statistical significance of only 2 components. Such components were interpreted as proxies for, respectively, (i) clausal/sentential embedding, length of major units (sentences, T-units), reading difficulty, and syntactic and lexical dissimilarity among units, and (ii) higher phrasal and lower clausal complexity. Of the initial inventory of 24 independent variables, 17 measures were declared by PCA and the regression analysis to be significantly explanatory in the model, which gives support to both the theoretical assumptions and the methodology on which this study was based.

In the current study, I hypothesised that proficiency and linguistic complexity intercorrelate. In other words, higher linguistic complexity could be assumed to be a proxy for better written linguistic production, and vice versa. However, as reported in Section 4, the statistical analysis of the complexity metrics applied to the learner and the native data has not given support to this hypothesis. First, my data showed that the learners' essays are linguistically more complex and contain longer grammatical units and more diverging structures than the writings by the native students. Second, as regards proficiency, the texts written by 'basic'-proficiency learners evinced higher phrasal complexity and contained longer phrases than the texts produced by intermediate or 'independent' students, and the academic texts by the most proficient learners showed higher levels of phrasal complexity, close to those attested in the native writings.[18] Thus, my findings have led to the conclusion that the assumed complexity/proficiency correlation is only partial. On the one hand, they favour Biber and colleagues' claim that, as Ortega (2003:516) puts it, "advanced proficiency groups should be expected to produce writing that capitalizes on complexification at the phrasal, rather than at the clausal, level". But, on the other hand, the trends per proficiency level suggested by the statistical model are considerably irregular. In particular, A2 essays evinced higher rates of embedding, dissimilar structures and longer units, a finding which is in keeping with Palloti's (2009:596) suggestion that learners maximise complexification deliberately (see Section 3). On the whole, my results also corroborate prior studies (Kim,

2004 and Hawkins & Filipović, 2012, among others) that investigated complexity in CEFR-rated writing and concluded that differences are not always regular and incremental. Pallotti (2009) also contended that viewing complexity as a by-product of linguistic proficiency is too simplistic, since L2 development is not linear.[19] This view is given support by, for example, Larsen-Freeman (2009) and Lambert and Kormos (2014).

Further cross-linguistic research might shed light on the influence of L1 Spanish on L2 English. As already mentioned, Reppen and Grabe (1993) have claimed that L1 Spanish students write in a more elaborate manner, with an extensive use of coordination and subordination.

Notes

1 I am grateful to the Spanish State Research Agency and the European Regional Development Fund (grant no. FFI2016-77018-P), and Xunta de Galicia (grant no. ED431C 2017/50) for generous financial support.

2 In her study of syntax-based indexes potentially evincing microscopic complexity variation, Ortega (2003:498) claims that L2 data must be controlled with native data.

3 As reported in Khushik and Huhta (2019:3), "[t]he CEFR contains some references to linguistic elements, even to [syntactic complexity], but they are unsystematic and ambiguous and not linkable with particular levels. The clearest references to [syntactic complexity] are found in the Overall written production scale (...), which mentions simple phrases and sentences at A1 and A2, and 'linking a series of shorter discrete elements into a linear sequence' at B1".

4 Housen and Simoens (2016:166) recognise that "the term *complex(ity)* as used in the L2 literature is polysemous and ambiguous (...). *Structural complexity* (also *linguistic* or *absolute complexity*) refers to the inherent linguistic properties of a language feature or (sub)system and is typically operationalized in terms of the number and variety of the discrete components of which a language feature consists, and the number and nature of their internal relationships and interconnections with other features. *Cognitive complexity* (also *relative complexity*) has to do with how costly, demanding, or difficult a given language feature is for a given language learner in a given learning context".

5 T-units, very similar to AS-units, are defined as the "shortest grammatically terminable units into which a connected discourse can be segmented without leaving any residue" (Hunt, 1964:34), more specifically as "one main clause plus any subordinate clause or nonclausal structure that is attached to or embedded in it" (Hunt, 1970:184; similarly in 1965:36). 'Clause' is defined as "a structure with a subject and a finite verb (...), and includes independent clauses, adjective clauses, adverbial clauses, and nominal clauses" in Lu (2010:481). To give an example, (i) illustrates a single T-unit (the whole utterance) consisting of one main clause (*I don't know ... to see something else*), which contains one embedded dependent clause (*why I was expecting...*), and the latter, in turn, includes the embedded dependent clause *to see something else*.

i I don't know [[why I was expecting [to see something else]]].

The concept of c-unit, close to that of T-unit, also includes non-clausal structures which have communicative value, like *Coffee, please*.

Lintunen and Mäkilä (2014:394) develop their concept of U-unit, which is valid for the segmentation of spoken productions. In their words, a U-unit is "one independent clause or several coordinated independent clauses, with all dependent clauses or fragmental structures attached to it, separated from the surrounding speech by a pause of 1.5 seconds or more, or, especially in occurrences of coordination, a clear change in intonation and a pause of 0.5 seconds or more (depending on the average length of boundary pauses in the sample), containing one semantic unity" (385). Their analysis of the indexes of written and spoken L2 productions leads to the conclusion that "the choice of segmentation unit strongly affected the results, and that spoken language complexity may not be as different from written language complexity as it had been claimed in several earlier studies".

6 Since the present study relies on the overt shape of linguistic productions, theoretical and/or developmental studies, which are usually associated with research in L1 acquisition, have been discarded as supportive sources in the selection of relevant features. To give some examples, first, studies of L1 writing proficiency based on complexity indexes such as Grant and Ginther (2000) have not been considered here because they investigate production rather than reception, and are focused on non-learners. Second, other well-known corpus-based approaches, such as Lu (2009), which provides a heuristics-based system for the automatic measurement of syntactic complexity using Covington et al.'s (2006) D-Level scale, are not relevant to the present study either, since they assess native linguistic development (from Level 0 – simple sentences – to Level 6 – including, for example, nonfinite adjuncts) in order to test whether D-Level scores and speaker age correlate. Third, Di Domenico (2017) provides a collection of papers on L1 (and bilingual) acquisition framed within the transformational tradition, thus relying on deep parsing levels of syntactic constructions, which falls beyond the scope of the current paper.

7 The influence of task type, genre (or text type), and mode of production on complexity has been investigated in Struc and Wood (2011) and Wijers (2018), for example. Such variables will not be examined in the present study since my data contain only academic essays.

8 Reppen and Grabe's (1993) low-scale quantitative contribution looked at how L1 Spanish elementary school students' writing in English compares with that of L1 English students. Their main finding is that these L1 Spanish students wrote in English in a manner consistent with the literature on L1 Spanish adult writers, that is, in a more elaborate manner, characterised, for instance, by the extensive use of coordination and subordination.

9 To give some examples of multi-feature analyses of L1 English, Hardy and colleagues have applied Douglas Biber's multidimensional analysis (for an introduction to this approach, see Conrad, 2019) to academic essays written by native students. Hardy and Römer (2013) replicate Biber's model and implemented it in the 2.6-million-word Michigan Corpus of Upper-level Student Papers (MICUSP). They ascertained a number of significant dimensions, different from Biber's, such as (i) 'Involved, Academic Narrative' versus 'Descriptive, Informational' discourse; (ii) Expression of Opinions and Mental Processes; (iii) 'Situation-Dependent, Non-Procedural Evaluation' versus 'Procedural Discourse'; and (iv) Production of Possibility Statement and Argumentation. They also undertook a qualitative analysis of the 50 texts that clearly characterise the positive and negative poles of each dimension. Hardy (2015) carried out a multidimensional analysis of native student writing based on A-graded, upper-level papers of different disciplines and paper types from MICUSP. In Hardy and Friginal (2016), rather than

using pre-established groups of texts (e.g. Biology versus Physics), single papers were analysed and it was confirmed that there is a continuum of paper types in a single dimension, such as those seen as more involved versus those which are less personal and more informational. Finally, Grant and Ginther's (2000) study, also cited in this chapter as an instance of research based on production rather than on perception, assessed L1 proficiency through the application of a long repertoire of research features to 90 native essays, written at three levels of proficiency as defined by TWE ratings. Among their findings, as proficiency features, they identified the higher frequency of connecting items (conjuncts, subordinators, and demonstratives), qualifiers (emphatics and amplifiers), nominalisations, modals, subordinated and complement clauses, and passive sentences.

10 Lu (2017:502) points out that "[t]he reliability of the measures generated by Coh-Metrix has not been explicitly reported. Coh-Metrix uses the Charniak parser for syntactic analysis, which has an average precision/recall of around 90%".

11 The indexes in Table 13.2 do not include prototypical measures of lexical sophistication, first, because the focus in this study is on processing and syntax, and, second, because, as shown in Treffers-Daller et al. (2018), for example, the traditional measures of lexical sophistication are biased by text length and lemmatisation (versus non-lemmatised textual sources) – see Crossley and Kyle (2018:48), where the lexical sophistication measures provided by TAALES (Tool for the Automatic Analysis of Lexical Sophistication) strongly predict writing quality both in L1 and L2.

12 See Lahmann et al. (2019) as an example of an empirical multivariate investigation of syntactic, morphological, and lexical complexity measures in a corpus of spontaneous speech by highly advanced bilinguals.

13 Interestingly, Palloti (2009:596) contends that "learners [aim] at complexification by default, as if they were eager to produce a subordinate clause or a rare lexical item whenever they have a pinch of free attentional resources".

14 Biber et al. (2013) corroborate that the type of complexity evinced not only in (personal, professional, and academic) spoken but also in popular written (novels, personal essays) genres is fundamentally clausal, whereas complexity in newspaper, magazine, and, above all, academic writing is mainly phrasal. In their words, "academic prose could almost be described as discourse without verbs!" (195). From a diachronic perspective, Gray and Biber (2018) pointed out that the use of phrasal complexity in academic writing, which is so dense in the present, was minimal in earlier historical periods.

15 The classification of texts according to widely accepted proficiency levels constitutes a strength of WRICLE with respect to, for example, the International Corpus of Learner English (ICLE, Centre for English Corpus Linguistics, Université catholique de Louvain), in which the students' mastery of English is not evaluated externally but simply reported by participants.

16 The variable CPT, which has a positive loading in component 3, provides the ratio of coordinated phrases per T-unit. The difficulty of accounting for the contribution of this measure to the interpretation of this component can be justified by its low coefficient (0.22) in comparison with the loadings of the other positive variables (0.45–0.52).

17 Jarvis et al. (2003) is an example of a feature-driven L2 study that compares proficiency levels of students from different backgrounds. They carried out an agglomerative hierarchical cluster analysis of the frequencies of 21 linguistic features representative of length (text length, mean word length), lexical diversity (type/token ratio), lexical reinforcement (hedges, amplifiers,

emphatics, downtoners), lexical involvement/objectification (nouns and nominalisations, personal/impersonal pronouns, verbal tenses, demonstratives), syntactic sophistication (frequency of conjuncts, passives, adverbial/ relative subordination, complementation), etc., in two sets of L2 English placement compositions and essays written by Arabic-, Chinese-, Japanese-, and Spanish-speaking university-level students. They concluded that highly rated L2 texts are not at all isometric and, in consequence, the relationship between the linguistic distribution of proficiency features and writing quality is not conclusive. In their words, "it is possible to find multiple profiles of quality texts that have been written in the same register, on the same topic, and in the same context" (2003:399). Similarly, Lintunen and Mäkilä (2014:394) observed that "[t]he individual examination of the samples revealed fairly great inter-individual and intra-individual variation".

18 In their study of L1 English, Taguchi et al. (2013:428) observe that "noun phrase modification (...) had a tendency to contribute to essay quality" and that differences in subordination measures are less apparent.

19 As regards the issue of whether syntactic diversity and linguistic complexity go hand in hand, Vercellotti (2019) analysed syntactic complexity in the speech of L2 learners over three academic semesters through measures of productive complexity (length of AS units, finite-clause length, subordination) and of structural complexity (syntactic variety or proportion of different clause types within texts, weighted complexity scores ranging from independent finite clause to clauses involving dependent clauses, frequency of nonfinite clauses). Her hierarchical linear and non-linear modelling of the data proved that "[a]ll measures showed growth over time, suggesting that learners are not forced to prioritize certain aspects of the construct at the expense of others (i.e., no trade-off effects) across development" (233), which contradicts the claims by Larsen-Freeman (2009), Pallotti (2009), and Lambert and Kormos (2014), summarised in the main text of the present study.

References

Ai, H. & Lu, X. (2013). A Corpus-based Comparison of Syntactic Complexity in NNS and NS University Students' Writing, in A. Díaz-Negrillo, N. Ballier & P. Thompson (eds.) *Automatic Treatment and Analysis of Learner Corpus Data*. Amsterdam: John Benjamins, 249–264.

Alexopoulou, Th., Michel, M., Murakami, A. & Meurers, D. (2017). Task Effects on Linguistic Complexity and Accuracy: A Large‐Scale Learner Corpus Analysis Employing Natural Language Processing Techniques. *Language Learning* 67, 180–208.

Biber, D. & Gray, B. (2011). Is Conversation More Grammatically Complex than Academic Writing?, in M. Konopka, J. Kubczak, Ch. Mair, F. Štícha & U.H. Waßner (eds.) *Grammatik und Korpora 2009: Dritte Internationale Konferenz. Grammar & Corpora 2009: Third International Conference.* Tübingen: Narr Verlag, 7–61.

Biber, D., Gray, B. & Poonpon, K. (2011). Should We Use Characteristics of Conversation to Measure Grammatical Complexity in L2 Writing Development? *TESOL Quarterly* 45/1, 5–35.

Biber, D., Gray, B. & Poonpon, K. (2013). Pay Attention to the Phrasal Structures: Going Beyond T-Units – A Response to WeiWei Yang. *TESOL Quarterly* 47/1, 192–201.

Biber, D., Gray, B. & Staples, S. (2016). Predicting Patterns of Grammatical Complexity across Language Exam Task Types and Proficiency Levels. *Applied Linguistics* 37/5, 639–668.

Bulté, B. & Housen, A. (2012). Defining and Operationalising L2 Complexity, in A. Housen, F. Kuiken & I. Vedder (eds.) *Dimensions of L2 Performance and Proficiency: Complexity, Accuracy and Fluency in SLA*. Amsterdam: John Benjamins, 21–46.

Casanave, Ch.P. (1994). Language Development in Students' Journals. *Journal of Second Language Writing* 3/3, 179–201.

Casal, J.E. & Leeb, J.J. (2019). Syntactic Complexity and Writing Quality in Assessed First-Year L2 Writing. *Journal of Second Language Writing* 44, 51–62.

Council of Europe. (2001). *Common European Framework of Reference for Languages: Learning, Teaching, Assessment*. Cambridge: Cambridge University Press.

Charniak, E. (2000). A Minimum-Entropy-Inspired Parser, in *Proceedings of the First Conference on North American Chapter of the Association for Computational Linguistics*. San Francisco: Morgan Kaufmann, 132–139.

Collentine, K. (2011). Learner Autonomy in a Task-based 3D World and Production. *Language Learning & Technology* 15/3, 50–67.

Conrad, S. (2019). Register in English for Academic Purposes and English for Specific Purposes. *Register Studies* 1/1, 168–198.

Covington, M.A., He, C., Brown, C., Naçi, L. & Brown, J. (2006). *How Complex Is that Sentence? A Proposed Revision of the Rosenberg and Abbeduto D-Level Scale*. CASPR Research Report 2006–01. Athens, GA: The University of Georgia, Artificial Intelligence Center.

Crossley, S.A. & Kyle, K. (2018). Assessing Writing with the Tool for the Automatic Analysis of Lexical Sophistication (TAALES). *Assessing Writing* 38, 46–50.

Crossley, S.A. & McNamara, D.S. (2012). Predicting Second Language Writing Proficiency: The Role of Cohesion, Readability, and Lexical Difficulty. *Journal of Research in Reading* 35/2, 115–135.

Crossley, S.A., Allen, L.K. & McNamara, D.S. (2014). A Multi-dimensional Analysis of Essay Writing. What Linguistic Features Tell Us about Situational Parameters and the Effects of Language Functions on Judgements of Quality, in T. Berber Sardinha & M. Veirano Pinto (eds.) *Multi-dimensional Analysis, 25 Years On: A Tribute to Douglas Biber*. Amsterdam: John Benjamins, 197–238.

Di Domenico, E. (ed.) (2017). *Syntactic Complexity from a Language Acquisition Perspective*. Newcastle upon Tyne: Cambridge Scholars.

Folkert, K. & Vedder, I. (2019). Syntactic Complexity across Proficiency and Languages: L2 and L1 Writing in Dutch, Italian and Spanish. *International Journal of Applied Linguistics* 29/2, 192–210.

Frase, LT., Faletti, J., Ginther, A. & Grant, L. (1999). *Computer Analysis of the TOEFL Test of Written English*. Princeton, NJ: Educational Testing Service.

Gardner, S., Nesi, H. & Biber, D. (2019). Discipline, Level, Genre: Integrating Situational Perspectives in a New MD Analysis of University Student Writing. *Applied Linguistics* 40/4, 646–674.

Graesser, A.C., Mcnamara, D.S., Louwerse, M.M. & Cai, Z. (2004). Coh-Metrix: Analysis of Text on Cohesion and Language. *Behavior Research Methods, Instruments, & Computers* 36/2, 193–202.
Granger, S. (1998). The Computer Learner Corpus: A Versatile New Source of Data for SLA Research, in S. Granger (ed.) *Learner English on Computer.* London: Addison Wesley Longman, 3–18.
Grant, L. & Ginther, A. (2000). Using Computer-Tagged Linguistic Features to Describe L2 Writing Differences. *Journal of Second Language Writing* 9/2, 123–145.
Gray, B. & Biber, D. (2018). Academic Writing as a Locus of Grammatical Change. The Development of Phrasal Complexity Features, in R.J. Whitt (ed.) *Diachronic Corpora, Genre, and Language Change.* Amsterdam: John Benjamins, 117–146.
Gyllstad, H., Granfeldt, J., Bernardini, P. & Källkvist, M. (2014). Linguistic Correlates to Communicative Proficiency Levels of the CEFR: The Case of Syntactic Complexity in Written L2 English, L3 French and L4 Italian. *EUROSLA Yearbook* 14, 1–30.
Hardy, J.A. (2015). Multi-dimensional Analysis of Academic Discourse, in P. Baker & T. McEnery (eds.) *Corpora and Discourse Studies: Integrating Discourse and Corpora.* London: Palgrave Macmillan, 155–174.
Hardy J.A. & Friginal, E. (2016). Genre Variation in Student Writing: A Multi-dimensional Analysis. *Journal of English for Academic Purposes* 22, 119–131.
Hardy, J.A. & Römer, U. (2013). Revealing Disciplinary Variation in Student Writing: A Multi-dimensional Analysis of the Michigan Corpus of Upper-level Student Papers (MICUSP). *Corpora* 8/2, 183–207.
Hawkins, J.A. & Filipović, L. (2012). *Criterial Features in L2 English: Specifying the Reference Levels of the Common European Framework.* Cambridge: Cambridge University Press.
Housen, A. & Simoens, H. (2016). Introduction: Cognitive Perspectives on Difficulty and Complexity in L2 Acquisition. *Studies in Second Language Acquisition* 38, 163–175.
Hunt, K.W. (1964). *Differences in Grammatical Structures Written at Three Grade Levels: The structures to Be Analyzed by Transformational Methods.* Report no. CRP-1998. Tallahasser: Florida State University.
Hunt, K.W. (1965). *Grammatical Structures Written at Three Grade Levels.* NCTE Research Report No. 3. Champaign, IL: National Council of Teachers of English.
Hunt, K.W. (1970). Recent Measures in Syntactic Development, in M. Lester (ed.) *Readings in Applied Transformational Grammar.* New York: Holt, Rinehert and Winston, 179–192.
Ishikawa, S. (1995). Objective Measurement of Low-proficiency EFL Narrative Writing. *Journal of Second Language Writing* 4/1, 51–69.
Jarvis, S., Grant, L., Bikowski, D. & Ferris, D. (2003). Exploring Multiple Profiles of Highly Rated Learner Compositions. *Journal of Second Language Writing* 12/4, 377–403.
Kim, S. (2004). *A Study of Development in Syntactic Complexity by Chinese Learners of English and Its Implications on the CEF Scales.* MA dissertation. Lancaster: Lancaster University.

Klein, D. & Manning, Ch.D. (2003). Fast Exact Inference with a Factored Model for Natural Language Parsing, in S. Becker, S. Thrun & K. Obermayer (eds.) *Advances in Neural Information Processing Systems*. Cambridge, MA: MIT Press, 3–10.

Khushik, G.A. & Huhta, A. (2019). Investigating Syntactic Complexity in EFL Learners' Writing across Common European Framework of Reference Levels A1, A2, and B1. *Applied Linguistics* amy064, 1–28. https://doi.org/10.1093/applin/amy064.

Kyle, K. & Crossley, S.A. (2018). Measuring Syntactic Complexity in L2 Writing Using Fine-grained Clausal and Phrasal Indices. *The Modern Language Journal* 102/2, 333–349.

Lahmann, C., Steinkrauss, R. & Schmid, M.S. (2019). Measuring Linguistic Complexity in Long-Term L2 Speakers of English and L1 Attriters of German. *International Journal of Applied Linguistics* 29/2, 173–191.

Lahuerta Martínez, A.C. (2018). Analysis of Syntactic Complexity in Secondary Education EFL Writers at Different Proficiency Levels. *Assessing Writing* 35, 1–11.

Lambert, C. & Kormos, J. (2014). Complexity, Accuracy, and Fluency in Task-based L2 Research: Toward More Developmentally Based Measures of Second Language Acquisition. *Applied Linguistics* 35/5, 607–614.

Lambert, C. & Nakamura, S. (2019). Proficiency-Related Variation in Syntactic Complexity: A Study of English L1 and L2 Oral Descriptive Discourse. *International Journal of Applied Linguistics* 29/2, 1–17.

Larsen-Freeman, D. (1978). An ESL Index of Development. *TESOL Quarterly* 12/4, 439–448.

Larsen-Freeman, D. (2009). The Emergence of Complexity, Fluency, and Accuracy in the Oral and Written Production of Five Chinese Learners of English. *Applied Linguistics* 30/4, 590–619.

Levy, R. & Andrew, G. (2006). Tregex and Tsurgeon: Tools for Querying and Manipulating Tree Data Structures, in *Proceedings of the Fifth International Conference on Language Resources and Evaluation*. Genoa: ELRA, 2231–2234.

Lintunen, P. & Mäkilä, M. (2014). Measuring Syntactic Complexity in Spoken and Written Learner Language: Comparing the Incomparable? *Research in Language* 12/4, 377–399.

Lu, X. (2009). Automatic Measurement of Syntactic Complexity in Child Language Acquisition. *International Journal of Corpus Linguistics* 14/1, 3–28.

Lu, X. (2010). Automatic Analysis of Syntactic Complexity in Second Language Writing. *International Journal of Corpus Linguistics* 15/4, 474–496.

Lu, X. (2011). A Corpus-based Evaluation of Syntactic Complexity Measures as Indices of College-level ESL Writers' Language Development. *TESOL Quarterly* 45, 36–62.

Lu, X. (2012). The Relationship of Lexical Richness to the Quality of ESL Learners' Oral Narratives. *The Modern Language Journal* 96/2, 190–208.

Lu, X. (2017). Automated Measurement of Syntactic Complexity in Corpus-based L2 Writing Research and Implications for Writing Assessment. *Language Testing* 34/4, 493–511.

McNamara, D.S., Graesser, A.C., McCarthy, P.M. & Cai, Z. (2014). *Automated Evaluation of Text and Discourse with Coh-Metrix*. Cambridge: Cambridge University Press.

Michel, M. (2017). Complexity, Accuracy, and Fluency in L2 production, in S. Loewen & M. Sato (eds.) *Routledge Handbook of Instructed Second Language Acquisition.* Oxon: Routledge, 50–68.

Michel, M., Murakami, A., Alexopoulou, Th. & Meurers, D. (2019). Effects of Task Type on Morphosyntactic Complexity across Proficiency: Evidence from a Large Learner Corpus of A1 to C2 Writings. *Instructed Second Language Acquisition* 3/2, 124–152.

Norrby, C. & Håkansson, G. (2007). The Interaction of Complexity and Grammatical Processability: The Case of Swedish as a Foreign Language. *IRAL – International Review of Applied Linguistics in Language Teaching* 45, 45–68.

Norris, J.M. & Ortega, L. (2009). Towards an Organic Approach to Investigating CAF in Instructed SLA: The Case of Complexity. *Applied Linguistics* 30/4, 555–578.

Ortega, L. (2003). Syntactic Complexity Measures and Their Relationship to L2 Proficiency: A Research Synthesis of College-level L2 Writing. *Applied Linguistics* 24/4, 492–518.

Pallotti, G. (2009). CAF: Defining, Refining and Differentiating Constructs. *Applied Linguistics* 30/4, 590–601.

Parkinson, J. & Musgrave, J. (2014). Development of Noun Phrase Complexity in the Writing of English for Academic Purposes Students. *Journal of English for Academic Purposes* 14, 48–59.

R Core Team. (2018). *R: A Language and Environment for Statistical Computing.* Vienna: R Foundation for Statistical Computing. <www.R-project.org>.

Reid, J. (1986). Using the Writer's Workbench in Composition Teaching and Testing, in Ch.W. Stansfield (ed.) *Technology and Language Testing.* Alexandria, VA: TESOL, 167–188.

Reppen, R. & Grabe, W. (1993). Spanish Transfer Effects in the English Writing of Elementary School Children. *Lenguas Modernas* 20, 113–128.

Rollinson, P. & Mendikoetxea, A. (2010). Learner Corpora and Second Language Acquisition: Introducing WriCLE, in J.L. Bueno Alonso et al. (eds.) *Analizar datos > Describir variación/ Analysing data > Describing variation.* Vigo: Universidade de Vigo, 1–12.

Staples, S., Egbert, J., Biber, D. & Gray, B. (2016). Academic Writing Development at the University Level: Phrasal and Clausal Complexity across Level of Study, Discipline, and Genre. *Written Communication* 33/2, 149–183.

Struc, N. & Wood, N. (2011). A Corpus-based Investigation of Syntactic Complexity, Fluency, Sentence Variety, and Sentence Development in L2 Genre Writing. *Reitaku University Journal* 93, 45–80.

Taguchi, N., Crawford, W. & Wetzel, D.Z. (2013). What Linguistic Features are Indicative of Writing Quality? A Case of Argumentative Essays in a College Composition Program. *TESOL Quarterly* 47, 420–430.

Treffers-Daller, J., Parslow, P. & Williams, S. (2018). Back to Basics: How Measures of Lexical Diversity Can Help Discriminate between CEFR Levels. *Applied Linguistics* 39/3, 302–327.

Venables, W.N. & Ripley, B.D. (2002, 4th ed). *Modern Applied Statistics with S.* New York: Springer.

Vercellotti, M.L. (2019). Finding Variation: Assessing the Development of Syntactic Complexity in ESL Speech. *International Journal of Applied Linguistics* 29/2, 233–247.

Verspoor, M., Schmid, M.S. & Xu, X. (2012). A Dynamic Usage-based Perspective on L2 Writing. *Journal of Second Language Writing* 21, 239–263.

Wijers, M. (2018). The Role of Variation in L2 Syntactic Complexity: A Case Study on Subordinate Clauses in Swedish as a Foreign Language. *Nordic Journal of Linguistics* 41/1, 1–42.

Wolfe-Quintero, K., Inagaki, S. & Kim, H-Y. (1998). *Second Language Development in Writing: Measures of Fluency, Accuracy, and Complexity.* Technical report no. 17. Honolulu: University of Hawai'i, Second Language Teaching and Curriculum Center.

14 New Linguistic Corpus in Catalan and the Teaching of Languages for Specific Purposes at University

Anna Montesinos-López and Francesca Romero-Forteza

1 Introduction

In this chapter, we present a new corpus, the Corpus for the Learning of Catalan for Specific Purposes, called CALEC in Catalan, developed at the Universitat Politècnica de València (UPV) (Spain). Development of CALEC entailed assembling a corpus of texts produced by university students studying degree courses in computer engineering and industrial engineering. The texts were collected systematically for the purposes of needs assessment within these subjects.

The study arose out of the importance that is currently placed on languages for specific purposes. Society is increasingly demanding multilingual professionals with sufficient language competence to handle communication in specific and specialised areas and for specific objectives. The courses in Catalan for specific purposes allow students to become familiar with texts which are characteristic of formal oral and written communicative situations in professional and academic settings, and to learn pertinent expressive and communicative strategies to perform properly and effectively.

As mentioned earlier, this research grew out of a needs assessment, carried out through the compilation of a linguistic corpus collected at the beginning of the academic year, which enabled the curricular content to be adapted to meet, as much as possible, the language and subject-matter needs of the group.

Although the students' development throughout the course was monitored through their oral and written production, here we only present the assessment of their first written text. As we will show, CALEC is an important aid for syllabus preparation and for devising educational activities in the teaching/learning of languages for specific purposes within the university framework. It should also be noted that studies which have been carried out in the field of computerised corpus linguistics intended for learning Catalan can be described as scarce.

A linguistic corpus in Catalan has very specific social and educational implications. In order to understand this background, in the next section, we give a brief overview of the history of Catalan corpus linguistics.

In Section "Educational framework of the CALEC corpus", we describe the educational setting in which the corpus was developed, together with the reasons for doing so and in Section "Importance of the CALEC", we address the importance of the linguistic corpus in the learning of Catalan for Specific Purposes. A brief description of the methodology used for making the CALEC corpus is given in Section "Objectives and Methodology", while next section includes a detailed description of the corpus and an analysis of the results. This chapter ends with some concluding remarks.

2 Research of Linguistic Corpora in Catalan

As mentioned earlier, the literature on Catalan linguistic corpora for language learning is not abundant, and there is even less concern with university teaching of Catalan for specific purposes. Nonetheless, during the second half of the 1990s, some conferences specialising in corpus linguistics took place, as Turell and Vallduví (1998) and Battaner and López (2000) report. Since then, a number of corpus linguistics studies for Catalan have been produced. Some of the most important include the following: the PAAU 92 corpus, managed since June 1992 by the Institut Universitari de Lingüística Aplicada (IULA) of the Universitat Pompeu Fabra de Catalunya. This corpus consists of texts produced by students during the entrance examinations held at various Spanish universities. IULA's main research project Projecte Corpus consists of texts written in five different languages (Catalan, Spanish, English, French, and German) in the areas of economics, law, the environment, medicine, computer science, and the language sciences. Through this corpus, the project tries to infer the laws that govern the behaviour of each language in each area (Cabré et al., 2006; Cabré and Gómez de Enterría, 2006). A further research line focuses on extracting data for second language (L2) teaching.

In the last few years, the creation of different language corpora in Catalan has increased significantly. Some of the most significant ones are shown below. AnCora is a corpus of Catalan and Spanish with different levels of entries: lemma and morphological categories; constituents and syntactic functions; argumentative structure and thematic roles; verb semantic class; denotative type of deverbal nouns; nominative WordNet meanings; named entities and co-reference relationships. Each language corpus comprises 500,000 words and is mostly made up of journalistic texts. As a result of the annotation process, two lexicons are available, AnCora-Verb, with 2,143 entries for Catalan and 2,647 for Spanish, and one of deverbal nominalisations, AnCora-Nom, with 1,600 entries for Spanish.

However, CesCa (the School Written Catalan in Catalonia) is a corpus whose aim has been to provide the educational community with a fundamental tool in order to know the language uses of their students:

a baseline corpus of school-written Catalan in Catalonia with the data obtained from their processing (Llauradó et al., 2012). The texts produced by 2,426 children have been compiled and processed. The children are all students from the last year of pre-school education to the last year of compulsory education, from 31 educational centres from different regions of Catalonia. This corpus consists of: the lexicon produced corresponding to five semantic fields (food names, pieces of clothing, natural phenomena, leisure activities, and personality features); and four different types of texts (definitions, narration of a film, argumentative recommendation, and telling a joke). Likewise, in the lexical section, you can find organised information about frequency of use of words (forms and lemmas), the relationship between the forms and the lemmas, and the distribution of lemmas following the school level. In the texts section, texts are accessed by selecting anyone according to the participant's age, to their type or to the combination of both values; you can look at the texts as the participants wrote them, and another version with corrections of separation of words. You can access definitions by selecting participants' age and type of text, as well as picking any of the defined words. You can also access any kind of text containing a specific word or a specific lemma. Finally, it's possible to choose the definitions corresponding to a particular word in its context or according to an age range.

Furthermore, Nident-Ca is a Catalan-language corpus with annotations in the form of labels of near-identity. Nident-Ca has been obtained from the corpus AnCora-Ca (Recasens & Martí, 2010) and consists of 51,622 words. It includes articles from the paper edition of the newspaper El Periódico as well as from the news agency ACN. The mentions of near-co-references represent 16% of the co-referential mentions (Recasens et al., 2012).

Additionally, CuCWeb is a corpus of Catalan that is built from the internet, with 208 million words (125,000 documents) automatically compiled from the web. The corpus has been automatically processed so as to provide additional linguistic information to the mere form of words, and a flexible research interface has been enabled that allows one to look for examples of certain constructions or words and also to extract usages frequencies. The purpose of the corpus is to know the Catalan language through linguistic studies and to know the use of the web in Catalan by means of sociolinguistic surveys (Badia & Boleda, 2008).

We can also consider the computerised Corpus of ancient Catalan (CICA), a rather unknown resource outside the specialised scope, but very useful for historical linguistics. This is a corpus of written texts containing works between the eleventh and eighteenth centuries.

The search allows one to select a sub-corpus or to narrow down the results to particular works or authors. Besides, you can look up words or word combinations and the punctuation is even regarded. The result of these searches shows the frequency of the found cases and enables the choice of parameters to be displayed. Once selected, the contexts appear sorted by chronology and work, but they can be rearranged by dialect, text typology, and the word preceding or following the searched term.

Another outstanding corpus is the Corpus of Contemporary Catalan of the University of Barcelona (CCCUB). It's an archive of corpora of contemporary oral Catalan language that has been conceived for the study of dialectal variations (COD: Dialectal Oral Corpus), social variations (COS: Corpus of Social Varieties), and functional variations (COC: Oral Corpus of colloquial conversation, COR: Oral Corpus of registers) of the Catalan language.

Finally, the Institute of Catalan Studies offers the Computerised textual corpus of the Catalan language, a compilation of texts in Catalan written between 1833 and 1988. This corpus contains 52,000,000 terms, from a wide range of texts written in the Catalan language, coming from literature records (narrative, theatre, poetry, essay) and non-literary sources (treatises and manuals of different disciplines, articles in specialised and disclosure publications, legal texts, daily press and various regular publications, etc.). The web allows one to connect the dictionary entries, offered by the IEC language resources portal, with the texts of the corpus, and the searches are limited to lemmas with their contexts, to their grammatical forms, and to the tracing of lemmas and forms in the works.

3 Educational Framework of the CALEC Corpus

The university where CALEC was developed exists within a bilingual community where Catalan and Spanish both are official languages. They are not used equally, however. According to Cabré (2000: 85), Spanish is much more consolidated socially and politically, while Catalan is socially weaker, due to the fact that it lacks full autonomy.

Catalan is a minority language that has suffered, since the early eighteenth century, a more or less systematic process of exclusion from formal (and so from informal) discourse. In the present century, there has been a process of language revival. The first period culminated in the *Normes de Castelló* in 1932, which set out the official standard accepted today. The dictatorship between 1939 and the mid-seventies attempted, unsuccessfully, to eradicate the use of Catalan, and since then, there has been a gradual revival of the language.

It is necessary to bear this background in mind to understand the complex relations between prescription and description in language studies in Catalan. That's why carrying out this corpus came from the need of knowing the learning group, because of the sociolinguistic context of the Catalan language within the Valencia area.

The presence of numerous languages coexisting at the international level, but also inside many states, doesn't imply that they enjoy a similar status. In different historical periods, multilingualism has lived with the fact that one of the languages found itself in a role of main usage with regard to the others, and it was used much more frequently than the others in the field of international relations (Generalitat Valenciana (Valencian Government), 2019: 42–43).

In this regard, a distinction is generally made between minoritised language and minoritising language (Hernàndez, 2016: 20). Thus, a minoritised language is the one presenting private use rates higher than public use rates, whereas the opposite happens in the case of minoritising languages, which cut back public use of the others, minoritising them. This is the case of Catalan and Spanish in the Valencia sphere. There is a situation of disglossia, since one language is used in a familiar and colloquial way and the other in a reputable way among speakers. According to a study made by a research team from the Generalitat Valencia (2019: 44), if a language has been defined as socially inferior, which is the case of many minority languages, this can make its acquisition harder (Generalitat Valenciana, 2019: 44). Following the study mentioned earlier, when the language perceived as inferior is the mother tongue, this status becomes a key factor in preventing people from investing their efforts in improving it at all levels, what has been named as linguistic intolerance.

As for competence, the students understand Catalan, both Catalan speakers and Spanish speakers. Nevertheless, some have Catalan as their mother tongue and others as a second language, L2. What is more, there are some with a very partial knowledge of the Catalan language, with reduced competence in passive skills like understanding and reading. There certainly exist situations of passive bilingualism, that is to say, they are so close as languages that one person can speak one of the languages and another person, the other, and both understand each other perfectly.

At this point, we have to distinguish between linguistic competence and the use of the language. In respect of the former, the students have mostly completed the compulsory studies and non-university post-compulsory studies, and they are considered to have a medium level in the four skills, which doesn't mean that they are language users. Neither should we forget that the competences are continuously improved by their use. In the case of the Politechnical University of Valencia, during the academic year 2016–2017, 7.24% of its teaching was provided in the Valencian language in the degree courses. Consequently, the linguistic use of the Catalan language at the university doesn't contribute to improving the students' linguistic competence.

Furthermore, broadly speaking, an expectable consequence of the language schooling process is the progressive *escripturització*, that is, raising the active writing competence when compared with the passive one: there are more and more people who can write than those who can read (Hernàndez, 2016: 54).

For this reason, the academic groups are usually very diversified with regard to the students' knowledge of the language and their linguistic competence. Therefore, this raises the need for carrying out a survey of linguistic behaviour as well as of the linguistic competence of students in these groups. Undertaking this analysis of needs will enable teachers in the classroom to adapt better to the linguistic reality of the groups.

We could say that the Catalan language is caught between two more dominant languages. On the one hand, it is 'squeezed out' as it were, by English, especially in scientific, technical, and cultural areas. For example, within the university, students usually know the specialist terms of their academic field of study in both English and Spanish but not in Catalan. Furthermore, the linguistic skills, uses, practices, and attitudes of the university student body towards the use of Catalan are similar to those of the Valencian population as a whole (Aparici & Castelló, 2011: 10). On the other hand, in everyday, colloquial uses, Catalan must compete with Spanish. The linguistic interference of Spanish in Catalan was first pointed out by Payrató (1985). This is especially noticeable in certain theme-restricted areas (Cabré, 2004: 192). As a result of all this, Catalan is a minoritised language and does not possess channels for the dissemination of science comparable to those of English or Spanish (Montesinos, 2013).

We can see, then, that the teaching–learning context is linguistically rather complex. Knowledge of the students' level of proficiency in Catalan, as well as of how both English and Spanish impact learners' attitudes to Catalan is extremely important and one of the reasons why the needs assessment is an important tool at the beginning of the learning process.

4 Importance of the CALEC Corpus for Learning Specialised Languages in Catalan

The teaching/learning of Catalan for specific purposes is now a consolidated field of research with its own considerable literature, both from discursive and cognitive approaches (Cabré & Bach, 2005), and more especially from the point of view of terminology which, from the beginning, was considered as the principal and most visible target of normalisation and standardisation (Cabré, 1992; Generalitat de Catalunya, 1992; Termcat, 2005, 2006). However, the study of the linguistic competence of students in Catalan for specific purposes is still in the process of development, since there are very few studies in this area.

The main objective of teaching/learning specialised language domains is to develop communicative competence (linguistic, textual, and pragmatic competence), linguistic skills, and strategic competence in the Catalan language (Alcón, 2007: 260), in specific areas of Engineering.

In this regard, according to Morell (1996: 39), the learning process of a language for a specific purpose has a cognitive, rather than an innatistic base, and both internal and external factors must be taken into account. The former are linked to the individual (aptitude, motivation, etc.), while the latter are mostly related, though not exclusively, to the nature of each specific domain. Given that it is the students themselves who choose to take our classes on Catalan for specific purposes, generally speaking, the level of motivation is high.

As Alcón (op. cit.) points out, both learning objectives and teaching methodology need to account for the raison d'être of languages for specific purposes. In other words, before any teaching takes place, an assessment should be made of the communicative needs linked to the specialist field, and the educational purposes should be specified in the form of goals. In order to do this, first an analysis of the contents pertaining to the training of future engineers is carried out, and the characteristics of the specialised languages are recorded (Biber, Conrad & Reppen, 1998: 157). Thus, text genres, text types, semantic fields, etc., are used to shape the aspects of communicative competence to be targeted.

There is unanimous agreement about the fact that the teaching of specialised languages in Catalan should address the following issues: the standard variety of the language, specific terminology and phraseology, the characteristic text types and genres, and the characteristic communicative strategies for each specialty (see, for example, Riera, 1992, 1994, 2005; Marquet, 1995).

It is also useful to take into account the linguistic performance of the students, since this tends to vary considerably. In fact, this is precisely why it is educationally very useful, even necessary, to make a needs assessment at the beginning of the process. As McEnery, Xiao, and Tono (2006: 97) point out, learner-based corpora are particularly useful in the teaching of languages for specific purposes and, as mentioned earlier, the CALEC corpus is based on a questionnaire plus the initial texts written by the students. Digitalising it offers several advantages (McEnery, Xiao & Tono, 2006: 5–6), such as broadening its availability to other text genres or to a greater number of students (Biber, Conrad & Reppen, 1998: 173).

5 Objectives and Methodology

As a result of what has been discussed earlier, the objective of the project we present here was to create and prepare a text corpus for studying the teaching/learning of specialised domain languages in Catalan using the written materials produced by students enrolled in classes for specific purposes at the UPV, in order to pinpoint areas of learning difficulty and the level of the students' communicative competence. Further work to be done with the text corpus includes computerising, storing, and analysing it.

There are different approaches to carrying out a linguistic analysis of students' writing. One of the most widely used, and also often questioned, is error analysis (Corder, 1967). In our work, in addition to error analysis, we also analysed correct formulations. Our corpus, then, based as it is on the students' written output, not only provides a means to specify their needs but also indicates where improvements should be made in the curriculum and corresponding activities (O'Donnell, 2012: 148).

The methodology we used combined direct observation with the preparation and study of the corpus (Corder, 1981: 36–37): selecting the corpus, identifying errors in the corpus, classifying errors (interference or interlanguage errors and intralinguistic errors), and error analysis.

6 Description and Analysis of the CALEC Corpus

The research was conducted with students who were enrolled in the elective subject *Technical Catalan*, in different degree programmes at UPV. As explained earlier, the corpus of texts was collected on the first day of class. The students wrote a descriptive text of approximately 300 words about a computer. The texts were written in electronic format with the spell checker deactivated. Nor were other linguistic consultations allowed.

It should be noted that the student body is very heterogeneous in terms of age, place of birth, etc., as well as their previous linguistic training, or the language(s) they use normally. We found that some students spoke Catalan at home, others Spanish, and some spoke both languages. Some students had done all their schooling using Catalan as the vehicular language; others had only studied it as an academic subject, and a minority had never studied it.

Of the total texts collected, 167 were used for our study. The rest did not comply with one or more of the established criteria, for example, regarding the length or type of text. This number may not seem very large, but according to Sinclair (1996, in Edo, 2010: 89), a corpus must meet four basic linguistic criteria: quantity, quality, simplicity, and documentation. However, it is an accepted fact among corpus linguists that it is impossible to define and create a fully representative corpus (Atkins, Clear & Ostler, 1992), although its goal must be to compile a corpus that is as representative as possible (Edo, 2010). We believe this is what we have done. The tools provided by the program Word Smith were used to analyse the CALEC corpus. After the first analysis, the total percentage of detected errors was 8% (see Figure 14.1).

If all the detected errors are reviewed in detail, we obtain the data shown in Table 14.1.

Detailed analysis of the results shows a variety of types of error, in particular those caused by the influence of Spanish – in the day-to-day

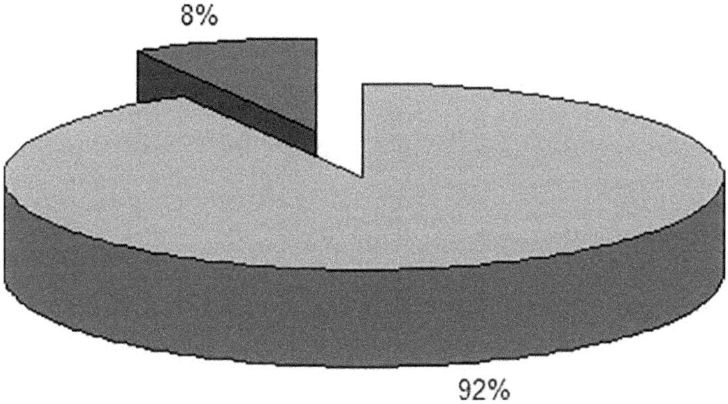

Figure 14.1 Presence of errors in the CALEC.

Table 14.1 Percentage of errors

Interlinguistic errors	
Linguistic interference of Spanish	
Phonetic and spelling level	4%
Morphosyntactic level	2%
Lexical level	10%
Linguistic interference of English	
Lexical level	21%
Intralinguistic errors	
Phonetic and spelling level	55%
Morphosyntactic level	3%
Lexical level	5%

sphere – and English – in the domain of science. By far, the greatest number of errors (55%) are intralinguistic and correspond to the phonetic and spelling levels. This high percentage is rather striking when one considers that these errors pertain to the surface level of the language and, as mentioned earlier, most of the students had received formal training in Catalan. A greater number of errors at a deeper language levels were expected. Errors found included incorrect use of consonants, such as **aprexiar, acavat, ahon, crissis, cualsevol, dessitge, engloven, enyinger, fatigosos, grosor, hàmbit, hutilitza, images, mitj*, or *multitut.*

In the same way, many errors are detected, due to the incorrect application of the rules of use of accentuation and diaeresis. Corresponding to these phenomena are errors such as **açó, desus, enten, etcetera, habitaciò, linia, majoritariament, mobils, monitor, principàls,* *or segóns*. As for the misuse of the rules of application of the diaeresis, we find examples such as **agraida, eïna, frequència, extraible, gratuitat, heïnes, introduida, introduïr, questió, reduïr*, or *reduïts*.

However, what would have been expected would have been to find a greater number of errors at a deeper level of the language. At the morphosyntactic level, the intralinguistic errors observed often occurred in very common structures in Catalan. These include, for example, the plural form of the masculine singular demonstrative **aquestos*, or the use of the imminential periphrasis **vaig a descriure*, which is incorrect in this language. Likewise, we find errors of incorrect application of the apostrophe rules *(*satisfeix, siguent, tinguent…)* among others.

There was also high lexical interference of English in the scientific-technical realm: 21% of errors correspond to this linguistic level. This is not surprising, however, given that the terminology of the subject-matter (computer technology) uses many words of Anglophone origin. Here, we can find, for instance, terms such as **big, desadvantages, core, express, host, markt, program, software, hardware, online, pack, chat, log in, password, router, wifi, etc.*

Regarding the linguistic interference of Spanish, the highest percentage of errors also occurred at the lexical level, with errors such as **actualmente, ahorrar, almacena, apretava, borra, casi, como, con, cotidians, cual, descifrar, ingles, interfaç, lento, juego, momento, ningún, rayos*... As for spelling, there was confusion in the use of consonants *(*accesos, cambia, compañies, conecta, cualsevol, cuatre, deixaba, estaba, haber, instalar, móvils, necesaria, ocupaba, realizar*... As well as non-observance of spelling rules, such as not separating the verb from the pronoun *(*adaptantse, adaptarse, agafarlo, cambiarme, durla, facilitarnos, ferles, mantenirlo…)* and the application to Catalan of Spanish accent rules *(*agradaría, algún, batería, d'audio, día, están, fotografíes, informática, industria, pero, podrán, Valencia, etc.)*. Interference at the morphosyntactic level was found in the use of text connectors, such as *per a què* or *doncs*, as well as errors that involved the use of the gerund, which is quite different in the two languages. In order to appreciate more clearly the extent of each type of error, Figure 14.2 shows a graphic representation of the errors found in the CALEC corpus.

The data provided by the Word Smith program only provides a partial view of the errors produced, as it does not detect deep aspects of communicative production. Two further observations are, therefore, in order. Firstly, the quality of the written texts varies widely, with those at the bottom end showing a poor command of text typology and appropriateness of the standard register in the Catalan language. Secondly, both errors and correct formulations were found in the corpus. For example, while the Anglicism *software* was used by the majority of students (68%), other students used the equivalent term in Catalan, *programari*.

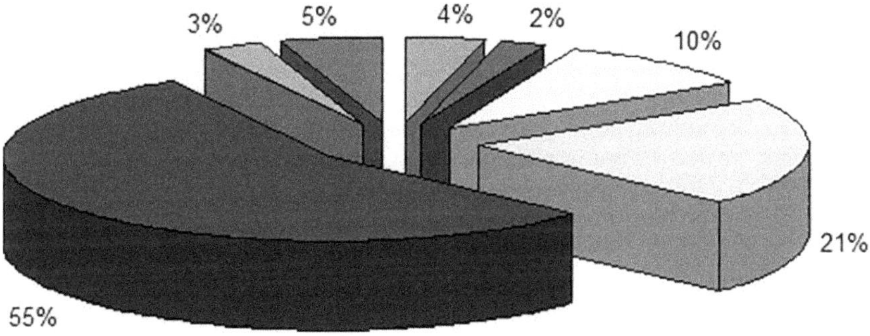

Figure 14.2 Detail of errors in the CALEC.

7 Conclusions

This chapter presents pioneer research on the use of a linguistic corpus for the learning of Catalan for Specific Purposes. As mentioned earlier, this is an innovative field within this area of study, and although each individual component of the research (language learning, the study of linguistic corpora, the analysis of errors, the Catalan language, and languages for specialised domains) is of great relevance, a study that takes a multifaceted approach, which brings together and reviews all the complexity of these aspects, constitutes a novel contribution.

Finally, this study has led to the creation of the CALEC, the Corpus for the Learning of Specialised Languages in Catalan, which is a compilation of texts produced by students of Catalan for specific purposes. This has allowed us to systematise students' errors, to know their weaknesses and needs and from there to design teaching strategies that address those needs. The two main findings of this research are that students have a very low command of spelling in Catalan, and that English has a high level of interference in the terminology of the subject-matter. On the basis of this assessment, we have designed a plan of educational action which we are implementing, and whose results will be presented in future research projects.

References

Alcón, E. (2007). La difusión didáctica de las lenguas de especialidad, in E. Alcaraz et al. (eds.), *Las lenguas profesionales y académicas*. Barcelona: Ariel, 259–270.

Aparici, A. & Castelló, R. (2011). *Els usos lingüístics a les universitats públiques valencianes*. València: Acadèmia Valenciana de la Llengua.

Atkins, S., Clear, J. & Ostler, N. (1992). Corpus design criteria. Literary and Linguistic Computing. *Journal of the Association for Literary and Linguistic Computing* 7/1, 1–16.

Badia, T. & Boleda, G. (2008). CuCWeb: A corpus of Catalan developed from the web. *Estudis Romànics*, 30, 291–293.

Battaner, M.P. & López, C. (Eds.). (2000). *VI Jornada de corpus lingüístics: corpus lingüístics i ensenyament de llengües*. Barcelona: Institut Universitari de Lingüística Aplicada.

Biber, D., Conrad, S., & Reppen, R. (1998). *Corpus linguistics. Investigating language structure and use*. Cambridge: Cambridge University Press.

Cabré, M. T. (1992). *La terminologia: la teoria, els mètodes, les aplicacions*. Barcelona: Les Naus d'Empúries.

Cabré, M.T. (2000). La neologia com a mesura de la vitalitat interna de les llengües, in M.T. Cabré, J. Freixa & E. Solé (eds.), *La neologia en el tombant de segle* (pp. 85–108). Barcelona: Universitat Pompeu Fabra.

Cabré, M.T. (2004). Terminologia i llengua catalana: funció social i cooperació, in J. Massot i Muntaner (Coord.), *Estudis de llengua i literatura catalanes XLVIII Miscel·lània Joan Veny* (pp. 181–208). Barcelona: Publicacions de l'Abadia de Montserrat.

Cabré, M.T. & Bach. C. (2005). *Coneixement, llenguatge i discurs especialitzat*. Barcelona: Institut Universitari de Lingüística Aplicada.

Cabré, M.T., Bach, C., & Vivaldi, J. (2006). *10 anys del corpus de l'IULA*. Barcelona: Institut Universitari de Lingüística Aplicada-Universitat Pompeu Fabra.

Cabré, M.T. & Gómez de Enterría. J. (2006). *Enseñanza de los lenguajes de especialidad. La simulación global*. Madrid: Gredos.

Corder, S.P. (1967). The significance of learner's errors. *IRAL*, 5, 161–170.

Corder, S.P. (1981). *Error analysis and interlanguage*. Oxford: Oxford University Press

Edo, N. (2010). How to exploit corpora in class: Making the most of ESP teaching and learning, in B. Bellés-Fortuño et al. (eds.), *Exploring corpus-based research in English language teaching*. Castelló de la Plana: Edicions de la Universitat Jaume I.

Generalitat de Catalunya (1992). *La terminologia en el seu entorn*. Barcelona: Departament de Cultura.

Generalitat Valenciana (2019). *Impacte i valor econòmic del valencià*. Collection Rafael L. Ninyoles. Valencia: Generalitat Valenciana.

Hernàndez, F.J. (2016). *El tio Canya ha mort. Notes sobre la mecànica sociolingüística del valencià*. Demos 9. Research and disclosure papers. Foundation Nexe.

Llauradó, A., Martí, M.A. & Tolchinsky, L. (2012). Corpus CesCa: Compiling a corpus of written Catalan produced by school children. *International Journal of Corpus Linguistics*, 17, 3, 428–441.

Marquet, L. (1995). *El llenguatge científic i tècnic*. Barcelona: Associació d'Enginyers Industrials de Catalunya.

McEnery, T., Xiao, R. & Tono, Y. (2006). *Corpus-based language studies: An advanced resource book*. London–New York: Routledge Applied Linguistics.

Montesinos, A. (2013). Enseñanza y aprendizaje de la terminología informática en lengua catalana en el contexto universitario, in *Actas del XI Congreso Internacional de la Asociación Europea de Lenguas para Fines Específicos*.

Morell, J. (1996). L'adquisició de la terminologia. *Articles de la llengua i de la literatura: Terminologia i ensenyament*, 9, 35–47.

O'Donnell, M. (2012). Using learner corpora to redesign universty-level ELF grammar education. *Revista Española de Lingüística Aplicada* [Special Issue], 25, 145–160.

Payrató, L. (1985). *La interferència lingüística. Comentaris i exemples català-castellà.* Barcelona: Universitat de València.

Recasens, M, & Martí, M. A. (2010). AnCora-CO: Coreferentially annotated corpora for Spanish and Catalan. *Language Resources and Evaluation*, 44(4), 315–345.

Recasens, M. et al. (2012). Annotating near-identity from coreference disagreements. A *Proceedings of LREC* 2012, 165–172.

Riera, C. (1992). *Manual de català científic.* Barcelona: Claret.

Riera, C. (1994). *El llenguatge científic català. Antecedents i actualitat.* Barcelona: Barcanova.

Riera, C. (2005). *Manual de redacció científica. El llenguatge de les ciències de la salut.* Barcelona: Claret.

Termcat. (2005). *Manlleus i calcs lingüístics en els treballs de terminologia catalana.* Barcelona: Termcat-Eumo.

Termcat. (2006). *La normalització terminològica en català: criteris i termes 1986–2004.* Barcelona: Termcat-Publicacions de l'Abadia de Montserrat.

Turell, M.T. & Vallduví, E. (ed.) (1998). *IV i V Jornades de Corpus Lingüístics 1996–1997.* Barcelona: Institut Universitari de Lingüística Aplicada.

15 Overused Bundles in the Written Academic English of Spanish EFL Students

Miguel Fuster-Márquez and Jesús Fernández-Domínguez

1 Introduction

Phraseology is a complex area that has attracted scholars in the fields of English for Academic and Specific Purposes and Second Language Acquisition. In the past decades, this area has grown as an important research field thanks to the advent of computers and the application of corpus methodologies. Instead of isolated words, different kinds of word sequences are increasingly being perceived as the building blocks of language usage. Thus, native speakers appear to follow by default what Sinclair (1991: 110) called the 'Idiom Principle'.

The aim of this article is to identify and analyse word sequences in written academic tasks of Spanish undergraduate students that might represent extreme cases of overuse, i.e. unconventional sequences which are practically absent from native corpora of similar registers. This research falls within what Granger (2002:11–12, 2015) calls *Contrastive Interlanguage Analysis* (CIA), which may involve quantitative and qualitative comparisons between L1 and different varieties of L2/L3 data, or between learners with different L1s.

This chapter is arranged as follows. Section 2 reviews the criteria for the identification and classification of lexical bundles (LBs), while Section 3 describes the corpora and methodology. Sections 4 and 5 include the experimental body: the analysis of learner production from the perspective of overused bundles (Section 4.1) and longer sequences (Section 4.2), and an assessment of the discourse features of these LBs: stance (Section 5.1), referential (Section 5.2), and discourse organising (Section 5.3). Section 6 offers the results and a summary of the main findings.

2 Identification and Classification of Lexical Bundles

The interest in the study of multiword units is not new; there is a good deal of work on the topic throughout the twentieth century (see Cortes, 2004:398–401). The term *lexical bundle* (LB) is one particular type of multiword unit that refers to uninterrupted sets of at least three words[1] which occur in natural language (Biber et al., 1999, 2004; Cortes, 2004;

Hyland, 2008). LBs are automatically extracted through a frequency-driven corpus technique; hence, statistical frequency and distribution lie at the heart of this notion given that LBs cannot be reliably obtained in a different way. Crucially, LBs are defined by their occurrence in a given register, that is, their frequency of occurrence and quality are highly dependent on discourse features. This explains why the study of LBs has been related to their relevance in particular registers, e.g. in conversation, academic prose (Biber et al., 1999; Conrad & Biber, 2004), classroom teaching and textbooks (Biber et al., 2004), L2/L3 writing (Chen & Baker, 2010; Salazar, 2014), or specific purposes (see Fuster-Márquez, 2014).

Different classifications of bundles have been proposed. For example, Hyland (2005; Hyland & Tse, 2004) classifies them according to metalinguistic functions of the relationship writer-reader. Hyland (2008) proposes three categories: (a) research-oriented, (b) text-oriented, and (c) participant-oriented. He also offers a revision of Biber's category of stance, which is, in his view, a superordinate category, to introduce the function of engagement (see Section 5). In this study, attention is directed to two variables: (1) native vs. non-native and (2) expert vs. non-expert. Our interest is in the overuse of LBs by Spanish EFL students (non-native and non-expert), whose production has been compared with that of native non-experts (BAWE) and native experts (ACUV; see Section 3). The relevance of this topic is justified by previous research which highlights problems caused by overuse of connectors (Granger & Tyson, 1996), the presence of features of spoken language in learner writing (Gilquin & Paquot, 2007), over-reliance on a limited number of linguistic items or a lack of register awareness in student essays (Gilquin et al., 2007). It has been pointed out that a sufficient number of conventional LBs in a text reflect the author's fluency and natural use of language, while absence or underuse may indicate a lack of control thereof (Biber et al., 2004; Hyland, 2008).

3 Description of Native and Learner Corpora, Methodology, and First Filtering of Results

The present study is based on data from three different corpora: the Academic Corpus of the University of Valencia (ACUV), the British Academic Written English (BAWE), and the Corpus of Learners of English as a Foreign Language (CASTLE).[2] Our procedure consisted of three stages: a quantitative computer-assisted first stage where LBs were extracted by means of a frequency-driven technique; the manual filtering of non-relevant or ill-formed sequences was the second stage. The third and final stage was the qualitative assessment of the resulting overused bundles in the learner corpus. We made use of AntConc 3.4.3 (Anthony, 2014) for the exploration and analysis of LBs.

The ACUV is an *ad hoc* corpus made up of articles from American/British journals published between 2007 and 2015, and amounts to 1,006,610 words. This corpus represents the variables 'native' and 'expert'; its usefulness lies in providing the so-called *target bundles*, i.e. "the most frequent LBs used by published authors" (Cortes, 2004:401–402) which students are likely to come across or need to be acquainted with. Regarding its content, all the texts in the ACUV corpus are of an argumentative kind in Humanities.

The BAWE corpus contains around 2,700 texts of proficient student writing amounting to 6.5 million words and collected between 2004 and 2007. A selection of BAWE (that we called Br-BAWE) was made, containing 1,004,147 words from 393 student assignments. Only argumentative compositions from the Humanities produced by writers whose L1 was British English were selected. Br-BAWE here represents the variables 'native' and 'non-expert'. It also provides *target bundles* or models for our students, since they may be thought to be native writers closer in age, experience, and academic context to the non-native Spanish learner in CASTLE.

The CASTLE corpus has 462,838 words and consists of 887 texts collected between 2008 and 2015. The written texts were produced by students from the Degree of English Studies and Translation Studies at the University of Valencia; most of them fall within intermediate or upper-intermediate proficiency levels. These assignments, collected via in-class controlled tasks or homework, mainly consisted in the writing of essays, usually of an argumentative kind (63.5%), but also of a narrative kind (36.5%). Given its compilation features, several units had to be filtered out from it for the present research.

Further, the CQP-edition of British National Corpus, BNC*Web* (Hoffmann & Evert, 1996–2008) was used to establish additional contrasts with the spoken conversational (demographically sampled) component (BNC*Conv*). The entire BNC is a reputed corpus of contemporary British English with around 100 million words. BNC*Conv* contains around four million words of transcribed conversational speech. Table 15.1 provides the basic features of the corpora we have just described.

Table 15.1 Overview of ACUV, Br-BAWE, and CASTLE

Corpus	*Features*	*No. of words*	*No. of texts*	*Average no. of words per text*
ACUV	Native, expert	1,006,610	146	6,894
Br-BAWE	Native, non-expert	1,004,147	393	2,555
CASTLE	Non-native, non-expert	462,863	887	522

Frequency is of paramount importance when generating lists of LBs. Biber et al. (1999:992) set a threshold of "at least ten times per million words" to consider a word sequence as an LB; in addition, the unit should appear in a minimum of 5 different texts in the corpus to avoid idiosyncratic usage. These parameters have been replicated elsewhere, although no general consensus on cut-off points has been reached (see Fuster-Márquez, 2014; Bychkovska & Lee, 2017). Threshold differences established by researchers greatly depend on the text-type and other discourse variables. The present study focuses on four-word LBs with at least 26 tokens which occur in at least 10 texts per million words in the target corpora. In the case of CASTLE, the thresholds were set to 12 LBs and a minimum of 6 texts.

An initial corpus search was carried out, the results of which are shown in Table 15.2. Please note that ACUV and Br-BAWE have around 1 million words, while the current selection of CASTLE goes up to roughly half a million words. Frequencies are normalised to 1 million.

Table 15.2 shows a marked contrast in the number of types between CASTLE and the two native corpora. It was decided to filter out the list of LBs in learner writing in order to get only a relevant inventory of overused items of an argumentative kind, to render it comparable with ACUV and Br-BAWE, which contained only argumentative texts. No less than 169,045 words in CASTLE belonged to narrative tasks, which represents 36.5% of that corpus. LBs that were left out on these grounds included, for example, purely narrative items. Likewise, bundles that were copied from prompts were excluded. Also, highly specific topic-related bundles or bundles that were found to cross punctuation boundaries were filtered out too.

Our results showed that quantitative similarities across the three corpora were not high after the filtering process in CASTLE. Out of the 65 bundles found in ACUV, 44 (67.7%) were not present in CASTLE, and 27 (41.5%) were not found in Br-BAWE. Target bundles like *in the context of* or *in the face of*, among others, did not occur in CASTLE. Strikingly, only two bundles occurred in ACUV and CASTLE, but not in Br-BAWE: *on the one hand* (13) and *when it comes to* (8). It has been pointed out that variation among native corpora may be caused by

Table 15.2 Preliminary four-word LB frequencies in ACUV, Br-BAWE, and CASTLE

	Raw		*Normalised per million words*	
Corpus	Types	Tokens	Types	Tokens
ACUV	45	2,046	44.7	2,032.5
Br-BAWE	64	2,960	63.7	2,947.7
CASTLE	384	8,059	829.6	17,411.1

different variables, such as genre, discipline, or communicative purpose (Gilquin et al., 2007: 321). In theory, great differences should not have been expected in phraseology when similar registers, disciplines, and communicative purposes by native writers were examined.

For this study, the LBs from ACUV were also compared with lists of LBs in published research to examine analogies. One of these inventories was taken from the analysis of professional writers in applied linguistics (Hyland, 2008), another from professional historians (Cortes, 2004), and from the pedagogical list in Martinez and Schmitt (2012). As these disciplines show similarities, high degrees of affinity were expected. As it turned out, only about half of the LBs in ACUV were present in the lists published in these sources. To be precise, there is a match of 51.2% with the bundles in Hyland's (2008) research, 48.9% with the bundles listed in Cortes (2004), and 31.1% with the pedagogical list in Martinez and Schmitt (2012). There were also important quantitative differences between ACUV and Br-BAWE, where novice writers used only 57.8% of the bundles in ACUV.

4 Lexical Bundles in Learner Language

The present section focuses on the LBs that were extracted from CASTLE, first by analysing overused bundles (Section 4.1) and then by paying attention to longer sequences (Section 4.2).

4.1 Overused Bundles by Learners

The quantification of usage differences between non-native and native writers (*overuse, underuse* and *similar use*) can be carried out in different ways. Our interest here is in sequences which, despite being grammatically correct, were clearly overused by EFL learners, in the sense of Hasselgren's (1994) *lexical teddy bears.* Our decision was to discard sequences such as *one of the most*, with 99 tokens in CASTLE, 35 tokens in ACUV, and 52 in Br-BAWE. When frequencies were normalised per million, it became apparent that this certainly was a case of overuse; however, the fact that it was present in CASTLE revealed that learners were acquainted with this native bundle. Another interesting case is afforded by sequences such as *on the one hand*, present in the learner corpus and in the repertoire of expert writers (ACUV); however, it was below the threshold established in the discourse of novice writers in Br-BAWE. Again, this might be interpreted as a case of Spanish learners' overuse when contrasted with novice writers' practice. Nonetheless, since such bundles were present in at least one of the two target corpora, it meant that learners were familiar with them; consequently, it was decided to discard them from our inventory.

Admittedly, many sequences posed difficulties in terms of overuse or underuse by simply comparing corpus figures. This is why we focused exclusively on extreme or indisputable cases of overuse, namely LBs with over 12 tokens present in at least 6 different texts in CASTLE, but which at the same time had the lowest frequencies, between 0 and 5 tokens, in the two native corpora (ACUV and Br-BAWE). Out of the initial 384 LB types in the learner corpus, our research became confined to 77 types of extreme overuse.

It has been often claimed that the argumentative prose of EFL learners includes sequences that belong to informal or typical of oral discourse (see Granger & Rayson, 1998; Gilquin & Granger, 2007; Gilquin et al., 2007; Luzón, 2010:87). This observation allegedly underscores the difficulty that learners have in the discrimination of registers, but, more specifically, their lack of familiarity with the style required in academic English writing. To test this observation, a comparison was performed for these sequences with the *Spoken Conversational subcorpus* of the BNC (BNC*Conv*). The BNC was accessed through the BNC*Web* interface (see Lehmann et al., 2000). Table 15.3 shows the frequencies of the 42 most frequently overused LBs in CASTLE, the corresponding frequencies in ACUV and Br-BAWE, and normalised frequencies per million words from the BNC*Conv*.[3]

Table 15.3 List of selected overused bundles by learners

Tokens in CASTLE	*Distribution In CASTLE*	***Four-word bundle***	*Tokens in ACUV*	*Tokens in Br-BAWE*	*BNC**Conv** norm. x million*
67	61	*my point of view*	1	0	1.65
57	45	*I think that the*	0	4	1.18
47	38	*the most important thing*	2	1	1.42
46	42	*from my point of*	0	0	1.42
45	39	*are a lot of*	2	1	4.25
44	39	*there are a lot*	2	1	4.25
42	34	*a lot of people*	2	0	39.92
38	32	*when we talk about*	0	0	0
37	36	*and I think that*	1	0	7.79
37	35	*going to talk about*	0	0	0.47
37	29	*a lot of things*	1	0	9.21
36	31	*I think that it*	0	0	1.89
35	35	*first of all I*	0	1	2.13
34	29	*if you want to*	5	0	51.25

(*Continued*)

Tokens in CASTLE	*Distribution In CASTLE*	***Four-word bundle***	*Tokens in ACUV*	*Tokens in Br-BAWE*	*BNC**Conv** norm. x million*
34	23	*we are going to*	1	0	3.31
33	33	*to sum up I*	0	0	0
31	30	*have a lot of*	0	0	13.23
31	28	*have to say that*	3	0	2.36
30	29	*in my opinion the*	1	4	0
30	29	*the truth is that*	0	2	0.24
30	25	*agree with the author*	0	0	0
29	26	*I have to say*	1	0	5.43
28	24	*I agree with the*	0	1	0
27	24	*think that it is*	0	2	0.47
26	26	*would like to say*	0	0	1.18
26	22	*I can say that*	0	0	0.47
25	24	*to say that I*	1	0	2.36
24	22	*as I said before*	0	0	0.71
24	22	*we can say that*	3	2	0
23	23	*am going to talk*	0	0	0
23	22	*I am sure that*	0	0	0.24
23	21	*we are talking about*	2	0	0.94
22	21	*is the most important*	4	4	3.55
21	21	*like to say that*	0	0	0.71
20	20	*in my opinion this*	1	2	0
20	20	*we have to take*	0	0	0.47
20	18	*as we can see*	0	3	0.76
20	16	*as far as I*	3	2	18.19
19	17	*one of the best*	5	5	3.31
18	18	*but I think that*	0	2	6.38
18	18	*I think that I*	0	0	1.42
18	14	*I do not think*	0	3	0*

The asterisk indicates that the alternative spoken sequence *I don't think* is extremely frequent. To decide whether sequences were typical of speech or writing, we adopted Biber et al. (2004)'s classification of bundles according to four bands of typicality:

Band 1: between 0–19 items per million (we understand as not typical).
Band 2: between 20-39 items per million, a star (*).
Band 3: between 40-99 items per million, two stars (**).
Band 4: 100 and over (***).

Higher frequencies clearly point to the membership of items to a specific register or more than one. It is part of our assumption that the selected overused bundles were fairly uncommon in the prose of native writers in ACUV and Br-BAWE. Strikingly, as shown in Table 15.3, only two learner bundles out of 42, namely *a lot of people* (39.92) and *if you want to* (51.25), appeared to be typical of conversational English. If the contracted form *I don't think*, equivalent to the four-word *I do not think*, was added, the total number of 'conversational' bundles would amount to 6. In all probability, learners in CASTLE used uncontracted forms by applying straightforwardly the instruction of using uncontracted forms in writing, in spite of the fact that *I do not think* is seldom used in academic writing. Briefly, 92% overused sequences cannot be said to be typical of conversational English, as shown by this comparison with the BNC*Conv* subcorpus. Moreover, a large number of these learner bundles had occurrences between 0 and 1 in conversational English. The orality of the units listed required further analysis vis-à-vis findings from research in EFL phraseology.

4.2 Longer and Overlapping Bundles

Careful examination of the data revealed that a number of bundles overused by our L2 writers overlapped with longer bundles. Table 15.4 shows all the relevant overlapping cases in CASTLE among these LBs.

The bundle *from my point of view* (46 instances in CASTLE) did not have a corresponding single occurrence in any of the two native corpora. This is in line with reports in the EFL literature that classifies it as an overused sequence in learner academic writing (Gilquin et al., 2007:331; Gilquin & Paquot, 2007; Luzón, 2010:89). The BNC*Conv* subcorpus only affords 1.42 tokens per million. *My point of view* is also extremely infrequent in the native corpora (3 cases in ACUV and none in Br-BAWE). By contrast, the shorter bundle *point of view* affords 131 cases in the learner corpus. Simpson-Vlach & Ellis (2010) mention this

Table 15.4 Overlapping four-word sequences in CASTLE and resulting longer sequences

Overlapping bundle 1	*Overlapping bundle 2*	*Overlapping bundle 3*	*Resulting longer bundles (tokens)*
from my point of (46)	*my point of view* (67)		*from my point of view* (46)
there are a lot (44)	*are a lot of* (45)		*there are a lot of* (44)
am going to talk (23)	*going to talk about* (37)		*(I) am going to talk about* (22)
I have to say (29)	*have to say that* (31)		*I have to say that* (23)
*I would like to** (128)	*would like to say* (26)	*like to say that* (21)	*I would like to say that* (21)
*I would like to** (128)	*would like to point* (12)	*like to point out* (12)	*I would like to point out (that)* (12)
I agree with the (28)	*agree with the author* (30)		*I agree with the author* (15)
as far as I (20)	*far as I am* (13)	*as I am concerned* (13)	*as far as I am concerned* (13)

sequence in combinations with variable elements in the formula *(from) (the) point of view (of)*. Its presence is also attested in ACUV with 45 occurrences and in Br-BAWE with 56 occurrences. Apparently, the difference lies in the full five-word bundle *from my point of view*, used by learners to alternate with *in my opinion* and some other sequences. In both cases, the need felt by the EFL writer to be present is in all probability at the heart of its peculiarity.

Another unusual sequence in native academic English is *there are a lot of*, with 44 occurrences in CASTLE. The shorter *a lot of* has been described as a speech-like sequence and as a case of learner overuse in academic writing (Paquot, 2013:2). It is to be noted that this bundle has 4.02 occurrences in BNC*Conv*, whereas the three-word bundle *a lot of* affords no less than 406.95 occurrences per million in the same subcorpus. This three-word bundle has 33 occurrences in Br-BAWE, 38 in ACUV, but 456 in CASTLE, which bears witness to its overuse by learners in the academic register. A set of analogue bundles is that made up by *are a lot of* (45), *there are a lot* (44), *a lot of people* (42), *a lot of things* (37), *have a lot of* (31), *with a lot of* (17), and *a lot of time* (12). Similarly, the six-word sequence *I am going to talk about* appears 22 times in CASTLE, but there were no occurrences in ACUV or Br-BAWE. The basic contrast in relation to expert writing seems to stem from the addition of *I am going to* to the sequence (*to*) *talk about*. Although it might be thought to be a feature widely favoured in speech, 13.93 occurrences of *to talk about* in the BNC*Conv* do not prove that this is typical of conversational English.

There are no occurrences in ACUV or Br-BAWE for the sequence *I have to say that*. Let us note that one of potential three-word bundles in this sequence, *I have to*, has very low frequencies in both native academic corpora, whereas CASTLE affords no less than 129 instances. In contrast, the BNC*Conv*, with over 100 instances per million, suggests the oral character of the sequence. However, the longer bundle *I have to say that* offers the meagre figure of 0.71 occurrences per million in that subcorpus. Once more, this five-word bundle does not seem to be typical of conversational English. Again, this suggests that many longer prefabricated chunks in CASTLE are instances of highly deviant preferences of learners.

The bundle *I would like to say that* is unattested in ACUV and Br-BAWE. One of its embedded bundles, *I would like to*, is not listed among the extreme cases of overuse given that more than five occurrences were found in ACUV and Br-BAWE. Biber et al. (2014) include it as a typical bundle of classroom teaching and conversation. The BNC*Conv* yields 10.63 occurrences per million, plus 52.2 more if its contracted equivalent *I'd like to* was added. These findings confirm the speech-like character of this sequence. Likewise, the longer sequence *I would like to say that* has poor results: 0.24 occurrences per million words in the BNC*Conv*.

The learner bundle *I would like to point out (that)*, containing the embedded sequence *I would like to*, has no occurrences in ACUV or Br-BAWE. The BNC*Conv* does not have any instances of this sequence, which there again bears witness to its foreignness.

The five-word bundle *I agree with the author* is not attested in any of the two native corpora or the BNC*Conv*. It is to be noted that the phrase frame *I * agree with the author* shows variations in CASTLE, where the slot is filled with emphatic adverbials which enhance the stance character of the sequence: *absolutely*, *completely*, *personally*, or *totally*.

The sequences *far as I am* and *as I am concerned*, embedded in the six-word bundle *as far as I am concerned*, were not found in the native corpora; only *as far as I* showed a few occurrences: 4 in ACUV and 2 in Br-BAWE. BNC*Conv* comprises no occurrences of this LB, which leads to the preliminary conclusion that it is untypical of academic English and spoken conversational English. Milton and Hyland (1999) demonstrate that Chinese non-native students use this LB frequently, but that no single occurrence was found in the native student corpus they compare it with.

5 Discourse Features of Learner Bundles

LBs fulfil major roles in discourse. For this functional classification, Biber et al. (2004), Conrad and Biber (2004), Cortes (2004), and Hyland (2008) have been followed. Their approach distinguishes three main discourse functions: (1) stance expressions, (2) referential expressions, and (3) discourse organising expressions. Biber et al.'s (2004) classification of bundles from four registers, classroom teaching, textbooks, conversation, and academic prose, proved especially useful in our analysis.

This section accounts for the discourse functions that overused bundles fulfil in texts. Figure 15.1 shows an overview of the distribution of LBs across the aforementioned functions. As shown, most bundles fall within the category of stance, while only a few have a discourse organising function. The ensuing subsections deal with each of such functions: stance (Section 5.1), referential (Section 5.2), and discourse organising (Section 5.3).

5.1 Overused Stance Bundles

Stance bundles, the most common, are used to "provide a frame for the interpretation of the following proposition" (Biber et al., 2004:389). The two major functional types in CASTLE were epistemic and attitudinal/modality.

Table 15.5 displays the categories and subcategories of overused stance bundles in CASTLE. An overwhelming majority of them belong to the epistemic category, by means of which learners express certainty,

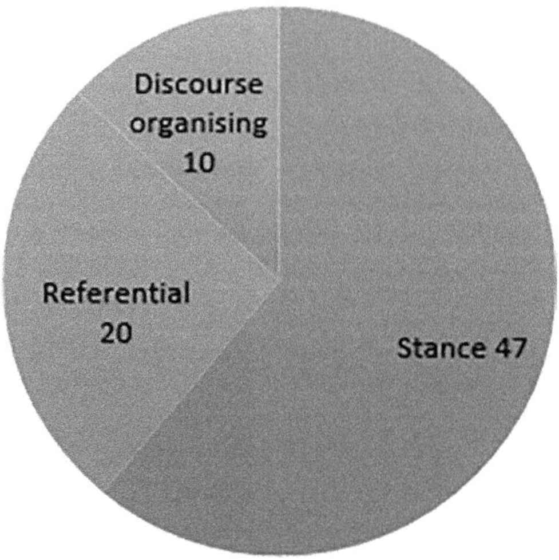

Figure 15.1 Distribution of LBs by discourse function.

Table 15.5 Overused stance bundles in CASTLE (frequencies 0–5 in ACUV and Br-BAWE)

Type	*Subtype*	*Bundles*
Epistemic		*Personal*: I think that the, and I think that, I think that it, think that it is, but I think that, I do not think, I think that I, I think that is, I think that this, I think that we, because I think that, tend to think that, I think that if, I am sure that, in my opinion the, in my opinion this, in my opinion it, my opinion it is, I do not know, as far as I, my point of view, from my point of, agree with the author, I agree with the, as far as I, far as I am, as I am concerned. *Impersonal*: the truth is that, it does not matter, is supposed to be.
Attitudinal/ Modality	*Desire*	if you want to, would like to say, like to say that, like to point out, would like to point.
	Prediction	is going to be.
	Ability	we can say that, I can say that, as we can see, we can see in, I do not see.
	Obligation/ directive	we have to take, have to take into, have to say that, I have to say, that we have to, we have to be, I must say that.

uncertainty, or probability regarding the information in the following proposition. In all the personalised sequences, the authorial first person pronoun *I* and the determiner *my* are used. In this category, CASTLE shows a large number of LBs containing *I think (that)*, which convey uncertainty (see Gilquin et al., 2007; Paquot, 2013:392). As shown earlier, ACUV, Br-BAWE, and BNC*Conv* show very low frequencies of these bundles. These findings confirm that the clausal unit *I think* is overused and undoubtedly typical of conversational English, but surprisingly the vast majority of these overused LBs are not typical of spoken register.

Likewise, *I do not know* is only listed by Biber et al. (2004) in contracted combinations such as *I don't know if*, found in conversation and classroom teaching. However, stronger epistemic sequences, e.g. *my opinion*, *my point of view*, and *as far as I am concerned*, or the frame *I * agree with the author*, are not mentioned for any of the four registers therein. These findings are in agreement with those in Luzón (2010:89), where Spanish engineering students of intermediate levels are found to overuse sequences such as *in my opinion*, or *from my point of view*. Gilquin and Paquot (2007) also report that the stance expression *from my point of view* is overused in EFL academic writing.

Attitudinal and modality stance bundles "[...] express speaker attitudes towards the actions or events described in the following proposition" (Biber et al., 2004:390). Most sequences in this category are also personal; in most cases, there is a first person singular *I*, although *we* is also used in some bundles. Hyland (2008) classifies a number of sequences where "you" and "we" are present as features of *engagement*, when the reader is rhetorically invited to participate. Several subcategories can be found here. One of these is represented by bundles where the writer expresses desire or inquires the readers. The sequences *would like to say* and *like to say that*, which demand a personal subject in context (*I*), are not listed by Biber et al. (2004) for any of the four registers. The sequence *if you want to* seems to be typical of classroom teaching and conversation (the spoken registers) in Biber et al.'s (2004) research. A second subcategory is that in which the writer predicts development of future events. This is represented by the impersonal bundle *is going to be*, listed as fairly typical of classroom teaching alone. The BNC*Conv* shows that it is somewhat frequent in that spoken register, with 51.25 tokens per million words.

Another subcategory is ability bundles. The personal sequences include *I can say that*, *I do not see*, and the engagement expressions *we can say that*, *as we can see*, *we can see in*, where "we" seems to invite the reader to participate, particularly in the last two sequences and may be classified as a discourse organiser too. None of these LBs are mentioned in Biber et al.'s (2004) study. Likewise, the BNC*Conv* has very low frequencies. Only the equivalent contracted form of *I do not see* (*I don't see*) may be interpreted as typical of conversational English according to BNC*Conv*. Bundles within the subcategory of obligation and directives have as a subject a second person pronoun rather than the first person personal pronoun. In CASTLE, the first person singular and plural are used by learners to express some kind of obligation by means of the modal verb *have to*. Biber et al. (2004) do not record any of these bundles used by learners: *we have to take*, *have to take into*, *have to say that*, *I have to say*, *that we have to*. However, the embedded sequences *I have to* and *we have to* seem to be typical of conversational English, according to BNC*Conv*. Therefore, these sequences might be interpreted as partly speech-like, but never in their four-word output.

5.2 Overused Referential Bundles

Referential bundles are those that "[...] identify an entity or single out some particular attribute of an entity as especially important" (Biber et al., 2004). The overused LBs in this referential group also fall into different subheadings as it can be seen in Table 15.6.

Identification and focus refer to LBs employed to single out or state a point in the argumentation as being important. These sequences have a discourse organising function: *the most important thing*, *is the most important*, *and this is a*, *is the case of*. Of all the overused bundles in this subheading, Biber et al. (2004) mention only *and this is a*, which they find to be typical of classroom teaching.

A number of sequences can be found as well within the subtype of specification, which are LBs that name attributes present in the following head noun. Some of these bundles indicate quantities: *the only thing*

Table 15.6 Overused referential bundles in CASTLE (frequencies 0–5 in ACUV and Br-BAWE)

Type	*Subtype*	*Bundle*
Identification/Focus		the most important thing, is the most important, and this is a, is the case of, point of view about.
Specification of attributes	*Quantity Specification*	the only thing I, all the things that, are a lot of, there are a lot, a lot of people, a lot of things, have a lot of, with a lot of, there are people who.
	Quality Specification	a good way to, one of the best.
	Intangible framing attributes	the problem is that, is a way to, is the reason why.
Time reference		a long time ago.

I, all the things that, are a lot of, there are a lot, a lot of people, a lot of things, have a lot of, with a lot of, there are people who. Interestingly, Biber et al. (2004) enumerate certain bundles containing *a lot of* as typical of the classroom teaching register; however, the only one in common with CASTLE is *have a lot of*; the others are not listed by these authors. Also, in spite of the importance of *a lot of* in speech, there again, none of the overused four-word LBs in CASTLE enjoys any significant frequency in that corpus. As to their presence in academic prose, *a lot of* affords 33 cases in Br-BAWE, and 38 in ACUV, but no less than 456 in learners.

Intangible framing attributes are represented in CASTLE by *the problem is that, is a way to* and *is the reason why*. These sequences are used to identify abstract features or to establish logical relationships in the text. None of these LBs are found in Biber et al. (2004). The sequence *the problem is that* has very low frequencies in the BNC*Conv*. Its embedded sequence *the problem is* also has a low frequency in the two native corpora, with 9 cases in both. There are no occurrences of *is a way to* or *is the reason why* in BNC*Conv*. Time reference is represented by the sequence *a long time ago*, which is not listed by Biber et al. (2004) for any of the four registers they analysed and, as seen in Table 15.4, it enjoys a low frequency in the BNC*Conv*. Consequently, none of these learner bundles can be said to be representative of native academic writing or even conversational English.

5.3 Overused Discourse Organising Bundles

The last category is that of discourse organising bundles (see Table 15.7).

Bundles in this group serve two major functions. One of them is topic introduction and focus, represented by the sequences *first of all I, the first thing that, am going to talk, we are going to, going to talk about*. EFL writers in CASTLE use them to announce the issue or topic of their text. It should be remarked that the embedded sequence *first of all*, present in *first of all I*, has only 6 occurrences in the native academic corpora, whereas it appears 86 times in CASTLE. The overused parallel bundle *the first thing that* is not commented on by any of these scholars,

Table 15.7 Overused discourse organising bundles in CASTLE (frequencies 0–5 in ACUV and Br-BAWE)

Type	*Bundle*
Topic introduction and focus	first of all I, the first thing that, am going to talk, we are going to, going to talk about.
Text Deixis	when we talk about, we are talking about, as I said before, to sum up I
Others	to say that I

and the distributional figures in BNC show that they are not frequent in conversational English. The embedded LB *the first thing* has one instance in ACUV, and 5 in Br-BAWE. BNC*Conv* shows a frequency of 13.93, which shows that it is atypical of that register.

Text deixis is represented by the sequences *when we talk about*, *we are talking about*, *as I said before* and *to sum up I*. By means of these expressions, writers summarise or remind their readers about the topic, where specific points are found in discourse: *when we talk about* and *we are talking about* direct the reader to statements made in other parts of the text, *as I said before* leads them to remind them and summarise, etc. None of these LBs are listed by Biber et al. (2004) and show very low frequencies in the BNC*Conv*. Two of these sequences, *when we talk about* and *as I said before*, are not found in ACUV and Br-BAWE. As to relevant embedded sequences, *when we talk* is not found in ACUV or Br-BAWE either; *we are talking* affords 2 instances in ACUV and 1 in Br-BAWE; *as I said* affords 3 instances in ACUV, and none in Br-BAWE, whereas *to sum up* 6 instances in each of the two native corpora.

Finally, the bundle *to say that I* has very low frequencies in the two subcorpora of the BNC. In ACUV, it is found once, but there are no cases in Br-BAWE. This LB is typically encountered in longer sequences containing a modal that expresses personal obligation, desire in the frame *I * to say that I.*

6 Discussion and Conclusion

The aforementioned results have shed light on several aspects of the phraseology of non-native learners of English. While statistical findings confirm the presence of overused phraseology by EFL writers, the strongest cases of overuse cannot be ignored. No less than 77 four-word bundles have been detected in CASTLE, and the reasons why learners use them in a divergent manner call for an explanation.

The inadequacy of these sequences may be due to the learners' familiarity with shorter sequences, and to the fact that learners have not grasped the pragmatic complexity of longer sequences (see Hasselgren 1994:237). Milton and Hyland (1999:148) point out that "[...] modal expressions are syntactically, semantically and pragmatically complex, and thus extremely difficult for learners to master". Another interesting observation is that a large number of overused sequences reflect personal stance features; however, such writer visibility is not a feature of native writing. In other words, the presence of *I* or *we* in many of these sequences is indicative of the foreignness or unusualness of the LBs. Let us recall that there is a 50% coincidence among the phraseological lists published on specific academic genres, which are the inventories to which learners may have been exposed. The gulf between professional academic writing and non-native writing in a foreign academic context is greater. Perhaps we cannot expect to find much of the expert phraseology in learners' production because, even at the university level, students are not sufficiently exposed to the language of journals. However, it has also been noted that much research on bundles has been devoted to the analysis of native academic and specific registers. These registers include tasks that are not usually demanded from non-native learners in L3 contexts. The literature in CIA has highlighted that not few English words or sequences overused by Spanish learners are shared by learners from different language backgrounds, so they may be assumed to be developmental (Gilquin et al., 2007:323). This only evidences, as suggested by one of the reviewers, the role played by L1 as a decisive influence over the language of EFL students (see Paquot, 2013).

In sum, more work is required in order to find out whether these LBs are shared with learners of English from different mother tongues. Some of the implications are that textbook material with relevant phraseology may be needed in EAP and ESP purposes, but careful attention should be paid to the phraseology that learners will need at different stages. Attention should also be paid to the level and nature of their exposure to LB inventories. We agree with various scholars (Luzón, 2010:79; Salazar, 2014:153–154; Bychkovska & Lee, 2017) that students should be familiar with the rhetorical preferences in their professional and academic genres, which can only be done through more intense contact with those registers over time.

Notes

1 In this context, *word* is used in the sense of *word-form* and not of lemma (see Biber et al. 1999: 990, Hyland 2008: 5).
2 BAWE is a well-known public corpus (see www2.warwick.ac.uk/fac/soc/al/research/collect/bawe). However, ACUV and CASTLE have been compiled at the University of Valencia.
3 The aforementioned procedure results in a list of 77 overused bundles, here cut down to 42 entries due to space limitations. The 35 bundles omitted from Table 3 are those with lowest frequencies and hence less representative of phraseological overuse.

References

Anthony, L. (2014). AntConc (Version 3.4.3) [Computer Software]. Tokyo, Japan: Waseda University. Available from www.laurenceanthony.net/.

Biber, D., Johansson, S., Leech, G., Conrad, S. & Finegan, E. (1999). *Longman grammar of spoken and written English.* London: Longman.

Biber, D., Conrad, S. & Cortes, V. (2004). *If you look at…*: Lexical bundles in university teaching and textbooks. *Applied Linguistics* 25(3), 371–405.

Bychkovska, T. & Lee, J. J. (2017). At the same time: Lexical bundles in L1 and L2 university student argumentative writing. *Journal of English for Academic Purposes* 30, 38–52.

Chen, Y. & Baker, P. (2010). Lexical bundles in L1 and L2 academic writing. *Language Learning and Technology* 14(2), 30–49.
Conrad, S. & Biber, D. (2004). The frequency and use of lexical bundles in conversation and academic prose. *Lexicographica* 20, 56–71.
Cortes, V. (2004). Lexical bundles in published and student disciplinary writing: Examples from history and biology. *English for Specific Purposes* 23(4), 397–423.
Fuster-Márquez, M. (2014). Lexical bundles and phrase frames in the language of hotel websites. *English Text Construction* 7(1), 84–121.
Gilquin, G. & Paquot, M. (2007). Spoken features in learner academic writing: Identification, explanation and solution, in M. Davies, Rayson, P., Hunston, S. & Danielsson, P. (Eds), *Proceedings of the Fourth Corpus Linguistics Conference,* University of Birmingham, 27–30. http://ucrel.lancs.ac.uk/publications/CL2007/ paper/204_Paper.pdf [Retrieved: August 28, 2015].
Gilquin, G., Granger, S. & Paquot, M. (2007). Learner corpora: The missing link in EAP pedagogy. *Journal of English for Academic Purposes* 6, 319–335.
Granger, S. (2002). A bird's eye view of learner corpus research, in S. Granger, Hung, J. & Petch-Tyson, S. (Eds.) *Computer learner corpora, second language acquisition and foreign language teaching.* Amsterdam & Philadelphia: John Benjamins, 3–33.
Granger, S. (2015). Contrastive interlanguage analysis. A reappraisal. *International Journal of Learner Corpus Research* 1(1), 7–24.
Granger, S. & Rayson, P. (1998). Automatic profiling of learner texts, in S. Granger (Ed.) *Learner English on computer.* London: Longman, 119–131.
Granger, S. & Tyson, S. (1996). Connector usage in the English essay writing of native and non-native EFL speakers of English. *World Englishes* 15, 19–29.
Hasselgren, A. (1994). Lexical teddy bears and advanced learners: a study into the ways Norwegian students cope with English vocabulary. *International Journal of Applied Linguistics* 4(2), 237–258.
Hoffmann, S. & Evert, S. (1996–2008). *BNCweb* (*CQP-edition*). URL http://bncweb.lancs.ac.uk (Last accessed November 29, 2017).
Hyland, K. (2005). Stance and engagement: A model of interaction in academic discourse. *Discourse Studies* 7(2), 173–192.
Hyland, K. (2008). *As can be seen*: Lexical bundles and disciplinary variation. *English for Specific Purposes* 27, 4–21.
Hyland, K. & Tse, P. (2004). Metadiscourse in academic writing: A reappraisal. *Applied Linguistics* 25(2), 156–177.
Lehmann, H.-M., Schneider, P. & Hoffmann, S. (2000). BNCweb, in J. Kirk (Ed.) *Corpora galore: Analysis and techniques in describing English.* Amsterdam: Rodopi, 259–266.
Luzón, M. J. (2010). Analysis of organizing and rhetorical items in a learner corpus of technical writing, in M. C. Campoy, B. Bellés-Fortuno & M. Ll. Gea-Valor (Eds.), *Corpus-based approaches to English language teaching.* London and New York: Continuum, 79–94.
Martinez, R. & Schmitt, N. (2012). A phrasal expressions list. *Applied Linguistics* 33(3), 299–320.
Milton, J. C. P. & Hyland, K. (1999). Assertions in students' academic essays: a comparison of English NS and NNS student writers, in *Language analysis,*

description and pedagogy, proceedings of international conference organized by Language Centre, HKUST (1996), HKUST, 147–161.

Paquot, M. (2013). Lexical bundles and L1 transfer effects. *International Journal of Corpus Linguistics* 18 (3), 391–417.

Salazar, D (2014). *Lexical bundles in native and non-native scientific writing.* Amsterdam and Philadelphia: John Benjamins.

Simpson-Vlach, R. & Ellis, N. C. (2010). An academic formulas list: New methods in phraseology research. *Applied Linguistics* 31(4), 487–512.

Sinclair, J. M. (1991). *Corpus, concordance, collocation.* Oxford: Oxford University Press.

16 Verbs of Vision in Academic Discourse

Variations in the Use of Their Non-literal Senses in L1 Expert, L1 Non-expert, and L2 Non-expert Writing

Hanna Skorczynska

1 Introduction

Studies of academic writing by English learners as compared to native professional and student writers have pointed towards many areas of difficulty requiring attention in the teaching of academic English. Unawareness of register, simplicity of lexical and grammatical structures, or a limited range of lexico-grammatical patterns, which are rich in academic texts written by native experts, are only some of the issues brought up by a number of scholars (Hyland, 1999; Hinkel, 2002, 2003, 2004; Charles, 2006a, 2006b; Hiltunen, 2006; Gilquin & Paquot, 2008; Granger & Paquot, 2009; Chen & Baker, 2010; Ädel & Ermann, 2011; Byrd & Coxhead, 2010). The use of lexical verbs performing major discourse functions in academic texts is a specific problematic area of English usage for non-native and non-expert writers. Difficulties in the use of grammatical forms as well as limitations of lexico-grammatical patterning were found to be the main areas of concern (Hinkel, 2002; Granger & Paquot, 2009). The present study follows this line of research and takes a step further by enquiring into the use of three specific verbs: 'regard', 'see', and 'view' in the corpora representing academic discourse produced by professional writers using English as the first language (L1), non-expert writers using English as L1, and non-expert writers with English as the second language (L2). As Granger and Paquot (2009) pointed out, each verb shows a specific pattern of usage in academic discourse, and therefore, the corpus data on those patterns should be carefully analysed so that the information obtained could easily find its way into teaching materials.

The present study also takes a cognitive linguistics view on the three verbs of vision, in the sense that it distinguishes between their literal and non-literal senses, and examines the patterns of use of the latter. The metaphorical or non-literal meanings of 'regard', 'see', and 'view' reveal recurrent associations between the human capacity of perceiving objects with eyes and human mental activities such as understanding, considering, or imagining, and point to the conceptual metaphor of MIND AS BODY (Lakoff & Johnson, 1980; Sweetser, 1990). These particular meanings of 'regard', 'see', and 'view' appear to be particularly relevant in the construction of academic discourse, as they perform functions reflecting the main mental activities involved. The universalist (Viberg, 1983; Sweetser, 1990) and variationist (Ibarretxe-Antuñano, 2002, 2008; Aikhenvald & Storch, 2013) views on the verbs of vision and the underlying conceptual metaphors provide an additional motivation for the present study, as it explores the extent to which native and non-native writers vary the use of the non-literal senses of 'regard', 'see', and 'view' in academic texts. Furthermore, and given that the non-literal uses of words and phrases in discourse tend to differ from their literal senses regarding the word form and co-text (Deignan, 2005), the present study provides useful corpus-based insights into precisely that type of usage. In this way, specific areas of difficulty for English L2 non-expert writers, as compared to the other two types of writer, will be identified.

The following section will present a cognitive linguistics perspective on the verbs of vision. Section 3 overviews the research conducted in the field of academic writing and the use of lexical verbs. Section 4 includes the description of the corpora examined and the steps taken in the analysis. Section 5 discusses the results obtained from the analysis of the corpora and is divided into three parts: the first part reports on the frequency findings; the second deals with the use of the different non-literal senses of 'see'; and the third part describes the syntactic structures in which the non-literal 'regard', 'see', and 'view' were identified. The article closes with conclusions.

2 Verbs of Vision and Their Non-literal Senses

From the cognitive linguistics perspective, the non-literal senses of verbs of vision, such as 'regard', 'see', and 'view' are based on the conceptual metaphor of MIND AS BODY (Lakoff & Johnson, 1980; Sweetser, 1990). A conceptual metaphor is understood as a mapping or correspondence between two conceptual domains, where properties from one domain (source domain) are transferred onto another domain (target domain). Following Lakoff and Johnson (1980: 135), this is how metaphors "allow us to understand one domain of experience in terms of another". The associations established through mappings in conceptual metaphors are considered to be universal, since they are grounded on an experientially bodily basis, that is, embodied human experience (Lakoff & Johnson, 1980, 1999; Johnson, 1987; Grady, 1997; Kövecses, 2010). In this sense, the non-literal or metaphorical senses of the three verbs studied here are established through mappings between the properties of our physical capacity of perceiving objects with eyes and pertaining to the source domain, and the properties of our intellectual capacity of understanding, imagining, or considering something belonging in the target domain.

The non-literal senses of the verbs of vision are lexicalised as their semantic extensions and are cases of polysemy. The rich polysemous structures and uses of different perception verbs have been largely studied in morpho-syntax (Dik & Hengeveld, 1991; Horie, 1993; Roegiest, 2003) and semantics (Viberg, 1983; Sweetser, 1990; Ibarretxe-Antuñano, 1999, 2002, 2008; Rojo & Valenzuela, 2004–2005; San Roque et al., 2015). Both Viberg (1983) and Sweetser (1990) made universalist claims about the verbs of vision. According to Viberg's hierarchy, based on a study of 50 languages, vision is the most salient sense modality across languages with a near-universal presence of a basic perception verb meaning 'see'. In the same way, San Roque et al. (2015) claimed that the apparent linguistic dominance of vision might be rooted in our biology, as humans display considerable visual specialisation. In a highly influential study, Sweetser (1990: 39) further argued that an association between intellect and sight in the language of the senses was universal, since vision is "our primary source of objective data about the world".

In her study of perception verbs, Ibarretxe-Antuñano (1999, 2002) provided a detailed analysis of the semantic extensions of the English verbs of vision, resulting from the lexicalisation of their non-literal senses. Depending on the mappings between the domains involved, Ibarretxe-Antuñano (1999) organised those senses into four categories: a) intellect and mental activity (e.g. understand, foresee); b) social relationships (e.g. meet, visit); c) reliability and assurance (e.g. find out, make sure); and d) miscellany (e.g. witness, refer). According to the author, all these groups except group (b) (social relationships) can be considered as sub-cases of the MIND-AS-BODY metaphor.

Regarding the first group of semantic extensions referring to intellect and mental activity (Ibarretxe-Antuñano, 2002: 96–98), which is the focus of this study, the mapping takes place between the domain of physical visual perception (seeing and looking) and the domain of mental processing (understanding, foreseeing, visualising, regarding, imagining, revising, and mediating). This mapping involves the following sub-mappings between:

- understanding and seeing (e.g. "I explained the problem but he could not see it"[1]),
- foreseeing and seeing (e.g. "I can see what will happen if you don't help"),
- imagining and seeing (e.g. "Do all your people see themselves as having a selling role?"),

- considering and seeing (e.g. "She thinks it is soft of him to see them as belonging to a universal latent hostility"), and
- studying/examining and seeing (e.g. "I have to see how I fix it").

With reference to the second group referring to reliability and assurance, Ibarretxe-Antuñano (2002: 98–100) mentions correspondences between finding out and seeing (e.g. "Please see who is knocking"), making sure and seeing (e.g. "See that it gets done right away"), and taking care of something and seeing something (e.g. "He looked after his younger brother"). Finally, for the fourth group (miscellany), the author (2002: 100–101) points to mappings between witnessing and seeing (e.g. "He has seen much happiness").

Verbs of vision, as can be observed, are complex in the number and type of semantic extensions derived from their non-literal or metaphorical senses. Even though considered as universal by some scholars, perception verbs, and among them, vision verbs, show cross-linguistic and cross-cultural variations, as reported in many studies (Classen, 1997; Ibarretxe-Antuñano, 1999, 2002, 2008; Aikhevald & Storch, 2013). The present research does not look precisely into this type of variation, but explores ways in which the use of the non-literal vision verbs correlates with the use of English as L1 or L2, and with the level of expertise in academic discourse writing. Such an approach draws upon cognitive linguistics, while at the same time provides a more context-specific and usage-based analysis of those verbs.

3 Lexical Verbs in Academic Writing

A substantial amount of research concerning academic writing has focused on the differences between three groups of writers: native professional, native student, and non-native student with the aim to provide corpus-based findings, which could be easily transferred to English language teaching materials. Recent studies have particularly focused on the differences in the use of lexical bundles (Chen & Baker, 2010; Byrd & Coxhead, 2010; Ädel & Ermann, 2011) pointing to a reduced range of those multi-word units in L2 student academic writing as compared to L1 professional and student writers. Other studies revealed that L2 academic writing shows certain influence of spoken language contributing to the simplicity of lexical and syntactic structures used (Hinkel, 2003). The features of speech reflected in L2 academic writing point to students' unawareness of register differences and to factors such as the influence of spoken language, L1 transfer, teaching-induced factors, and developmental causes (Gilquin & Paquot, 2008).

Lexical verbs have been viewed as significantly involved in expressing major discourse functions in academic texts, such as conveying personal stance, reviewing literature, quoting, expressing cause and effect, summarising, and contrasting (Granger & Paquot, 2009). Hinkel (2004) classified lexical verbs into five categories: activity verbs (make, use, give), reporting verbs (suggest, discuss, argue, propose), mental/emotive verbs (know, think, see), linking verbs (appear, become, keep, prove), and logico-semantic relationship verbs (contrast, follow, cause, illustrate). Reporting verbs and 'coming-to-know verbs' have received much attention in academic discourse studies (Meyer, 1997; Hyland, 1999; Charles, 2006a, 2006b; Hiltunen, 2006). The specific difficulties for English language learners pointed by scholars with regard to the verb usage have been their grammatical forms, such as tense, aspect, mood, and voice (Hinkel, 2002), but also their lexico-grammatical patterns (Granger & Paquot, 2009). Granger and Paquot (2009:194) rightly claimed:

> Presenting learners with lists of EAP verbs and the exact meanings they convey is (...) undoubtedly an important first step but unless it is complemented with a detailed description of their use, results are bound to be highly disappointing.

Granger and Paquot (2009) offered a general overview of the use of lexical verbs in academic writing by L1 expert writers, L1 novice writers, and L2 learners. The study revealed that English learners significantly underuse the majority of verbs characteristic for academic discourse, such as 'include', 'report', or 'relate', and at the same time they resort to verbs typical of informal speech, for example 'think' or 'like'. The use of academic verbs by those writers tends to be restricted to a very limited range of phraseological patterns, which contrasts with the rich patterning of expert writing. For instance, language learners predominantly used the verb 'conclude' in the sentence-initial position signalling a conclusion: 'to conclude, ...', while expert writers employed a wide range of different patterns: 'it must be therefore concluded', 'he concludes', or 'we must conclude'. Finally, L1 and L2 novice writers share a number of problems; for instance, they all draw more often on high-frequency verbs (e.g. get, want, feel, state, realise, think) and employ a more limited number of lexico-grammatical patterns as compared to professional academic writers. On the whole, the use of lexical verbs in academic writing reported in Granger and Paquot (2009) shows variations among the three groups of writers with the problems of usage frequency as well as the range of phraseological patterns, which were exclusive for L2 writers.

Of the verbs under examination in this study, 'see' and 'regard' were included in the top 100 verb lemma list extracted from the French L1 writer component of the ICLE (International Corpus of Learner English) and the ACAD, and English L1 expert writing corpus (Granger & Paquot, 2009). 'See' appeared 14th on the list extracted from the learner corpus and the second in the expert corpus, which confirms that this verb is one of the most frequently used in those two types of academic writing. 'Regard' did not appear on the list of the top 100 verb lemmas from the learner corpus, but it was listed as number 80 in the expert corpus. 'View' was not included in either of those two lists. The list of the top 100 verb forms from the learner corpus (Granger & Paquot, 2009) included 'see' in the infinitive form (position 14), the base form (position 47), and the past participle (position 65). A similar list extracted from the expert corpus included four forms of 'see', but in higher positions than in the learner corpus (past participle – the fourth, base form – the sixth, infinitive – the 14th, simple past – the 74th). The only form of 'regard', i.e. the past participle, was included in position 53 in the expert corpus. The study by Granger and Paquot (2009) supports the choice of the verbs for the present research: 'see' and 'regard' have been considered characteristic for expert academic writing, while 'see' has also been found to be relatively frequent in learner writing. Even though 'view' was not included in the lists mentioned, it was selected for this study as a near-synonym of 'see' and 'regard' in both their senses: literal and non-literal.

In the context of the previous studies on the variations of learner and expert academic writing, and particularly with reference to lexical verbs, the present research provides data on the usage of three verbs expressing mental activities in their non-literal senses. As Granger and Paquot (2009) have shown, each lexical verb presents its own pattern of usage in academic discourse both with regard to the choice of its forms and its co-text. The approach adopted here allows for a detailed analysis of the selected verbs in three corpora, based on their frequencies and the syntactic structures used, and in this way furthers the research on lexical verbs in academic discourse.

4 Corpora and Procedure

This section provides a detailed description of the corpora used for the study and the steps taken in the identification and analysis of the non-literal senses of the three verbs of vision.

4.1 Description of Corpora

Two corpora were used in the present research: the British Academic Written English (BAWE) Corpus, accessed from www.sketchengine.com and the Professional English Research Consortium (PERC) Corpus, formerly known as the "Corpus of Professional English", available at http://scn.jkn21.com/~percinfo/.

The BAWE Corpus contains 2,761 pieces of proficient assessed student writing, produced between 2000 and 2007 at universities in the UK. The texts range from about 500 to 5,000 words and represent four broad disciplinary areas (Arts and Humanities, Social Sciences, Life

Sciences, and Physical Sciences) and four levels of study (undergraduate and taught masters levels). The corpus contains samples of the following academic genres: case study, design specification, essay, exercise, explanation, literature survey, methodology recount, problem question, proposal and research report. The total number of words is 6,968,089 and of tokens, 8,336,262.

The PERC Corpus contains 50,000 word samples of scientific articles from the top 20% impact factor academic journals indexed in the Science Edition of the Journal Citation Index (JCR), as of 2001. It covers the period from 1995 to 2002 and includes a broad range of domains from the so-called 'hard' science and technology:[2] the corpus includes the regional varieties of English, such as American or British English, among others. It contains 17 million words. For the clarity of the analysis, this corpus will be referred to as L1 expert corpus from now on.

Additionally, two sub-corpora of the BAWE were created: L1 non-expert corpus and L2 non-expert corpus. The first criterion in the compilation of those two sub-corpora was the thematic scope: it was narrowed so that it could match L1 expert corpus as much as possible.[3] The second criterion concerned the writer's use of English as L1 or L2. L1 non-expert corpus accounted for 25.51% of the main corpus with 1,777,789 words and 2,126,855 tokens. L2 non-expert corpus included texts written by students with 41 different L1. It represented 11.29% of the BAWE corpus with 786,719 words and 941,191 tokens. The creation of these two sub-corpora allowed for two types of comparison: on the one hand, L2 non-expert writing with L1 non-expert writing; and on the other hand, L2 non-expert writing with L1 expert writing. Additionally, there was a possibility to contrast L1 writing at different levels of mastery: expert and non-expert. Such an approach responds to claims made in the past to use L1 non-expert writing as a reference in the studies of L2 student writing (Hyland & Milton, 1997; Lorenz, 1999). Following Ädel (2006), however, and taking into account possible pedagogical implications of this research, the professional writer corpus was also considered as a point of reference. In this way, broader insights into the use of the non-literal senses of the three verbs of vision in different types of academic writing could be gained.

4.2 Identification and Analysis

The three corpora were queried for 'see', 'regard', and 'view'. First of all, the non-literal senses listed by Macmillan Dictionary (online edition) recommended for metaphor identification in corpora (Steen et al., 2010) were considered. The non-literal senses of those verbs derive from their basic meaning, which in general terms could be defined as noticing something with eyes. The non-literal senses were established using Macmillan Dictionary and selected, in case there were various listed, after a preliminary overview of the corpora samples. In the case of 'see', three non-literal senses were chosen, and one non-literal sense was included for 'regard' and 'view'. All the non-literal senses reflect mental processes involved in academic enquiry and writing:

- see – 1) understand something; 2) consider something in a particular way; 3) find something out,
- regard – 1) think of someone or something in a particular way,
- view – 1) think about or consider a subject or issue in a particular way.

The concordances containing these verbs were manually analysed for the identification of their non-literal senses. In the case of 'regard' and 'view', all of the concordances were examined as they included less than 1,000 hits per corpus and verb. For 'see', a random sample of 1,000 was created for both the L1 expert and the L1 non-expert corpus, as the total number of occurrences was high above 1,000 (approximately 2,000 for the former and 9,000 for the latter). Regarding the L2 non-expert corpus, there were fewer than 1,000 hits for 'see', and thus all of the occurrences were analysed.

In the next step, the frequency of the non-literal senses was calculated for each verb and corpus. In the case of 'regard' and 'view' in all the corpora, as well as 'see' in the L2 non-expert corpus, the relative frequency was normalised by 1,000. For 'see' in the L1 non-expert corpus and L1 expert corpus (PERC), a predicted frequency was calculated first and then, it was normalised per 1,000 words as follows:

$$ef = (f/1000 * n)/g * 1000$$

where f is the number of non-literal occurrences, n is the number of all occurrences in the corpus, and g is the number of tokens in each corpus. In this way, comparable frequencies were obtained for each corpus.

In the following stage, the different non-literal senses of 'see' were identified in order to determine the degree of variation depending on the corpus studied. The occurrences were grouped according to the non-literal sense and the percentages were calculated for each non-literal sense and corpus.

Finally, the syntactic structures containing the verbs analysed, such as 'something is seen to be', 'something is regarded as', or 'somebody views something as', were manually identified and the percentages of use were calculated in each case.

All of the data compiled for the three corpora were finally compared in order to detect possible variations.

5 Results and Discussion

This section reports on and discusses the quantitative findings and includes the analysis of selected examples.

5.1 Frequency of Use

The overall normalised frequency of the three verbs varies significantly in the three corpora (see Table 16.1). L2 non-expert writers most frequently used 'regard' and 'view', while L1 non-expert writers used 'see' most often. By corpus, 'see' was in all cases the most frequent verb, as compared to 'regard' and 'view'.

The frequency of the non-literal senses of the three verbs followed a similar pattern of use, as shown in Table 16.2, even though certain variations can be observed.

If we compare the non-literal uses to the overall uses of each verb in the corpora studied, it should be noted that for 'regard', the frequency of the non-literal uses (Table 16.2) and the overall uses (Table 16.1) is the same in all the corpora, that is, no occurrence of a literal use was found in the L1 expert corpus and the L2 non-expert corpus. With reference to 'see' and 'view', the non-literal uses registered significantly lower frequencies than the overall uses in the three corpora. This reveals many literal occurrences with uses such as 'viewing data on a screen' or 'see Table 16.1', which may reflect a more experiment-based type of research reported in the corpora.

If the frequencies of the non-literal senses are compared across the corpora (Table 16.2), L2 non-expert writers used 'regard' twice as often (0.064) as L1 expert and non-expert writers, who, in turn, used it with similar frequencies (0.035 and 0.030, respectively). This is an interesting finding that points to a notable overuse of the non-literal sense of 'regard' by L2 non-expert writers. Different factors may cause such a use: English learners may tend to choose this verb as a way of making their writing more formal, as recommended on academic writing

Table 16.1 Overall normalised (per 1,000 words) frequencies of 'regard', 'see', and 'view'

	L1 expert	*L1 non-expert*	*L2 non-expert*
regard	0.035	0.030	0.064
See	0.688	1.071	0.851
View	0.046	0.078	0.093

Table 16.2 Normalised frequency (per 1,000 words) of the non-literal sense of 'regard', 'see', and 'view'

	L1 expert	*L1 non-expert*	*L2 non-expert*
Regard	0.035	0.030	0.064
See	0.133	0.363	0.211
View	0.024	0.026	0.018

courses, or there might be some L1 influence, as indicated by Gilquin and Paquot (2008). The following examples show how different types of writer used 'regard' meaning 'thinking of someone or something in a particular way'.

> (1) The age estimate has a very large uncertainty, and glass is not generally regarded as reliable for IVAr dating because hydration and devitrification of glass may cause loss of radiogenic argon, and hence underestimation of the true age (Kaneoka, 1972; McDougall and Harrison, 1988). We therefore **regard** the WAr age as unreliable. (L1 expert, Geology)
>
> (2) It is interesting to compare these two papers [3] and [4] and to **regard** how the understanding and technology has progress in the intervening two decades. (L1 non-expert, Biological Sciences)
>
> (3) Capacity planning is **regarded** as most important activity in manufacturing planning and control system. (L2 non-expert, Engineering)

L2 non-expert writers also overused the non-literal 'see' as compared to L1 expert writers (0.211 and 0.133, respectively), in the same way as L1 non-expert writers did with an even higher frequency of 0.366. It can be clearly observed that non-expert writers, with either English L1 or L2, notably overuse the non-literal 'see' in comparison to expert writers. This is another significant finding, which seems to confirm earlier research on the influence of the informal speech on academic writing for less experienced and certainly younger writers (Hinkel, 2003; Gilquin & Paquot, 2008). The examples that follow (from 4 to 6) show the different uses of the non-literal 'see' in the three corpora.

> (4) Increased information, then, must be **seen** as a statistical measure for directing research towards the quantification of an identifying feature. (L1 expert, Biomedical Engineering)
>
> (5) It can be **seen**, according to Dyson (p259) that "if the trend is upwards, then the investment in fixed assets is beginning to pay off." (L1 non-expert, Engineering)
>
> (6) We can **see** how this particular corollary leads us to the issue of the quintic. (L2 non-expert, Mathematics)

Finally, the non-literal 'view' (Table 16.2) shows a rather distinct pattern of use from its overall uses (Table 16.1). If the overall frequency of 'view' was the highest in the L2 non-expert corpus (0.093), the frequency of its non-literal sense was the lowest in that particular corpus (0.018) in comparison to the L1 expert and non-expert writers. The latter used the non-literal 'view' with similar frequencies of 0.024 and 0.026, respectively (see examples 7 and 8). L2 non-expert writers used it less often (0.018), which points to a slight underuse (see example 9).

(7) We **view** a network as a large, distributed control system, in which a congestion control scheme is a (distributed) control policy executed at each node (hosts or switches) of the network in order to maintain a certain level of stable conditions. (L1 expert, Telecommunications)

(8) Schizophrenia is **viewed** as a neurodevelopmental disorder caused by an interaction of genetic and environmental factors. (L1 non-expert, Medicine)

(9) Project Management literature should not be **viewed** as a static medium. (L2 non-expert, Computer Science)

From the perspective of L2 non-expert academic writing, the use of the non-literal senses of the verbs of vision differs both from L1 expert and non-expert writing, particularly with reference to 'regard', which was overused and 'view', which was slightly underused. In addition, L2 non-expert writers clearly overused 'see' in comparison to L1 expert writers, but underused it regarding L1 non-expert writer. This last finding creates quite a complex picture. It also challenges the approaches postulating that L2 non-expert writing should solely be compared to L1 non-expert writing because of being fairer and more realistic (Hyland & Milton, 1997; Lorenz, 1999). If the ultimate objective of academic writing teaching is to assist L2 non-expert student in reaching a high level of competency, then clearly, the L1 expert writing should be the point of reference, as the findings on the non-literal 'see' confirm.

The section that follows will further examine the case of 'see', which was used with different non-literal senses in the corpora studied.

5.2 'See': Variations of the Non-literal Sense across the Corpora

As has been mentioned in Section 4.2, three non-literal senses of 'see', as listed in Macmillan Dictionary (online edition), were identified in the corpora: 1) understand something; 2) consider something in a particular way; 3) find something out. Table 16.3 shows the percentage of use of those senses in each corpus.

'Understand' registered the highest percentage of all the non-literal uses of 'see' in the three corpora: 57.7% in the L1 expert corpus, 49.7% in the L2 non-expert corpus, and 38.6% in the L1 non-expert corpus. Therefore, this particular non-literal meaning is the most frequent in each corpus and a common feature of the use of the non-literal 'see' in academic discourse produced by the different types of writer (examples 10, 11, and 12).

Table 16.3 Percentages of use of the non-literal senses of 'see'

Non-literal senses of 'see'	*L1 expert (%)*	*L1 non-expert (%)*	*L2 non-expert (%)*
Understand	57.7	38.6	49.7
find out	25.8	25.4	18.1
Consider	16.5	36.6	32.2

(10) The difference between the scientific and industrial approach is best **seen** with an example. (L1 expert, Computer Science)

(11) It can be **seen**, according to Dyson (p259) that "if the trend is upwards, then the investment in fixed assets is beginning to pay off." (L1 expert, Engineering)

(12) So we **see** that the icosahedral inverse solves the Brioschi quintic, and inverting involves solving the Brioschi quintic. (L2 non-expert, Mathematics)

'Consider' registered the second highest percentage in the two non-expert corpora (36.6% and 32.2%, respectively), but not in the expert corpus, where 'find out' was more frequent than 'consider'. This particular variation may be interpreted in terms of the content differences between the expert and non-expert corpora. A greater proportion and range of experimental disciplines in the expert corpus, containing detailed research reports, is possibly the main reason for a higher percentage of 'find out' than of 'consider' in that particular corpus. Example 13 shows the use of the meaning 'find out' in the L1 expert writing, while examples 14 and 15 illustrate the use of the meaning 'consider' in the two types of non-expert writing.

(13) However, though trends were **seen**, the identification of most clinical syndromes by such varied electrical parameters has not been realized (Frost, 1979; Frost et al., 1986; Lemieux and Blume, 1983). (L1 expert, Biomedical Engineering)

(14) Previous studies in aquaponics have often been carried out as aquaculture-based research projects, the hydroponic crop being **seen** as a by-product of the low-tech biological filtration. (L1 non-expert, Biological Sciences)

(15) In the past, it [manufacturing strategy] always been **seen** as a tool to provide cooperate request. (L2 non-expert, Engineering)

Interestingly, the data reported here reveal variations between L1 expert writing on the one hand, and L1 and L2 non-expert writing, on the other, in what refers to two senses of 'see': 'find out' and 'consider'. In all the three corpora, the predominant sense used was that of seeing as understanding, which provides additional corpus-based evidence for the universalist view of vision verbs and their non-literal meaning related to human intellectual capacities (Sweetser, 1990; Ibarretxe-Antuñano, 2008).

5.3 'Regard', 'See', and 'View': Variations in Syntactic Structures across the Corpora

As has been previously mentioned, lexico-grammatical patterns in which verbs are used by L2 non-expert writers have been of concern in the field of academic writing, where significant differences with L1 writers have been largely attested (Hinkel, 2002,2003, 2004; Granger & Paquot, 2008). This section reports on the variations in the syntactic structures involving the non-literal vision verbs under study. Identifying full lexico-grammatical patterns of such uses requires a close manual scrutiny of a large amount of data, and therefore has been left for future research.

Table 16.4 includes the syntactic structures in which the non-literal 'regard' was used, along with the corresponding percentages by corpus. The base forms of the verbs used in those structures have been highlighted in italics, signalling that different tenses were employed.

'Regard' was found in a number of syntactic structures, which registered varying proportions of use in the three corpora. The passive construction 'something/somebody (modal) *be* regarded as' was the most frequent in each corpus with the highest percentages recorded. The most notable variation was detected for 'somebody *regard* something', which accounted for 9.5% of all uses in the L1 non-expert corpus, a much lower 2.5% in the L1 expert corpus (see examples 16–18), and with no occurrences in the L2 non-expert corpus.

Table 16.4 Syntactic structure with the non-literal 'regard': percentage of use by corpus

Regard	*L1 expert (%)*	*L1 non-expert (%)*	*L2 non-expert (%)*
something/somebody (modal) *be* regarded as	78.3	58.7	71.6
somebody *regard* something as	12.7	16.0	20.0
something/somebody *be* regarded (adjective, adverb, prepositional phrase)	2.2	7.9	5.0
something/somebody *regard* something	2.5	9.5	–
something *be* regarded to have/to be	2.3	1.6	1.7
Other	2.0	6.3	1.7

(16) In particular the improvement **regarded** items C, E, I. and J.: bathing, dressing the lower body and transferring the body. (L1 expert, Neuroscience)

(17) Another main factor contributing to the isomer shift **regards** the density of the non s-electrons. (L1 non-expert, Physics)

(18) There are many things in this situation that I feel powerless to change but there are also areas I have control over, not least my attitude to patients. In future I will try not to label people or **regard** them with negativity. (L1 non-expert, Health)

The non-literal 'see' was found to be used in a broader range of syntactic structures, as can be seen in Table 16.5.

In the L1 expert corpus, the most frequent phrase was the impersonal "it *be* seen that" (18.6%), introducing a subordinate clause. It was followed by the personal 'somebody *see*' introducing a range of subordinate clauses starting with 'that', 'if', 'how', 'which', and 'why' (17.5%). The third most frequent structure was a passive construction 'something *be* seen as' (16.5%). The L2 non-expert corpus shows a very similar pattern with the three structures mentioned as the most frequent, but used in varying proportions. The L2 non-expert writers clearly preferred the personal 'somebody see' followed by clause starting with 'that', 'why', 'if', and 'how' (34.7%), to other impersonal or passive structures (example 19).

(19) Through the following study of culture's four elements, we could **see** why culture is one of the reasons for Oticon's success. (L2 non-expert, Engineering)

Table 16.5 Syntactic structures with the non-literal 'see': percentage of use by corpus

See	*L1 expert (%)*	*L1 non-expert (%)*	*L2 non-expert (%)*
it *be* seen + that-clause	18.6	20.1	17.3
somebody *see* + clause (that/if/how/what/which/why)	17.5	12.4	34.7
something *be* seen as	16.5	22.4	18.9
as it *be* seen	16.0	3.2	2.6
Other	14.9	5.9	2.6
something *be* seen to be	8.2	11.2	6.1
(in order) to see + clause (that/why/whether/which/how/if)	6.7	18.6	8.7
somebody *see* something as	1.5	3.2	7.7
somebody *see* something through/by	–	2.9	1.5

Like L1 expert writers, L1 non-expert writers used the passive and impersonal phrases: 'something *be* seen as' and 'it *be* seen + that-clause' with significant percentages (22.4% and 20.1%). In addition, they resorted to the non-finite purpose clause: '(in order) to see that/why/whether/which/how/if' with a high 18.6% of all the uses (examples 20 and 21).

> (20) A visual observation of the samples was undertaken. The liquid samples were smelled to **see** if any off notes could be detected. (L1 non-expert, Food Sciences)
>
> (21) After the extensive debate on the banning of fox hunting with hounds it will be interesting to **see** how much an effect it will have on fox populations, at present there is no confirmed data available. (L1 non-expert, Biological Sciences)

Another relevant difference between the expert and non-expert writers concerns the use of the causal clause 'as it *be* seen', which accounts for 16% in the expert corpus and 3.2% and 2.6% in the L1 and L2 non-expert corpora, respectively. Despite certain differences detected, we can observe some similarities among the three types of writer, especially L1 expert and L2 non-expert writers.

Finally, and with reference to the non-literal 'view', further variations can be observed in the three corpora (see Table 16.6).

The most frequent structure with the non-literal 'view' in the L1 expert corpus was the passive construction 'something/somebody *be* viewed as'; for instance "the balancing condition can be **viewed**, (…), as a two-sided symmetry condition" (L1 expert corpus, Engineering). It accounted for 68.6% of all uses; a very similar proportion was found for that structure in the L2 non-expert corpus (68.8%). This phrase was also the most frequent in the L1 non-expert corpus but with a lower 44.6%. The active structure 'somebody *view* something as' was the second most frequent

Table 16.6 Syntactic structures with the non-literal 'view': percentage of use by corpus

View	*L1 expert (%)*	*L1 non-expert (%)*	*L2 non-expert (%)*
something/somebody *be* viewed as	68.6	44.6	68.8
somebody *view* something as	15.1	23.2	18.7
Other	6.9	3.6	0.0
something *be* viewed + adverb/prepositional phrase	6.3	26.8	–
somebody *view* something	3.1	1.8	12.5

both in the L1 expert corpus and the L2 non-expert corpus with 15.1% and 18.7%, respectively. This pattern resembles the similarities found between these two corpora in the use of the syntactic structures with the non-literal 'regard' (Table 16.4).

Apart from the similarities described, significant differences can also be observed in Table 16.6. A passive structure, 'something *be* viewed', followed by an adverb or a prepositional phrase (e.g. negatively, favourably, with caution) was the second most frequent in the L1 non-expert corpus (example 22), while it was the fourth in the L1 expert corpus (6.3%) and was not used at all by L2 non-expert writers.

(22) Research and development lacks funding in line with the general growth of the business and should be **viewed** carefully over the coming year. (L1 non-expert, Engineering)

Another variation was observed in the use of the structure 'somebody *view* something', which registered a high 12.5% (the third most frequent) in the L2 non-expert corpus (examples 23 and 24), but a significantly lower proportion in the L1 expert corpus (3.1%) and the L1 non-expert corpus (1.8%).

(23) Everyone uses stereotypes. People use it in their humour, in their beliefs, in the way they **view** occupations and even ideas. (L2 non-expert, Medicine)

(24) A variety of shocks occurring throughout markets have radically changed the way managers **view** their environments. (L2 non-expert, Engineering)

On the whole, the data obtained in the analysis of the corpora revealed common patterns of use of the non-literal senses of 'regard', 'see', and 'view', especially in the L1 expert and the L2 non-expert corpora. Surprisingly, the main variations were found between those two corpora and the English L1 non-expert corpus, where certain syntactic structures registered notably higher proportions. From the perspective of English L2 non-expert writing, the absence of some structures, such as 'something/somebody *regard* something' and 'something *be* viewed + adverb/prepositional phrase', draws attention and should be taken into account in academic writing teaching contexts.

In this section, we have looked into the frequencies of the non-literal senses of the three verbs of vision, the proportion of use of the different meanings of the non-literal 'see', and the syntactic structures involving those verbs. The quantitative data have shed light on the overuse of the non-literal 'regard' and the underuse of the non-literal 'view' by L2 non-expert writers. Their use of the non-literal 'see' also differed from L1 expert and non-expert writers. These aspects certainly deserve being paid attention in teaching academic writing to L2 learners. Regarding other features, fewer differences between L2 non-expert writers, on the one hand, and L1 expert and non-expert writers, on the other, were found. However, and as it has been pointed out in previous research (Granger & Paquot, 2009), L1 expert writers used a broader range of syntactic structures (Tables 16.5 and 16.6): the category of 'other' for both 'see' and 'view' included additional structures which were used on a more ad-hoc basis contributing to a greater richness of the structures used.

6 Conclusions

This study enquired into the use of the non-literal senses of three verbs of vision in academic discourse produced by L1 expert, L1 non-expert, and L2 non-expert writers. It has provided further data on learner uses as compared to native speaker uses, and has pointed to the problematic areas, in line with the previous research in the field of academic writing. Adopting a cognitive linguistics perspective has allowed for a more fine-grained analysis of those verbs when they are used to reflect intellectual processes involved in scientific enquiry and when they serve to construct academic discourse. Focusing on non-literal or metaphorical senses has also ensured that specific uses were closely scrutinised. Finally, examining three types of discourse, as represented by the corpora examined, has provided a broad view of variations in the use of those verbs.

The findings reported here create a rather complex picture of variations among the three types of writer. There are certainly areas that should be paid attention to in the teaching of academic English such as the overuse of the non-literal 'regard' and 'see', or the overuse and the lack of certain syntactic structures involving the non-literal vision verbs. However, similarities between L1 expert writers and L2 non-expert writers, and at the same time their differences with L1 non-expert writers were also found, especially in the case of the syntactic structures used. This type of variation should be further examined, as factors such as the corpus contents or the genres included could have influenced the results obtained. Future research should also look into the lexico-grammatical patterns of the different non-literal verbs of vision by means of analysing their collocates or lexical bundles, so that more corpus-based evidence on the use of these verbs would be obtained.

Notes

1 All of the examples were taken from Ibarretxe-Antuñano (2002).
2 Agriculture, Biology, Chemistry, Civil Engineering, Computer Science, Construction & Building Technology, Earth Science, Electrical & Electronic engineering, Engineering, Environmental Sciences, Fisheries, Food Science, Forestry, General Science, Materials Science, Mathematics, Medicine, Metallurgy & Metallurgical Engineering, Nuclear Science & Technology, Oceanography, Physics, Telecommunications.

3 Agriculture, Biological Sciences, Chemistry, Computer Science, Cybernetics, Electronic Engineering, Engineering, Food Sciences, Health, Mathematics, Medicine, Meteorology, and Physics.

References

Ädel, A. (2006). *The Use of Metadiscourse in Argumentative Texts by Advanced Learners and Native Speakers of English.* Amsterdam & Philadelphia: John Benjamins Publishing Company.

Ädel, A. & Erman, B. (2011). Recurrent word combinations in academic writing by native and non-native speakers of English: A lexical bundles approach. *English for Specific Purposes* 31, 81–92.

Aikhenvald, A.Y. & Storch, A. (2013). Linguistic expression of perception and cognition: A typological glimpse, in A.Y. Aikhenvald & A. Storch (eds.) *Perception and Cognition in Language and Culture.* Leiden: Brill, 1–46.

Byrd, P. & Coxhead, A. (2010). *On the other hand*: Lexical bundles in academic writing and in the teaching of EAP. *University of Sydney Papers in TESOL* 5/31, 31–64.

Charles, M. (2006a). Phraseological patterns in reporting clauses used in citation: A corpus-based study of theses in two disciplines. *English for Specific Purposes* 25, 310–331.

Charles, M. (2006b). The construction of stance in reporting clauses: A cross-disciplinary study of theses. *Applied Linguistics* 27, 492–518.

Chen, Y.-H. & Baker, P. (2010). Lexical bundles in L1 and L2 academic writing. *Language Learning & Technology* 14/2, 30–49.

Classen, C. (1997). Foundations for an anthropology of the senses. *International Social Science Journal* 49/153, 401–412.

Deignan, A. (2005). *Metaphor and Corpus Linguistics* (Vol. 6). Amsterdam & Philadelphia: John Benjamins Publishing Company.

Dik, S. & Hengveld, K. (1991). The hierarchical structure of the clause and the typology of perception verb complements. *Linguistics* 29, 231–159.

Gilquin, G. & Paquot, M. (2008). Too chatty: Learner academic writing and register variation. *English Text Construction* 1/1, 41–61.

Grady, J. (1997). THEORIES ARE BUILDINGS revisited. *Cognitive Linguistics* 8, 267–90.

Granger, S. & Paquot, S. (2009). Lexical verbs in academic discourse: A corpus-driven stud of learner use, in M. Charles, D. Pecorari & S. Hunston (eds.) *Academic Writing: At the Interface of Corpus and Discourse.* London and New York: Continuum, 193–214.

Hiltunen, (2006). Coming-to-know verbs in research articles in three academic disciplines. *Proceedings of the 5th International AELFE Conference*, 246–251. Available from http://www.unizar.es/aelfe2006.

Hinkel, E. (2002). *Second Language Writers' Text. Linguistic and Rhetorical Features.* Mahwah, New Jersey & London: Lawrence Erlbaum Associates.

Hinkel, E. (2003). Simplicity without elegance: Features of Sentences in L1 and L2 Academic texts. *TESOL Quarterly* 37/2, 275–301.

Hinkel, E. (2004). *Teaching Academic ESL Writing: Practical Techniques in Vocabulary and Grammar.* Mahwath, New Jersey & London: Lawrence Erlbaum Associates.

Horie, K. (1993). *A Cross-Linguistic Study of Perception and Cognition Verb Complements: A Cognitive Perspective.* Unpublished Ph.D. thesis. University of Southern California.

Hyland, K. (1999). Academic attribution: Citation and the construction of disciplinary knowledge. *Applied Linguistics* 20, 341–367.

Hyland, K. & Milton, J. (1997). Qualification and certainty in L1 and L2 students' writing. *Journal of Second Language Writing* 6/2, 183–205.

Ibarretxe-Antuñano, I. (1999). *Polysemy and Metaphor in Perception Verbs: A Cross-Linguistic Study.* Unpublished Ph.D. thesis. University of Edinburgh.

Ibarretxe-Antuñano, I. (2002). MIND-AS-BODY as a Cross-Linguistic Conceptual Metaphor. *Miscelánea. A Journal of English and American Studies* 25, 93–119.

Ibarretxe-Antuñano, I. (2008). Vision metaphor for the intellect: Are they really cross-linguistic? *ATLANTIS. Journal of the Spanish Association of Anglo-American Studies* 30/1, 15–33.

Johnson, M. (1987). *The Body in the Mind. The Bodily Basis of Meaning, Reason and Imagination.* Chicago: Chicago University Press.

Kövecses, Z. (2010). *Metaphor: A Practical Introduction (2nd edition).* Oxford: Oxford University Press.

Lakoff, G. & Johnson, M. (1980). *Metaphors We Live By.* Chicago: Chicago University Press.

Lakoff, G. & Johnson, M. (1999). *Philosophy in the Flesh. The Embodied Mind and its Challenge to Western Thought.* New York: Basic Books.

Lorenz (1999). "Learning to cohere: Causal links in native vs. non-native argumentative writing", in W. Bublitz, U. Lenk & E. Ventola (eds.) *Coherence in Spoken and Written Discourse. How to create it and how to describe it.* Amsterdam & Philadelphia: John Benjamins Publishing Company, 55–75.

Macmillan Dictionary (online edition). Macmillan Publishers Limited 2009–2018. Available from www.macmillandictionary.com/.

Meyer, P.G. (1997). *Coming to Know: Studies in the Lexical Semantics and Pragmatics of Academic English.* Tübingen: Gunter Narr Verlag Tübingen.

Roegiest, E. (2003). Argument structure of perception verbs and actance variation of the Spanish Direct Object, in G. Fiorentino (ed.) *Romance Objects. Transitivity in Romance Languages.* Berlin: Mouton de Gruyter, 299–322.

Rojo, A. & Valenzuela, J. (2004–2005). Verbs of sensory perception: An English-Spanish comparison. *Languages in Contrast* 5/2, 219–243.

San Roque, L., Kendrick, K.H., Norcliffe, E., Brown, P., Defina, R., Dingemanse, M., Dirksmeyer, T., Enfield, N.J., Floyd, S., Hammond, J., Rossi, G., Tufvesson, S., van Putten, S. & Majid, A. (2015). Vision verbs dominate in conversation across cultures, but the ranking of non-visual verbs varies. *Cognitive linguistics* 26/1, 31–60.

Steen, G. J., Dorst, A. G., Herrmann, J. B., Kaal, A., Krennmayr, T., & Pasma, T. (2010). *A Method for Linguistic Metaphor Identification: From MIP to MIPVU* (Vol. 14). Amsterdam: John Benjamins Publishing

Sweetser, E. (1990). *From Etymology to Pragmatics. Metaphorical and Cultural Aspects of Semantic Structure.* Cambridge: Cambridge University Press.

Viberg, A. (1983). The verbs of perception: A typological study. *Linguistics* 21/1, 123–162.

17 Showing Emotion in Academic Discourse. A Pragmatic Analysis

Eva M. Mestre-Mestre

1 Introduction

Academic discourse (AD) in English can no longer be merely described as objective and impersonal. As the field for academic writing enlarges, it diversifies and apparently seems to consent to greater variation. This not only concerns research articles (RAs); it is becoming increasingly common to write PhD Theses (PhDT) or Master's Theses (MT) in English in Non-native English (NNE) environments. Learners of English find the pragmatic competence of utmost difficulty to learn, particularly at the highest levels of competence (Thomas, 1983; Rose & Kasper, 2001). As it has proven to be a major challenge for learners with a medium-to-advanced level of language, it is one of the main concerns for teachers.

Indeed, when students in their last year as undergraduates write their MT, they need to comply with the specifications learned as to how to write academically in English. However, some aspects of language, which were scarce in AD up to now, such as first-person authorial presence or emotion, are becoming more common in AD, and now this can be traced in the texts.

The acquisition of pragmatic competence, described as the 'ability to produce and comprehend [...] discourse that is adequate to the L2 socio-cultural context in which interaction takes place' (Kecskes, 2013:64), is currently one of the most thriving fields of research in language learning. Particularly with regard to pragmatic competence, the approach in the study of emotions is possibly one of the most theoretically insightful nowadays. Within the model, two main approaches exist: the ethno-pragmatic perspective (Wierzbicka, 2004; Gladkova and Romero-Trillo, 2014; Goddard, 2014) and the intercultural pragmatics perspective (Kecskes & Romero-Trillo, 2013). The present research presents a study of the expression of emotion from an intercultural pragmatics perspective, in which a series of MT written by NE speakers is compared to a similar set written by NNE speakers, to analyse whether they are using the same resources.

New formulae, showing new attitudes and new concerns, are appearing in the texts written by expert scholars. In this setting, a stimulating field of research are MT, which differ from work presented by accomplished researchers (Tang & John, 1999; Hyland, 2002) and yet are AD texts produced by students in their final years. Some students choose to write them in English as their L2. In this regard, there seem to be differences in MT written by students with English as L1 and as L2 (Mestre-Mestre, 2017).

In the study presented here, MT have been chosen as materials for the study of the expression of emotions in formal contexts, and specifically, AD, from an intercultural perspective. MT are a particularly interesting field for study, as it is a genre in which students must defend their work and prove a niche for research, thus showing their involvement in the field. It also provides an educational background, since students are entering and becoming familiar with the world of AD. This work is an analysis of the expression of emotions (through verbs, self-references, and adjectives). This chapter attempts at bringing some light into new strategies used by L1 authors in AD, so that L2 students can be made aware of their significance and improve their pragmatic competence by introducing them in their own production in order to obtain appropriate, improved texts. Thus, findings have relevance, among others, for the teaching of pragmatic competence for research writing.

The text is organised as follows: first, there is a section in which the theoretical background is detailed, including, on the one hand, AD, MT, and changes in AD, and on the other, pragmatic competence and emotion. Then, the objectives of the research presented are introduced, followed by the methodology used to attain them, and the results and conclusions of the work.

2 Theoretical Background

2.1 Academic Discourse

Traditionally, it has been accepted that AD, and in particular scientific texts have their own unique form of expression. Extensive amount of literature gives a proof of this (Bazerman, 1988; Crismore, 1989; Swales, 1990; Hyland, 1999; Hunston & Thompson, 2000; Hartley, 2008). Unambiguous descriptions have described the main characteristics of this type of language, offering a very clear image of what is or what is not acceptable. Of the most recurrent features used to describe AD, a few will be mentioned: (1) impersonal, objective language, (2) third party expression, (3) passive-structured times, (4) complex concepts, (5) notes and reference systems, or (6) simple, understandable, and objective expression. These characteristics are very specific so that scientific texts are easily recognisable; at a different level, terms and structures shape a sort of concept map in the written text in which proficient readers jump from one known concept to the next. Because of this, experienced readers can follow a path of common places, and move from one part of the manuscript to the next; they can foresee what is ahead, because texts follow predictable structures and conventions. Scientific texts must not only be structured and written for their identification as knowledge, but also for knowledge dissemination. This is a premise that the researcher must know and satisfy.

Research dedicated to AD is broad, mainly in the case of RAs. However, MT are a much lesser studied aspect. Related to this, we can mention some works that look into Swales' (2004) move-steps (Soler-Monreal, 2016), and particular sections of these texts (Samraj, B., 2008; Kwan, B. S. C. & Chan, H., 2014), metadiscourse (Hyland, K., 2004; Ozdemir, N. O. & Longo, B., 2014), or into the comparison between different types of AD productions, which include MT (Taş, E. E. I., 2008; Lim, J. M. H., 2010; Carrió-Pastor, M. L., 2013). Finally, other research work focuses on the educational part of these texts, looking for pedagogic results (Balcı, A. et al., 2013; Uccelli, P. et al., 2013).

As early as 1990, Swales explained the different communicative functions carried out by discourse, namely, referential, when the aim is to represent the world (content), literary, when focus is set on the form, persuasive, when most attention is paid to the receiver of the text, and expressive, when emphasis is put on the sender. In AD, the most important of these functions are referential and persuasive, since the aim of the writings is to convince the scientific community of the interest of new discoveries.

2.1.1 Some Changes in Academic Discourse

Obviously, nothing remains immutable, not even AD. There has recently been some interest in the analysis of AD from a long-term perspective, which tries to investigate new developments and possible alterations in this type of discourse. In particular, Hyland and Jiang (2017) have investigated novel (greater) degrees of informality in academic writing. For them, informality can no longer be considered as deviation from traditional notions of objectivity, nor inappropriate use of colloquial language, but "the expression of a more personal tenor which implies a closer relationship to readers, a willingness to negotiate claims and a positive attitude towards subjectivity" (Hyland & Jiang, 2017:42). According to these authors, formality and informality can be measured by tracing a set of rhetorical characteristics which exist – or not – in a text. The following features (Chang & Swales, 1999) are taken as a representative of informality (Table 17.1).

In their analysis, they conclude that academic writing is indeed varying, although at different rates, depending on the features analysed here. We will just mention some of the aspects highlighted. It appears that interpersonal engagement is one of the most distinctive aspects of change,

Table 17.1 List of informal features (Chang & Swales, 1999)

1	First-person pronouns to refer to the author(s) (I and we) e.g., "I will approach this issue in a roundabout way."
2	Unattended anaphoric pronouns (this, these, that, those, it) that can refer to antecedents of varying length e.g., "This is his raw material."
3	Split infinitives – an infinitive that has an adverb between to and the verb stem e.g., "The president proceeded to sharply admonish the reporters."
4	Sentence initial conjunctions or conjunctive adverbs e.g., "And I will blame her if she fails in these ways."
5	Sentence final preposition e.g., "A student should not be taught more than he can think about."
6	Listing expressions ('and so on', 'etc', 'and so forth' used when ending a list) e.g., "These semiconductors can be used in robots, CD players, etc."
7	Second person pronouns/determiners to refer to the reader (you and your) e.g., "Suppose you are sitting at a computer terminal which assigns you role R"
8	Contractions e.g., "Export figures won't improve until the economy is stronger."
9	Direct questions e.g., "What can be done to lower costs?"
10	Exclamations e.g., "This is not the case!"

as authors try to be closer to their readers, and thus involve them in their research. Another aspect that is really shifting is the use of pronouns. Hyland and Jiang mention the use of *you* instead of *one* to refer to the impersonal, for instance, as a desire to shorten the distance with the reader. However, Breeze, when comparing essays written in English by Spanish students and essays written by English students some time ago, concluded that the use of *you* by Spanish students was due to lack of formality: "This phenomenon again points to lack of awareness of genre conventions" (2007:20).

In this process of slow transformation, another feature that could be in the process of appearing in academic texts is the expression of feelings and emotions, as will be seen in the analysis presented here. This might pose a greater challenge for NNE students who wish to publish their work in English, and need to know and follow the particularities of English AD, as the square cut difference between informal language and formal AD no longer strictly applies.

2.2 *Master's Thesis*

Although the amount of research work dedicated to AD is enormous, there are not many references related to the analysis of MT. The reason for this might be that they are texts produced by postgraduate students and are therefore still considered as part of their education process, and not by acknowledged academics. Another reason could be that they have restricted access and represent a smaller contribution to the world of science, since their objective is to prove the student's accomplishment. In general, studies about MT have mainly been based on a small number of texts for analysis. Some studies that have been carried out focus on the analysis of MT and PhD dissertations from single disciplines produced in Britain (Paltridge, 2002), focusing on their overall organisation. Other studies have examined a disciplinary variation in writing produced by graduate students, as a source for information about differences among branches of knowledge, and approaches to the presentations of research and results (Prior, 1998; Samraj, 2002, 2008). Claims are that some disciplines use much more traditional approaches than others.

The greatest variations between AD work produced by researchers and that written by students are a different approach to the presentation of their own and previous research (Samraj 2002, 2008; Carrió-Pastor & Mestre-Mestre, 2014). In academic investigation, an author's contribution is presented as relevant to the research interests of other researchers in a given disciplinary field. That is the niche (following Swales, 2004) they attempt to fill. However, students include in their dissertations a great number of references – as a proof of knowledge of existing research – which masks their own contributions. In addition, the second biggest difference found in the texts refers to authorial presence. Indeed, it seems clear that undergraduate students don't create a strong authorial presence (Tang & John, 1999; Mestre-Mestre, 2017). Researchers authoring RAs use first-person pronoun markers to project themselves and their ideas (Clark & Ivanic, 1997; Ivanič & Camps, 2001; Hyland, 2002), to state the objectives, to outline procedures, and to make a knowledge claim (Kuo, 1999; Hyland, 2002; Harwood, 2005), whereas undergraduate writers make a lesser use of the first-person pronoun, and they make themselves present in the texts with a narrower range of functions:

> "Whereas the expert writers used authorial pronouns to underline the personal source of their contributions, in these student essays they mainly occurred when writers acknowledged assistance, stated their purposes, or explained procedures".
>
> (Hyland, 2002:354)

As has been seen, the interest of this type of texts is twofold: MT can be studied from the point of view of their contribution to the world of science, and AD can be considered as the pedagogical implications they have in the field of English as a Second Language (ESL). Indeed, they are also part of academic instruction, part of the training that students receive before they finish their education.

2.3 Pragmatic Competence. Emotion and Feeling from a Pragmatic Perspective

When dealing with emotion, one can study it from an ethnopragmatic perspective (Wierzbicka, 2004; Gladkova & Romero-Trillo, 2014; Goddard, 2014; Romero-Trillo & Fuentes, 2014), in the search for the alphabet of human thoughts, which should be explicitly linked to the search for lexical universals, that is, lexicalised concepts which would express emotions worldwide. In the search for semantic primitives, it is crucial to analyse the role a given concept plays in defining other concepts, and the range of languages in which a given concept has been lexicalised (usually departing from English).

Another usual perspective to analyse emotion, which we use here, is the intercultural perspective (Kecskes, 2013; Kecskes & Romero-Trillo, 2013), in which emotion is analysed for every language, assuming that in L2 interactions, speakers cannot exclusively rely on norms and conventions the way they do in L1 communication. A communicator needs to know that beliefs, models, and norms vary, not only depending on the L2, but also on the community of use. Members of a speech community increasingly develop common norms of conduct. That is so for NNE speakers, who need to master English to comply with the requirements of AD in issues such as self-mention, use of pronouns, or even involvement discourse markers (Romero-Trillo, 2007). In fact, Langlotz and Locher (2013) point to the fact that it is not so much that there is no emotion in academic texts, but that they are subtly masked, and are still necessary in the audience–author relationship. In Hyland's words:

> we are learning that such interpersonal aspects of writing are not simply an optional extra to be brushed up when students have gained control of summarizing, synthesizing, handling citations, and so on; they are central to academic argument, and to university success.
>
> (Hyland, 2002: 357)

It is therefore crucial for students to be aware of the effects of correctly recognising and introducing the expression of emotions in their texts, so that they can become true members, not only of the English-speaking community, but also of the scientific community.

3 Objectives

The main aim of this study is to trace and analyse the basic expression of emotions in MT. Three secondary objectives are derived from this: first, to carry out a comparison between texts written by NE and NNE speakers, in order to identify similarities and differences and advert divergences in the findings in these two sets of texts; secondly, the elucidation of the items for analysis, which helps us to identify emotion in an academic text. Our third secondary objective is the issuing of some improvement proposals for pedagogical purposes in relation to the acquisition and enhancement of the pragmatic competence.

4 Methodology

4.1 Corpora

For the research presented here, two corpora were gathered and analysed. On the one hand, 15 MT were written by NE speakers, presented by students in the Universities of South Carolina, Ottawa, and southern California, in the period of 2010–2015. All these MT were written on subjects related to health, engineering, or natural sciences, except for one set which was written on human sciences. In particular, the fields were medicine, veterinary, sociology, mechanical engineering, electronic engineering, and marine science. They added up a total of 536,321 words.

The second set of texts was written by NNE speakers, all students of the Universitat Politècnica de València, and presented during the period of 2008–2013. Similarly, the subjects chosen for analysis were mainly engineering, natural sciences, and one set on human sciences. In this case, the chosen fields were environmental science, computer engineering, artificial intelligence, chemical engineering, and business administration. The total number of words analysed was 362,115.

4.2 Analysis

Having applied a corpus-driven analysis, without any conclusive results, due to the large amount of data, a corpus-based approach was the method chosen to analyse the corpora. Because of this, prior to examining the two corpora, a key issue to consider was to decide upon what elements would be suitable and could be used to identify emotion on AD, since traces of emotion were expected to be little, despite the abovementioned changes. An extensive list of hedges and boosters, adapted by Friginal et al. (2017:279) from Hyland's classification of metadiscourse markers (Hyland, 2005:49), was used. As is well known, Hyland proposed a model in which he classified interpersonal resources as interactive and interactional. Following this author, the part dedicated to interactional relations (involving the reader in the text) includes hedges, boosters, attitude markers, self-mentions, and engagement markers. Hedges were chosen, as they are used in the text to withhold commitment and open dialogue, whereas boosters were chosen because they are used to emphasise certainty or close dialogue. Friginal et al. (2017) listed extensively the type of words that could be included under each category, and, in the case of hedges, sub-divided this list into content-oriented and audience-oriented. Table 17.2 shows both hedges and boosters included in the analysis.

In addition to this, the list of stative verbs that relate to emotion was also included in the analysis: adore, appreciate, care, desire, dislike, enjoy, envy, fear, feel, hate, hope, like, love, mind, need, prefer, value, want, and wish, as well as modal verbs: can, could, be able to, may, might, shall, should, must, have to, will, would.

Table 17.2 Hedges and boosters included in the analysis

Hedges	*Boosters*
Content-oriented: accuracy-oriented About, almost, apparent, apparently, approximately, around, bit, broadly, certain amount, certain extent, certain level, could, couldn't, could not, doubt, doubtful, essentially, estimate, estimated, fairly, frequently, generally, guess, in general, in most cases, in most instances, just, kind of, largely, likely, little, mainly, may, maybe, might, mostly, often, on the whole, perhaps, plausible, plausibly, possible, possibly, presumable, presumably, pretty probable, probably, quite, rather X, relatively, roughly, slightly, sometimes, somewhat, sort of, tend to, tended to, typical, typically uncertain, uncertainly, unclear, unclearly, unlikely, usually Content-oriented: speaker-oriented Argue, argued, appear, appeared, assume, assumed, claim, claimed, indicate, indicated, postulate, postulated, seem, seemed, suggest, suggested, suppose, supposed, suspect, suspected Audience-oriented Believe, believed, feel, felt, from my perspective, from our perspective, from this perspective, in my opinion, in our opinion, in my view, in our view, in this view, ought, should, think, thought, to my knowledge, would, wouldn't, would not.	Actually, beyond doubt, certain, clear, definite, demonstrate, demonstrated, doubtless, establish, established, evident, find, found, in fact, incontestable, incontrovertible, indeed, indisputable, know, known, must, do doubt, obvious, of course, prove, proved, realise, realised, really, show, showed, shown, sure, truly, true, undeniable, without doubt, without a doubt, A lot, lots, absolutely, always, certainly, clearly, completely, conclusively, decidedly, definitely, evidently, incontestably, incontrovertibly, indisputably, never, obviously, so, surely, too, totally, undeniably, undisputedly, undoubtedly, very,

Source: Based on Friginal et al. (2017).

Table 17.3 List of Words for emotions

Merriam-Webster Learner's Dictionary		
acceptance	Dislike	Love
admiration	dismay	lust
affection	distress embarrassment	malice
aggravation	enthusiasm	misery optimism
anger	envy	panic
anguish	excitement	patience
anxiety	fear	pessimism
attraction	frustration	pity
boredom	fury	pleasure
caution	generosity	pride
certainty	greed	rage
compassion	grief	relief
confidence	guilt	sadness
confusion	hate	satisfaction
contentment	hatred	scorn
courage	hope	shame
curiosity	horror	sorrow
defeat	hostility	sympathy
defiance	impatience	terror
delight	jealousy	unhappiness
dependence	joy	wonder
depression	kindness	wrath
desire	loneliness	
disappointment	longing	

Source: Merriam-Webster learner's dictionary.

Finally, a list elaborated from the Merriam-Webster Learner's Dictionary including "words for emotions" was added to the study for the analysis of the corpora. Table 17.3 includes these words used in the analysis.

For the concordancing and the analysis of frequency in the texts, L. Anthony's (2017) ProtAnt and AntCon tools were used.

5 Results

From the texts analysed, the following results were obtained. First, we will compare the type/token rations for NE and NNE speaker production. Figure 17.1 displays the different results in this matter.

It can be seen here that, although the number of words and file sizes is much greater for NE texts, if we look at the type/token ratio, there is a significant difference between NNE (around 58%) and NE (around 42%), which is then counterweighed in the number of tokens which actually appeared in the list to be analysed.

Secondly, it is interesting to look at correlations. The results for tokens that are coincidental in both corpora with the highest frequencies are shown below. Figure 17.2 presents the results for modal and emotion

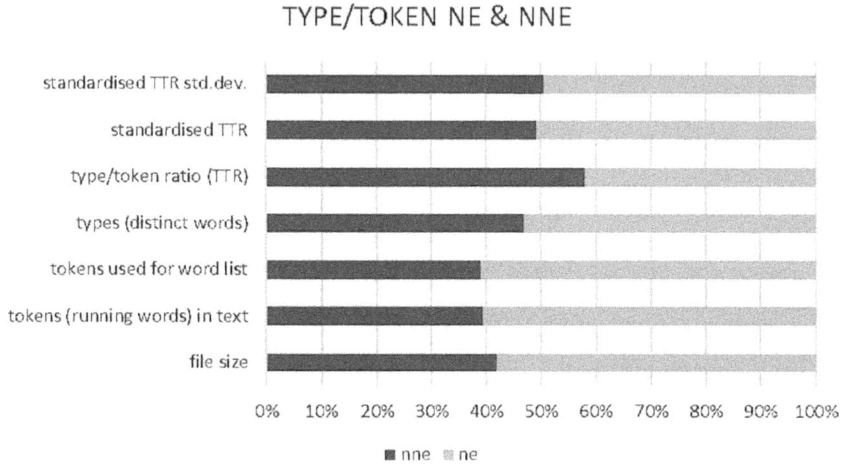

Figure 17.1 Type/Token for NE and NNE.

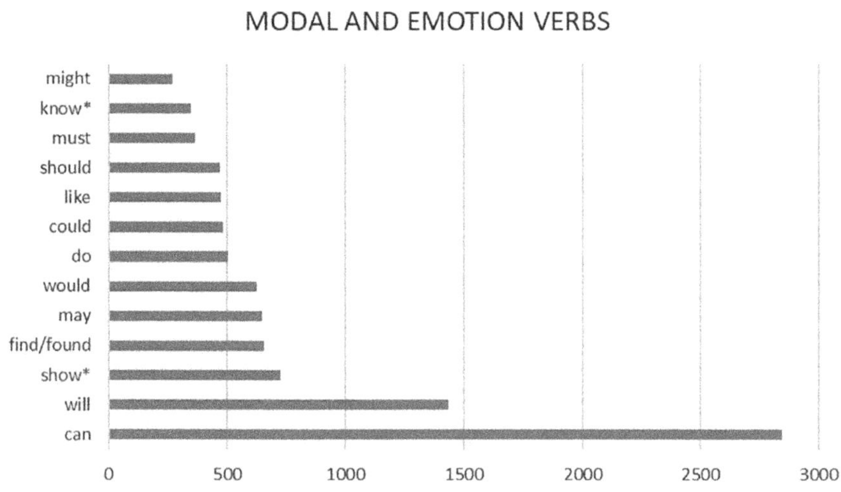

Figure 17.2 Frequency of modal verbs and emotion verbs in the texts in both corpora.

verbs. In it, it can be clearly seen that, with a big difference with the rest, the most widely used modal is *can*. Verbs like *would*, *could*, or *should*, more clearly identifying emotion (see contexts of appearance), also appear in the rank of 500 manifestations.

Figure 17.3 shows the total frequencies obtained for hedges, boosters, and emotion words in the texts, only for coincidental cases, as before. The interesting things to study in this graph are not only tokens that appear at the greatest frequencies, adding up utterances both in the NE corpus and in the NNE corpus, such as *certain*, *completely*, or *establish* (for lemmatised words), but also open-class words; adjectives and nouns that clearly identify emotion (see contexts), *interested, confidence, satisfy, evident, hope, fear, love, desire, depression*, etc.

To understand whether the list used is identifying the way emotions are expressed, and to establish a comparison of use between the two corpora, we must look at the results obtained for the ten most used words in both corpora, so that an evaluation about the word use frequency can be carried out. Figure 17.4 clearly shows that, in the cases where one term appears in both corpora, there is greater frequency of use among NE speakers than among NNE speakers, except for the case of *true* and *always*, where the opposite is the case.

In Table 17.4, samples of the contexts of appearance of these items can be found, both for texts written by NE and for texts written by

Figure 17.3 Frequency of modal boosters, hedges, and emotion words in both corpora.

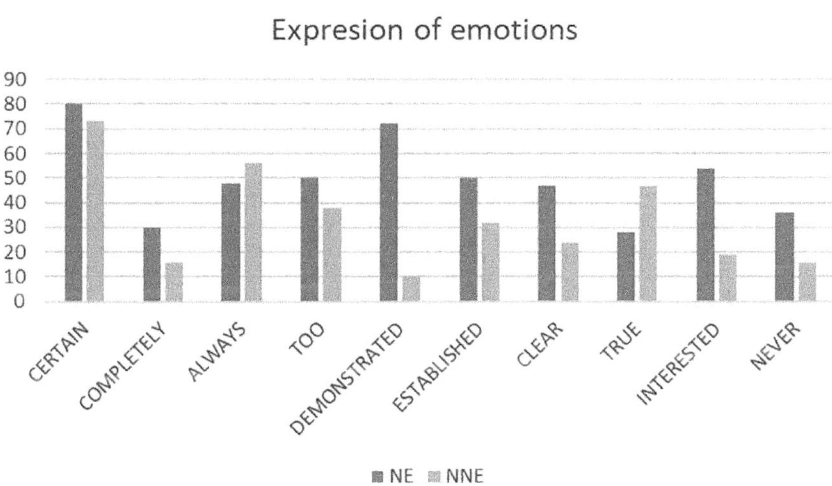

Figure 17.4 Comparison of emotion words in two corpora.

Table 17.4 Contexts of appearance of tokens in both corpora

NE	through the National Bank of Malawi. However, it is	**clear** from the interviews that MMCT was involved in the
	states that, "The increased beekeeping activities are a	**clear** indication that the initiative is empowering people
	local communities and the mining company. It is not	**clear** how this is possible since some of the people
NNE	Lake Liambezi. The reason for that is not yet	**clear**, but there are various possible scenarios that caused
	having a (total) weight of zero, wn, should be	**clear**. The former means that this node did not cause
	and both are query-optimal. However, it should be	**clear** that our technique is not incompatible with any of
NE	with VETs. This solves the time scalability problem as	**demonstrated** by our experiments. In our implementation
	distribution of the runoff and rainfall was already	**demonstrated**. Looking at the flow duration curve for
	crops, reducing the amount of water needed. As is	**demonstrated** by the conclusions above, floods play an
NNE	sub-groups within these communities. As I have	**demonstrated** above, this type of detailed analysis allows
	and looking towards the future. This dissertation has	**demonstrated** the value that can come from a detailed
	recovery is discussed and reviewed. It has been	**demonstrated** to be a promising technology capable of
NE	Since we are	**interested** in managing resources efficiently, it
	(or non-existent) data, the implications for those	**interested** in the well-being of the MMFR were
	as the main heterogeneous condition, we were also	**interested** in learning whether some these
NNE	(completed or not), and so on. We refer the	**interested** reader to the source code of our
	are always real bugs. We refer all readers	**interested** in the implementation to the webpage
	of the programme. Normally, a programmer is not	**interested** in debugging all the pro- gram, but

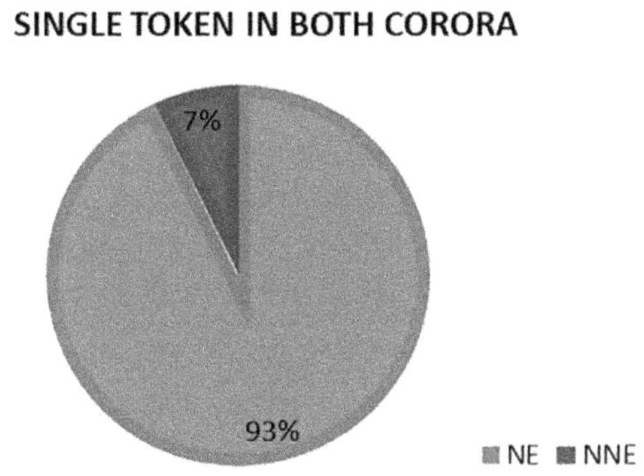

Figure 17.5 Comparison between tokens only in NE and in NNE.

NNE, so that it can be more clearly understood the way authors use these expressions of emotion. Occurrences are similar in the examples provided.

The identification of tokens which have very few (one or two) occurrences is also worth studying. We present below the results for the 15 most used words only appearing either in texts written by NE or NNE speakers, which are shown in Figure 17.5. Here, the graph indicates that most of the terms, which only appear in one of the corpora, are used exclusively in the NE corpus, and not in the NNE corpus. In fact, the proportion is almost 9 to 1.

All the words obtained for the corpus under this category and their contexts are shown in Table 17.5. Unsurprisingly, the great majority of utterances in this list are again open-class words, nouns, or adjectives. They refer to both positive and negative emotions (*optimism, tired*), and from very simple emotions (*anger*), to more elaborate ones (*frustration*). The only one used in the NNE is *doubt.*

Making this analysis extensive to words that only appear twice in the same corpus and in the entire corpora, to see whether this is a common pattern, almost the exact 9-1 proportion of words, which only appear in the NE corpus, can be seen in Figure 17.6.

Again, Table 17.6 presents all the words that were found twice in the corpora analysed in the context. Interestingly enough, there are no coincidences across corpora, i.e. terms are either used by NE speakers, or by NNE speakers. The only word that can only be found in the NNE corpus, and not in the NE corpus is *indisputable.*

6 Conclusions

This study aimed at shedding some light into some variations that are being introduced in the world of AD. The initial focus was set on finding

Table 17.5 Single tokens in the corpora

NE	and providing generous help of all sorts. Your	**optimism** has guided me through some difficult
	With the dogs. I	**enjoyed** my day... I am definitely coming back to adopt
	les significant. Also, the students were likely	**tired** because the IAS scale was at the end of
	appeal to different students. The slightly higher	**dislike** of lesson 6 is most likely due to a graphi
	a vegetarian (as in the empathy score, which could	**anger** or upset a farming community
	the people's facial expressions of happiness,	**sadness**, joy, contentment and fatigue. These are
	facial expressions of happiness, sadness, joy,	**contentment** and fatigue. These are the same,
	individual is just like her, with emotions and	**longing** to find their way home. After some time
	and read a couple of them. The visitor is	**fascinated** to read and see the different perspectives of
	second (Hurley, 2001). This research suggests that	**caution** must be taken when integrating math and
	During his travels Dr. Livingstone became	**horrified** by the slave trading operations that he
	for successfully gaining the information I desired.	**Jealousy** and favouritism are real concerns for many
	and the issue was never resolved, much to the	**frustration** of MMCT and other managers (Wisborg and
	social and environmental awareness. I had the	**pleasure** of seeing one of this group's rehearsals during
NNE	Expected Transmission Count (ETX) is without any	**doubt**, the most well-known metric for characterising

Note: NE vs. NNE.

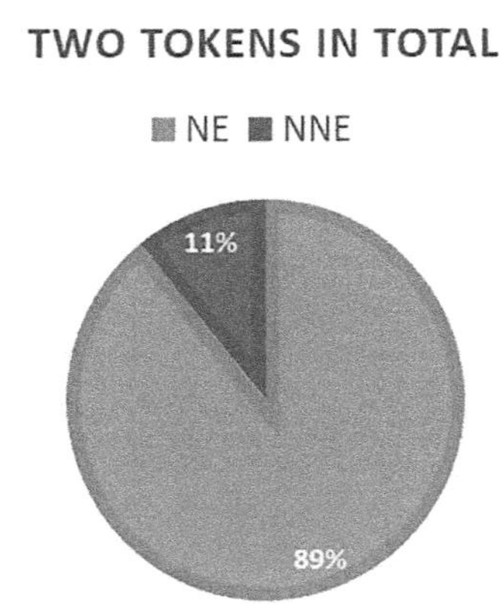

Table 17.6 Two tokens in the corpora

NE	it was, "a life changing thought… that it just	**amazed** me that for some of these people, some of
	. And I remember just being shocked by that and	**amazed** that people could be living so differently than
	the teacher's lack of preparedness. The extreme	**disappointment** from participating CAS staff indicates
	can make the audience feel restricted, which leads to	**disappointment** story of homelessness fro
	had interesting discussion on pharmacology and even	**entertained** the adventurous idea of setting up a biotech
	to have animals fight just so people can be	**entertained**. If a neighbour's cat scratches a baby.
	lex projects and this can also be a deterrent.	**Excitement** from instruction via outside sources is.
	student had a positive interaction with science and her	**excitement** never tapered, whereas two other students
	with teachers that followed the criteria examined, but	**frustrated** and stressed by other classrooms. One
	to the curriculum. Concerns include students being	**frustrated** that the shells did not match the gun found.
	describes that besides having her social worker, the	**generosity** of a couple that gave her a used car
	themselves highly dependent on farm residues and the	**generosity** of others or assistance from their children for.
	read a brief description. The text informs her how	**loneliness** accompanies those who are homeless, and
	for social motives including new friends, alleviating	**loneliness**, and social pressure
	again, you got a lot... I mean, personally, the	**pride** issue is very, very strong with me" (Personal,
	looked like everybody in the store. She emphasises the	**pride** was a big key issue she had to deal
	fragility of this management regime is brought into	**relief** by recent events around MMFR. Below, I highlight
	diversity and rusted rough texture, and stand in strong	**relief** to the ornate neoclassical garden features of the
	of characters), Empathetic Concern (EC feelings of	**sympathy**/concern for others), personal distress (PD—
	had more	**sympathy**, gave more consistent care to living animals
	monkey they had just killed. The men were not	**worried** about getting caught since it was Sunday and
	populations that hunting involves, they are even more	**worried** about the use of fire in some traditional hunting
NNE	but their preeminence in engineering design is	**indisputable**. As such, they are the natural starting point
	effect in wireless mesh networks, is something	**indisputable**. Since the industrial, scientific and medical (

Note: NE vs. NNE.

out whether NNE students express emotions in their MT, the same way NE students, and accomplished writers, are starting to do. If so, it intended to study the kind of expressions and terms the latter use, and to compare these usages with those of NNE students.

As expected, most occurrences found for both NE texts and NNE texts were boosters and hedges, or modal verbs. However, apart from this, other types of expressions (emotion verbs, emotion adjectives, and nouns) could be found in the corpora. In all the cases where there was coincidence, the use of these is much greater in the case of NE texts than in the case of NNE texts. From the results, it seems that NE speakers are less concerned about showing their opinions or feelings in a stronger, more visible way, than NNE speakers; they are introducing the similar trends to those mentioned in other studies for the writing of expert AD. This also agrees with the lesser use of first-person pronouns, and lesser authorial presence in NNE texts than in NE texts, mentioned in previous studies. Indeed, NNE students follow more traditional patterns when writing AD in English. Indeed, the analysis of results shows that NNE students use far less boosters, hedges, and emotion words than NE. Also that some very commonly used words in MT written by NE to show conviction, aimed to persuade the reader, such as *demonstrated* or *clear*, are not very popular among NNE students, who never utilise them in their writings, probably, in an attempt to avoid sharp, emphatic words.

It has been seen that the expression of some emotions can be traced in MT, as compared to what seemed to be the rule not too long ago. Indeed, emotions such as *disappointment* or *pride* can be found in the MT analysed. However, there is a very dissimilar use of them between NE and NNE students (9 to 1).

These new strategies, that are slowly being introduced in the way AD is written, need to be incorporated to the language classroom and instructions for the writing of academic English by speakers of other languages. To achieve this, pragmatic awareness should be raised on this matter, so that students become familiar with the changes and the new possibilities that arise. It would also be advisable for them to work with real texts in order to find out the type of expressions, which more clearly reflect each discipline of work.

Acknowledgements

This work was sponsored by the Spanish Ministerio de Economía y Competitividad, in the framework of the project "La expresión de las emociones: análisis contrastivo basado en córpora de la competencia pragmática en la interlengua de aprendices de inglés" (Project: FFI2016–75160-R).

References

Anthony, L. (2017). AntConc (Version 3.5.0) [Computer Software]. Tokyo, Japan: Waseda University. Available from http://www.antlab.sci.waseda.ac.jp/.

Anthony, L. (2017). ProtAnt (Version 1.2.1) [Computer Software]. Tokyo, Japan: Waseda University. Available from http://www.antlab.sci.waseda.ac.jp/.

Balcı, A., Coşkun, E., & Özçakmak, H. (2013). Trends in reading education: An analysis of postgraduate theses written in Turkey. *Procedia - Social and Behavioral Sciences*, 93, 1574–1579.

Bazerman, C. (1988): *Shaping written knowledge*. Madison: University of Wisconsin Press.

Breeze, R. (2007). How personal is this text? Researching writer and reader presence in student writing using Wordsmith Tools. *CORELL: Computer Resources for Language Learning* 1, 14–21

Carrió-Pastor, M.L. & Mestre-Mestre, E.M. (2014). Estudio intercultural de la argumentación: la referencia al autor in Goes, J, J.-M. Mangiante, F. Olmo and C. Pineira-Tresmontant (Eds.), *Le langage manipulateur. Pourquoi et comment argumenter?* Artois Presses Université, Arras,

Carrió-Pastor, M.L. (2013). A contrastive study of the variation of sentence connectors in academic English. *Journal of English for Academic Purposes*, 12(3), 192–202. doi:10.1016/j.jeap.2013.04.002.

Chang, Y.-Y., & Swales, J. (1999). Informal elements in English academic writing: Threats or opportunities for advanced non-native speakers? In C. Candlin, & K. Hyland (eds.), *Writing: Texts, processes and practices*. London: Longman.

Clark, R., & Ivanic, R. (1997). *The politics of writing*. New York: Routledge.

Crismore, A. (1989). *Talking with readers: Metadiscourse as rhetorical act*. New York, NY: Peter Lang. Flowerdew.

Friginal, E, Lee, J.J., Polat, B. & Roberson, A. (2017). *Exploring Spoken English Learner Language Using Corpora: Learner Talk*. Cham: Springer International Publishing.

Gladkova, A. & Romero-Trillo, J. (2014). Ain't it beautiful? The conceptualization of beauty from an ethnopragmatic perspective. *Journal of Pragmatics* 60, 140–159.

Goddard, C. (2014). Interjections and emotion with special reference to "surprise" and "disgust". *Emotion Review* 6, 53–63.

Hartley, J. (2008). *Academic writing and publishing - A practical handbook*. New York and London: Routledge.

Harwood, N. (2005). 'We do not seem to have a theory… The theory I present here attempts to fill this gap': Inclusive and exclusive pronouns in academic writing. *Applied linguistics*, 26(3), 343–375.

Hunston, S. & Thompson, G. (2000). *Evaluation in Text: Authorial stance and the construction of discourse*. Oxford: Oxford University Press.

Hyland, K. (1999). Academic attribution: Citation and the construction of disciplinary knowledge. *Applied Linguistics*, 20(3), 341–367.

Hyland, K. (2002). Options of identity in academic writing. *ELT Journal*, 56(4), 351–358. doi:10.1093/elt/56.4.351.

Hyland, K. (2004). Disciplinary interactions: metadiscourse in L2 postgraduate writing. *Journal of Second Language Writing*, 13(2), 133–151. doi:10.1016/j.jslw.2004.02.001.

Hyland, K. (2005). *Metadiscourse: Exploring interaction in writing*. London: Continuum.
Hyland, K., & Jiang, F. (Kevin). (2017). Is academic writing becoming more informal? *English for Specific Purposes*, 45(October), 40–51.
Ivanič, R., & Camps, D. (2001). I am how I sound: Voice as self-representation in L2 writing. *Journal of Second Language Writing*, 10(1–2), 3–33. doi:10.1016/S1060-3743(01)00034-0.
Kecskes, I. & Romero-Trillo, J. (Eds.) (2013) *Research Trends in Intercultural Pragmatics*. Berlin, Boston: de Gruyter.
Kecskes, I. (2013). *Intercultural pragmatics*. Oxford: Oxford University Press.
Kuo, C-H (1999). The use of personal pronouns: Role relationships in scientific journal articles. *English for Specific Purposes,* 18, 121–138.
Kwan, B.S.C. & Chan, H. (2014). An investigation of source use in the results and the closing sections of empirical articles in Information Systems: In search of a functional-semantic citation typology for pedagogical purposes. *Journal of English for Academic Purposes*, 14, 29–47. doi:10.1016/j.jeap.2013.11.004.
Langlotz, A. & Locher, M. A. (2013). The role of emotions in relational work. *Journal of Pragmatics,* 58, 87–107. doi:10.1016/j.pragma.2013.05.014.
Lim, J.M.H. (2010). Commenting on research results in applied linguistics and education: A comparative genre-based investigation. *Journal of English for Academic Purposes,* 9(4): 280–294. doi:10.1016/j.jeap.2010.10.001.
Mestre-Mestre, E.M. (2017). An analysis of interactive and interactional strategies in Conclusions and Discussion sections in Masters Theses. *Pragmalingüística*, 25, 416–438.
Ozdemir, N. O., & Longo, B. (2014). Metadiscourse use in thesis abstracts: A cross-cultural study. *Procedia - Social and Behavioral Sciences*, 141, 59–63. doi:10.1016/j.sbspro.2014.05.011.
Paltridge, B. (2002). Thesis and dissertation writing: An examination of published advice and actual practice. *English for Specific Purposes*, 21, 125–143.
Prior, P. (1998). *Writing disciplinary: A sociohistoric account of literate activity in the academy*. Mahwah, NJ: Lawrence Erlbaum.
Romero-Trillo, J. (2007). Adaptive management in discourse: The case of involvement discourse markers in English and Spanish conversations. *Catalan Journal of Linguistics*, 6, 81–94.
Romero-Trillo, J. & Fuentes, V. (2014). What is pretty cannot be beautiful? A corpus-based analysis of the aesthetics of nature, in J. Blochowiak, C. Grisot, S. Durrleman-Tame, C. Laenzlinger. (eds.), *Papers dedicated to Jacques Moeschler*. Genève: Université de Genève, pp. 1–19.
Rose, K R. & Kasper, G. (2001). *Pragmatics in language teaching*. Cambridge: Cambridge University Press.
Samraj, B. (2002). Introductions in research articles: Variations across disciplines. *English for Specific Purposes*, 21, 1–17.
Samraj, B. (2008). A discourse analysis of master's theses across disciplines with a focus on introductions. *Journal of English for Academic Purposes*, 7(1), 55–67. doi:10.1016/j.jeap.2008.02.005.
Soler-Monreal, C. (2016.). A move-step analysis of the concluding chapters in computer science PhD theses. *Ibérica* (32), 105–132.
Swales, J. (1990). *Genre analysis: English in academic and research settings*. Cambridge, England: Cambridge University Press.

Swales, J. (2004): *Research genres: Exploration and applications.* Cambridge, England: Cambridge University Press.

Tang, R., & John, S. (1999). The „I" in identity: Exploring writer identity in student academic writing through the first person. *English for Specific Purposes*, 18, S23–S39.

Taş, E.E.I. (2008). A corpus-based analysis of genre-specific discourse of research: The Phd Thesis and the Research Article in Elt, 276. Retrieved from http://etd.lib.metu.edu.tr/upload/3/12609375/index.pdf [15/02/2019].

Thomas, J. (1983). 'Cross-cultural pragmatic failure'. *Applied Linguistics* 4, 91–112.

Uccelli, P., Dobbs, C. L., & Scott, J. (2013). Mastering academic language. *Written Communication* (30). doi:10.1177/0741088312469013.

Wierzbicka, A. (2004). Preface: Bilingual lives, bilingual experience. *Journal of Multilingual and Multicultural Development*, 25(2–3), 94–104.

18 Proofreading, the Net and Foreign Language Anxiety in the Use of Apology Formulae in an Online Forum. A Learner Corpus Study[1]

Milagros Torrado-Cespón

1 Introduction

Nowadays, the frantic rhythm of the Internet asks students to set correctness aside. Every day, there are posts in the social networks with spelling and grammar mistakes which could be easily avoided if the text was read before pressing enter key, what is more: social networks include the possibility of editing when an incongruence is noticed. However, the number of incorrect texts, linguistically speaking, found online is high. In fact, it can be considered too high to think that the authors are not aware of their mother tongue grammar rules. Moving to the field of second and foreign language (L2 or FL), the number of mistakes is expected to increase, as the users are not at the same level as native speakers. This study takes a look at the online interventions of university students in the process of learning English as a foreign language (EFL) and using it as the vehicular language in the classroom and how some of them act when they realise that they have made a grammar or spelling mistake. Instead of proofreading before sending, their solution is to reread their posts once published and apologise if something incorrect is detected. This is something they would not do if the task was handed to the teacher, so the phenomenon can be considered as an online medium characteristic.

Just observing for some minutes the language used on the Internet, everybody notices how the quality of the language is decreasing. As teachers, we should put an emphasis on the need of proofreading, not just at school but also in using the net by students in their free time. Previous studies about the wrong use of language in contexts related to information and communication technology (ICT) (Dansieh, 2011; Plester, Wood & Bell, 2008; Wood, Kemp & Plester, 2013; Wood, Kemp & Waldron, 2014; Torrado-Cespón, 2015) have shown that students are aware of these mistakes, but it seems they do not really care when it is an online medium, especially if language correctness is not among the main correction criteria. Now, when adding the variable of using an FL, the boundary between the lack of proofreading and the lack of awareness becomes a little blurred. In the case of the subject in this study, another factor enters the scene as they are using an FL which they do not master, as their level varies from a B1 to a C1. The lack of command provokes a certain level of anxiety which is alleviated by writing an apology which seems to be the solution when text editing is not possible, even though this could be solved with a previous revision. ICT use must be normalised in the classroom as another via offering accurate texts, no matter what students do in their free time and teachers must be aware of the problematic situation that may arise in academic contexts and, as an extension, in the correct use of a given language in other everyday contexts.

2 Objectives

The main aim of this study is being aware of the need to provide students with techniques to overcome two main problems when writing online. On the one hand, taking into account the influence of technology, the need to revise their writings is to prevent an incorrect use of the language caused by laziness and hurry and/or lack of knowledge. On the other hand, advise both students and teacher about the importance of foreign language anxiety (FLA), which, even though its presence is lower in asynchronous than in synchronous communication, plays a role in the need of excuse bad English. For this, their productions need a closer look so that the teacher can provide the most suitable solutions for this new generation of students

3 Theoretical Background

Writing online is not just merely writing, so even though the factors involved in online writing seem to be similar to those of pencil and paper, processing is rather different, and teachers need to be aware of this to better understand their students' productions. The circumstances under which this type of texts are written also need to be rethought in order to understand the way the students work and, thus, help them to improve in their online performances. Online writing in an FL is not just a matter of using a computer to transform thoughts into written words. The process the brain goes through when using computer-mediated communication (CMC) is far more complex than pressing a memorised keyboard.

3.1 Handwriting vs. Typing

It is interesting to revise the role of ICT in writing, but handwriting needs to be revised first in order to understand how the brain processes both systems. Handwriting is a rather complex task: there is one-to-one correspondence between the movement of our hand and the resulting shape. In order to achieve proficiency in handwriting, a person needs to practise since childhood and keep on improving until adulthood. Handwriting strokes also show individual characteristics, which are not present in typing. When typing in a keyboard, the process is different in all senses: first, the subject recognises the character, then memorises its position so that s/he does not need to look at it when typing and practice makes him/her faster and more efficient. Typewriting has more to do with visuomotor ability than visual recognition; it is less precise and makes the relationship between the input and output more abstract and disconnected (Velay & Longcamp, 2012: 371; Magen & Velay, 2014: 76). When using ICT, the system is simpler and less demanding in terms of processing. The complex procedure that involves handwriting is underestimated and the result is a text, which does not care that much about rules neither in grammar nor in spelling, or at least that is what the Internet is showing us. The research carried out by Longcamp, Boucard, Gilhode, and Veley (2006) proves how the different way of processing also affects the learning of new letters in adults, supporting the idea that EFL users may have more problems related to spelling when new words are learned by just using a keyboard. This adds a new turning point to sole online instruction, which could be contributing to the lowering of the acquisition of new FL words regarding spelling. In addition, the expansion of typing is also related to a decrease in the precision of arm–hand movements and fine motor skills (Sülzenbrück, Hegele, Rinkenauer, Heuer, 2011), not being a good idea using it in the first stages of writing instruction.

Nowadays, typing is closely related to the use of Internet. As noted in any social network, the use of ICT influences the written productions of both native speakers and learners. The language found in chats or any other type of synchronous and asynchronous ways of online communication tends to be simpler and abbreviated, even the capitalisation of first-person singular pronoun is often ignored (Crystal, 2004: 164). So, it seems that the influence of the keyboards is not actually related to the command of the language but adds an extra factor to its quality. This is something teachers need to be aware of to better instruct their students. On the side of the student, consequently, when they are being assessed by the quantity and quality of their written productions, more emphasis is needed in revision as processing is rather different from the one they are used to doing in handwritten tasks.

3.2 Computer-Mediated Communication (CMC) and Writing

The power of the computers as learning tools is unquestionable. Thanks to them and the Internet, students have nowadays the possibility of accessing to a huge amount of resources, which, years ago, involved hours in a library or even research stays at other universities. It is obvious that the net is present in more and more fields of education in all levels, providing both teachers and pupils with what this society values the most: quickness. However, when using resources such as e-mails or forums, the student starts seeing the difference between instruction and leisure a little intermingled. Actually, the usage of the net for instruction is not a widely extended procedure, even though it is getting more and more ground each year, so students are used to employing the net, especially posts in a forum, for personal questions and not for given accurate academic opinions. As Baron noted (2003: 86–87), the contact between teacher and students through an e-mail is a mix of formal and informal languages or, according to Danet (1997: 8–9), more intangible and ephemeral than traditional letters. Therefore, it is expectable to find more informal communication when the students are alone in a forum as this is the type of language they usually employ in this channel. What is more, CMC also includes the variable of cultural background and this needs some exploration to understand the way students express themselves (Yates, 2000: 242). Register is also important, as the writer usually adapts its computer-mediated discourse to the type of online genre demands, being a social network, such as Facebook, the most informal and an e-mail, the most formal (Pérez Sabater, 2011). In addition, CMC had proved to combine both characteristics of oral and written communication, as already analysed by Yates and Orlikowski (1993), so the language is simpler and less academic.

Together with informality, there is carelessness. In 1994, Angell and Heslos (Crystal, 2004: 112) already pointed out the unprofessional aspect of e-mails full of grammatical mistakes and misspellings, which offered an untidy image to the reader. More than twenty-five years later, this written inaccuracy is found in the palm of our hand in everyday synchronous communication through smartphones. The netspeak (Crystal, 2004), that is, the language used on the Internet, is not really the problem. Informal as it may look, it is correct within its paradigm; Crystal (2004: 111) even states that misspellings are to be considered as a natural feature of e-mail writing. Baron (2003: 92) points out at the fact that misspellings and grammatical inaccuracies are not just a matter of proofreading, which has been left to a second place, but of sloppiness in writing. In fact, even though students in these forums are not really using netspeak, emoticons appear in some cases. As these are FL users, the real issue is not paying attention to what has been written because the user does not know the rules, but because of laziness to revise and the attributed informality to the medium.

When using a computer or a smartphone for writing, it is also necessary to add the variable of the autocorrector present in word processors. Now that writing is not linked to the previous mental process that used to go through in handwriting, word processors simplify it even more by adding the extra help of their internal dictionaries. The first editions limited themselves to underline mistakes related to misspelling, but nowadays most misspelling mistakes are autocorrected while writing and some grammatical incongruences are also noted, underlined, and an alternative is offered. Having all this help on the computer side is a good reason to consider that people (no matter whether they are native or non-native) make mistakes because they got used to the autocorrections when using ICT. Actually, computer users can even be considered as dependents of autocorrectors (Penny, 2003).

In the same way, writing online is not the same as writing on paper; reading is also different. So, the student does not put much emphasis on intensive reading nor in extensive reading and, as a result, the information which is not relevant during skimming is not even noticed. Therefore, being aware of mistakes when writing online implies the subject has gone through the text a second time and has paid attention properly to it for the first occasion. In the cases this research analyses, sometimes, students realise that these are not mere twits or Facebook posts, but it is too late for editing.

3.3 Foreign Language Anxiety

Online tasks are to be considered as an important part in the process of using FL as a vehicular language in nowadays society. It is not a matter of having an exclusively online teaching method, but all universities resort to online tasks at a given moment or to the use of online media to send them (e-mail, online storage services). When students use the net for their tasks, they feel more confident even though they make mistakes, especially when talking about interacting with other classmates. The reason is that students' interactions in online discussions can ease a learner-centred approach to teaching and provide them with opportunities to practise and learn in a supportive and encouraging environment (Stacey, 2002; Birch & Volkov, 2007), but this is not always so. If these interactions are a source of material for the teacher, the student should think it twice before publishing any text. Within this situation, it is necessary taking into account the extensive use of English in the Internet which has favoured the use of less standard varieties of English and their informal or even slang vocabulary worldwide (Androutsopoulos, 2006: 429), even for non-native speakers. The way is paved for a good environment where the students feel free to express themselves fluently even if they make mistakes, but there is a further factor to bear in mind: FLA.

Traditional teaching methods (grammar-translation method as the major representative) have risen generations of learners who were centred on grammar rather than the fluent use of language, being the production of correct written language the main objective of instruction.

When talking about speaking, students usually found themselves a little bit lost, as written language is not to be equalled to spoken language. As a consequence, students traditionally feel worried about their performance, especially regarding speaking, but this is not just a matter of level and nervousness in the learner: the teacher also plays an important role as the conductor of the learning process. It is the teacher's responsibility to make the student feel comfortable when using the FL. As Horwitz (2001: 122) pointed out, teachers need to tailor instruction to the specific needs of their specific learners. The idea, even though awfully helpful, could be too time-consuming in cases of overcrowded classrooms and needs commitment from both teachers and institutions. Motivated teachers who are really able to motivate students can solve this situation somehow in spite of the poor conditions regarding the regulated language exposition or the teaching conditions. Motivation and affect were considered as an important part of the writing process (Hayes, 1996), so that they should not be forgotten in any case. Moreover, as the classroom is not an authentic environment, students feel, traditionally, under correctness pressure. Therefore, motivation on both parts needs to be enhanced to promote an environment as free from stress as possible, where the student does not feel embarrassed by the misuse of the FL but learns from it. When the situation is not comfortable for the student, FLA appears.

Anxiety related to the FL deals with three subcomponents: test anxiety, communication apprehension, and the fear of negative evaluation (Horwitz, Horwitz & Cope, 1986). It is important to note that anxiety is then part of cyclic process: students feel anxious because their performances are poor due to anxiety (Horwitz, 2001: 117). Also, FLA deals with the fact that learners perceive language use as a way to test themselves, instead as a means of communication (Daud, Daud & Kassim, 2005). In the case of written language, the level of anxiety seems to lower, but it does not disappear. Actually, FLA regarding writing should be looked as a distinct form of anxiety (Cheng, 2002: 648). However, as this chapter analyses an online forum and every classmate can see it, the embarrassment of the lack of a third-person singular present inflexion almost equals the situation to that of a live contribution where all the eyes are signalling the error. What is more, the mistake is permanent as it is written, so it can be considered as a greater source of anxiety. Therefore, in the same way as writing in a synchronous system cannot be considered at the same level as merely written language, the anxiety of seen one's mistakes in public can be equally or even more frustrating for the learner. This self-awareness about mistakes is linked to the conscious learning of language most Spanish students have gone through in academic environment. The fact that English is usually learned in Spain and not acquired adds extra anxiety to the presence of an error, which could have been easily solved with previous revision. However,

Aida (1994: 159) noted that second language learners fear negative evaluation during their performances in almost 38% of the cases in her study, so it could be considered as significative but not decisive. In the case of native speakers, this type of failures is rather unconscious (Schmidt, 1990: 133), so although they may correct them, it is not really a source of anxiety or they even do not care about them and make mistakes on purpose because it is faster (Torrado-Cespón, 2018: 47). In this case, apologising by adding an extra post could be considered as the equivalent to an oral "sorry" in real life, that is, a way of relieving anxiety.

4 Participants and Data

This article is part of an ongoing research about the use of English as a vehicular language by university students. As English is not their first language and their level varies from B1 to C1, they, obviously, make mistakes and, as the sample exemplifies, some students are aware of them, even though they find out late. However, it is not just a problem of lack of proficiency: it is the Internet revolution, and anything needs to be faster, no matter whether it could be better. After going through the literature review, the influence of typing, CMC, ICT, and, as a consequence, the usual relaxed use of accurate text on the social networks has influenced the way students also expressed themselves in academic settings. Are those tools which were created to ease online communication are destroying the language in the name of quickness?

This preliminary research takes a look at the online posts of English teachers-to-be (primary and pre-school) who use English as a language of instruction. As part of their assessment, they participate in online forums where they express their ideas about a given topic and discuss it among themselves with no intervention from the lecturer. The corpus used is being compiled by the research group ENTELEARN at Universidad Internacional de La Rioja (Spain). Currently, the corpus ENTERCOR has been compiled using two different subjects and degrees. It is divided into two sub-corpora: TICOR and TRAINCOR with a total of 470,088 word tokens. The first one (see Table 18.1) is used in this study and is also divided into two components: ICT (from pre-school education degree) and TIC (from primary education degree).

Table 18.1 Sub-corpus TICOR

	Component 1: ICT	*Component 2: TIC*	*Corpus TICOR*
Number of participants	155	511	620
Word types	4,816	9,320	14,136
Word tokens	107,042	317,759	367,790

The aim of this compilation is analysing these productions in order to be able to provide practical solutions for common mistakes made by the students who combine the use of an FL with technology. However, even though this is an online university, the results may be applied to other methodologies, as the use of ICT for tasks is present in most institutions. During this research, there were some mistakes which were expected, such as the misuse of prepositions (Serrano Moya & Rubio Martínez, 2015), frequency adverbs (Stefanova & Bobkina, 2015), false friends (López Pérez & Taouis, 2015), initialisms (Torrado-Cespón & Díaz-Lage, 2017), or problems with capitalisation in words which differ from the students L1 (Torrado-Cespón & Font Paz, 2016) and which could be easily attributed to the lack of proficiency or the role of interlanguage. It was interesting to note that, sometimes, students realised they had made a mistake after pressing enter and no editing is possible, which offered the possibility of including the influence of CMC to the equation. As these are online forums, they do not work as a text processor where some grammatical constructions and spelling mistakes are underlined. As a consequence, the lack of self-editing before sending is a risk the student undertakes. Being content subjects, the correct use of language remains in the background as the teacher does not consider it as decisive when marking even though students are advised to produce correct language. This should be considered as a way of minimising FLA, but this is not the case in all instances.

5 Methodology and Results

After revising the data using corpus analysis software (AntConc 3.2), the results may be classified into two categories of apologies:

- Group A: Being sorry because typing was wrong (Table 18.2).
- Group B: Being sorry because their level of English is low (Table 18.3).

As it was expected, in some cases, it is difficult to discern whether it is a matter of lack of proficiency or the use of ICT plays a role, especially in group A, as fast typing can easily be the one to blame in spelling mistakes. In group B, they really put the blame on proficiency forgetting the influence of the ICT, even though its role is equally important as it has been revised in the theoretical background.

When looking at the students' apologies, considering the number of word tokens, they may not seem significant statistically speaking. However, the number of spelling and grammar mistakes in the forums is significantly high as already analysed by other members of ENTELEARN (see "Participants and Data"). Why do some students apologise? These students had revised their posts; they feel embarrassed and suffer FLA. Therefore, there are three types of attitudes observed in these forums.

Table 18.2 Group A

Student	*Utterance*	*Mistake*
23TOENICTA	Hello again, I wanted to say flashcards.	flashacards
23TOENICTA	I wanted to say ICT is not are, sorry	
23TOENICTA	(This contribution is repeated, take into account the second one please, the first one has a spelling mistake)	
133TOENICTA	(Sorry, in my previous intervention I confused convergent & divergent. I wanted to say divergent	
55TOENICTA	Oh my God! I\x92m going to correct to myself some mistakes... they have just learnt* resources**	
200TOENTICB	I'm really sorry, I have forgotten to post the link! Here you have it: www.bbc.co.uk/iplayer/tv/categories/childrens	
418TOENTICB	Sorry, a little typing mistake in my previous post; in my last sentence I meant...one of our greatest challenges	
424TOENTICA	sorry tools	tolos
455TOENTICA	Sorry for the spelling mistake! I meant to say ICT! Have a nice weekend!	ITC
457TOENTICA	Sorry, It's Don't YOU (not yoy) think this might be?	

Table 18.3 Group B

Student	*Utterance*
136TOENTICA	Sorry for my English
349TOENTICA	First of all, I have to say sorry for my mistakes because I am rushing myself to complete this task for all of you, given that yesterday It was my first encounter with the platform because I have many problems to face before I went with that.
362TOENTICA	First of all I would like to apologise for my bad English, I still have much to learn.
374TOENTICA	I apologise for my English, I am still learning.
133TOENICTA	I am sorry, I have discovered some mistakes in my previous contribution. ICT means Information and communication technology, not technologies, so, the correct spelling is: ICT offers a good way... / ICT also has... / ICT is important

Those who are worried about their posts and revise them even if it is late to mend any mistake or are just aware that their level of English is not high enough to write fluently. These are the ones who have made the teacher pay attention to the apology and think about the problem of

CMC and learning. A second group is that which sprouts in any type of CMC, the one who does not revise and is not really worried about that. Finally, although not very abundant, those who have revised before sending. The teacher's objective is to move everybody to the last group.

6 Conclusions

Taking into account the concepts revised in the theoretical background, the boundary between academic work and free time is not really clear in this type of activity. The students feel rather comfortable writing from home with apparently no pressures, even forgetting the anxiety state of a face-to-face session. In fact, students are aware of how to produce accurate written posts, but it seems that they do not really care when it is an online medium (Torrado-Cespón, 2015). When they realise the teacher is looking at these productions, as it is too late for proofreading, their solution is apologising, mostly to impress the teacher and relieve the anxiety of seeing their errors permanently on the forum. Their apparent indifference disappears, and anxiety comes back in some cases because, as English teachers-to-be, having their mistakes exposed to the whole class is a source of peer embarrassment. So, the rhythm which technologies have imposed on them in their daily lives contributes to a strange connection between correctness and speed which, as a result, provokes FLA in a written environment. Thus, FLA in online written tasks could be classified as a new form of FLA; in the same way, the language used in these forums is also a mixture of written and spoken languages.

Since the net entered the scene of education, the quality of the language is decreasing (Baron, 2003) and this also reflected in what the students send as tasks. Although the length of an essay (or a post, in this case) is not significatively affected (Mogey, Paterson, Burk & Purcell, 2016), their productions are less cared. However, the Internet itself should not be blamed nor the teaching methodology, as students have a correct instruction in the FL. The fact of being aware or not of a typographic mistake seems to largely depend on the process our brain goes through when typing instead of using pen and paper (Velay & Longcamp, 2012; Magen & Velay, 2014). Consequently, by using typing, significantly less time-consuming than handwriting, students need to employ the saved time in revising, which is something they are not really used to in online environments. When adding the variable of using an FL to this equation, the boundary between the lack of proofreading and the lack of awareness becomes a little unclear, especially when dealing with the anxiety of using it in a correct way. The characteristics attributed to the process of writing in handwriting seem to be an important factor to consider, especially among users of EFL as a vehicular language. It is then necessary doing further analysis of the errors committed by the students to reach a more solid conclusion about the importance of handwriting in the learning/acquisition of an FL.

Thinking about the medium and the problem, a good solution seems to be resorting to explicitly advise them of proofreading or, even, emphasise the fact that the teacher will take spelling mistakes into account in the final mark. However, the latter could contribute to increase the levels of anxiety. Another solution is the advantage of autocorrective software, so it could also be useful asking students to download an online resource for this end. In this way, the students will feel less anxiety and, consequently, be more motivated to express themselves without the pressure of perfect written productions. This also supports the conclusions in Cheng (2002: 652), who stated that teachers should be aware that students' perceptions of competence are more relevant in their experience of FL writing anxiety than their actual writing competence. These two ideas are quite different from each other, so a new study with two control groups could generate a clearer view on the relief of FLA.

Through an analysis of the students' productions, it is noticeable that the number of apologies or autocorrections may not be significant from a statistical point of view. However, its mere presence is something to take into account. Teachers must be aware of the need to advise students regarding the correct use of the language, even if they are content teachers.

From the point of view of the affective filter hypothesis (Krashen, 1985), FL users feel more confident online, so they use expressions and vocabulary they would not use in face-to-face discussions. This is to be considered as an advantage of the online setting. In contrast, the resulting texts are careless due to a lack of proofreading or, maybe, an excess of confidence hidden behind the screen. This is what the era of multitasking has created. Saving seconds in writing and proofreading no matter the grammatical rules until the subject is aware that the written production is part of an assignment. In a non-academic environment, these extra seconds imply the possibility of pressing "like" in a Facebook post before than any other person. Maybe it is time to breathe for a while and think if this compensates the poor writing or if, academically, we should accept netspeak as the correct production of an FL in an online medium, even if this implies some mistakes. The special characteristics of CMC and the use of ICT are calling for a new reclassification of written production of language and teachers' attitudes towards them. In the case of an FL, less pressure on grammar and spelling correction should not be against the interest of the students in producing the most correct language within their level.

Note

1 This work has been carried out in the frame of the emerging research project "Detección y análisis del comportamiento lingüístico de producciones escritas de estudiantes universitarios" (Project reference: B0036-1617-104-ETEL. Universidad Internacional de La Rioja, 2016-2018).

References

Aida, Y. (1994). Examination of Horwitz, Horwitz, and Cope's Construct of Foreign Language Anxiety: The Case of Students of Japanese. *The Modern Language Journal*, 78/2, 155–168.

Androutsopoulos, J. (2006). Introduction: Sociolinguistics and Computer-Mediated Communications. *Journal of Sociolinguistics* 10/4: 419–438.

Baron, N.S. (2003). Why E-mail Looks like Speech: Proofreading, Pedagogy and Public Face, in J. Aitchison & D. Lewis (eds.), *New Media Language*. London: Routledge, 102–113.

Birch, D. & Volkov, M. (2007). Assessment of Online Reflections: Engaging English as a Second Language (ESL) Students. *Australasian Journal of Educational Technology*, 23/3, 291–306.

Cheng, Y. (2002). Factor Associated with Foreign Language Writing Anxiety. *Foreign Language Annals*, 35/5, 647–657.

Crystal, D. (2004). *Language and the Internet*. Cambridge: CUP.

Danet, B. 1997. Books, Letters, Documents: The Changing Aesthetics of Texts in Late Print Culture. *Journal of Material Culture* 2/1: 5–38.

Dansieh, S.A. (2011). SMS Texting and Its Potential Impacts on Students' Written Communication Skills. *International Journal of English Linguistics*, 1, 222–229.

Daud, N.S.M., Daud, N.M., & Kassim, N.K.A. (2005). Second Language Writing Anxiety: Cause or Effect? *Malaysian Journal of ELF Research*, 1/1, 1–19.

Hayes, J.R. (1996). A New Framework for Understanding Cognition and Affect in Writing, in C.M. Levy and S. Ransdell (eds.), *The Science of Writing: Theories, Methods, Individual Differences, and Applications*. Mahwah: Laurence Erlbaum, 1–27.

Horwitz, E.K. (2001). Language Anxiety and Achievement. *Annual Review of Applied Linguistics*, 21, 112–126. DOI:10.1017/S0267190501000071

Horwitz, E.K., Horwitz, M.B., & Cope, J. (1986). Foreign Language Classroom Anxiety. *The Modern Language Journal*, 70/2, 125–132.

Krashen, S.D. (1985). *The Input Hypothesis: Issues and Implications*. New York: Longman.

Longcamp, M., Boucard, C., Gilhodes, J., & Velay, J. (2006). Remembering the Orientation of Newly Learned Characters Depend on the Associated Writing Knowledge: A Comparison between Handwriting and Typing. *Human Movement Science*, 25, 646–656.

López Pérez, S. & Taouis, H. (2015). Identifying the Misuse of False Friends: Evidence form a Learner Corpus. *Revista Académica liLETRAd*, 1, 631–638.

Magen, A. & Velay, J. (2014). Cognitive Implications of New Media, in M. Ryan, L. Emerson, and B. Robertson (eds.), *The Johns Hopkins Guide to Digital Media*. Baltimore: John Hopkins University Press, 73–77.

Mogey, N., Paterson, J., Burk, J., & Purcell, M. (2016). Typing Compared with Handwriting for Essay Examination at University: Letting the Students Choose. *ALT-J*, 18/1, 29–47. DOI: 10.1080/09687761003657580

Penny J. (2003). Reading High Stakes Writing Samples: My life as a Reader. *Assessing Writing*, 8/3, 192–215

Pérez Sabater, C. (2011). Cartas por internet: las implicaciones lingüísticas y estilísticas de los mensajes de correo electrónico y los comentarios del sito de redes sociales Facebook. *Resla*, 24, 111–130.

Plester, B., Wood, C., & Bell, V. (2008). Txt Msg n School Literacy: Does Texting and Knowledge of Text Abbreviations Adversely Affect Children's Literacy Attainment? *Literacy* 42, 137–144. DOI: 10.1111/j.1741–4369.2008.00489.

Schmidt, R. W. (1990). The Role of Consciousness in Second Language Learning. *Applied Linguistics*, 11/2, 129–158.

Serrano Moya, E. & Rubio Martínez, B. (2015). The Use of Prepositions at/on/in in Spontaneous Writing Productions by Digital Immigrants. *Actas del XXX Congreso internacional de la Asociación de Jóvenes Lingüistas.*

Stacey, E. (2002). Learning Links Online: Establishing Constructivist and Collaborative Learning Environment: Relationships and Critical Factors. *Computers and Education*, 51/1, 318–33.

Stefanova, S. & Bobkina, J. (2015). A Corpus-based Study of Adverbs of Frequency in EFL Students' Writing: a Case of Distance Learning. *EDULEARN Proceedings*, 2562–2568.

Sülzenbrück, S., Hegele, M., Rinkenauer, G., & Heuer, H. (2011). The Death of Handwriting: Secondary Effects of Frequent Computer Use on Basic Motor Skills. *Journal of Motor Behaviour*, 43/2, 247–251.

Torrado-Cespón, M. (2015). Uso del Smartphone y su reflejo en la escritura entre estudiantes de secundaria bilingües gallego-español. *Digital Education Review*, 28, 77–90 http://revistes.ub.edu/index.php/der/article/viewFile/14374/pdf.

Torrado-Cespón, M. (2018). Interlanguage or Technology when Using English as Vehicular Language: What Influences Students Productions Online? *The Eurocall Review*, 26/2, 41–49. https://doi.org/10.4995/eurocall.2018.9924.

Torrado-Cespón, M. & J.M. Díaz-Lage (2017). Error Analysis and Interlanguage in the Use of the Term 'ICT' in an Online Learner Corpus. *Complutense Journal of English Studies* 25, 105–123. https://revistas.ucm.es/index.php/CJES/article/view/56354/52479.

Torrado-Cespón, M. & Font Paz, C. (2016). Interlanguage or technology? Capitalization in a learner corpus of English as a Foreign Language. *Opción*, 32/12, 784–793 www.redalyc.org/articulo.oa?id=31048903037.

Velay, J. & Longcamp, M. (2012). Handwriting versus Typewriting: Behavioral and Cerebral Consequences in Letter Recognition, in M. Torrance, D. Alamargot, M. Castelló, F. Ganier, O. Kruse, A. Mangen, L. Tolchinsky and L. van Waes (eds.), *Learning to Write Effectively: Current Trends in European Research.* UK: Emerald, 371–373.

Wood, C., Kemp, N., & Plester, B. (2013). *Text Messaging and Literacy – The Evidence.* Londres: Routledge.

Wood, C., Kemp, N., & Waldron, S. (2014). Exploring the Longitudinal Relationships between the Use of Grammar in Text Messaging and Performance on Grammatical Tasks. *British Journal of Developmental Psychology*, 32, 4, 415–429. DOI: 10.1111/bjdp.12049.

Yates, S. J. (2000). Computer-mediated Communication, the Future of the Letter? in D. Barton and N. Hall (eds.), *Letter Writing as a Social Practice.* Amsterdam/Philadelphia: John Benjamins, 233–252.

Yates, J. and Orlikowski, W. J. (1993). Knee-jerk Anti-LOOPism and Other E-mail Phenomena: Oral, Written and Electronic Patterns in Computer-mediated Communication. *MIT Sloan School Working Paper,* 3578–3593.

Index

www.ingramcontent.com/pod-product-compliance
Ingram Content Group UK Ltd.
Pitfield, Milton Keynes, MK11 3LW, UK
UKHW022115190926
475702UK00013B/1456
* 9 7 8 0 3 6 7 4 9 9 9 3 8 *